STERLING
Test Prep

SAT
Physics
Practice Questions

3rd edition

www.Sterling-Prep.com

3 2 1

ISBN-13: 978-1-5141101-6-4

Sterling Test Prep products are available at special quantity discounts for sales, promotions, academic counseling offices and other educational purposes.

For more information contact our Sales Department at:

Sterling Test Prep
6 Liberty Square #11
Boston, MA 02109

info@sterling-prep.com

Congratulations on choosing this book as part of your SAT Physics preparation!

Scoring high on SAT subject tests is important for admission to college. To achieve a high score on SAT Physics, you need to develop skills to properly apply the science knowledge you have to solving each question. To be able to do this, you must solve numerous practice questions, because understanding how to apply key physical relationships and formulas is more valuable on the test than simple memorization.

This book provides 881 physics practice questions that test your knowledge of all topics tested on SAT Physics subject test. It contains four diagnostic tests (with eight more available online) to help you identify the topics you are not well prepared for. It also contains eleven sections of topical practice questions, so you can selectively work with the topic you need to study and master. In the second part of the book, you will find answer keys and explanations for the problems in the diagnostic tests and topical practice questions.

The explanations provide step-by-step solutions for qualitative questions and detailed explanations for conceptual questions. The explanations include the foundations and important details needed to answer related questions on the SAT Physics. By reading these explanations carefully and understanding how they apply to solving the question, you will learn important physical concepts and the relationships between them. This will prepare you for the exam and you will be able to maximize your score.

All the questions in this book are prepared by physics instructors with years of experience in applied physics, as well as in academic settings. This team of physics experts analyzed the content of the test, released by the College Board, and designed practice questions that will help you build knowledge and develop the skills necessary for your success on the exam. The questions were reviewed for quality and effectiveness by our science editors who possess extensive credentials, are educated in top colleges and universities and have years of teaching and editorial experience.

We wish you great success in your future academic achievements and look forward to being an important part of your successful preparation for the SAT Physics!

Sterling Test Prep Team   160916gdx

How to Use This Book

To extract the maximum benefit from this book, we recommend that you start by doing the first diagnostic test and use the answer key to identify the topics you need to spend more time on. Spend some time going through the explanations to this diagnostic test. Review all the explanations, not only those that you got right. After this, practice with the topical questions for those topics you identified as your weak areas – take your time and master those questions.

Next, take the second diagnostic test. You should see a dramatic improvement in your performance on the topics that you practiced prior to this. Analyze your performance on the second diagnostic test and find new topics that you can improve on. Work with the corresponding topical practice questions.

Finally, take the third and fourth diagnostic tests. At this point, you should be very strong on all topics. If you still find weaknesses, spend extra time going through the solutions and do more practice. You may also find three additional diagnostic tests on our web site.

Ultimately, your goal should be to complete all three diagnostic tests, all topical practice questions and go through all the explanations.

We want to hear from you

Your feedback is important to us because we strive to provide the highest quality prep materials. If you have any questions, comments or suggestions, email us, so we can incorporate your feedback into future editions.

Customer Satisfaction Guarantee

If you have any concerns about this book, including printing issues, contact us and we will
resolve any issues to your satisfaction.

info@sterling-prep.com

To access these and other SAT questions online at a special pricing for book owners, see page 412

Our Commitment to the Environment

Sterling Test Prep is committed to protecting our planet's resources by supporting environmental organizations with proven track records of conservation, environmental research and education and preservation of vital natural resources. A portion of our profits is donated to support these organizations so they can continue their important missions. These organizations include:

 Ocean Conservancy For over 40 years, Ocean Conservancy has been advocating for a healthy ocean by supporting sustainable solutions based on science and cleanup efforts. Among many environmental achievements, Ocean Conservancy laid the groundwork for an international moratorium on commercial whaling, played an instrumental role in protecting fur seals from overhunting and banning the international trade of sea turtles. The organization created national marine sanctuaries and served as the lead non-governmental organization in the designation of 10 of the 13 marine sanctuaries. In twenty five years of International Coastal Cleanups, volunteers of Ocean Conservancy have removed over 144 million pounds of trash from beaches. Ocean Conservancy mobilizes citizen advocates to facilitate change and protect the ocean for future generations.

 For 25 years, Rainforest Trust has been saving critical lands for conservation through land purchases and protected area designations. Rainforest Trust has played a central role in the creation of 73 new protected areas in 17 countries, including Falkland Islands, Costa Rica and Peru. Nearly 8 million acres have been saved thanks to Rainforest Trust's support of in-country partners across Latin America, with over 500,000 acres of critical lands purchased outright for reserves. Through partnerships and community engagement, Rainforest Trust empowers indigenous people to steward their own resources offering them education, training, and economic assistance.

 Since 1980, Pacific Whale Foundation has been saving whales from extinction and protecting our oceans through science and advocacy. As an international organization, with ongoing research projects in Hawaii, Australia and Ecuador, PWF is an active participant in global efforts to address threats to whales and other marine life. A pioneer in non-invasive whale research, PWF was an early leader in educating the public, from a scientific perspective, about whales and the need for ocean conservation. In addition to critically important whale education and research, PWF was instrumental in stopping the operation of a high-speed ferry in whale calving areas, prohibiting smoking and tobacco use at all Maui County beaches and parks, banning the display of captive whales and dolphins in Maui County, and supporting Maui County's ban on plastic grocery bags.

Thank you for choosing our products to achieve your educational goals.

With your purchase you support environmental causes around the world.

Table of Contents

Table of Contents *(continued)*

About SAT Physics Test

Recommended Preparation

- One-year introductory physics course on the college-preparatory level

- Laboratory experience: even though the test can measure lab skills only in a limited way (e.g. data analysis), lab skills are a significant factor in developing reasoning and problem-solving competencies.

Content

College Board divided the test into six categories. Below is the breakdown of these topical categories with their respective percentages on the test. Keep in mind that these percentages are estimations and can vary from test to test. This simply serves as a way to know where to focus your studies if you are particularly weak in a certain topic. Practice questions in this book cover all tested topics.

Content Category / Topic	% of the test

Mechanics:
    Kinematics
    Dynamics
    Energy and momentum
    Circular motion
    Simple harmonic motion
    Gravity
	36–42%

Electricity and magnetism:
    Electric fields, forces and potentials
    Capacitance
    Circuit elements and DC circuits
    Magnetism
	18–24%

Waves and optics:
    General wave properties
    Reflection and refraction
    Ray optics
    Physical optics
	15–19%

Heat and thermodynamics:
    Thermal properties
    Laws of thermodynamics
	6–11%

Modern physics:
    Quantum phenomena
    Atomic structure
    Nuclear and particle physics
    Relativity
	6–11%

Miscellaneous:
    General history of physics and questions that overlap several major topics
    Analytical skills (graphical analysis, measurement and math skills)
    Contemporary Physics
	4–9%

Questions on the SAT Physics test topics that are covered in any standard high school physics course. However, there are many differences that depend on your school's curriculum, and many students will discover that there are topics that are not familiar to them. By using this book, you can fill in the gaps in your knowledge and maximize your score.

Format of the Test

There are 75 questions on the test that must be completed in 60 minutes. The test is divided into two parts. The first is Part A, which contains classification questions. The second is Part B, which contains five-choice completion questions. Part A is 12–13 questions and Part B is 62–63 questions.

Part A: Classification Questions

Classification questions are essentially multiple-choice questions. You are provided with five answer choices that pertain to a group of few questions. These types of questions require you to have a more broad understanding of the topic because they present multiple questions on a single topic.

The difficulty level within each set of questions can vary. The beginning question won't always be easier than the last. However, with each set of classifications, the difficulty level increases as you go through the test. This means that questions 1–4 will normally be easier than questions 11–13.

Part B: Five-Choice Completion Questions

Part B consists of regular multiple-choice questions with five answer choices. This part of the test has no specific structure in terms of the topic order. You might find questions that are similar or questions that test completely different topics near each other. Questions usually increase in difficulty as you progress through the test.

How Your Knowledge is Tested

To better prepare yourself for the test, you should know that three different skills will be tested. Certain topics of physics will be tested in different ways. For example, kinematics questions often require the use of a formula, but questions on atomic structure may ask to name a particular concept.

Skills covered in the context of physics:

1) Recalling and understanding the application of major physics concepts to solve specific problems.

   - *Fundamental knowledge*: remembering and understanding concepts or information (approximately 12%–20% of test). These questions test your understanding of basic knowledge. Either you know these questions or you don't. There is no need for equations or calculations to solve these questions.

- *Single-concept problems*: applying a single physical formula or concept (about 48%–64% of test). These questions require you to recall physical relationships, formulas or equations to solve the problem. You might need to plug numbers into an equation or simply recall the equation and solve for a variable. These questions focus on your knowledge of important functions and how to use them.

- *Multiple-concept problems*: integrating two or more physical formulas or concepts (about 20%–35% of test). These questions require you to combine two or more formulas or equations. These could be formulas from the same or different topics. These questions tests your knowledge of relationships in physics and how to integrate more than one formula to solve a problem.

2) Understanding simple algebraic, trigonometric and graphical relationships, the concepts of ratio and proportion and the application of these to physics problems.

3) Application of laboratory skills in the context of the physics content

Fundamental knowledge questions are not always the easiest, and the multiple-concept questions are not always the most difficult. All three types of questions are found throughout the test with varying difficulty levels. Every question ultimately tests the same thing – whether you understand the basic principles of physics.

Scoring on SAT Physics

The scaled score on SAT Physics test ranges from 200 to 800. These scaled scores are converted from raw scores and the formula is developed by ETS at the time of the exam.

The raw score is comprised of 1 point for each correctly answered question (regardless of its difficulty) with 0.25 points subtracted for each question answered incorrectly. Questions without a response neither earn nor subtract any points.

On the next page is the approximate raw-to-scaled score conversion table for SAT Physics. This conversion formula is only an approximation and not an absolute measure.

Raw Score	Scaled Score	Raw Score	Scaled Score	Raw Score	Scaled Score
75	800	43	680	11	480
74	800	42	670	10	480
73	800	41	670	9	470
72	800	40	660	8	470
71	800	39	650	7	460
70	800	38	640	6	450
69	800	37	640	5	450
68	800	36	630	4	440
67	800	35	620	3	440
66	800	34	610	2	430
65	790	33	610	1	430
64	790	32	600	0	420
63	790	31	600	−1	410
62	780	30	590	−2	410
61	780	29	590	−3	400
60	780	28	580	−4	400
59	770	27	580	−5	390
58	770	26	570	−6	380
57	760	25	560	−7	380
56	760	24	560	−8	370
55	750	23	550	−9	360
54	740	22	540	−10	360
53	740	21	540	−11	360
52	730	20	530	−12	350
51	720	19	530	−13	350
50	720	18	520	−14	340
49	710	17	520	−15	340
48	700	16	510	−16	330
47	690	15	510	−17	320
46	690	14	500	−18	310
45	680	13	490	−19	310
44	680	12	490		

Test-Taking Strategies For SAT Physics

The best way to do well on SAT Physics is to be really good at physics. There is no way around that. Prepare for the test as much as you can, so you can answer with confidence as many questions as possible. With that being said, for multiple choice questions the only thing that matters is how many questions were answered correctly, not how much work you did to come up with those answers. A lucky guess will get you the same points as an answer you knew with confidence.

Below are some test-taking strategies to help you maximize your score. Many of these strategies you already know and they may seem like common sense. However, when a student is feeling the pressure of a timed test, these common sense strategies might be forgotten.

Mental Attitude

If you psych yourself out, chances are you will do poorly on the test. To do well on the test, particularly physics, which calls for cool, systemic thinking, you must remain calm. If you start to panic, your mind won't be able to find correct solutions to the questions. Many steps can be taken before the test to increase your confidence level. Buying this book is a good start because you can begin to practice, learn the information you should know to master the topics and get used to answering physics questions. However, there are other things you should keep in mind:

Study in advance. The information will be more manageable, and you will feel more confident if you've studied at regular intervals during the weeks leading up to the test. Cramming the night before is not a successful tactic.

Be well rested. If you are up late the night before the test, chances are you will have a difficult time concentrating and focusing on the day of the test, as you will not feel fresh and alert.

Come up for air. The best way to take this hour-long test is not to keep your head down, concentrating the full sixty minutes. Even though you only have 48 seconds per question and there is no time to waste, it is recommended to take a few seconds between the questions to take a deep breath and relax your muscles.

Time Management

Aside from good preparation, time management is the most important strategy that you should know how to use on any test. You have an average time of 48 seconds for each question. You will breeze through some in fifteen seconds and others you may be stuck on for two minutes.

Don't dwell on any one question for too long. You should aim to look at every question on the test. It would be unfortunate to not earn the points for a question you could have easily answered just because you did not get a chance to look at it. If you are still in the first half of the test and find yourself spending more than a minute on one question and don't see yourself getting closer to solving it, it is better to move on. It will be more productive if you come back to this question with a fresh mind at the end of the test. You do not want to lose points because you were stuck on one or few questions and did not get a chance to work with other questions that are easy for you.

Nail the easy questions quickly. On SAT subject tests, you get as many points for answering easy questions as you do for answering difficult questions. This means that you get a lot more points for five quickly answered questions than for one hard-earned victory. The questions do increase in difficulty as you progress throughout the test. However, each student has their strong and weak points, and you might be a master on a certain type of questions that are normally considered difficult. Skip the questions you are struggling with and nail the easy ones.

Skip the unfamiliar. If you come across a question that is totally unfamiliar to you, skip it. Do not try to figure out what is going on or what they are trying to ask. At the end of the test, you can go back to these questions if you have time. If you are encountering a question that you have no clue about, most likely you won't be able to answer it through analysis. The better strategy is to leave such questions to the end and use the guessing strategy on them at the end of the test.

Set a Target Score

The task of pacing yourself will become easier if you are aware of the number of questions you need to answer to reach the score you want to get. Always strive for the highest score, but also be realistic about your level of preparation. It may be helpful if you research what counts as a good score for the colleges you are applying to. You can talk to admissions offices at colleges, research college guidebooks or specific college websites, or talk to your guidance counselor. Find the average score received by students that were admitted to the colleges of your choice and set your target score higher than the average. Take a look at the chart we provided earlier to see how many questions you would need to answer correctly to reach this target score. You can score:

> 800 if you answered 68 right, 7 wrong, and left 0 blank
> 750 if you answered 58 right, 12 wrong, and left 5 blank
> 700 if you answered 51 right, 13 wrong, and left 11 blank
> 650 if you answered 43 right, 16 wrong, and left 16 blank
> 600 if you answered 36 right, 19 wrong, and left 20 blank

If the average score on SAT Physics for the school you're interested in is 700, set your target at about 750. To achieve that score, you need to get 58 questions right, which leaves you room to get 12 wrong and leave 5 blank. Therefore, you can leave a number of questions blank, get some wrong, and still achieve 750. If you have an idea of how many questions you need to answer correctly, you can pace yourself accordingly. Keep in mind that you'll likely get some answered questions wrong.

Understanding the Question

It is important that you know what the question is asking before you select your answer choice. This seems obvious, but it is surprising how many students don't read a question carefully because they rush through the test and select a wrong answer choice.

A successful student will not just read the question, but will take a moment to understand the question before even looking at the answer choices. This student will be able to separate the important information from distracters and will not get confused on the questions that are asking to identify a false statement (which is the correct answer). Once you've identified what you're dealing with and what is being asked, you should be able to spend less time on picking the right answer. If the question is asking for a general concept, try to answer the question before looking at the answer choices, then look at the choices. If you see a choice that matches the answer you thought of, most likely it is the correct choice.

Correct Way to Guess

Random guessing won't help you on the test, but educated guessing is the strategy you should use in certain situations if you can eliminate at least one (or even two) of the five possible choices.

On SAT subject tests, you lose ¼ of a point for each wrong answer. This is done to prevent blind guessing, but not to punish you for making an educated guess. For example, if you just randomly entered responses for the first 20 questions, there is a 20% chance of guessing correctly on any given question. Therefore, the odds are you would guess right on 4 questions and wrong on 16 questions. Your raw score for those 20 questions would then be 0 because you get 4 points for 4 correct answers and lose 4 points for 16 wrong answers. This would be the same as leaving all 20 questions blank.

However, if for each of the 20 questions you can eliminate one answer choice because you know it to be wrong, you will have a 25% chance of being right. Therefore, your odds would move to 5 questions right and 15 questions wrong. This gives a raw score of 1.25 (gain 5 points and lose 3.75 points).

Guessing is not cheating and should not be viewed that way. Rather it is a form of "partial credit" because while you might not be sure of the correct answer, you do have relevant knowledge to identify one or two choices that are wrong.

SAT Physics Tips

Tip 1: Know the formulas

Since 70–80% of the test requires that you know how to use the formulas, it is imperative that you memorize and understand when to use each one. It is not permitted to bring any papers with notes to the test. Therefore you must memorize all the formulas you will need to solve the questions on the test, and there is no way around it.

As you work with this book, you will learn the application of all the important physical formulas and will use them in many different question types. If you are feeling nervous about having a lot of formulas in your head and worry that it will affect your problem-solving skills, look over the formulas right before you go into the testing space and write them down before you start the test. This way, you don't have to worry about remembering the formulas throughout the test. When you need to use them, you can refer back to where you wrote them down earlier.

Tip 2: Know how to manipulate the formulas

You must know how to apply the formulas in addition to just memorizing them. Questions will be worded in ways unfamiliar to you to test whether you can manipulate equations that you know to calculate the correct answer. Knowing that $F = ma$ is not helpful without understanding that $a = F/m$ because it is very unlikely that a question will ask to calculate the force acting on an object with a given mass and acceleration. Rather you will be asked to calculate the acceleration of an object of a given mass with the force acting on it.

Tip 3: Estimating

This tip is only helpful for quantitative questions. For example, estimating can help you choose the correct answer if you have a general sense of the order of magnitude. This is especially applicable to questions where all answer choices have different orders of magnitude and you can save time that you would have to spend on actual calculations.

Tip 4: Draw the question

Don't hesitate to write, draw or graph your thought process once you have read and understood the question. This can help you determine what kind of information you are dealing with. Draw the force and velocity vectors, ray/wave paths, or anything else that may be helpful. Even if a question does not require a graphic answer, drawing a graph (for example, a sketch of a particle's velocity) can allow a solution to become obvious.

Tip 5: Eliminating wrong answers

This tip utilizes the strategy of educated guessing. You can usually eliminate one or two answer choices right away in most questions. In addition, there are certain types of questions for which you can use a particular elimination method.

By using logical estimations for quantitative questions, you can eliminate the answer choices that are unreasonably high or unreasonably low.

In classification questions (Part A), the same five answer choices apply to several questions. It is helpful to keep in mind that it is not often that one answer choice is correct for more than one question (though it does happen sometimes). Some answer choices that you are confident to be correct for some questions are good elimination candidates for other questions where you're trying to use a guessing strategy. It is not a sure bet, but you should be aware of this option if you have to resort to guessing on some questions.

Roman numeral questions are the type of multiple-choice questions that list a few possible answers with five different combinations of these answers. Supposing that you know that one of the Roman numeral choices is wrong, you can eliminate all answer choices that include it. These questions are usually difficult for most test takers because they tend to present more than one potentially correct statement which is often included in more than one answer choice. However, they have a certain upside if you can eliminate at least one wrong statement.

Last helpful tip: fill in your answers carefully

This seems like a simple thing, but it is extremely important. Many test takers make mistakes when filling in answers whether it is a paper test or computer-based test. Make sure you pay attention and check off the answer choice you actually chose as correct.

Common Physics Formulas & Conversions

Constants and Conversion Factors

1 unified atomic mass unit	$1\ u = 1.66 \times 10^{-27}\ kg$
	$1\ u = 931\ MeV/c^2$
Proton mass	$m_p = 1.67 \times 10^{-27}\ kg$
Neutron mass	$m_n = 1.67 \times 10^{-27}\ kg$
Electron mass	$m_e = 9.11 \times 10^{-31}\ kg$
Electron charge magnitude	$e = 1.60 \times 10^{-19}\ C$
Avogrado's number	$N_0 = 6.02 \times 10^{23}\ mol^{-1}$
Universal gas constant	$R = 8.31\ J/(mol \cdot K)$
Boltzmann's constant	$k_B = 1.38 \times 10^{-23}\ J/K$
Speed of light	$c = 3.00 \times 10^8\ m/s$
Planck's constant	$h = 6.63 \times 10^{-34}\ J \cdot s$
	$h = 4.14 \times 10^{-15}\ eV \cdot s$
	$hc = 1.99 \times 10^{-25}\ J \cdot m$
	$hc = 1.24 \times 10^3\ eV \cdot nm$
Vacuum permittivity	$\varepsilon_0 = 8.85 \times 10^{-12}\ C^2/N \cdot m^2$
Coulomb's law constant	$k = 1/4\pi\varepsilon_0 = 9.0 \times 10^9\ N \cdot m^2/C^2$
Vacuum permeability	$\mu_0 = 4\pi \times 10^{-7}\ (T \cdot m)/A$
Magnetic constant	$k' = \mu_0/4\pi = 10^{-7}\ (T \cdot m)/A$
Universal gravitational constant	$G = 6.67 \times 10^{-11}\ m^3/kg \cdot s^2$
Acceleration due to gravity at Earth's surface	$g = 9.8\ m/s^2$
1 atmosphere pressure	$1\ atm = 1.0 \times 10^5\ N/m^2$
	$1\ atm = 1.0 \times 10^5\ Pa$
1 electron volt	$1\ eV = 1.60 \times 10^{-19}\ J$
Balmer constant	$B = 3.645 \times 10^{-7}\ m$
Rydberg constant	$R = 1.097 \times 10^7\ m^{-1}$
Stefan constant	$\sigma = 5.67 \times 10^{-8}\ W/m^2 K^4$

Units			Prefixes	
Name	**Symbol**	**Factor**	**Prefix**	**Symbol**
meter	m	10^{12}	tera	T
kilogram	kg	10^{9}	giga	G
second	s	10^{6}	mega	M
ampere	A	10^{3}	kilo	k
kelvin	K	10^{-2}	centi	c
mole	mol	10^{-3}	mili	m
hertz	Hz	10^{-6}	micro	μ
newton	N	10^{-9}	nano	n
pascal	Pa	10^{-12}	pico	p
joule	J			
watt	W			
coulomb	C			
volt	V			
ohm	Ω			
henry	H			
farad	F			
tesla	T			
degree Celsius	°C			
electronvolt	eV			

Values of Trigonometric Functions for Common Angles

θ	$\sin \theta$	$\cos \theta$	$\tan \theta$
0°	0	1	0
30°	1/2	$\sqrt{3}/2$	$\sqrt{3}/3$
37°	3/5	4/5	3/4
45°	$\sqrt{2}/2$	$\sqrt{2}/2$	1
53°	4/5	3/5	4/3
60°	$\sqrt{3}/2$	1/2	$\sqrt{3}$
90°	1	0	∞

Newtonian Mechanics

		a = acceleration
	$v = v_0 + at$	
		A = amplitude
	$x = x_0 + v_0t + \frac{1}{2}at^2$	
Translational Motion		E = energy
	$v^2 = v_0^2 + 2a\Delta x$	F = force
	$\vec{a} = \dfrac{\sum \vec{F}}{m} = \dfrac{\vec{F}_{net}}{m}$	f = frequency
		h = height
	$\omega = \omega_0 + \alpha t$	I = rotational inertia
	$\theta = \theta_0 + \omega_0 t + \frac{1}{2}\alpha t^2$	J = impulse
Rotational Motion		K = kinetic energy
	$\omega^2 = \omega_0^2 + 2\alpha\Delta\theta$	k = spring constant
	$\vec{\alpha} = \dfrac{\sum \vec{\tau}}{I} = \dfrac{\vec{\tau}_{net}}{I}$	ℓ = length
		m = mass
Force of Friction	$\left\|\vec{F}_f\right\| \leq \mu\left\|\vec{F}_n\right\|$	N = normal force
Centripetal Acceleration	$a_c = \dfrac{v^2}{r}$	P = power
		p = momentum
Torque	$\tau = r_\perp F = rF\sin\theta$	L = angular momentum
		r = radius of distance
Momentum	$\Delta\vec{p} = m\vec{v}$	T = period
Impulse	$J = \Delta\vec{p} = \vec{F}\Delta t$	t = time
		U = potential energy
Kinetic Energy	$K = \dfrac{1}{2}mv^2$	v = velocity or speed
		W = work done on a system
Potential Energy	$\Delta U_g = mg\Delta y$	
Work	$\Delta E = W = F_\| d = Fd\cos\theta$	x = position
		y = height
Power	$P = \dfrac{\Delta E}{\Delta t} = \dfrac{\Delta W}{\Delta t}$	α = angular acceleration

Simple Harmonic Motion	$x = A \cos(\omega t) = A \cos(2\pi f t)$	*μ = coefficient of*
Center of Mass	$x_{cm} = \dfrac{\sum m_i x_i}{\sum m_i}$	*friction*
		θ = angle
Angular Momentum	$L = I\omega$	*τ = torque*
		ω = angular speed
Angular Impulse	$\Delta L = \tau \Delta t$	
Angular Kinetic Energy	$K = \dfrac{1}{2}I\omega^2$	
Work	$W = F\Delta r \cos\theta$	
Power	$P = Fv \sin\theta$	
Spring Force	$|\vec{F_s}| = k|\vec{x}|$	
Spring Potential Energy	$U_s = \dfrac{1}{2}kx^2$	
Period of Spring Oscillator	$T_s = 2\pi\sqrt{m/k}$	
Period of Simple Pendulum	$T_p = 2\pi\sqrt{\ell/g}$	
Period	$T = \dfrac{2\pi}{\omega} = \dfrac{1}{f}$	
Gravitational Body Force	$|\vec{F_g}| = G\dfrac{m_1 m_2}{r^2}$	
Potential Energy of Gravitational Body	$U_G = -\dfrac{Gm_1 m_2}{r}$	

Electricity and Magnetism

Electric Field Strength	$\vec{E} = \dfrac{\vec{F}_E}{q}$	A = area
		B = magnetic field
		C = capacitance
Electric Field Strength	$\left|\vec{E}\right| = \dfrac{1}{4\pi\varepsilon_0}\dfrac{|q|}{r^2}$	d = distance
		E = electric field
Electric Field Strength	$\left|\vec{E}\right| = \dfrac{|\Delta V|}{|\Delta r|}$	ϵ = emf
		F = force
Electric Field Force	$\left|\vec{F}_E\right| = \dfrac{1}{4\pi\varepsilon_0}\dfrac{|q_1 q_2|}{r^2}$	I = current
		l = length
Electric Potential Energy	$\Delta U_E = q\Delta V$	P = power
		Q = charge
Voltage	$V = \dfrac{1}{4\pi\varepsilon_0}\dfrac{q}{r}$	q = point charge
		R = resistance
Capacitor Voltage	$\Delta V = \dfrac{Q}{C}$	r = separation
		t = time
Capacitance	$C = \kappa\varepsilon_0\dfrac{A}{d}$	U = potential energy
		V = electric potential
Capacitor Electric Field	$E = \dfrac{Q}{\varepsilon_0 A}$	v = speed
		κ = dielectric constant
Capacitor Potential Energy	$U_C = \frac{1}{2}Q\Delta V = \frac{1}{2}C(\Delta V)^2$	ρ = resistivity
		θ = angle
Current	$I = \dfrac{\Delta Q}{\Delta t}$	Φ = flux
Resistance	$R = \dfrac{\rho l}{A}$	
Power	$P = I\Delta V$	

Current $\qquad$ $I = \dfrac{\Delta V}{R}$

Resistors in Series $\qquad$ $R_s = \displaystyle\sum_i R_i$

Resistors in Parallel $\qquad$ $\dfrac{1}{R_p} = \displaystyle\sum_i \dfrac{1}{R_i}$

Capacitors in Parallel $\qquad$ $C_p = \displaystyle\sum_i C_i$

Capacitors in Series $\qquad$ $\dfrac{1}{C_s} = \displaystyle\sum_i \dfrac{1}{C_i}$

Magnetic Field Strength $\qquad$ $B = \dfrac{\mu_0 I}{2\pi r}$

Magnetic Force

$$\vec{F}_M = q\vec{v} \times \vec{B}$$

$$\vec{F}_M = |q\vec{v}||\sin\theta||\vec{B}|$$

$$\vec{F}_M = I\vec{l} \times \vec{B}$$

$$\vec{F}_M = |I\vec{l}||\sin\theta||\vec{B}|$$

Magnetic Flux

$$\Phi_B = \vec{B} \cdot \vec{A}$$

$$\Phi_B = |\vec{B}| \cos\theta \, |\vec{A}|$$

Electromagnetic Induction

$$\epsilon = \dfrac{-\Phi_B}{\Delta t}$$

$$\epsilon = Blv$$

Fluid Mechanics and Thermal Physics

Density	$\rho = \dfrac{m}{V}$	A = area
		c = specific heat
Pressure	$P = \dfrac{F}{A}$	d = thickness
		e = emissivity
Absolute Pressure	$P = P_0 + \rho g h$	F = force
Buoyant Force	$F_b = \rho V g$	h = depth
Fluid Continuity Equation	$A_1 v_1 = A_2 v_2$	k = thermal conductivity
		K = kinetic energy
Bernoulli's Equation	$P_1 + \rho g y_1 + \dfrac{1}{2}\rho v_1^2 = P_2 + \rho g y_2 + \dfrac{1}{2}\rho v_2^2$	l = length
		L = latent heat
Heat Conduction	$\dfrac{Q}{\Delta t} = \dfrac{kA\Delta T}{d}$	m = mass
		n = number of moles
		n_c = efficiency
Thermal Radiation	$P = e\sigma A(T^4 - T_C^4)$	N = number of molecules
Ideal Gas Law	$PV = nRT = Nk_BT$	P = pressure or power
		Q = energy transferred to
Average Energy	$K = \dfrac{3}{2}k_BT$	a system by heating
		T = temperature
Work	$W = -P\Delta V$	t = time
Internal Energy	$\Delta U = Q + W$	U = internal energy
Linear Expansion	$\Delta l = \alpha l_o \Delta T$	V = volume
Heat Engine Efficiency	$n_c = |W/Q_H|$	v = speed
		W = work done on a
Carnot Heat Engine Efficiency	$n_c = \dfrac{T_H - T_c}{T_H}$	system
		y = height
		σ = Stefan constant
Energy of Temperature Change	$Q = mc\Delta T$	α = coefficient of linear expansion
Energy of Phase Change	$Q = mL$	ρ = density

Optics

Wavelength to Frequency	$\lambda = \dfrac{v}{f}$	d = separation
Index of Refraction	$n = \dfrac{c}{v}$	f = frequency or focal length
		h = height
Snell's Law	$n_1 \sin \theta_1 = n_2 \sin \theta_2$	L = distance
		M = magnification
Thin Lens Equation	$\dfrac{1}{s_i} + \dfrac{1}{s_0} = \dfrac{1}{f}$	m = an integer
		n = index of refraction
		R = radius of curvature
Magnification Equation	$\|M\| = \left\|\dfrac{h_i}{h_o}\right\| = \left\|\dfrac{s_i}{s_o}\right\|$	s = distance
		v = speed
Double Slit Diffraction	$d \sin \theta = m\lambda$	x = position
	$\Delta L = m\lambda$	λ = wavelength
		θ = angle
Critical Angle	$\sin \theta_c = \dfrac{n_2}{n_1}$	
Focal Length of Spherical Mirror	$f = \dfrac{R}{2}$	

Acoustics

Standing Wave/ Open Pipe Harmonics	$\lambda = \dfrac{2L}{n}$	f = frequency
		L = length
Closed Pipe Harmonics	$\lambda = \dfrac{4L}{n}$	m = mass
		M = molecular mass
Harmonic Frequencies	$f_n = nf_1$	n = harmonic number
Speed of Sound in Ideal Gas	$v_{sound} = \sqrt{\dfrac{yRT}{M}}$	R = gas constant
		T = tension
Speed of Wave Through Wire	$v = \sqrt{\dfrac{T}{m/L}}$	v = velocity
		y = adiabatic constant
Doppler Effect (Approaching)	$f_{observed} = \left(\dfrac{v}{v - v_{source}}\right) f_{source}$	λ = wavelength
Doppler Effect (Receding)	$f_{observed} = \left(\dfrac{v}{v + v_{source}}\right) f_{source}$	

Modern Physics

Photon Energy	$E = hf$	B = Balmer constant
		c = speed of light
Photoelectric Electron Energy	$K_{max} = hf - \phi$	E = energy
		f = frequency
Electron Wavelength	$\lambda = \dfrac{h}{p}$	K = kinetic energy
		m = mass
Energy Mass Relationship	$E = mc^2$	p = momentum
Rydberg Formula	$\dfrac{1}{\lambda} = R\left(\dfrac{1}{n_f^2} - \dfrac{1}{n_i^2}\right)$	R = Rydberg constant
		v = velocity
Balmer Formula	$\lambda = B\left(\dfrac{n^2}{n^2 - 2^2}\right)$	λ = wavelength
		ϕ = work function
Lorentz Factor	$\gamma = \dfrac{1}{\sqrt{1 - \dfrac{v^2}{c^2}}}$	γ = Lorentz factor
Relativistic Mass	$m_R = m_0\gamma$	

Geometry and Trigonometry

Rectangle	$A = bh$	A = area
		C = circumference
Triangle	$A = \dfrac{1}{2}bh$	V = volume
		S = surface area
Circle	$A = \pi r^2$	b = base
	$C = 2\pi r$	h = height
		l = length
Rectangular Solid	$V = lwh$	
		w = width
Cylinder	$V = \pi r^2 l$	r = radius
	$S = 2\pi rl + 2\pi r^2$	θ = angle
Sphere	$V = \dfrac{4}{3}\pi r^3$ $S = 4\pi r^2$	
Right Triangle	$a^2 + b^2 = c^2$ $\sin\theta = \dfrac{a}{c}$ $\cos\theta = \dfrac{b}{c}$ $\tan\theta = \dfrac{a}{b}$	

SAT Physics

Diagnostic Tests

Diagnostic Test #1

Answer Sheet

#	Answer:					Mark for review	#	Answer:					Mark for review
1:	A	B	C	D	E	___	31:	A	B	C	D	E	___
2:	A	B	C	D	E	___	32:	A	B	C	D	E	___
3:	A	B	C	D	E	___	33:	A	B	C	D	E	___
4:	A	B	C	D	E	___	34:	A	B	C	D	E	___
5:	A	B	C	D	E	___	35:	A	B	C	D	E	___
6:	A	B	C	D	E	___	36:	A	B	C	D	E	___
7:	A	B	C	D	E	___	37:	A	B	C	D	E	___
8:	A	B	C	D	E	___	38:	A	B	C	D	E	___
9:	A	B	C	D	E	___	39:	A	B	C	D	E	___
10:	A	B	C	D	E	___	40:	A	B	C	D	E	___
11:	A	B	C	D	E	___	41:	A	B	C	D	E	___
12:	A	B	C	D	E	___	42:	A	B	C	D	E	___
13:	A	B	C	D	E	___	43:	A	B	C	D	E	___
14:	A	B	C	D	E	___	44:	A	B	C	D	E	___
15:	A	B	C	D	E	___	45:	A	B	C	D	E	___
16:	A	B	C	D	E	___	46:	A	B	C	D	E	___
17:	A	B	C	D	E	___	47:	A	B	C	D	E	___
18:	A	B	C	D	E	___	48:	A	B	C	D	E	___
19:	A	B	C	D	E	___	49:	A	B	C	D	E	___
20:	A	B	C	D	E	___	50:	A	B	C	D	E	___
21:	A	B	C	D	E	___	51:	A	B	C	D	E	___
22:	A	B	C	D	E	___	52:	A	B	C	D	E	___
23:	A	B	C	D	E	___	53:	A	B	C	D	E	___
24:	A	B	C	D	E	___	54:	A	B	C	D	E	___
25:	A	B	C	D	E	___	55:	A	B	C	D	E	___
26:	A	B	C	D	E	___							
27:	A	B	C	D	E	___							
28:	A	B	C	D	E	___							
29:	A	B	C	D	E	___							
30:	A	B	C	D	E	___							

This Diagnostic Test is designed for you to assess your proficiency on each topic. Use your test results and identify areas of your strength and weakness to adjust your study plan and enhance your fundamental knowledge.

The length of the Diagnostic Tests is proven to be optimal for a single study session.

Our guarantee – the highest quality preparation materials.

We expect our books to have the highest quality content and be error-free.

Be the first to report an error, typo or inaccuracy and receive a
$10 reward for a content error or
$5 reward for a typo or grammatical mistake.

info@sterling-prep.com

1. What property of matter determines an object's resistance to change in its state of motion?

    I. mass   II. density   III. volume

A. I only   **B.** II only   **C.** III only   **D.** I and II only   **E.** I and III only

2. Two forces of equal magnitude act on an object. If each force is 4.6 N and the angle between them is 40°, what is the magnitude and direction of a third force for the object to be in equilibrium?

    A. 2.3 N, to the right   **C.** 6.5 N, to the right

    B. 4.3 N, to the right   **D.** 0.6 N, to the right

    E. 8.6 N, to the right

3. A thermally-isolated system is made up of a hot piece of aluminum and a cold piece of copper, with the aluminum and copper in thermal contact. The specific heat capacity of aluminum is more than double that of copper. Which object experiences the greater magnitude of gain or loss of heat during the time the system takes to reach thermal equilibrium?

    A. Aluminum   **C.** Neither, because both undergo the same magnitude of gain or loss of heat

    B. Copper   **D.** Requires knowing the masses

                      E. Requires knowing the volumes

4. In the absence of friction, how much work would a boy do while pulling a 10 kg sled a distance of 3.5 m with a 20 N force?

    A. 57 J   **B.** 70 J   **C.** 1.8 J   **D.** 85 J   **E.** 280 J

5. Total constructive interference is observed when two waves with the same frequency and wavelength are at a:

    A. 45° phase difference   **C.** 180° phase difference

    B. 90° phase difference   **D.** –90° phase difference   **E.** 0° phase difference

6. The Doppler shift occurs when the source of waves and a detector are moving relative to each other. There is an increase in the detected frequency when the source and detector are approaching each other, and a decrease in the detected frequency when they are moving away from each other. A commuter train is moving rapidly at 50 m/s towards Kevin who is standing still. The train sounds its horn at 420 Hz. The speed of sound is 350 m/s at a temperature of 29 °C. What frequency does Kevin hear after the train passes?

    A. 335 Hz   **B.** 368 Hz   **C.** 424 Hz   **D.** 446 Hz   **E.** 295 Hz

7. If the speed of a moving object doubles, then what else doubles?

        I. Acceleration   II. Kinetic energy   III. Momentum

  A. I only   **B.** II only   **C.** III only   **D.** I and II only   **E.** I and III only

8. A charged particle that is moving in a uniform static magnetic field:

  A. may experience a magnetic force, but its speed does not change
  B. may experience a magnetic force, but its direction of motion does not change
  C. always experiences a magnetic force, and its direction of motion does change
  D. always experiences a magnetic force, and its speed does not change
  E. always experiences a magnetic force, and its direction of motion does not change

9. Two objects, I and II, have equal charge and mass. Because of equal gravitational and electrostatic forces between them, neither body is in motion. If the mass of object I is halved, equilibrium is maintained if which change occurs for object II:

  A. mass is quadrupled   **C.** charge is doubled
  B. mass is halved   **D.** charge is halved   **E.** charge is increased by $\sqrt{2}$

10. What is the focal length of a lens if a candle is viewed at a distance of 4 m from the lens and the image is 2 m from the other side of the lens?

  A. –2 m   **B.** –4/3 m   **C.** 3/4 m   **D.** 2 m   **E.** 4/3 m

11. When a nucleus captures a β^- particle, the atomic number of the nucleus:

  A. increases by two   **C.** increases by one
  B. decreases by one   **D.** remains the same   **E.** decreases by two

12. How far from the heavier end must the fulcrum of a massless 10 m seesaw be if an 800 N father on one side is to balance his 200 N son at the other end?

  A. 0.5 m   **B.** 2 m   **C.** 1 m   **D.** 8 m   **E.** 6 m

13. A ball bounces on the floor three times, whereby it loses 20% of its energy with each bounce due to heating. How high is the third bounce, provided the ball was released 250 cm from the floor?

  A. 115 cm   **B.** 150 cm   **C.** 75 cm   **D.** 180 cm   **E.** 128 cm

14. What is the period of a wave if its frequency is 10 Hz?

A. 0.1 s   **B.** 1 s   **C.** 100 s   **D.** 10 s   **E.** 0.01 s

15. What is the frequency of a pressure wave with a wavelength of 2.5 m that is traveling at 1,600 m/s?

A. 640 Hz   **B.** 5.6 kHz   **C.** 0.64 Hz   **D.** 4 kHz   **E.** 64 Hz

16. What type of radioactive decay produces a daughter nuclide that is the same element as the parent nuclide?

    I. Alpha   II. Gamma   III. Beta

A. I only   **B.** II only   **C.** III only   **D.** I and II only   **E.** I and III only

17. Which characteristic is required for a mass spectrometer?

A. Perpendicular electric and gravitational fields
B. Perpendicular gravitational and magnetic fields
C. Perpendicular magnetic and electric fields
D. Collinear magnetic and electric fields
E. Collinear gravitational and magnetic fields

18. What is the peak current for a 26 μF capacitor connected across a 120 V_{rms} 60 Hz source?

A. 1.2 A   **B.** 7.3 A   **C.** 2.7 A   **D.** 0 A   **E.** 0.13 A

19. A light ray in glass arrives at the glass-water interface at an angle of $\theta = 48°$ with respect to the normal. The refracted ray in the water makes an angle of $\phi = 61°$ with respect to the normal. If the angle of incidence changes to $\theta = 25°$, what is the new angle of refraction ϕ in the water? (Use index of refraction of water = 1.33)

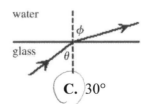

    A. 16°   **B.** 54°   **C.** 30°   **D.** 24°   **E.** 38°

20. What is the name of the type of radiation that has the atomic notation $^{0}_{0}\gamma$?

A. Gamma   **B.** Neutron   **C.** Alpha   **D.** Beta   **E.** Proton

21. As a solid goes through a phase change to a liquid, heat is absorbed and the temperature:

A. fluctuates   C. decreases

B. remains the same   D. increases   E. depends on the heat absorbed

22. Which of the following statements is TRUE regarding the acceleration experienced by a block moving down a frictionless plane that is inclined at a 20° angle?

A. It decreases as the block moves down the plane

B. It increases as the block moves down the plane

C. It increases at a rate proportional to the incline

D. It decreases at a rate proportional to the incline

E. It remains constant

23. Which of the following statements is FALSE?

A. Waves from a vibrating string are transverse waves

B. Sound travels much slower than light

C. Sound waves are longitudinal pressure waves

D. Sound can travel through a vacuum

E. In music, pitch and frequency have approximately the same meaning

24. A 15 kg block on a table is connected by a string to a 60 kg mass, which is hanging over the edge of the table. Ignoring the frictional force, what is acceleration of the 15 kg block when the 60 kg block is released? (Use acceleration due to gravity $g = 10$ m/s^2)

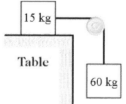

A. 9.5 m/s^2 C. 10.5 m/s^2

B. 7.5 m/s^2 D. 8 m/s^2 E. 6 m/s^2

25. Two charges, $Q_1 = 3.4 \times 10^{-10}$ C and $Q_2 = 6.8 \times 10^{-9}$ C, are separated by a distance of 1 cm. Let F_1 be the magnitude of the electrostatic force felt by Q_1 due to Q_2 and let F_2 be the magnitude of the electrostatic force felt by Q_2 due to Q_1. What is the ratio of F_1 / F_2?

A. 2   B. 1   C. 16   D. 8   E. 4

26. The electric power of a lamp that carries 2 A at 120 V is:

A. 24 W   B. 2 W   C. 60 W   D. 120 W   E. 240 W

27. What happens to an atom when it absorbs energy?

A. The atom re-emits the energy as light
B. The atom re-emits the energy as heat
C. The extra energy decreases the speed of the electrons in their orbitals
D. The atom stores the energy as kinetic energy
E. The atom re-emits the energy as an electron

28. A sievert is the SI unit for:

A. measuring the amount of low radiation absorbed per kilogram of tissue
B. measuring the energy of different types of radiation
C. measuring the amount of radiation absorbed per gram of tissue
D. the amount of radiation that produces one unit charge in 1 cm^3 of water
E. the amount of radioactive substance for 1×10^{10} disintegrations per second

29. Ignoring air resistance, how long does it take a coin to reach the ground when it is dropped from a 42 m building?   Use $g = 10$ m/s^2

  A. 1.4 s   **B.** 2.9 s   **C.** 3.6 s   **D.** 5.4 s   **E.** 4.7 s

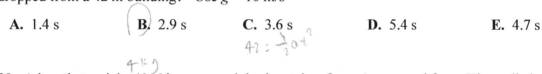

30. A box that weighs 40 N is on a rough horizontal surface. An external force *F* is applied horizontally to the box. A normal force and a friction force are also present. When force *F* equals 8.8 N, the box is in motion at a constant velocity. The box decelerates when force *F* is removed. What is the magnitude of the acceleration of the box? (Use acceleration due to gravity $g = 10$ m/s^2)

  A. 0.55 m/s^2 **B.** 1.1 m/s^2 **C.** 4.4 m/s^2 **D.** 2.2 m/s^2 **E.** 0 m/s^2

31. A bullet shot from a gun with a longer barrel has a greater muzzle velocity because the bullet receives a greater:

    I. force   II. impulse   III. acceleration

  A. I only   **B.** II only   **C.** III only   **D.** I and II only   **E.** II and III only

32. A 1,000 kg car is traveling at 30 m/s on a level road when the driver slams on the brakes, bringing the car to a stop. What is the change in kinetic energy during the braking, if the skid marks are 35 m long?

  A. –4.5 × 10^5 J   **B.** 0 J   **C.** –9 × 10^{10} J   **D.** 4.2 × 10^5 J   **E.** 9 × 10^{10} J

33. The graph shows the position (x) as a function of time (t) for a system undergoing simple harmonic motion. Which of the following graphs represents the acceleration of this system as a function of time?

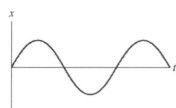

A.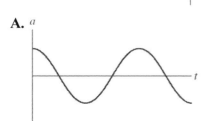

C.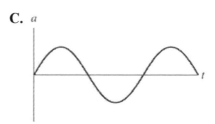

B.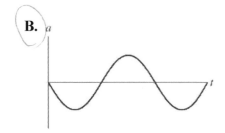

D.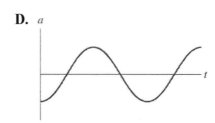

E. none of the above

34. What is the average kinetic energy of an ideal gas at 740 K? (Use Boltzmann's constant $k = 1.38 \times 10^{-23}$ J/K)

A. 3.9×10^{-19} J   **C.** 5.8×10^{-21} J

B. 2.4×10^{-17} J   **D.** 1.5×10^{-20} J   **E.** 4.5×10^{-22} J

35. If two converging lenses with focal lengths of 10 cm and 20 cm are placed in contact, what is the power of the combination?

A. 10 D   **B.** 15 D   **C.** 20 D   **D.** 30 D   **E.** 25 D

36. What is the capacitance of a capacitor with a resistance of 4 kΩ at a frequency of 0.6 kHz?

A. 96 µF   **B.** 2.4 µF   **C.** 0.15 µF   **D.** 0.024 µF   **E.** 0.066 µF

37. A 3 Ω and a 1.5 Ω resistor are connected in parallel within a circuit. If the voltage drop across the 3 Ω resistor is 2 V, what is the sum of the currents through these two resistors?

   A. 4/3 amps   **B.** 3/2 amps   **C.** 2 amps   **D.** 2/3 amps   **E.** 3/4 amps

38. Ignoring air resistance, what is the speed of a rock as it hits the ground if it was dropped from a 50 m cliff? (Use acceleration due to gravity $g = 10$ m/s^2)

   A. 21 m/s   **B.** 14 m/s   **C.** 32 m/s   **D.** 42 m/s   **E.** 9 m/s

39. Sound can undergo refraction in:

   I. air   II. water   III. a vacuum

   A. I only   **B.** II only   **C.** III only   **D.** I and II only   **E.** I and III only

40. Crests of an ocean wave pass a pier every 10 s. What is the wavelength of the ocean waves if the waves are moving at 4.6 m/s?

   A. 4.4 m   **B.** 0.46 m   **C.** 4.6 m   **D.** 2.2 m   **E.** 46 m

41. How much work is done on a crate if it is pushed 2 m with a force of 20 N?

   A. 10 J   **B.** 20 J   **C.** 30 J   **D.** 40 J   **E.** 50 J

42. Two friends are standing on opposite ends of a canoe which is initially at rest with respect to the lake. Steve is on the right when he throws a very massive ball to the left, and Mike, on the left, catches it. Ignoring friction between the canoe and the water, after the ball is caught, the canoe:

   A. moves to the right before reversing direction   **C.** remains stationary
   B. moves to the left before reversing direction   **D.** moves to the right
                                                      E. moves to the left

43. Lisa is standing in a moving truck, and she suddenly falls backward because the truck's:

   A. speed remained the same   **C.** acceleration remained the same
   B. velocity decreased   **D.** velocity increased
                                                      E. velocity remained the same

44. At terminal velocity, an object falling toward the surface of the Earth has a velocity that:

   A. depends on the mass of the object   **C.** remains constant
   B. depends on the weight of the object   **D.** increases   **E.** decreases

---

45. Aluminum has a positive coefficient of thermal expansion. Consider a round hole that has been drilled in a large sheet of aluminum. As the temperature increases and the surrounding metal expands, the diameter of the hole:

    A. either increases or decreases, depending on how much metal surrounds the hole

    B. remains constant

    C. decreases

    D. increases

    E. either increases or decreases, depending on the total change in temperature

46. Which statement is correct when a flower pot of mass m falls from rest to the ground for a distance h below?

    A. The speed of the pot when it hits the ground is proportional to m

    B. The KE of the pot when it hits the ground does not depend on h

    C. The KE of the pot when it hits the ground is proportional to h

    D. The speed of the pot when it hits the ground is proportional to h

    E. The speed of the pot when it hits the ground is inversely proportional to h

47. Two speakers placed 3 m apart are producing in-phase sound waves with a wavelength of 1 m. A microphone is placed between the speakers to determine the intensity of the sound at various points. What kind of point exists exactly 0.5 m to the left of the speaker on the right? (Use speed of sound $v = 340$ m/s)

    A. Antinode   **C.** Node and antinode

    B. Node   **D.** Destructive interference   **E.** None of the above

48. What causes an object to become electrostatically charged?

    A. Charge is created   **C.** Electrons are transferred

    B. Protons are transferred   **D.** Protons and electrons are transferred

                                        E. Charge is destroyed

49. The rear-view mirror on the passenger side of many cars has a warning: *objects in mirror are closer than they appear*. This implies that the mirror must be:

    A. convex   **B.** transparent   **C.** concave   **D.** plane   **E.** magnifying

50. A small boat is moving at a velocity of 3.35 m/s when it is accelerated by a river current perpendicular to the initial direction of motion. Relative to the initial direction of motion, what is the new velocity of the boat after 33.5 s if the current acceleration is 0.75 m/s^2?

    A. 62 m/s at 7.6°   **C.** 25 m/s at 7.6°

    B. 62 m/s at 82.4°   **D.** 25 m/s at 82.4°   **E.** 40 m/s at 82.4°

51. A machinist turns the power on for a stationary grinding wheel at time $t = 0$ s. The wheel accelerates uniformly for 10 s and reaches the operating angular velocity of 58 radians/s. The wheel is run at that angular velocity for 30 s before the power is shut off. The wheel slows down uniformly at 1.4 radians/s^2 until it stops. What is the approximate total number of revolutions for the wheel?

   A. 460   **B.** 320   **C.** 380   **D.** 510   **E.** 720

52. The total distance traveled by an object in one complete cycle of simple harmonic motion is how many times the amplitude?

   A. two   **B.** three   **C.** half   **D.** one   **E.** four

53. Which of the following is a TRUE statement?

   A. It is impossible to convert work entirely into heat
   B. It is impossible to transfer heat from a cooler to a hotter body
   C. The second law of thermodynamics is a consequence of the first law of thermodynamics
   D. It is possible for heat to flow spontaneously from a hot body to a cold one or vice versa, depending on whether the process is reversible or irreversible
   E. All of these statements are false

54. Initially, for the circuit shown, the switch S is open and the capacitor voltage is 80 V. The switch S is closed at time $t = 0$. What is the charge on the capacitor when the current in the circuit is 33 μA?

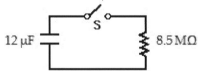

   A. 2,200 μC   **B.** 2,600 μC   **C.** 3,000 μC   **D.** 1,800 μC   **E.** 3,400 μC

55. The nuclear particle described by the symbol ^4_2He is a(n):

   A. positron   **C.** electron
   B. neutron   **D.** alpha particle   **E.** proton

Check your answers using the answer key. Then, go to the explanations section and review the explanations in detail, paying particular attention to questions you didn't answer correctly or marked for review. Note the topic that those questions belong to.

We recommend that you do this BEFORE taking the next Diagnostic Test.

Diagnostic test #1

1	A	Translational Motion		31	B	Equilibrium & momentum
2	E	Force, motion, gravitation		32	A	Work & energy
3	C	Heat & thermodynamics		33	B	Waves & periodic motion
4	B	Work & energy		34	D	Heat & thermodynamics
5	E	Waves & periodic motion		35	B	Light & optics
6	B	Sound		36	E	Circuit elements & DC circuits
7	C	Equilibrium & momentum		37	C	Electrostatics & electromagnetism
8	A	Electrostatics & electromagnetism		38	C	Translational Motion
9	D	Circuit elements & DC circuits		39	D	Sound
10	E	Light & optics		40	E	Waves & periodic motion
11	B	Atomic & nuclear structure		41	D	Work & energy
12	B	Equilibrium & momentum		42	C	Equilibrium & momentum
13	E	Work & energy		43	D	Force, motion, gravitation
14	A	Waves & periodic motion		44	C	Translational Motion
15	A	Sound		45	D	Heat & thermodynamics
16	B	Atomic & nuclear structure		46	C	Work & energy
17	C	Electrostatics & electromagnetism		47	B	Sound
18	A	Circuit elements & DC circuits		48	C	Electrostatics & electromagnetism
19	C	Light & optics		49	A	Light & optics
20	A	Atomic & nuclear structure		50	D	Translational Motion
21	B	Heat & thermodynamics		51	D	Equilibrium & momentum
22	E	Force, motion, gravitation		52	E	Waves & periodic motion
23	D	Sound		53	E	Heat & thermodynamics
24	D	Force, motion, gravitation		54	E	Circuit elements & DC circuits
25	B	Electrostatics & electromagnetism		55	D	Atomic & nuclear structure
26	E	Circuit elements & DC circuits				
27	A	Light & optics				
28	A	Atomic & nuclear structure				
29	B	Translational motion				
30	D	Force, motion, gravitation				

Diagnostic Test #2

Answer Sheet

#	Answer:					Mark for review	#	Answer:					Mark for review
1:	A	B	C	D	E	___	31:	A	B	C	D	E	___
2:	A	B	C	D	E	___	32:	A	B	C	D	E	___
3:	A	B	C	D	E	___	33:	A	B	C	D	E	___
4:	A	B	C	D	E	___	34:	A	B	C	D	E	___
5:	A	B	C	D	E	___	35:	A	B	C	D	E	___
6:	A	B	C	D	E	___	36:	A	B	C	D	E	___
7:	A	B	C	D	E	___	37:	A	B	C	D	E	___
8:	A	B	C	D	E	___	38:	A	B	C	D	E	___
9:	A	B	C	D	E	___	39:	A	B	C	D	E	___
10:	A	B	C	D	E	___	40:	A	B	C	D	E	___
11:	A	B	C	D	E	___	41:	A	B	C	D	E	___
12:	A	B	C	D	E	___	42:	A	B	C	D	E	___
13:	A	B	C	D	E	___	43:	A	B	C	D	E	___
14:	A	B	C	D	E	___	44:	A	B	C	D	E	___
15:	A	B	C	D	E	___	45:	A	B	C	D	E	___
16:	A	B	C	D	E	___	46:	A	B	C	D	E	___
17:	A	B	C	D	E	___	47:	A	B	C	D	E	___
18:	A	B	C	D	E	___	48:	A	B	C	D	E	___
19:	A	B	C	D	E	___	49:	A	B	C	D	E	___
20:	A	B	C	D	E	___	50:	A	B	C	D	E	___
21:	A	B	C	D	E	___	51:	A	B	C	D	E	___
22:	A	B	C	D	E	___	52:	A	B	C	D	E	___
23:	A	B	C	D	E	___	53:	A	B	C	D	E	___
24:	A	B	C	D	E	___	54:	A	B	C	D	E	___
25:	A	B	C	D	E	___	55:	A	B	C	D	E	___
26:	A	B	C	D	E	___							
27:	A	B	C	D	E	___							
28:	A	B	C	D	E	___							
29:	A	B	C	D	E	___							
30:	A	B	C	D	E	___							

This Diagnostic Test is designed for you to assess your proficiency on each topic. Use your test results and identify areas of your strength and weakness to adjust your study plan and enhance your fundamental knowledge.

The length of the Diagnostic Tests is proven to be optimal for a single study session.

We want to hear from you

Your feedback is important to us because we strive to provide the highest quality prep materials. If you have any questions, comments or suggestions, email us, so we can incorporate your feedback into future editions.

Customer Satisfaction Guarantee

If you have any concerns about this book, including printing issues, contact us and we will resolve any issues to your satisfaction.

info@sterling-prep.com

1. Determine both the distance traveled and the magnitude of the displacement when an object moves 16 m to the North and then moves 12 m to the South.

    A. 4 m, 4 m   **C.** 28 m, 4 m

    B. 28 m, 28 m   **D.** 4 m, 28 m   **E.** 16 m, 12 m

2. A potted plant of mass M is resting on a flat board. One end of the board is lifted slowly until the potted plant begins to slide. What does the angle θ that the board must make for sliding to occur depend on?

    A. M **C.** μ_k, kinetic friction

    B. μ_s, static friction   **D.** g, acceleration due to gravity   **E.** all of the above

3. Objects 1 and 2 are heated from the same initial temperature (T_i) to the same final temperature (T_f). Object 1 has three times the specific heat capacity of Object 2 and four times the mass. If Object 1 absorbs heat Q during this process, what is the amount of heat absorbed by Object 2?

    A. $(4/3)Q$ **B.** $(3/4)Q$ **C.** $6Q$ **D.** $12Q$ **E.** $(1/12)Q$

4. A 20 kg object is dropped from a height of 100 m. Ignoring air resistance, how much gravitational PE has the object lost when its speed is 30 m/s?

    A. 2,050 J   **B.** 2,850 J   **C.** 9,000 J   **D.** 5,550 J   **E.** 6,750 J

5. What is the approximate wavelength of a wave that has a speed of 360 m/s and a period of 4.2 s?

    A. 85.7 m   **B.** 1.86 m   **C.** 1,512 m   **D.** 288.6 m   **E.** 422.1 m

6. What is the effect on a system's mechanical energy if only the amplitude of a vibrating mass-and-spring system is doubled?

    A. Increases by a factor of 2   **C.** Increases by a factor of 3

    B. Increases by a factor of 4   **D.** Remains the same

                                  E. Increases by a factor of $\sqrt{2}$

7. Cart 1 (2 kg) and Cart 2 (2.5 kg) run along a frictionless, level, one-dimensional track. Cart 2 is initially at rest, and Cart 1 is traveling 0.6 m/s toward the right when it encounters Cart 2. After the collision, Cart 1 is at rest. What is the efficiency of the collision with respect to kinetic energy?

    A. 16%   **B.** 65%   **C.** 80%   **D.** 25%   **E.** 53%

8. If the distance between two electrostatic charges is doubled, how is the force between them affected?

A. Increases by 2   **C.** Decreases by $\sqrt{2}$

B. Increases by 4   **D.** Decreases by 4   **E.** Remains the same

9. When fully charged, a particular battery provides 1 mW of power at 9 V. What is the current that it delivers?

A. 0.13 kA   **B.** 9 kA   **C.** 0.11 mA   **D.** 18 mA   **E.** 0.55 mA

10. A girl of height h stands in front of a plane mirror. What must the minimum length of the mirror be, so she can view her entire body?

A. ¼h **C.** ½h

B. 2h **D.** h **E.** Depends on her distance from the mirror

11. The fission of an atom that has a larger atomic number (e.g. uranium) can be induced by bombarding the atom with:

A. electrons   **B.** positrons   **C.** neutrons   **D.** protons   **E.** gamma rays

12. A 1 kg chunk of putty moving at 1 m/s collides and sticks to a stationary 6 kg box. What is the total momentum of the box and putty? (Assume the box rests on a frictionless surface)

A. 0 kg·m/s   **B.** 1 kg·m/s   **C.** 2 kg·m/s   **D.** 3 kg·m/s   **E.** 5 kg·m/s

13. Which statement correctly describes the situation when a 6 kg mass moving at 2 m/s and a 3 kg mass moving at 4 m/s are gliding over a horizontal frictionless surface? A horizontal force F, which directly opposes their motion, results in the objects coming to rest.

A. The 6 kg mass travels twice the distance of the 3 kg mass before stopping
B. The 3 kg mass travels farther, but less than twice the distance of the 6 kg mass before stopping
C. The 3 kg mass travels twice the distance of the 6 kg mass before stopping
D. The 6 kg mass loses four times more KE than the 3 kg mass before stopping
E. The 6 kg mass loses two times more KE than the 3 kg mass before stopping

14. Which statement is correct for the separation between adjacent maxima in a double-slit interference pattern for monochromatic light?

A. Greatest for red light   **C.** Greatest for yellow light
B. Greatest for violet light   **D.** Greatest for blue light
                                       E. The same for all colors of light

15. If a 25 cm violin string is vibrating at its fundamental frequency of 860 Hz, what is the speed of transverse waves on the string?

    A. 220 m/s   **B.** 430 m/s   **C.** 880 m/s   **D.** 1,680 m/s   **E.** 2,260 m/s

16. The two strongest forces that act between protons in a nucleus are the:

    A. electrostatic and gravitational forces
    B. strong nuclear and electrostatic forces
    C. weak nuclear and electrostatic forces
    D. strong nuclear and gravitational forces
    E. weak nuclear and gravitational forces

17. A conductor differs from an insulator in that a conductor has:

    A. slower moving molecules   **C.** more protons than electrons
    B. tightly-bound outer electrons   **D.** more electrons than protons
                                                E. none of the above

18. Which statement is true for two conductors that are joined by a long copper wire?

    A. One conductor must have a lower potential than the other conductor
    B. Shortening the wire increases the potential of both conductors
    C. Each conductor must have the same potential
    D. The potential on the wire is the sum of the potentials of each conductor
    E. The potential on the wire is the average of the potentials of each conductor

19. Two antennas 130 m apart on a North-South line radiate in phase at a frequency of 3.6 MHz, and all radio measurements are recorded far away from the antennas. What is the smallest angle, East of North from the antennas, for constructive interference of the two radio waves? (Use speed of light $c = 3 \times 10^8$ m/s)

    A. 45°   **B.** 60°   **C.** 50°   **D.** 30°   **E.** 90°

20. According to the quantum mechanical model of the He atom, if the orbital angular momentum quantum number is ℓ, how many magnetic quantum numbers are possible?

    A. $2\ell + 1$ **B.** $2\ell - 1$ **C.** 2ℓ **D.** $\ell/2$ **E.** 3ℓ

21. The transfer of energy from molecule to molecule is:

    A. conduction   **C.** convection
    B. equilibrium   **D.** radiation   **E.** dissipation

22. At constant speed, an object following a straight-line path has:

A. decreasing acceleration   **C.** unbalanced forces

B. no forces acting on it   **D.** increasing velocity   **E.** zero acceleration

23. The intensity of a sound wave is proportional to the:

A. Doppler shift   **C.** decibel level

B. power   **D.** wavelength   **E.** frequency

24. In an air-free chamber, a pebble is thrown horizontally and, at the same instant, a second pebble is dropped from the same height. Compare the time it took for the two pebbles to hit the ground:

A. They hit at the same time

B. Requires values for the initial velocities of both pebbles

C. The thrown pebble hits first

D. The dropped pebble hits first

E. Requires the height from which they were released

25. Two parallel metal plates, separated by a 0.05 m distance, are charged to produce a uniform electric field between them that points down. What is the magnitude of the force experienced by a proton between the two plates? (Use acceleration due to gravity $g = 10$ m/s^2, charge of a proton = 1.6×10^{-19} C and uniform electric field = 4×10^4 N/C)

A. 6.4×10^{-10} N   **C.** 3.2×10^{-15} N

B. 3.2×10^{-10} N   **D.** 6.4×10^{-15} N   **E.** 2.5×10^{-5} N

26. The resistance of an object equals:

A. length × resistivity × cross-sectional area   **C.** current / voltage

B. length / (resistivity × cross-sectional area)   **D.** voltage / current

E. voltage × current

27. Optical density is proportional to:

A. index of refraction   **C.** mass density

B. index of reflection   **D.** light speed   **E.** wavelength

28. Which radiation type penetrates about 1 cm of human tissue and requires a minimum protective shielding made of wood or aluminum?

A. Gamma   **C.** Alpha

B. Beta   **D.** Nuclide   **E.** None of the above

29. Which is a unit of measuring resistance to a change of motion?

A. N   **B.** ohm   **C.** $\sec^{-1}$ **D.** volt   **E.** kg

30. What is the tension in a cable that pulls a 900 kg object straight upward at an acceleration of 0.6 m/s^2? (Use acceleration due to gravity $g = 9.8$ m/s^2)

A. 8,280 N   **B.** 980 N   **C.** 9,800 N   **D.** 9,360 N   **E.** 930 N

31. The masses of the blocks and the velocities before and after a collision are:

1.8 m/s	0.2 m/s		0.6 m/s	1.4 m/s
4 kg	6 kg		4 kg	6 kg
Before			After	

In this example, the collision is:

A. completely inelastic   **C.** characterized by an increase in KE

B. completely elastic   **D.** characterized by a decrease in momentum

E. characterized by an increase in PE

32. What is Amanda's mass if Steve does 174 J of work while pulling her backwards on a swing that has a 5.1 m chain until the swing makes an angle of 32° with the vertical? (Use acceleration due to gravity $g = 9.8$ m/s^2)

A. 17.4 kg   **B.** 22.9 kg   **C.** 29.8 kg   **D.** 37.8 kg   **E.** 14.4 kg

33. For an object that exhibits simple harmonic motion (SHM), what is the frequency of the motion, if the shortest time interval between the two extremes of the object's displacement from its equilibrium position is 2 s?

A. 0.25 cycle/s   **C.** 2.5 cycles/s

B. 0.5 cycle/s   **D.** 5 cycles/s   **E.** 1 cycle/s

34. A few 10 cm long aluminum rods and 8 cm long steel rods are at 5 °C temperature and are joined together to form a 60 cm long rod. What is the increase in the length of the joined rod when the temperature is raised to 80 °C? (Use coefficient of linear expansion for aluminum = 2.4×10^{-5} K^{-1} and coefficient of linear expansion for steel = 1.2×10^{-5} K^{-1})

A. 0.3 mm   **B.** 0.5 mm   **C.** 1.8 mm   **D.** 0.72 mm   **E.** 1.4 mm

35. Relative to the mirror, where is the resulting image when a light source is placed 12 m in front of a diverging mirror that has a focal length of 6 m?

A. 2 m in front   **C.** 4 m in front

B. 2 m behind   **D.** 4 m behind   **E.** 0.5 m in front

36. When connected to household voltage of 120 V, a light bulb draws 2 A of current. How many watts is the light bulb?

   A. 30 W   **B.** 120 W   **C.** 180 W   **D.** 240 W   **E.** 60 W

37. What is the current through a 12 ohm resistor connected to a 120 V power supply?

   A. 1 A   **B.** 8 A   **C.** 10 A   **D.** 20 A   **E.** 0.1 A

38. An object travels along the x-axis at a constant speed of 3 m/s in the $-x$ direction. If the object is on $x = 4$ m at $t = 0$, where is it at time $t = 4$ s?

   A. $x = -16$ m   **B.** $x = -12$ m   **C.** $x = -8$ m   **D.** $x = -6$ m   **E.** $x = -2$ m

39. A commuter train is moving at a speed of 50 m/s directly toward Daud, who is whistling at 420 Hz while standing. If a passenger on the train hears him, what frequency would she hear? (Use the speed of sound $v = 350$ m/s)

   A. 300 Hz   **B.** 360 Hz   **C.** 480 Hz   **D.** 500 Hz   **E.** 520 Hz

40. Both constructive and destructive interference are necessary to produce the sound phenomena:

   I. beats   II. resonance   III. refraction

   A. I only   **B.** II only   **C.** III only   **D.** I and II only   **E.** I and III only

41. Determine the resting length of a spring if one end of the spring (spring constant $k = 40$ N/m) is fixed at point P, while the other end is connected to a 7 kg mass. The fixed end and the mass sit on a horizontal frictionless surface, and the mass and the spring are able to rotate about P. The mass moves in a circle with $r = 2$ m and the force on the mass is 12 N.

   A. 0.1 m   **B.** 1.7 m   **C.** 0.8 m   **D.** 2.3 m   **E.** 3.8 m

42. An electrical motor spins at a constant 2,640 rpm. What is the acceleration of the edge of the motor if the armature radius is 7.2 cm?

   A. 87 m/s^2 **B.** 1,690 m/s^2 **C.** 8,432 m/s^2 **D.** 2,420 m/s^2 **E.** 5,451 m/s^2

43. As in the figure, when a 100 kg block is released from rest from a height of 1 m, it takes 0.51 s to hit the floor. Assuming no friction and that the pulley is massless, what is the mass of the block on the other end? (Use acceleration due to gravity $g = 9.8$ m/s^2)

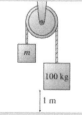

   A. 9 kg   **B.** 23 kg   **C.** 16 kg   **D.** 12 kg   **E.** 19 kg

44. A rock from a volcanic eruption is propelled straight up into the air. Ignoring air resistance, which of the statements is correct about the rock while it is in the air?

    A. Throughout its motion, the acceleration is always negative

    B. Throughout its motion, the acceleration is always negative and the velocity is always increasing

    C. On the way up, its velocity is increasing and its acceleration is positive

    D. On the way down, its velocity is increasing and its acceleration is negative

    E. At the highest point, both its velocity and acceleration are zero

45. The process whereby heat flows by the mass movement of molecules from one place to another is known to as:

    A. inversion   **C.** convection

    B. radiation   **D.** conduction   **E.** evaporation

46. An object weighing 50 N is traveling vertically upward from the Earth without air resistance at a constant velocity of 10 m/s. What is the power required to keep the object in motion?

    A. 0 W   **B.** 10 W   **C.** 50 W   **D.** 100 W   **E.** 500 W

47. Which statement is correct for a pipe with a length of L, that is closed at one end, and is resonating at its fundamental frequency?

    A. The wavelength is $2L$ and there is a displacement node at the pipe's closed end

    B. The wavelength is $2L$ and there is a displacement antinode at the pipe's open end

    C. The wavelength is $4L$ and there is a displacement antinode at the pipe's closed end

    D. The wavelength is $4L$ and there is a displacement antinode at the pipe's open end

    E. The wavelength is $4L$ and there is a displacement node at the pipe's open end

48. Which statement regarding the electric charge is NOT correct if the electric charge is conserved?

    A. Will not interact with neighboring electric charges

    B. Can neither be created nor destroyed

    C. Is a whole-number multiple of the charge of one electron

    D. May occur in an infinite variety of quantities

    E. Can only occur in restricted (i.e. allowable) quantities

49. Light refracts when traveling from air into glass because light:

    A. has a frequency that is greater in air than in glass
    B. travels slower in air than in glass
    C. has a frequency that is greater in glass than in air
    D. travels at the same speed in glass and in air
    E. travels slower in glass than in air

50. The area under the curve in a velocity vs. time graph determines:

    A. position   **B.** displacement   **C.** velocity   **D.** acceleration   **E.** time

51. Which statement is correct if two hockey pucks, each with a nonzero velocity, undergo an elastic collision as they slide toward each other on a surface of frictionless ice and collide head on?

    A. Both momentum and KE are doubled
    B. Neither momentum nor KE is conserved
    C. Momentum is conserved but KE is not conserved
    D. Momentum is not conserved but KE is conserved
    E. Both momentum and KE are conserved

52. A gamma ray is a pulse of electromagnetic energy with a frequency of 2.4×10^{20} Hz. What is the ratio of its wavelength to the radius of the nucleus which produced it? (Use speed of light $c = 3 \times 10^8$ m/s and radius of the nucleus = 5×10^{-13} cm)

    A. 0.028   **B.** 1.33×10^7 **C.** 38.2   **D.** 250   **E.** 2.58×10^{-7}

53. Which is an important feature of the Carnot cycle?

    A. Efficiency is determined only by the properties of the working substance used
    B. It is an irreversible process that can be analyzed exactly without approximations
    C. Efficiency can be 100%
    D. Efficiency depends only on the absolute temperature of the hot reservoir used
    E. It is the most efficient engine operating between two temperatures

54. Which of the following diagrams is correct for a circuit with a battery connected to four resistors, R_1, R_2, R_3, and R_4? Resistors R_1 and R_2 are connected in parallel, resistors R_3 and R_4 are connected in parallel, and both parallel sets of resistors are connected in series across the battery.

A.
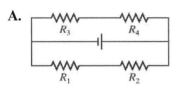

C.
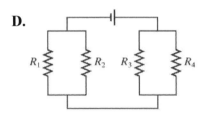

B.
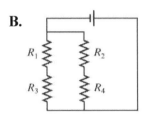

D.
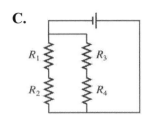

E. none of the above

55. Monochromatic light is incident on a metal surface and electrons are ejected. How do the ejection rate and maximum energy of the electrons change if the intensity of the light is increased?

A. Same rate; same maximum energy

B. Greater rate; greater maximum energy

C. Same rate; lower maximum energy

D. Greater rate; same maximum energy

E. Greater rate; lower maximum energy

Check your answers using the answer key. Then, go to the explanations section and review the explanations in detail, paying particular attention to questions you didn't answer correctly or marked for review. Note the topic that those questions belong to.

We recommend that you do this BEFORE taking the next Diagnostic Test.

Diagnostic test #2

1	C	Translational Motion
2	B	Force, motion, gravitation
3	E	Heat & thermodynamics
4	C	Work & energy
5	C	Waves & periodic motion
6	B	Sound
7	C	Equilibrium & momentum
8	D	Electrostatics & electromagnetism
9	C	Circuit elements & DC circuits
10	C	Light & optics
11	C	Atomic & nuclear structure
12	B	Equilibrium & momentum
13	C	Work & energy
14	A	Waves & periodic motion
15	B	Sound
16	B	Atomic & nuclear structure
17	E	Electrostatics & electromagnetism
18	C	Circuit elements & DC circuits
19	C	Light & optics
20	A	Atomic & nuclear structure
21	A	Heat & thermodynamics
22	E	Force, motion, gravitation
23	B	Sound
24	A	Force, motion, gravitation
25	D	Electrostatics & electromagnetism
26	D	Circuit elements & DC circuits
27	A	Light & optics
28	B	Atomic & nuclear structure
29	E	Translational motion
30	D	Force, motion, gravitation

31	B	Equilibrium & momentum
32	B	Work & energy
33	A	Waves & periodic motion
34	D	Heat & thermodynamics
35	D	Light & optics
36	D	Circuit elements & DC circuits
37	C	Electrostatics & electromagnetism
38	C	Translational motion
39	C	Sound
40	A	Waves & periodic motion
41	B	Work & energy
42	E	Equilibrium & momentum
43	D	Force, motion, gravitation
44	A	Translational motion
45	C	Heat & thermodynamics
46	E	Work & energy
47	D	Sound
48	A	Electrostatics & electromagnetism
49	E	Light & optics
50	B	Translational Motion
51	E	Equilibrium & momentum
52	D	Waves & periodic motion
53	E	Heat & thermodynamics
54	D	Circuit elements & DC circuits
55	D	Atomic & nuclear structure

Diagnostic Test #3

Answer Sheet

#	Answer:					Mark for review	#	Answer:					Mark for review
1:	A	B	C	D	E	___	31:	A	B	C	D	E	___
2:	A	B	C	D	E	___	32:	A	B	C	D	E	___
3:	A	B	C	D	E	___	33:	A	B	C	D	E	___
4:	A	B	C	D	E	___	34:	A	B	C	D	E	___
5:	A	B	C	D	E	___	35:	A	B	C	D	E	___
6:	A	B	C	D	E	___	36:	A	B	C	D	E	___
7:	A	B	C	D	E	___	37:	A	B	C	D	E	___
8:	A	B	C	D	E	___	38:	A	B	C	D	E	___
9:	A	B	C	D	E	___	39:	A	B	C	D	E	___
10:	A	B	C	D	E	___	40:	A	B	C	D	E	___
11:	A	B	C	D	E	___	41:	A	B	C	D	E	___
12:	A	B	C	D	E	___	42:	A	B	C	D	E	___
13:	A	B	C	D	E	___	43:	A	B	C	D	E	___
14:	A	B	C	D	E	___	44:	A	B	C	D	E	___
15:	A	B	C	D	E	___	45:	A	B	C	D	E	___
16:	A	B	C	D	E	___	46:	A	B	C	D	E	___
17:	A	B	C	D	E	___	47:	A	B	C	D	E	___
18:	A	B	C	D	E	___	48:	A	B	C	D	E	___
19:	A	B	C	D	E	___	49:	A	B	C	D	E	___
20:	A	B	C	D	E	___	50:	A	B	C	D	E	___
21:	A	B	C	D	E	___	51:	A	B	C	D	E	___
22:	A	B	C	D	E	___	52:	A	B	C	D	E	___
23:	A	B	C	D	E	___	53:	A	B	C	D	E	___
24:	A	B	C	D	E	___	54:	A	B	C	D	E	___
25:	A	B	C	D	E	___	55:	A	B	C	D	E	___
26:	A	B	C	D	E	___							
27:	A	B	C	D	E	___							
28:	A	B	C	D	E	___							
29:	A	B	C	D	E	___							
30:	A	B	C	D	E	___							

This Diagnostic Test is designed for you to assess your proficiency on each topic. Use your test results and identify areas of your strength and weakness to adjust your study plan and enhance your fundamental knowledge.

The length of the Diagnostic Tests is proven to be optimal for a single study session.

Our guarantee – the highest quality preparation materials.

We expect our books to have the highest quality content and be error-free.

Be the first to report an error, typo or inaccuracy and receive a
$10 reward for a content error or
$5 reward for a typo or grammatical mistake.

info@sterling-prep.com

1. A projectile is fired at time $t = 0$ s from point O of a ledge. It has initial velocity components of $v_{ox} = 30$ m/s and $v_{oy} = 300$ m/s with a time in flight of 75 s. The projectile lands at point P. What is the horizontal distance that the projectile travels?

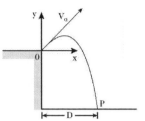

A. 3,020 m   C. 2,420 m

B. 2,880 m   D. 2,250 m   E. 3,360 m

2. A car of mass m is traveling along the roadway up a slight incline of angle θ to the horizontal when the driver sees a deer and suddenly applies the brakes. The car skids before coming to rest. Which expression gives the force of friction on the car if the coefficient of static friction between the tires and the road is μ_s, and the coefficient of kinetic friction is μ_k?

A. $\mu_k N$ B. $\mu_s N$ C. mg D. $mg \sin \theta$ E. $(\mu_s - \mu_k)N$

3. Once a steady-state heat flow is established, the thickness of a wall built from solid uniform material is doubled. Relative to the original value, what is the result for the rate of heat loss for a given temperature difference across the wall?

A. $1 / \sqrt{2}$ B. ¼   C. 2 times   D. ½   E. 4 times

4. Energy is the:

    I. ability to do work

    II. work that can be done by an object with potential or kinetic energy

    III. work needed to generate potential or kinetic energy

A. I only   B. II only   C. III only   D. I and III only   E. I, II and III

5. The displacement of a vibrating tuning fork and the resulting sound wave is related to:

A. period   B. wavelength   C. resonance   D. frequency   E. amplitude

6. The decibel level of sound is related to its:

A. velocity   B. frequency   C. wavelength   D. intensity   E. pitch

7. A 6.5 g bullet was fired horizontally into a 2 kg wooden block that is suspended on a 1.5 m string. The bullet becomes embedded in the block of wood, and immediately after that, the block and the bullet move at 2 m/s. The suspended wooden block with embedded bullet swings upward by height h. How high does the block with bullet swing before it comes to rest? (Use acceleration due to gravity $g = 9.8$ m/s^2)

A. 5.5 cm   B. 20 cm   C. 12 cm   D. 44 cm   E. 56 cm

8. Which statement(s) is/are correct?

    I. Current results in voltage
    II. Current flows through a circuit
    III. Voltage flows through a circuit

   A. I only   **B.** II only   **C.** III only   **D.** I and II only   **E.** I and III only

9. What is the voltage across a 5.5 Ω resistor if the current through it is 10 A?

   A. 1 V   **B.** 5 V   **C.** 55 V   **D.** 5.5 V   **E.** 100 V

10. Which of the following types of electromagnetic radiation has the highest energy per photon?

    I. Microwave   II. Infrared   III. Ultraviolet

   A. I only   **B.** II only   **C.** III only   **D.** I and II only   **E.** I and III only

11. This is an example of what type of nuclear reaction: $^{126}_{50}\text{Sn} \rightarrow {}^{126}_{51}\text{Sb}$?

   A. Transmutation   **C.** Fusion
   B. Gamma particle   **D.** Fission   **E.** Beta emission

12. A torque of 14 N·m is applied to a solid, uniform disk with a radius of 0.6 m. What is the mass of the disk if it accelerates at 5.3 rad/s^2?

   A. 7.6 kg   **B.** 4.2 kg   **C.** 14.7 kg   **D.** 21.4 kg   **E.** 13.8 kg

13. Marshall drops a water balloon from the top of a building onto Peter on the sidewalk below. Ignoring air resistance, how tall is the building if the balloon is traveling at 29 m/s when it strikes Peter's head? (Use acceleration due to gravity $g = 10$ m/s^2 and the distance of Peter's head above the ground = 1 m)

   A. 50.5 m   **B.** 37.5 m   **C.** 43 m   **D.** 26 m   **E.** 33 m

14. Assuming no change in the system's mass m, increasing the spring constant k of a spring system causes what kind of change in the resonant frequency of the system?

   A. No change   **C.** Decrease only if the ratio k/m is > 1
   B. Increase   **D.** Increase only if the ratio k/m is ≥ 1
                   E. Decrease

15. Assuming that all other factors remain constant, what happens to the velocity of sound as the temperature of the air increases?

   A. Does not change because it is dependent only on the state of the substance

   B. Increases when atmospheric pressure is high and decreases when the pressure is low

   C. Increases

   D. Decreases

   E. Decreases when atmospheric pressure is high and increases when the pressure is low

16. In a transition from one vibrational state to another, a molecule emits a photon of wavelength 6.5 μm. What is the energy difference between these two states? (Use speed of light $c = 3 \times 10^8$ m/s and Planck's constant $h = 4.136 \times 10^{-15}$ eV·s)

   A. 11.1 eV   **B.** 11.1 MeV   **C.** 0.28 MeV   **D.** 2.6 MeV   **E.** 0.19 eV

17. A likely cause for the existence of Earth's magnetic field is:

     I. moving charges in the liquid part of Earth's core

     II. convection currents in the liquid part of Earth's core

     III. great numbers of very slow moving charges in the Earth

   A. I only   **B.** II only   **C.** III only   **D.** I and III only   **E.** I, II and III

18. How often does the polarity of the voltage reverse in a 60 Hz circuit?

   A. 60 times/s   **C.** 90 times/s

   B. 120 times/s   **D.** 1/60 times/s   **E.** 30 times/s

19. A blue object appears black when illuminated with which color of light?

   A. Green   **B.** Yellow   **C.** Cyan   **D.** Blue   **E.** None of the above

20. What type of radiation is released when $^{224}_{86}Rn \rightarrow {}^{220}_{84}Po$?

     I. Gamma   II. Beta   III. Alpha

   A. I only   **B.** II only   **C.** III only   **D.** I and II only   **E.** I and III only

21. According to the laws of thermodynamics:

   A. entropy decreases as more energy is consumed

   B. heat flows naturally from a region of lower to a region of higher temperature

   C. mechanical energy cannot be completely converted into heat

   D. entropy of a system approaches zero as the temperature approaches absolute zero

   E. heat energy cannot be completely converted into mechanical energy

22. What is the net force on a 1,200 kg Alfa Romeo that is moving at a constant speed of 3.5 m/s and turning to the left on a curve of the road that has an effective radius of 4 m?

    A. 1,550 N   **B.** 2,160 N   **C.** 3,600 N   **D.** 8,465 N   **E.** 5,830 N

23. A guitar has a 14 cm string and sounds a 440 Hz musical note when played without fingering. How far from the end of the string should Samantha place her fingers to play a 520 Hz note?

    A. 5.8 cm   **B.** 0.8 cm   **C.** 1.6 cm   **D.** 2.2 cm   **E.** 3.4 cm

24. A 200 g hockey puck slides up a metal ramp that is inclined at a 30° angle. The coefficients of static and kinetic friction between the hockey puck and the metal ramp are μ_s = 0.4 and μ_k = 0.3, respectively. The initial speed of the hockey puck is 14 m/s. What vertical height does the puck reach above its starting point? (Use acceleration due to gravity g = 9.8 m/s^2)

    A. 11 m   **B.** 4.8 m   **C.** 6.6 m   **D.** 14 m   **E.** 14.3 m

25. Consider two current-carrying circular loops. Both are made from one strand of wire each and both carry the same amount of current, but one has double the radius. Compared to the magnetic moment of the smaller loop, the magnetic moment of the larger loop is:

    A. $\sqrt{2}$ times stronger   **C.** $\sqrt{2}$ times weaker
    B. 4 times stronger   **D.** 2 times stronger   **E.** 3 times stronger

26. What is the equivalent resistance of the circuits if each has a resistance of 600 Ω?

    A. 60 Ω   **C.** 600 Ω
    B. 1,200 Ω   **D.** 175 Ω   **E.** 350 Ω

27. A simple compound microscope normally uses a:

    A. long focal length objective and a longer focal length eyepiece
    B. long focal length objective and a short focal length eyepiece
    C. focal length objective and focal length eyepiece of the same length
    D. short focal length objective and a shorter focal length eyepiece
    E. short focal length objective and a long focal length eyepiece

28. What happens to the de Broglie wavelength for a particle as it increases its velocity?

    A. Increases   **C.** Remains constant
    B. Decreases   **D** Increases by $\sqrt{\Delta v}$ **E.** Increases by Δv^2

29. The slope of a line at a single point on a position vs. time graph gives:

    A. average acceleration   **C.** instantaneous velocity

    B. change in acceleration   **D.** average velocity   **E.** displacement

30. What is the reaction force if, as a ball falls, the action force is the pull of the Earth's mass on the ball?

    A. None present   **C.** The downward acceleration due to gravity

    B. The pull of the ball's mass on Earth   **D.** The air resistance acting against the ball

    E. Less than the action force

31. An irregularly-shaped object 10 m long is placed with each end on two nearby scales. If the scale on the right reads 94 N and the scale on the left reads 69 N, how far from the left is the object's center of gravity? (Use acceleration due to gravity $g = 9.8$ m/s^2)

    A. 6.8 m   **B.** 6.3 m   **C.** 7.7 m   **D.** 8.1 m   **E.** 5.8 m

32. Is it possible for a system to have negative potential energy?

    A. Yes, because the choice of the zero for potential energy is arbitrary

    B. No, because this has no physical meaning

    C. Yes, if the kinetic energy is positive

    D. Yes, if the total energy is positive

    E. No, because the kinetic energy of a system must be equal to its potential energy

33. What is the speed of 2 m long water waves as they pass by a floating piece of cork that bobs up and down for one complete cycle each second?

    A. 8 m/s   **B.** 0.5 m/s   **C.** 1 m/s   **D.** 2 m/s   **E.** 4 m/s

34. When 110 J of heat is added to a system that performs 40 J of work, the total thermal energy change of the system is:

    A. 2.8 J   **B.** 40 J   **C.** 70 J   **D.** 0 J   **E.** 150 J

35. The image of a real object from a plane mirror has the following characteristics:

    A. real, erect, with magnification = 1   **C.** real, erect, with magnification > 1

    B. real, inverted, with magnification = 1   **D.** virtual, erect, with magnification = 1

    E. virtual, erect, with magnification < 1

36. What is the current through the 2 Ω resistor if the current through the 8 Ω resistor is 0.8 A?

A. 15.2 A

B. 18.7 A

C. 1.5 A

D. 6.6 A

E. 8.8 A

37. A proton is traveling to the right and encounters region Y that contains an electric field where the proton speeds up. In what direction does the electric field in region Y point?

A. To the left

B. To the right

C. Down into the page

D. Up from the page

E. To the left and into the page

38. A ball is projected horizontally with an initial speed of 5 m/s from an initial height of 50 m. Ignoring air resistance, how far has the ball traveled horizontally from its original position when it lands? (Use acceleration due to gravity $g = 10$ m/s^2)

A. 11 m   B. 16 m   C. 20 m   D. 7 m   E. 27 m

39. Simple harmonic motion (SMH) is characterized by acceleration that:

A. is proportional to displacement

B. is proportional to velocity

C. decreases linearly

D. is inversely proportional to displacement

E. is inversely proportional to velocity

40. A simple pendulum has a bob of mass M and a period T. If M is doubled, what is the new period?

A. T/√2   B. T   C. T√2   D. 2T   E. T/2

41. Susan pulls on a wagon with a force of 70 N. What is the average power generated by Susan if the wagon moves a total of 45 m in 3 min?

A. 18 W   B. 27 W   C. 14 W   D. 21 W   E. 28 W

42. Shawn, with a mass of 105 kg, sits 5.5 m to the left of the center of a seesaw. Mark and John, each with a mass of 20 kg, are seated on the right side of the seesaw. If Mark sits 10 m to the right of the center, how far to the right from the center should John sit to balance the seesaw? (Use acceleration due to gravity $g = 10$ m/s^2)

A. 5 m   B. 10 m   C. 19 m   D. 20 m   E. 25 m

43. What is true about the acceleration of an object that travels at constant speed in a circular path?

    A. It is equal to zero because the speed is constant

    B. It is not equal to zero and is always directed tangent to the path

    C. It is not equal to zero and is always directed behind the radius of the path

    D. It is not equal to zero and is always directed in front of the radius of the path

    E. It is not equal to zero and is always directed toward the center of the path

44. How long does it take for a rock to reach the maximum height of its trajectory if a boy throws it with an initial velocity of 3.13 m/s at 30° above the horizontal? (Use acceleration due to gravity $g = 9.8$ m/s^2)

    A. 0.16 s   **B.** 0.28 s   **C.** 0.333 s   **D.** 0.446 s   **E.** 0.84 s

45. In the equation $PV = NkT$, k is known as:

    A. the spring (compressibility) constant   **C.** Planck's constant

    B. Boltzmann's constant   **D.** Avogadro's number

    E. the strain constant

46. A hammer of mass m is dropped from a roof and falls a distance h before striking the ground. How does the maximum velocity of the hammer, just before it hits the ground, change if h is doubled? Assume no air resistance.

    A. It is multiplied by $\sqrt{2}$ **C.** It is increased by 200%

    B. It is multiplied by 2   **D.** It is multiplied by 4   **E.** It remains constant

47. Color depends on what characteristics of light?

    I. frequency   II. wavelength   III. amplitude

    A. I only   **B.** II only   **C.** III only   **D.** I and II only   **E.** I and III only

48. The water fountain pump recirculates water from a pool and pumps it up to a trough, where it flows along the trough and passes through a hole in the bottom of it. As the water falls back into the pool, it turns a water wheel. What aspect of this water fountain is analogous to an electric current within an electric circuit?

    A. Volume flow rate   **C.** Density of water

    B. Height of water   **D.** Flow velocity   **E.** Volume of the trough

49. Light in a vacuum has a speed of 3×10^8 m/s as it enters a liquid with a refractive index of 2. What is the speed of light in this liquid?

A. 7.5×10^8 m/s   **C.** 6×10^8 m/s

B. 0.75×10^8 m/s   **D.** 3×10^8 m/s   **E.** 1.5×10^8 m/s

50. What is the shape of the line on a position vs. time graph for constant linear acceleration?

A. curve   **C.** sinusoidal graph

B. sloped line   **D.** horizontal line   **E.** vertical line

51. A steel ball A is thrown in the air with a speed of 4 m/s at an angle of 60° from the horizontal. It drops onto steel ball B which is 1.4 times the mass of A. If ball A comes to rest after the collision and ball B bounces, what is the horizontal component of ball B's velocity?

A. 0.4 m/s   **B.** 0.6 m/s   **C.** 1.4 m/s   **D.** 1.8 m/s   **E.** 1.1 m/s

52. The phenomena of compressions and rarefactions are characteristic of:

     I. longitudinal waves   II. transverse waves   III. standing waves

A. I only   **B.** II only   **C.** III only   **D.** I and II only   **E.** I, II and III

53. If 60 g of material at 100 °C is mixed with 200 g of water at 0 °C, the final temperature is 40 °C. What is the specific heat of the material?

A. 2.2 kcal/kg·°C   **C.** 0.4 kcal/kg·°C

B. 6.3 kcal/kg·°C   **D.** 4.6 kcal/kg·°C   **E.** 1.6 kcal/kg·°C

54. Which statement is accurate?

A. The magnetic force on a moving charge does not change its energy

B. The magnetic force on a current-carrying wire is minimal when the wire is perpendicular to the magnetic field

C. All magnetic fields originate from the North and South poles

D. By definition, a magnetic field line is tangent to the direction of the magnetic force on a moving charge at a given point in space

E. A current-carrying loop of wire tends to line up with its plane parallel to an external magnetic field in which it is positioned

55. In β– decay, the number of protons in the nucleus:

A. increases by 2   **C.** decreases by 2

B. increases by 1   **D.** decreases by 1   **E.** remains unchanged

Check your answers using the answer key. Then, go to the explanations section and review the explanations in detail, paying particular attention to questions you didn't answer correctly or marked for review. Note the topic that those questions belong to.

We recommend that you do this BEFORE taking the next Diagnostic Test.

Diagnostic test #3

1	D	Translational motion
2	A	Force, motion, gravitation
3	D	Heat & thermodynamics
4	E	Work & energy
5	E	Waves & periodic motion
6	D	Sound
7	B	Equilibrium & momentum
8	B	Electrostatics & electromagnetism
9	C	Circuit elements & DC circuits
10	C	Light & optics
11	E	Atomic & nuclear structure
12	C	Equilibrium & momentum
13	C	Work & energy
14	B	Waves & periodic motion
15	C	Sound
16	E	Atomic & nuclear structure
17	E	Electrostatics & electromagnetism
18	B	Circuit elements & DC circuits
19	B	Light & optics
20	C	Atomic & nuclear structure
21	E	Heat & thermodynamics
22	C	Force, motion, gravitation
23	D	Sound
24	C	Force, motion, gravitation
25	B	Electrostatics & electromagnetism
26	C	Circuit elements & DC circuits
27	E	Light & optics
28	B	Atomic & nuclear structure
29	C	Translational motion
30	B	Force, motion, gravitation
31	E	Equilibrium & momentum
32	A	Work & energy
33	D	Waves & periodic motion
34	C	Heat & thermodynamics
35	D	Light & optics
36	A	Circuit elements & DC circuits
37	B	Electrostatics & electromagnetism
38	B	Translational motion
39	A	Waves & periodic motion
40	B	Waves & periodic motion
41	A	Work & energy
42	C	Equilibrium & momentum
43	E	Force, motion, gravitation
44	A	Translational motion
45	B	Heat & thermodynamics
46	A	Work & energy
47	D	Sound
48	A	Electrostatics & electromagnetism
49	E	Light & optics
50	A	Translational motion
51	C	Equilibrium & momentum
52	A	Waves & periodic motion
53	A	Heat & thermodynamics
54	A	Circuit elements & DC circuits
55	B	Atomic & nuclear structure

Diagnostic Test #4

Answer Sheet

#	Answer:					Mark for review	#	Answer:					Mark for review
1:	A	B	C	D	E	___	31:	A	B	C	D	E	___
2:	A	B	C	D	E	___	32:	A	B	C	D	E	___
3:	A	B	C	D	E	___	33:	A	B	C	D	E	___
4:	A	B	C	D	E	___	34:	A	B	C	D	E	___
5:	A	B	C	D	E	___	35:	A	B	C	D	E	___
6:	A	B	C	D	E	___	36:	A	B	C	D	E	___
7:	A	B	C	D	E	___	37:	A	B	C	D	E	___
8:	A	B	C	D	E	___	38:	A	B	C	D	E	___
9:	A	B	C	D	E	___	39:	A	B	C	D	E	___
10:	A	B	C	D	E	___	40:	A	B	C	D	E	___
11:	A	B	C	D	E	___	41:	A	B	C	D	E	___
12:	A	B	C	D	E	___	42:	A	B	C	D	E	___
13:	A	B	C	D	E	___	43:	A	B	C	D	E	___
14:	A	B	C	D	E	___	44:	A	B	C	D	E	___
15:	A	B	C	D	E	___	45:	A	B	C	D	E	___
16:	A	B	C	D	E	___	46:	A	B	C	D	E	___
17:	A	B	C	D	E	___	47:	A	B	C	D	E	___
18:	A	B	C	D	E	___	48:	A	B	C	D	E	___
19:	A	B	C	D	E	___	49:	A	B	C	D	E	___
20:	A	B	C	D	E	___	50:	A	B	C	D	E	___
21:	A	B	C	D	E	___	51:	A	B	C	D	E	___
22:	A	B	C	D	E	___	52:	A	B	C	D	E	___
23:	A	B	C	D	E	___	53:	A	B	C	D	E	___
24:	A	B	C	D	E	___	54:	A	B	C	D	E	___
25:	A	B	C	D	E	___	55:	A	B	C	D	E	___
26:	A	B	C	D	E	___							
27:	A	B	C	D	E	___							
28:	A	B	C	D	E	___							
29:	A	B	C	D	E	___							
30:	A	B	C	D	E	___							

This Diagnostic Test is designed for you to assess your proficiency on each topic. Use your test results and identify areas of your strength and weakness to adjust your study plan and enhance your fundamental knowledge.

The length of the Diagnostic Tests is proven to be optimal for a single study session.

We want to hear from you

Your feedback is important to us because we strive to provide the highest quality prep materials. If you have any questions, comments or suggestions, email us, so we can incorporate your feedback into future editions.

Customer Satisfaction Guarantee

If you have any concerns about this book, including printing issues, contact us and we will resolve any issues to your satisfaction.

info@sterling-prep.com

1. An object starting from rest accelerates uniformly along a straight line until its final velocity is *v*, while traveling a distance *d*. What would be the distance traveled if the object accelerated uniformly from rest until its final velocity was 4*v*?

   A. 2*d*   **B.** 4*d*   **C.** 6*d*   **D.** 12*d*   **E.** 16*d*

2. Satellite #1 has mass *M*, which takes time T to orbit Earth. If satellite #2 has twice the mass, how long does it take for satellite #2 to orbit Earth?

   A. T/2   **B.** T   **C.** 2T   **D.** 4T   **E.** T/4

3. An engineer is studying the rate of heat loss, $\Delta Q / \Delta t$ through a sheet of insulating material as a function of the thickness of the sheet. Assuming fixed temperatures on the two faces of the sheet and steady-state heat flow, which of the graphs best represents the rate of heat transfer as a function of the thickness of the insulating sheet?

A.
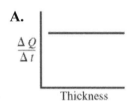

C.
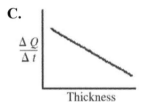

B.
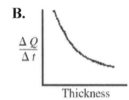

D.
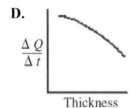

E.
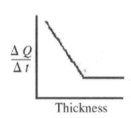

4. Two identical arrows, one with twice the kinetic energy, are fired into a hay bale. Compared to the slower arrow, the faster arrow penetrates:

   A. the same distance   **C.** four times as far

   B. twice as far   **D.** more than four times as far

   E. less than twice as far

5. On the Moon, the acceleration of gravity is *g* / 6. If a pendulum has a period T on Earth, what will be the period on the Moon?

   A. 6T   **B.** T/6   **C.** T/√6   **D.** T/3   **E.** T√6

6. What is the decibel level of a sound with an intensity of 10^{-7} W/m²?

   A. 10 dB   **B.** 20 dB   **C.** 30 dB   **D.** 50 dB   **E.** 70 dB

7. A child is trying to throw a ball over a fence that is 2 m high. She throws the ball at an initial speed of 8 m/s at an angle of 40° above the horizontal. The ball leaves her hand 1 m above the ground. How far is the child from the fence, if the ball just clears the fence and experiences no significant air resistance? (Use acceleration due to gravity $g = 9.8$ m/s^2)

   A. 1.6 m   **B.** 2.4 m   **C.** 3.9 m   **D.** 4.6 m   **E.** 8.8 m

8. A positive charge Q is held fixed at the origin. A positive charge z is let go from point p on the positive x-axis. Ignoring friction, which statement describes the velocity of z after it is released?

   A. Increases indefinitely   **C.** Increases, then decreases, but never reaches zero
   B. Decreases to zero   **D.** Increases, but never exceeds a certain limit
   E. Increases, then decreases forever to zero

9. A 9 V battery is connected to two resistors in a series. One resistance is 5 ohms and the other is 10 ohms. Which is true about the current for the locations (A, B, C, D) marked along the circuit?

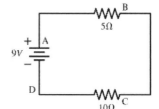

   A. Current at A > current at B > current at C > current at D
   B. Current at A > current at B = current at C = current at D
   C. Current at A = current at B = current at C = current at D
   D. Current at A = current at B = current at C > current at D
   E. Current at A = current at B > current at C = current at D

10. Which expression describes the critical angle for the interface of water with air? (Use index of refraction for water n = 1.33 and index of refraction for air n = 1)

   A. $\sin^{-1}(1/3)$ **C.** $\sin^{-1}(2/3)$
   B. $\sin^{-1}(3/4)$ **D.** $\sin^{-1}(4/3)$ **E.** $\sin^{-1}(3/2)$

11. What is the amount of energy required to ionize a hydrogen atom from the ground state? (Use Rydberg formula where $E_0 = -13.6$ eV)

   A. 4.1 eV   **B.** 9.8 eV   **C.** 13.6 eV   **D.** 22.3 eV   **E.** ∞

12. Sonja is sitting on the outer edge of a carousel that is 18 m in diameter. What is the velocity of Sonja in m/s if the carousel makes 5 rev/min?

   A. 3.3 m/s   **B.** 0.8 m/s   **C.** 8.8 m/s   **D.** 4.7 m/s   **E.** 3.2 m/s

13. A projectile weighing 120 N is traveling horizontally with respect to the surface of the Earth at a constant velocity of 6 m/s. Ignoring air resistance, what is the power required to maintain this motion?

    A. 0 W   **B.** 20 W   **C.** 120 W   **D.** 2 W   **E.** 12 W

14. A 0.4 kg harmonic oscillator has a total oscillation energy of 10 J. What is the oscillation frequency if the oscillation amplitude is 20 cm? (Use 1 J = 1 N·m)

    A. 3 Hz   **B.** 4.3 Hz   **C.** 2.1 Hz   **D.** 5.6 Hz   **E.** 9.9 Hz

15. Electromagnetic waves consist of:

    A. particles of heat energy
    B. high-frequency gravitational waves
    C. compressions and rarefactions of electromagnetic pulses
    D. low-frequency gravitational waves
    E. oscillating electric and magnetic fields

16. A β^- decay occurs in an unstable nucleus when a neutron is converted to a:

    A. beta particle by the weak force   **C.** neutron by the strong force
    B. positron by the weak force   **D.** proton by the strong force
                                    E. proton by the weak force

17. Two solenoids are close to each other with the switch S open. In which direction does the induced current flow through the galvanometer in the left-hand solenoid when the switch is closed?

    A. From left to right
    B. From right to left
    C. There will be no induced current through the galvanometer
    D. It depends on the amount of the induced current
    E. Closing the switch has no effect on the left-hand solenoid because they are independent

18. If the length and cross-sectional diameter of a wire are both doubled, the resistance is:

    A. halved   **C.** doubled
    B. increased fourfold   **D.** decreased by one fourth   **E.** unchanged

19. Using a mirror with a focal length of 10 m, an object is viewed at various distances. What is its magnification and orientation when the object is 5 m in front of the mirror?

A. Twice as large and upright

B. Twice as large and inverted

C. Half as large and upright

D. Same size and inverted

E. Same size and upright

20. Which energy source provides most of a person's annual exposure to radiation?

A. Cell phones and hand-held electronic devices

B. Televisions (i.e. cathode ray tubes)

C. Background radiation

D. Sunlight and UV rays

E. Dental and medical X rays

21. Which two temperature scales have the same interval size?

A. Kelvin and Celsius

B. Fahrenheit and Centigrade

C. Celsius and Fahrenheit

D. Fahrenheit and Kelvin

E. Rankine and Celsius

22. A 5.5 kg box slides down an inclined plane that makes an angle of 40° with the horizontal. At what rate does the box accelerate down the slope if the coefficient of kinetic friction μ_k is 0.19? (Use acceleration due to gravity $g = 9.8$ m/s^2)

A. 7.5 m/s^2　　　B. 6.4 m/s^2　　　C. 4.9 m/s^2　　　D. 5.9 m/s^2　　　E. 6.5 m/s^2

23. Assume that the sound level of a whisper is 20 dB and a shout is 90 dB. How many times greater is the intensity of a shout than a whisper, given that the decibel level of a sound wave is related to the intensity I of the wave by:

$$dB = 10 \log(I / I_0), \text{ where } I_0 = 10^{-12} \text{ W/m}^2$$

A. Seven

B. Seventy thousand

C. Seventy million

D. Seven million

E. Ten million

24. The reason an astronaut in one of Earth's satellites feels weightless is because:

A. gravity does not affect the astronaut because there is no atmospheric pressure

B. the forces acting on the astronaut are negative

C. the astronaut is beyond the range of the Earth's gravity

D. the astronaut is in free fall

E. the astronaut's acceleration is zero

25. A magnet is always surrounded by a(n):

　　　I. electric field　　　II. magnetic field　　　III. declination field

A. I only　　　B. II only　　　C. III only　　　D. I and II only　　　E. I and III only

26. Which quantity is expressed in units of Ω·m?

   A. Flow   **B.** Capacitance   **C.** Resistivity   **D.** Potential   **E.** Current

27. A candle is viewed through a lens. What is the magnification of the image when the candle is 6 m from the lens, and the image is 3 m from the lens on the other side?

   A. Twice as large and upright   **C.** Half as large and upright
   B. Same size and inverted   **D.** Half as large and inverted
                              E. Same size and upright

28. Uranium has an atomic number of 92, but often contains 146 or more neutrons and undergoes radioactive decay. Which statement describes why this occurs?

     I. The electromagnetic repulsion overcomes the strong nuclear force
     II. Excess neutrons increase the electromagnetic repulsion
     III. The strong nuclear force has a limited range

   A. I only   **B.** II only   **C.** III only   **D.** I and III only   **E.** I, II and III

29. A yacht moving initially at 10.7 m/s N, drifts due NE at the same speed. The captain, to correct the yacht's bearing, accelerates the engine and turns the rudder NW. How long does it take to cross the original line of longitude if the engine delivers a constant acceleration of 4.4 m/s^2?

   A. 1.3 s   **B.** 1.8 s   **C.** 3.3 s   **D.** 3.6 s   **E.** 2.4 s

30. A 100 kg lion sees an antelope and, from rest, accelerates uniformly to 20 m/s in 10 s. How much distance does the lion cover in 10 s?

   A. 100 m   **B.** 200 m   **C.** 180 m   **D.** 50 m   **E.** 150 m

31. An object is released from rest at a height h above the surface of the Earth, where h is much smaller than the radius of the Earth. The object's speed is v as it strikes the ground. Ignoring air resistance, at what height should the object be released from rest for it to strike the ground with a speed of $2v$? (Use g = acceleration due to gravity)

   A. $4gh$ **B.** $4h$ **C.** $2gh$ **D.** $2h$ **E.** h

32. A 4 kg ball is attached to one end of a 1.4 m light rod, while the other end is loosely affixed at a frictionless pivot. The rod is raised until it is vertical, with the ball above the pivot. The ball moves in a circle when the rod is released. What is the tension in the rod as the ball moves through the bottom of the circle? (Use acceleration due to gravity g = 9.8 m/s^2)

   A. 30.0 N   **B.** 84.8 N   **C.** 46.6 N   **D.** 120.0 N   **E.** 196.0 N

33. The crests of ocean waves pass a pier every 12 s. What is the wavelength of the ocean waves if the waves are moving at 4.5 m/s?

    A. 84 m   **B.** 66 m   **C.** 54 m   **D.** 38 m   **E.** 47 m

34. Compared to a giant iceberg, a hot cup of coffee has:

    A. a higher temperature, but more thermal energy
    B. a greater specific heat and more thermal energy
    C. a higher temperature, but less thermal energy
    D. more thermal energy and lower temperature
    E. a higher temperature and the same amount of thermal energy

35. What is the focal length of the mirror if, when an object is 24 cm in front of a concave spherical mirror, the image is formed 3 cm in front of the mirror?

    A. 1.5 cm   **B.** 2.7 cm   **C.** 5 cm   **D.** 6.3 cm   **E.** 7.4 cm

36. Which diagram represents a circuit with two batteries that connects a negative pole to a positive pole, a resistor between them, and a capacitor in parallel with the resistor?

A.
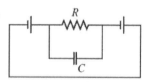

C.
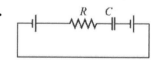

B.
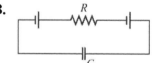

D.
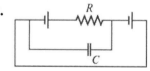

    E. none of the above

37. By what magnitude does a magnetic field produced by a wire decrease when the distance from a long current-carrying wire is doubled?

    A. $1/\sqrt{2}$ **B.** ½   **C.** ¼   **D.** 1/6   **E.** $\sqrt{(½)}$

38. A change in the state of motion is evidence of:

    I. a force that is wearing down
    II. an applied force that is unbalanced
    III. an increase in total force

    A. I only   **B.** II only   **C.** III only   **D.** I and II only   **E.** I and III only

39. If the intensity of sound increases by a factor of 100, the decibel level increases by:

A. 20 **B.** 1,000 **C.** $\log_{100}$ **D.** 100 **E.** 0.1

40. What is the tension on an aluminum wire with a diameter of 4.4 mm and a density of 2,600 kg/m^3 when transverse waves propagate at 42 m/s?

A. 15 N **B.** 24 N **C.** 46 N **D.** 68 N **E.** 76 N

41. A 5 kg box of books slides 10 m down a ramp inclined at 30° from the horizontal. What is the work done by gravity if the box slides at a constant velocity of 4 m/s? (Use acceleration due to gravity $g = 9.8$ m/s^2)

A. 0 J **B.** −32 J **C.** 245 J **D.** 32 J **E.** 133 J

42. What is the average momentum of a 65 kg runner who travels 400 m in 50 s?

A. 19 kg·m/s
B. 63 kg·m/s
C. 520 kg·m/s
D. 112 kg·m/s
E. 386 kg·m/s

43. What is a 10 kg wagon's acceleration when a girl pulls it with a constant force of 40 N?

A. 0.4 m/s^2 **B.** 4 m/s^2 **C.** 400 m/s^2 **D.** 40 m/s^2 **E.** 0.04 m/s^2

44. An object is traveling uniformly at a v of 5 m/s. What is its final velocity if it experiences a uniform acceleration of 2 m/s^2 for 6 s?

A. 12 m/s **B.** 28 m/s **C.** 24 m/s **D.** 32 m/s **E.** 17 m/s

45. A 830 g meteor impacts the Earth at a speed of 1,250 m/s. If its kinetic energy is entirely converted to heat of the meteorite, by what temperature does it increase? (Use specific heat for the meteor = 108 cal/kg·°C and 1 cal = 4.186 Joules)

A. 1,728 °C **B.** 1,346 °C **C.** 2,628 °C **D.** 7,142 °C **E.** 4,286 °C

46. Mary and Brittany throw identical balls vertically upward. Mary throws her ball with an initial speed of twice Brittany's ball. The maximum height of Mary's ball will be:

A. higher than Brittany's ball, but less than two times as high
B. equal to the maximum height of Brittany's ball
C. two times higher than the maximum height of Brittany's ball
D. four times higher than the maximum height of Brittany's ball
E. higher than twice Brittany's ball, but less than four times as high

47. An organ pipe is a cylindrical tube open at both ends. The air column is set to vibrate by air flowing through the pipe. The length of the pipe is 0.2 m and the diameter is 0.04 m. What is the wavelength of the fundamental? (Use v of sound at 23 °C = 340 m/s)

    A. 0.1 m   **B.** 2 m   **C.** 1 m   **D.** 0.4 m   **E.** 0.8 m

48. A proton, moving in a uniform magnetic field, moves in a circle perpendicular to the field. If the proton's speed is tripled, what happens to the time needed to complete a circular path?

    A. Increases   **C.** Decreases

    B. Remains constant   **D.** Doubles   **E.** Triples

49. A sodium emission tube produces a light of frequency 4.9×10^{14} Hz. Which is true of the image if it is placed 6 m from a converging lens of focal length 2 m?

    A. Inverted and virtual   **C.** Upright and virtual

    B. Inverted and real   **D.** Upright and real

                                 E. Same as if it were 1 m away

50. With all other factors equal, if the mass of an object is doubled while a constant unbalanced force is applied, its acceleration is:

    A. increased by $\sqrt{2}$ **C.** doubled

    B. decreased by $\sqrt{2}$ **D.** halved   **E.** divided by four

51. A 6 kg ball collides head on with a stationary 8 kg ball. Which statement is true if the collision between the balls is inelastic?

    A. Δp that the 6 kg ball experiences is greater than the Δp of the 8 kg ball

    B. Δp that the 6 kg ball experiences is equal to the Δp of the 8 kg ball

    C. Δv that the 6 kg ball experiences is greater than the Δv of the 8 kg ball

    D. Δv that the 6 kg ball experiences is less than the Δv of the 8 kg ball

    E. Δp that the 6 kg ball experiences is less than the Δp of the 8 kg ball

52. A pendulum of length L is suspended from the ceiling of an elevator. When the elevator is at rest, the period of the pendulum is T. How does the period of the pendulum change when the elevator moves upward with constant acceleration?

    A. Remains the same

    B. Decreases

    C. Increases

    D. Decreases only if the upward acceleration is less than $g / 2$

    E. Increases only if the upward acceleration is greater than $g / 2$

53. An auto mechanic needs to remove a tight-fitting pin of material X from a hole in a block made of material Y. The mechanic heats both the pin and the block to the same high temperature and removes the pin easily. What statement relates the coefficient of thermal expansion of material X to that of material Y?

    A. Material Y has a negative coefficient of expansion and material X has a positive coefficient of expansion

    B. Material Y has the same coefficient of expansion as material X

    C. The situation is not possible, heating material Y shrinks the hole in the material as the material expands with increasing temperature

    D. Material Y has a greater coefficient of expansion than material X

    E. Material X has a greater coefficient of expansion than material Y

54. Which of the following is an accurate statement?

    A. The magnetic force on a current-carrying wire is the smallest when the wire is perpendicular to the magnetic field

    B. The magnetic force on a moving charge does not change its energy

    C. A magnetic field line is, by definition, tangent to the direction of the magnetic force on a moving charge at a given point in space

    D. All magnetic fields have North and South poles as their sources

    E. A current-carrying loop of wire tends to line up with its plane parallel to an external magnetic field in which it is positioned

55. The isotope $^{238}_{92}U$ is most likely to emit:

    A. a γ ray   **C.** an α particle

    B. a β particle   **D.** both an α and β particle   **E.** both a β particle and a γ ray

Diagnostic test #4

1	E	Translational motion	31	B	Equilibrium & momentum
2	B	Force, motion, gravitation	32	E	Work & energy
3	B	Heat & thermodynamics	33	C	Waves & periodic motion
4	B	Work & energy	34	C	Heat & thermodynamics
5	E	Waves & periodic motion	35	B	Light & optics
6	D	Sound	36	A	Circuit elements & DC circuits
7	B	Equilibrium & momentum	37	B	Electrostatics & electromagnetism
8	D	Electrostatics & electromagnetism	38	B	Translational motion
9	C	Circuit elements & DC circuits	39	A	Sound
10	B	Light & optics	40	D	Waves & periodic motion
11	C	Atomic & nuclear structure	41	C	Work & energy
12	D	Equilibrium & momentum	42	C	Equilibrium & momentum
13	A	Work & energy	43	B	Force, motion, gravitation
14	D	Waves & periodic motion	44	E	Translational motion
15	E	Sound	45	A	Heat & thermodynamics
16	E	Atomic & nuclear structure	46	D	Work & energy
17	B	Electrostatics & electromagnetism	47	D	Sound
18	A	Circuit elements & DC circuits	48	B	Electrostatics & electromagnetism
19	A	Light & optics	49	B	Light & optics
20	C	Atomic & nuclear structure	50	D	Translational motion
21	A	Heat & thermodynamics	51	C	Equilibrium & momentum
22	C	Force, motion, gravitation	52	B	Waves & periodic motion
23	E	Sound	53	D	Heat & thermodynamics
24	D	Force, motion, gravitation	54	B	Circuit elements & DC circuits
25	B	Electrostatics & electromagnetism	55	C	Atomic & nuclear structure
26	C	Circuit elements & DC circuits			
27	D	Light & optics			
28	D	Atomic & nuclear structure			
29	E	Translational motion			
30	A	Force, motion, gravitation			

SAT Physics

Topical
Practice Questions

Kinematics and Dynamics

1. Starting from rest, how long does it take for a sports car to reach 60 mi/h, if it has an average acceleration of 13.1 mi/h·s?

   A. 6.6 s   **B.** 3.1 s   **C.** 4.5 s   **D.** 4.6 s   **E.** 13.1 s

2. A cannon ball is fired with an initial speed of 20 m/s at a 30° angle with the horizontal. Ignoring air resistance, how long does it take the cannon ball to reach the top of its trajectory? (Use acceleration due to gravity $g = 10$ m/s^2)

   A. 0.5 s   **B.** 1 s   **C.** 1.5 s   **D.** 2 s   **E.** 2.5 s

3. Darlene starts her car from rest and accelerates at a constant 2.5 m/s^2 for 9 s to get to her cruising speed. She then drives for 15 minutes at constant speed. She arrives at her destination, which is a straight-line distance of 31.5 km away, exactly 1.25 hours later. What is her average velocity during the interval of 1.25 hours?

   A. 3 m/s   **B.** 7 m/s   **C.** 18 m/s   **D.** 22.5 m/s   **E.** 2.5 m/s

4. Which of the following cannot be negative?

   A. Instantaneous speed   **C.** Acceleration of gravity
   B. Instantaneous acceleration   **D.** Displacement   **E.** Position

5. How far does a car travel while accelerating from 5 m/s to 21 m/s at a rate of 3 m/s^2?

   A. 15 m   **B.** 21 m   **C.** 69 m   **D.** 105 m   **E.** 210 m

6. Acceleration is sometimes expressed in multiples of g, where g is the acceleration due to gravity. How many g are experienced, on average, by the driver in a car crash if the car's velocity changes from 30 m/s to 0 m/s in 0.15 s? (Use acceleration due to gravity $g = 9.8$ m/s^2)

   A. 22 g **B.** 28 g **C.** 16 g **D.** 14 g **E.** 20 g

7. Ignoring air resistance, how many forces are acting on a bullet fired horizontally after it leaves the rifle?

   A. Two (one from the gunpowder explosion and one from gravity)
   B. One (from the motion of the bullet)
   C. One (from the gunpowder explosion)
   D. One (from the pull of gravity)
   E. None; it is in freefall and unaffected by any forces

8. Suppose that a car traveling to the East begins to slow down as it approaches a traffic light. Which of the following statements about its acceleration is correct?

    A. The acceleration is towards the East

    B. The acceleration is towards the West

    C. Since the car is slowing, its acceleration is positive

    D. The acceleration is zero

    E. Since the car is slowing, its acceleration cannot be determined

9. On a planet where the acceleration due to gravity is 20 m/s^2, a freely falling object increases its speed each second by about:

    A. 20 m/s   **B.** 10 m/s   **C.** 30 m/s   **D.** 40 m/s   **E.** depends on its initial speed

10. What is a car's acceleration if it accelerates uniformly in one dimension from 15 m/s to 40 m/s in 10 s?

    A. 1.75 m/s^2 **B.** 2.5 m/s^2 **C.** 3.5 m/s^2 **D.** 7.6 m/s^2 **E.** 4.75 m/s^2

11. If the fastest a person can drive is 65 mi/h, what is the longest time she can stop for lunch if she wants to travel 540 mi in 9.8 h?

    A. 1 h   **B.** 2.4 h   **C.** 1.5 h   **D.** 2 h   **E.** 0.5 h

12. What is a racecar's average velocity if it completes one lap around a 500 m track in 10 s?

    A. 10 m/s   **B.** 0 m/s   **C.** 5 m/s   **D.** 20 m/s   **E.** 15 m/s

13. What is a ball's net displacement after 5 s if it is initially rolling up a slight incline at 0.2 m/s and decelerates uniformly at 0.05 m/s^2?

    A. 0.4 m   **B.** 0.6 m   **C.** 0.9 m   **D.** 1.2 m   **E.** 2.4 m

14. What does the slope of a line connecting two points on a velocity vs. time graph represent?

    A. Change in acceleration   **C.** Average acceleration

    B. Instantaneous acceleration   **D.** Instantaneous velocity   **E.** Displacement

15. An airplane needs to reach a speed of 210.0 km/h to take off. On a 1,800.0 m runway, what is the minimum acceleration necessary for the plane to reach this speed?

    A. 0.78 m/s^2 **B.** 0.95 m/s^2 **C.** 1.47 m/s^2 **D.** 1.1 m/s^2 **E.** 2.5 m/s^2

16. A test rocket is fired straight up from rest with a net acceleration of 22 m/s^2. What maximum elevation does the rocket reach if the motor turns off after 4 s, but the rocket continues to coast upward? (Use acceleration due to gravity $g = 10$ m/s^2)

    A. 408 m   **B.** 320 m   **C.** 357 m   **D.** 563 m   **E.** 260 m

17. Without any reference to direction, how fast an object moves refers to its:

    A. acceleration   **C.** momentum
    B. impulse   **D.** velocity   **E.** speed

18. Ignoring air resistance, a 10 kg rock and a 20 kg rock are dropped at the same time. If the 10 kg rock falls with acceleration a, what is the acceleration of the 20 kg rock?

    A. $a / 2$ **B.** a **C.** $2a$ **D.** $4a$ **E.** $a / 4$

19. As an object falls freely, its magnitude of:

      I. velocity increases   II. acceleration increases   III. displacement increases

    A. I only   **B.** I and II only   **C.** II and III only   **D.** I and III only   **E.** I, II and III

20. What forces are acting on the suitcase when Jack carries a 25 kg suitcase at a constant velocity of 1.7 m/s across a room for 12 s?

    A. Gravity pointing downward; normal force pointing upward; Jack's force pointing forward
    B. Gravity pointing downward and the normal force pointing upward
    C. Gravity pointing downward and Jack's force pointing upward
    D. Gravity pointing downward
    E. Gravity pointing downward; normal force pointing downward; Jack's force pointing forward

21. A football kicker is attempting a field goal from 44 m away, and the ball just clears the lower bar with a time of flight of 2.9 s. What was the initial speed of the ball if the angle of the kick was 45° with the horizontal?

    A. 37 m/s   **B.** 2.5 m/s   **C.** 18.3 m/s   **D.** 7.2 m/s   **E.** 21.4 m/s

22. Ignoring air resistance, if a rock, starting at rest, is dropped from a cliff and strikes the ground with an impact velocity of 14 m/s, from what height was it dropped? (Use acceleration due to gravity $g = 10$ m/s^2)

    A. 10 m   **B.** 30 m   **C.** 45 m   **D.** 70 m   **E.** 90 m

23. An SUV is traveling at 20 m/s. Then Joseph steps on the accelerator pedal, accelerating at a constant 1.4 m/s^2 for 7 s. How far does he travel during these 7 s?

A. 205 m   B. 174 m   C. 143 m   D. 158 m   E. 115 m

24. Which of the following is NOT a scalar?

A. temperature   B. distance   C. mass   D. force   E. time

25. Two identical balls (A and B) fall from rest from different heights to the ground. Ignoring air resistance, what is the ratio of the heights from which A and B fall if ball B takes twice as long as ball A to reach the ground?

A. 1 : √2   B. 1 : 4   C. 1 : 2   D. 1 : 8   E. 1 : 9

26. How far does a car travel in 10 s when it accelerates uniformly in one direction from 5 m/s to 30 m/s?

A. 65 m   B. 25 m   C. 250 m   D. 650 m   E. 175 m

27. Which graph represents an acceleration of zero?

I.   II.   III.

A. I only
B. II only
C. I and II only
D. II and III only
E. I and III only

28. Doubling the distance between an orbiting satellite and the Earth results in what change in the gravitational attraction between the two?

A. Twice as much
B. Four times as much
C. One half as much
D. One fourth as much
E. Remains the same

29. An object is moving in a straight line. Consider its motion during some interval of time: under what conditions is it possible for the instantaneous velocity of the object at some point during the interval to be equal to the average velocity over the interval?

I. When velocity is constant during the interval
II. When velocity is increasing at a constant rate during the interval
III. When velocity is increasing at an irregular rate during the interval

A. II only
B. I and III only
C. II and III only
D. I, II and III
E. I and II only

30. A freely falling object on Earth, 10 s after starting from rest, has a speed of about: (Use acceleration due to gravity $g = 10$ m/s^2)

A. 10 m/s   B. 20 m/s   C. 80 m/s   D. 150 m/s   E. 100 m/s

31. A truck travels a certain distance at a constant velocity v for time t. If the truck travels three times as fast, covering the same distance, then by what factor does the time of travel in relation to t change?

A. Increases by 3

B. Decreases by 3

C. Decreases by $\sqrt{3}$

D. Increases by 9

E. Decreases by 1/9

32. Assuming equal rates of acceleration, how much farther would Steve travel if he braked from 58 mi/h to rest than from 29 mi/h to rest?

A. 2 times farther

B. 16 times farther

C. 4 times farther

D. 3.2 times farther

E. 1.5 times farther

33. What is the average speed of a racehorse if the horse makes one lap around a 400 m track in 20 s?

A. 0 m/s B. 7.5 m/s C. 15 m/s D. 20 m/s E. 25 m/s

34. What was a car's initial velocity if the car is traveling up a slight slope while decelerating at 0.1 m/s^2 and comes to a stop after 5 s?

A. 0.02 m/s B. 0.25 m/s C. 2 m/s D. 1.5 m/s E. 0.5 m/s

35. Average velocity equals the average of an object's initial and final velocity when acceleration is:

A. constantly decreasing

B. constantly increasing

C. constant

D. equal to zero

E. equal to the reciprocal of the initial velocity

36. Ignoring air resistance, compared to a rock dropped from the same point, how much earlier does a thrown rock strike the ground, if it is thrown downward with an initial velocity of 10 m/s from the top of a 300 m building? (Use acceleration due to gravity $g = 9.8$ m/s^2)

A. 0.75 s B. 0.33 s C. 0.66 s D. 0 s E. 0.95 s

37. With all other factors equal, what happens to the acceleration if the unbalanced force on an object of a given mass is doubled?

A. Increased by one fourth

B. Increased by one half

C. Increased fourfold

D. Doubled

E. Remains the same

38. How fast an object is changing speed or direction of travel is a property of motion known as:

A. velocity B. acceleration C. speed D. flow E. momentum

39. Which statement concerning a car's acceleration must be correct if a car traveling to the North (+y direction) begins to slow down as it approaches a stop sign?

- **A.** Acceleration is positive
- **B.** Acceleration is zero
- **C.** Cannot be determined from the data provided
- **D.** Acceleration decreases in magnitude as the car slows
- **E.** Acceleration is negative

40. For the velocity vs. time graph of a basketball player traveling up and down the court in a straight-line path, what is the total distance run by the player in the 10 s?

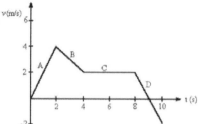

- **A.** 24 m
- **C.** 14 m
- **B.** 22 m
- **D.** 18 m
- **E.** 20 m

41. At the same time that a bullet is dropped into a river from a high bridge, another bullet is fired from a gun, straight down towards the water. Ignoring air resistance, the acceleration just before striking the water:

- **A.** is greater for the dropped bullet
- **B.** is greater for the fired bullet
- **C.** is the same for each bullet
- **D.** depends on how high the bullets started
- **E.** depends on the mass of the bullets

42. Sarah starts her car from rest and accelerates at a constant 2.5 m/s^2 for 9 s to get to her cruising speed. What was her final velocity?

- **A.** 22.5 m/s
- **B.** 12.3 m/s
- **C.** 4.6 m/s
- **D.** 8.5 m/s
- **E.** 1.25 m/s

43. A bat hits a baseball, and the baseball's direction is completely reversed and its speed is doubled. If the actual time of contact with the bat is 0.45 s, what is the ratio of the acceleration to the original velocity?

- **A.** −2.5 s^{-1} : 1
- **C.** −9.8 s^{-1} : 1
- **B.** −0.15 s^{-1} : 1
- **D.** −4.1 s^{-1} : 1
- **E.** −6.7 s^{-1} : 1

44. A 2 kg weight is thrown vertically upward from the surface of the Moon at a speed of 3.2 m/s and it returns to its starting point in 4 s. What is the magnitude of acceleration due to gravity on the Moon?

- **A.** 0.8 m/s^2
- **B.** 1.6 m/s^2
- **C.** 3.7 m/s^2
- **D.** 8.4 m/s^2
- **E.** 12.8 m/s^2

45. What is the change in velocity for a bird that is cruising at 1.5 m/s and then accelerates at a constant 0.3 m/s^2 for 3 s?

- **A.** 0.9 m/s
- **B.** 0.6 m/s
- **C.** 1.6 m/s
- **D.** 0.3 m/s
- **E.** 1.9 m/s

46. All of the following are vectors, except:

A. velocity   **B.** displacement   **C.** acceleration   **D.** mass   **E.** force

> Questions **47-49** are based on the following:

A toy rocket is launched vertically from ground level where $y = 0$ m, at time $t = 0$ s. The rocket engine provides constant upward acceleration during the burn phase. At the instant of engine burnout, the rocket has risen to 64 m and acquired a velocity of 60 m/s. The rocket continues to rise in unpowered flight, reaches maximum height and then falls back to the ground. (Use acceleration due to gravity $g = 9.8$ m/s^2)

47. What is the maximum height reached by the rocket?

    A. 274 m   **B.** 205 m   **C.** 223 m   **D.** 120 m   **E.** 248 m

48. What is the upward acceleration of the rocket during the burn phase?

    A. 9.9 m/s^2 **B.** 4.8 m/s^2 **C.** 28 m/s^2 **D.** 11.8 m/s^2 **E.** 8.6 m/s^2

49. What is the time interval during which the rocket engine provides upward acceleration?

    A. 1.5 s   **B.** 1.9 s   **C.** 2.3 s   **D.** 2.1 s   **E.** 2.6 s

50. A car accelerates uniformly from rest along a straight track that has markers spaced at equal distances along it. As it passes Marker 2, the car reaches a speed of 140 km/h. Where on the track is the car when it is traveling at 70 km/h?

A. Close to Marker 2   **C.** At Marker 1

B. Between Marker 1 and Marker 2   **D.** Close to the starting point

                                               E. Before Marker 1

51. What are the two measurements necessary for calculating average speed?

    A. Distance and time   **C.** Velocity and time

    B. Distance and acceleration   **D.** Velocity and acceleration

                                               E. Acceleration and time

52. A pedestrian traveling at speed v covers a distance x during a time interval t. If a bicycle travels at speed $3v$, how much time does it take the bicycle to travel the same distance?

    A. $t / 3$ **B.** $t - 3$ **C.** $t + 3^2$ **D.** $3t$ **E.** $t + 3^3$

53. Ignoring air resistance, how much time passes before a ball strikes the ground if it is thrown straight upward with a velocity of 39 m/s? (Use acceleration due to gravity $g = 9.8$ m/s^2)

    A. 2.2 s   **B.** 1.4 s   **C.** 12 s   **D.** 4 s   **E.** 8 s

54. A particle travels to the right along a horizontal axis with a constantly decreasing speed. Which one of the following describes the direction of the particle's acceleration?

    A. ↑   **B.** ↓   **C.** →   **D.** ←   **E.** None of the above

55. Larry is carrying a 25 kg package at a constant velocity of 1.8 m/s across a room for 12 s. What is the work done by Larry on the package during the 12 s? (Use acceleration due to gravity $g = 10$ m/s^2)

    A. 0 J   **B.** 280 J   **C.** 860 J   **D.** 2,200 J   **E.** 1,125 J

56. What does the slope of a tangent line at a time value on a velocity vs. time graph represent?

    A. Instantaneous acceleration   **C.** Instantaneous velocity
    B. Average acceleration   **D.** Position   **E.** Displacement

57. A car is traveling North at 17.7 m/s. After 12 s, its velocity is 14.1 m/s in the same direction. What is the magnitude and direction of the car's average acceleration?

    A. 0.3 m/s^2, North   **C.** 0.3 m/s^2, South
    B. 2.7 m/s^2, North   **D.** 3.6 m/s^2, South   **E.** 2.5 m/s^2, South

58. The graph below shows the position of an object as a function of time. The letters A – E represent particular moments in time. At which moment in time is the speed of the object the highest?

    A. A   **C.** C
    B. B   **D.** D   **E.** E

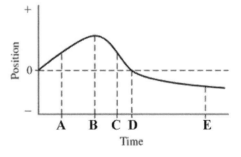

59. Ignoring air resistance, at a speed less than terminal velocity, what is happening to the speed of an object falling towards the surface of the Earth?

    A. Increasing at a decreasing rate   **C.** Decreasing
    B. Decreasing at an increasing rate   **D.** Constant   **E.** Increasing

60. How far does a car travel if it starts from rest and accelerates at a constant 2 m/s^2 for 10 s, then travels with the constant speed it has achieved for another 10 s and finally slows to a stop with constant deceleration of magnitude 2 m/s^2?

    A. 150 m   **B.** 200 m   **C.** 350 m   **D.** 400 m   **E.** 500 m

Kinematics & Dynamics – Answer Key

1: D	11: C	21: E	31: B	41: C	51: A
2: B	12: B	22: A	32: C	42: A	52: A
3: B	13: A	23: B	33: D	43: E	53: E
4: A	14: C	24: D	34: E	44: B	54: D
5: C	15: B	25: B	35: C	45: A	55: A
6: E	16: D	26: E	36: E	46: D	56: A
7: D	17: E	27: C	37: D	47: E	57: C
8: B	18: B	28: D	38: B	48: C	58: C
9: A	19: D	29: D	39: E	49: D	59: E
10: B	20: C	30: E	40: E	50: E	60: D

Force, Motion, Gravitation

1. A boy attaches a weight to a string, which he swings counter-clockwise in a horizontal circle. Which path does the weight follow when the string breaks at point P?

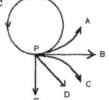

    A. path A   **C.** path C

    B. path B   **D.** path D   **E.** path E

2. A garment bag hangs from a clothesline. The tension in the clothesline is 10 N on the right side of the garment bag and 10 N on the left side of the garment bag. The clothesline makes an angle of 60° from vertical. What is the mass of the garment bag? (Use the acceleration due to gravity $g = 10.0$ m/s^2)

    A. 0.5 kg   **B.** 8 kg   **C.** 4 kg   **D.** 10 kg   **E.** 1 kg

3. A sheet of paper can be withdrawn from under a milk carton without toppling the carton if the paper is jerked away quickly. This demonstrates that:

    A. the milk carton has enough inertia

    B. gravity tends to hold the milk carton secure

    C. there is an action-reaction pair of forces

    D. the milk carton has no acceleration

    E. none of the above

4. A car of mass m is going up a shallow slope with an angle θ to the horizontal when the driver suddenly applies the brakes. The car skids as it comes to a stop. The coefficient of static friction between the tires and the road is μ_s, and the coefficient of kinetic friction is μ_k. Which expression represents the normal force on the car?

    A. $mg \tan \theta$ **B.** $mg \sin \theta$ **C.** $mg \cos \theta$ **D.** mg **E.** $mg \sec \theta$

5. A 27 kg object is accelerated at a rate of 1.7 m/s^2. How much force does the object experience?

    A. 62 N   **B.** 74 N   **C.** 7 N   **D.** 18 N   **E.** 46 N

6. How are two identical masses moving if they are attached by a light string that passes over a small pulley? Assume that the table and the pulley are frictionless.

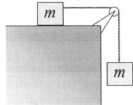

    A. With an acceleration equal to g

    B. With an acceleration greater than g

    C. At a constant speed

    D. With an acceleration less than g

    E. Not moving because the masses are equal

7. An object is moving to the right in a straight line. The net force acting on the object is also directed to the right, but the magnitude of the force is decreasing with time. What happens to the object?

    A. Continues to move to the right with its speed increasing with time

    B. Continues to move to the right with a constant speed

    C. Continues to move to the right with its speed decreasing with time

    D. Continues to move to the right, slowing quickly to a stop

    E. Stops and then begins moving to the left with its speed decreasing with time

8. A crate is sliding down an inclined ramp at a constant speed of 0.55 m/s. Where does the vector sum of all the forces acting on this crate point?

    A. Perpendicular to the ramp   **C.** Vertically upward

    B. Vertically downward   **D.** Across the ramp   **E.** None of the above

9. Consider an inclined plane that makes an angle θ with the horizontal. What is the relationship between the length of the ramp L and the vertical height of the ramp h?

    A. $h = L \sin \theta$ **C.** $L = h \sin \theta$

    B. $h = L \tan \theta$ **D.** $h = L \cos \theta$ **E.** $L = h \cos \theta$

10. Why is it just as difficult to accelerate a car on the Moon as it is to accelerate the same car on Earth?

       I. Moon and Earth have the same gravity

       II. weight of the car is independent of gravity

       III. mass of the car is independent of gravity

    A. I only   **B.** II only   **C.** III only   **D.** I and II only   **E.** I and III only

11. Sean is pulling his son in a toy wagon. His son and the wagon together are 60 kg. For 3 s Sean exerts a force which uniformly accelerates the wagon from 1.5 m/s to 3.5 m/s. What is the acceleration of the wagon with his son?

    A. 0.67 m/s^2 **B.** 0.84 m/s^2 **C.** 1.66 m/s^2 **D.** 15.32 m/s^2 **E.** 20.84 m/s^2

12. When an object moves in uniform circular motion, the direction of its acceleration is:

    A. directed away from the center of its circular path

    B. dependent on its speed

    C. in the opposite direction of its velocity vector

    D. in the same direction as its velocity vector

    E. directed toward the center of its circular path

13. What happens to a moving object in the absence of an external force?

   A. Gradually accelerates until it reaches its terminal velocity, at which point it continues at a constant velocity

   B. Moves with constant velocity

   C. Stops immediately

   D. Slows and eventually stops

   E. Moves with a constant speed in a circular orbit

14. A force of 1 N causes a 1 kg mass to have an acceleration of 1 m/s². From this information, a force of 9 N applied to a 9 kg mass would have what magnitude of acceleration?

   A. 18 m/s²   **B.** 9 m/s²   **C.** 1 m/s²   **D.** 3 m/s²   **E.** 27 m/s²

15. Which of the following statements is true about an object in two-dimensional projectile motion with no air resistance?

   A. The acceleration of the object is zero at its highest point

   B. The horizontal acceleration is always positive, regardless of the vertical acceleration

   C. The velocity is always in the same direction as the acceleration

   D. The acceleration of the object is +g when the object is rising and –g when it is falling

   E. The horizontal acceleration is always zero, and the vertical acceleration is always a nonzero constant downward

16. A can of paint with a mass of 10 kg hangs from a rope. If the can is to be pulled up to a rooftop with a constant velocity of 0.5 m/s, what must the tension on the rope be? (Use acceleration due to gravity $g = 10$ m/s²)

   A. 100 N   **B.** 40 N   **C.** 0 N   **D.** 120 N   **E.** 160 N

17. What is the magnitude of the force exerted on a 1,000 kg object that accelerates at 2 m/s²?

   A. 500 N   **B.** 1,000 N   **C.** 1,200 N   **D.** 2,000 N   **E.** 2,200 N

18. A 1,300 kg car is driven at a constant speed of 4 m/s and turns to the right on a curve on the road, which has an effective radius of 4 m. What is the acceleration of the car?

   A. 0 m/s²   **B.** 3 m/s²   **C.** 4 m/s²   **D.** 9.8 m/s²   **E.** 8 m/s²

19. A block of mass m is resting on a 20° slope. The block has coefficients of friction $\mu_s = 0.55$ and $\mu_k = 0.45$ with the surface. Block m is connected via a massless string over a massless, frictionless pulley to a hanging 2 kg block. What is the minimum mass of block m so that it does not slip? (Use acceleration due to gravity $g = 9.8$ m/s²)

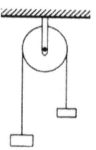

   A. 0.8 kg   **B.** 1.3 kg   **C.** 3.7 kg   **D.** 4.1 kg   **E.** 2.3 kg

20. As shown in the figure to the right, two identical masses, attached by a light cord passing over a massless, frictionless pulley on an Atwood's machine, are hanging at different heights. If the two masses are suddenly released, then the:

   A. lower mass moves down   **C.** higher mass moves down

   B. masses remain stationary   **D.** motion is unpredictable

                                     E. masses oscillate uniformly

21. When Victoria jumps up in the air, which of the following statements is the most accurate?

   A. The ground cannot exert the upward force necessary to lift her into the air, because the ground is stationary. Rather, Victoria is propelled into the air by the internal force of her muscles acting on her body

   B. When Victoria pushes down on the Earth with a force greater than her weight, the Earth pushes back with the same magnitude force and propels her into the air

   C. Victoria is propelled up by the upward force exerted by the ground, but this force cannot be greater than her weight

   D. The Earth exerts an upward force on Victoria that is stronger than the downward force she exerts on the Earth, therefore Victoria is able to spring up

   E. Because gravity is what keeps her on the ground, the internal force of her muscles acting on her body needs to be greater than the force of gravity in order to propel her into the air

22. If a feather is pounded with a hammer, which experiences a greater force?

   A. The magnitude of the force is always the same on both

   B. If the feather moves, then it felt the greater force

   C. Depends on the force with which the hammer strikes the feather

   D. Always the hammer

   E. Always the feather

23. A block is moving down a slope of a frictionless inclined plane. Compared to the weight of the block, what is the force parallel to the surface of the plane experienced by the block?

A. Greater   **C.** Less than

B. Unrelated   **D.** Equal   **E.** Requires more information

24. A package falls off a truck that is moving at 30 m/s. Ignoring air resistance, the horizontal speed of the package just before it hits the ground is:

A. 0 m/s   **B.** 15 m/s   **C.** $\sqrt{60}$ m/s   **D.** $\sqrt{30}$ m/s   **E.** 30 m/s

25. A carousel with the radius r is turning counterclockwise at a frequency f. How does the velocity of a seat on the carousel change when f is doubled?

A. Increases by a factor of $2r$ **C.** Remains unchanged

B. Increases by a factor of r **D.** Doubles

         E. It depends on the mass of the chair

26. What is the mass of a car if it takes 4,500 N to accelerate it at a rate of 5 m/s^2?

A. 900 kg   **B.** 1,320 kg   **C.** 620 kg   **D.** 460 kg   **E.** 1,140 kg

27. Steve is standing facing forward in a moving bus. What force causes Steve to suddenly move forward when the bus comes to an abrupt stop?

A. Force due to the air pressure inside the previously moving bus

B. Force due to kinetic friction between Steve and the floor of the bus

C. Force due to stored kinetic energy

D. Force of gravity

E. No forces were responsible for Steve's movement

28. A plastic ball in a liquid is acted upon by its weight and a buoyant force. The weight of the ball is 4.4 N. The buoyant force of 8.4 N acts vertically upward. An external force acting on the ball maintains it in a state of rest. What is the external force?

A. 4 N, upward   **C.** 4.4 N, upward

B. 8.4 N, downward   **D.** 4 N, downward   **E.** 2 N, downward

29. A passenger on a train traveling on a horizontal track notices that a piece of luggage starts to slide directly toward the front of the train. From this, it can be concluded that the train is:

A. slowing down   **C.** moving at a constant velocity forward

B. speeding up   **D.** changing direction

         E. moving at a constant velocity in the reverse direction

30. An object has a mass of 36 kg and weighs 360 N at the surface of the Earth. If this object is transported to an altitude that is twice the Earth's radius, what is the object's mass and weight, respectively?

A. 9 kg and 90 N   C. 4 kg and 90 N

B. 36 kg and 90 N   D. 36 kg and 40 N   E. 9 kg and 40 N

31. A truck is moving at constant velocity. Inside the storage compartment, a rock is dropped from the midpoint of the ceiling and strikes the floor below. The rock hits the floor:

A. just behind the midpoint of the ceiling

B. exactly halfway between the midpoint and the front of the truck

C. exactly below the midpoint of the ceiling

D. just ahead of the midpoint of the ceiling

E. exactly halfway between the midpoint and the rear of the truck

32. Jason takes off across level water on his jet-powered skis. The combined mass of Jason and his skis is 75 kg (the mass of the fuel is negligible). The skis have a thrust of 200 N and a coefficient of kinetic friction on water of 0.1. If the skis run out of fuel after only 67 s, how far has Jason traveled before he stops?

A. 5,428 m   B. 3,793 m   C. 8,224 m   D. 7,642 m   E. 10,331 m

33. A 200 g hockey puck is launched up a metal ramp that is inclined at a 30° angle. The puck's initial speed is 63 m/s. What vertical height does the puck reach above its starting point? (Use acceleration due to gravity $g = 9.8$ m/s^2, the coefficient of static friction $\mu_s = 0.40$ and kinetic friction $\mu_k = 0.30$ between the hockey puck and the metal ramp)

A. 66 m   B. 200 m   C. 170 m   D. 130 m   E. 48 m

34. When a 4 kg mass and a 10 kg mass are pushed from rest with equal force:

A. 4 kg mass accelerates 2.5 times faster than the 10 kg mass

B. 10 kg mass accelerates 10 times faster than the 4 kg mass

C. 4 kg mass accelerates at the same rate as the 10 kg mass

D. 10 kg mass accelerates 2.5 times faster than the 4 kg mass

E. 4 kg mass accelerates 10 times faster than the 10 kg mass

35. If a person were to move into outer space far from any stars or planets, her:

A. weight and mass decrease   C. weight remains the same but her mass changes

B. weight and mass remain the same   D. weight changes, but her mass remains the same

                                                     E. weight and mass increase

36. Which of the following statements must be true when a 20 ton truck collides with a 1,500 lb car?

   A. During the collision, the force on the truck is equal to the force on the car

   B. The truck did not slow down during the collision, but the car did

   C. During the collision, the force on the truck is greater than the force on the car

   D. During the collision, the force on the truck is smaller than the force on the car

   E. The car did not slow down during the collision, but the truck did

37. A block is on a frictionless table on Earth. The block accelerates at 3 m/s^2 when a 20 N horizontal force is applied to it. The block and table are then transported to the Moon. What is the weight of the block on the Moon? (Use acceleration due to gravity at the surface of the Moon = 1.62 m/s^2)

   A. 5.8 N   **B.** 14.2 N   **C.** 8.5 N   **D.** 11 N   **E.** 17.5 N

38. What is the weight of a 0.4 kg bottle of wine? (Use acceleration due to gravity $g = 9.8$ m/s^2)

   A. 0.4 N   **B.** 4 N   **C.** 40 N   **D.** 20 N   **E.** 2 N

39. Car A starts from rest and accelerates uniformly for time t to travel a distance of d. Car B, which has four times the mass of car A, starts from rest and also accelerates uniformly. If the magnitudes of the forces accelerating car A and car B are the same, how long does it take car B to travel the same distance d?

   A. t **B.** $2t$ **C.** $t/2$ **D.** $16t$ **E.** $4t$

40. A 1,100 kg vehicle is traveling at 27 m/s when it starts to decelerate. What is the average braking force acting on the vehicle, if after 578 m it comes to a complete stop?

   A. –440 N   **B.** –740 N   **C.** –690 N   **D.** –540 N   **E.** –880 N

41. An ornament of mass M, is suspended by a string from the ceiling inside an elevator. What is the tension in the string holding the ornament when the elevator is traveling upward with a constant speed?

   A. Equal to Mg **C.** Greater than Mg

   B. Less than Mg **D.** Equal to M/g **E.** Less than M/g

42. An object that weighs 75 N is pulled on a horizontal surface by a force of 50 N to the right. The friction force on this object is 30 N to the left. What is the acceleration of the object? (Use acceleration due to gravity $g = 9.8$ m/s^2)

   A. 0.46 m/s^2 **B.** 1.7 m/s^2 **C.** 2.6 m/s^2 **D.** 10.3 m/s^2 **E.** 12.1 m/s^2

43. While flying horizontally in an airplane, a string attached from the overhead luggage compartment hangs at rest 15° away from the vertical toward the front of the plane. From this observation, it can be concluded that the airplane is:

A. accelerating forward

B. accelerating backward

C. accelerating upward at 15° from horizontal

D. moving backward

E. not moving

44. An object slides down an inclined ramp with a constant speed. If the ramp's incline angle is θ, what is the coefficient of kinetic friction (μ_k) between the object and the ramp?

A. $\mu_k = 1$

B. $\mu_k = \cos\theta / \sin\theta$

C. $\mu_k = \sin\theta / \cos\theta$

D. $\mu_k = \sin\theta$

E. $\mu_k = \cos\theta$

45. What is the magnitude of the net force on a 1 N apple when it is in free fall?

A. 1 N   **B.** 0.1 N   **C.** 0.01 N   **D.** 10 N   **E.** 100 N

46. What is the acceleration of a 105 kg tiger that accelerates uniformly from rest to 20 m/s in 10 s?

A. 4.7 m/s^2 **B.** 1.5 m/s^2 **C.** 2 m/s^2 **D.** 3.4 m/s^2 **E.** 16.7 m/s^2

47. Yania tries to pull an object by tugging on a rope attached to the object with a force of F. If the object does not move, what does this imply?

A. The object has reached its natural state of rest and can no longer be set into motion

B. The rope is not transmitting the force to the object

C. There are no other forces acting on the object

D. The inertia of the object prevents it from accelerating

E. There are one or more other forces that act on the object with a sum of $-F$

48. If a force F is exerted on an object, the force which the object exerts back:

A. depends on the mass of the object

B. depends on the density of the object

C. depends on if the object is moving

D. depends on if the object is stationary

E. equals $-F$

49. What is the mass of an object that experiences a gravitational force of 685 N near Earth's surface? (Use acceleration due to gravity $g = 9.8 \text{ m/s}^2$)

A. 76 kg   **B.** 62 kg   **C.** 70 kg   **D.** 81 kg   **E.** 54 kg

50. Sarah and her father Bob (who weighs four times as much) are standing on identical skateboards (with frictionless ball bearings), initially at rest. For a short time, Bob pushes Sarah on the skateboard. When Bob stops pushing:

A. Sarah and Bob move away from each other, and Sarah's speed is four times that of Bob's
B. Sarah and Bob move away from each other, and Sarah's speed is one fourth of Bob's
C. Sarah and Bob move away from each other with equal speeds
D. Sarah moves away from Bob, and Bob is stationary
E. Sarah and Bob move away from each other and Bob's speed is less than one fourth that of Sarah's

51. Which best describes the motion of an object along a surface when considering friction?

A. Less force is required to start than to keep the object in motion at a constant velocity
B. The same force is required to start as to keep the object in motion at a constant velocity
C. More force is required to start than to keep the object in motion at a constant velocity
D. Once the object is set in motion, no force is required to keep it in motion at constant velocity
E. More information is needed about the surface before the amount of force can be determined

52. On the surface of Jupiter, the acceleration due to gravity is about three times that as on Earth. What is the weight of a 100 kg rock when it is taken from Earth to Jupiter? (Use acceleration due to gravity $g = 10$ m/s^2)

A. 1,800 N   **B.** 3,000 N   **C.** 3,300 N   **D.** 4,000 N   **E.** 9,000 N

53. Joe and Bill are playing tug-of-war. Joe is pulling with a force of 200 N, while Bill is simply holding onto the rope. What is the tension of the rope if neither person is moving?

A. 75 N   **B.** 0 N   **C.** 100 N   **D.** 200 N   **E.** 50 N

54. A 4 kg wooden block A slides on a frictionless table pulled by a hanging 5 kg block B via a massless string and pulley system as shown. What is the acceleration of block A as it slides? (Use acceleration due to gravity $g = 9.8$ m/s^2)

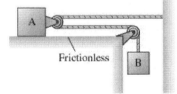

A. 2.8 m/s^2 **C.** 3.4 m/s^2
B. 1.6 m/s^2 **D.** 4.9 m/s^2 **E.** 4.1 m/s^2

55. Which of the following best describes the direction in which the force of kinetic friction acts relative to the interface between the interacting bodies?

A. Parallel to the interface and in the same direction as the relative velocity
B. Parallel to the interface and in the opposite direction of the relative velocity
C. Perpendicular to the interface and in the same direction as the relative velocity
D. Perpendicular to the interface and in the opposite direction of the relative velocity
E. Because kinetic friction depends on movement, there is no way to estimate it unless given a description of a body's velocity

56. A person who normally weighs 600 N is standing on a scale in an elevator. The elevator is initially moving upwards at a constant speed of 8 m/s and starts to slow down at a rate of 6 m/s^2. What is the reading of the person's weight on the scale in the elevator during the slowdown? (Use acceleration due to gravity $g = 9.8$ m/s^2)

    A. 600 N   **B.** 588 N   **C.** 98 N   **D.** 231 N   **E.** 61 N

57. Which object feels the greater force when a satellite is in orbit around the Moon?

    A. It depends on the distance of the satellite from the Moon
    B. The Moon and the satellite feel exactly the same force
    C. The Moon because the satellite has a smaller mass
    D. The satellite because the Moon is much more massive
    E. The Moon if the satellite has a mass less than the square root of the Moon's mass

58. What is the acceleration of a 40 kg crate that is being pulled along a frictionless surface by a force of 140 N that makes an angle of 30° with the surface?

    A. 1.5 m/s^2 **B.** 2 m/s^2 **C.** 2.5 m/s^2 **D.** 3 m/s^2 **E.** 3.5 m/s^2

59. A force is a vector quantity because it has both:

    I. action and reaction counterparts
    II. mass and acceleration
    III. magnitude and direction

    A. I only   **B.** II only   **C.** III only   **D.** I and II only   **E.** I and III only

Questions **60-61** are based on the following:

Alice pulls her daughter on a sled by a rope on level snow. Alice is 70 kg and her daughter is 20 kg. The sled has a mass of 10 kg, which slides along the snow with a coefficient of kinetic friction of 0.09. The tension in the rope is 30 N, making an angle of 30° with the ground. They are moving at a constant 2.5 m/s for 4 s. (Use acceleration due to gravity $g = 10$ m/s^2)

60. What is the work done by the force of gravity on the sled?

    A. –3,000 J   **B.** 0 J   **C.** 1,000 J   **D.** 3,000 J   **E.** –1,500 J

61. What is the work done by the rope on the sled?

    A. 0 J   **B.** 130 J   **C.** 65 J   **D.** 520 J   **E.** 260 J

Force, Motion, Gravitation – Answer Key

1: B	11: A	21: B	31: C	41: A	51: C
2: E	12: E	22: A	32: E	42: C	52: B
3: A	13: B	23: C	33: D	43: B	53: D
4: C	14: C	24: E	34: A	44: C	54: E
5: E	15: E	25: D	35: D	45: A	55: B
6: D	16: A	26: A	36: A	46: C	56: D
7: A	17: D	27: E	37: D	47: E	57: B
8: E	18: C	28: D	38: B	48: E	58: D
9: A	19: E	29: A	39: B	49: C	59: C
10: C	20: B	30: D	40: C	50: A	60: B
					61: E

Equilibrium and Momentum

1. When is the angular momentum of a system constant?

    A. When no net external torque acts on the system
    B. When the linear momentum and the energy are constant
    C. When no net external force acts on the system
    D. When the total kinetic energy is positive
    E. When the moment of inertia is positive

2. When a rock rolls down a mountainside at 7 m/s, the horizontal component of its velocity vector is 1.8 m/s. What was the angle of the mountain surface above the horizontal?

    A. 15°   **B.** 63°   **C.** 40°   **D.** 75°   **E.** 9.5°

3. A 200 N sled slides down a frictionless hill at an angle of 37° to the horizontal. What is the magnitude of the force that the hill exerts on the sled parallel to the surface of the hill?

    A. 170 N   **B.** 200 N   **C.** 74 N   **D.** 37 N   **E.** 0 N

4. Water causes a water wheel to turn as it passes by. The force of the water is 300 N, and the radius of the wheel is 10 m. What is the torque around the center of the wheel?

    A. 0 N·m   **B.** 300 N·m **C.** 3,000 N·m   **D.** 3 N·m   **E.** 30 N·m

5. Through what angle, in degrees, does a 33 rpm record turn in 0.32 s?

    A. 44°   **B.** 94°   **C.** 113°   **D.** 32°   **E.** 63°

6. A freight train rolls along a track with considerable momentum. What is its momentum if it rolls at the same speed but has twice the mass?

    A. Zero   **C.** Quadrupled
    B. Doubled   **D.** Unchanged   **E.** Cannot be estimated

> Questions **7-9** are based on the following:

Three carts run along a level, frictionless one-dimensional track. Furthest to the left is a 1 kg cart I, moving at 0.5 m/s to the right. In the middle is a 1.5 kg cart II moving at 0.3 m/s to the left. Furthest to the right is a 3.5 kg cart III moving at 0.5 m/s to the left. Consider the three carts as a system because they collide and stick together. Use the direction to the right as positive.

7. What is the total momentum of the system before the collision?

A. −2.6 kg·m/s   **C.** 0.6 kg·m/s

B. 1.4 kg·m/s   **D.** −1.7 kg·m/s   **E.** 1.1 kg·m/s

8. Assuming cart I and cart II collide first and cart III is still independent, what is the total momentum of the system just after cart I and cart II collide?

A. −1.7 kg·m/s   **C.** 0.9 kg·m/s

B. 0.1 kg·m/s   **D.** −0.9 kg·m/s   **E.** −0.11 kg·m/s

9. What is the final velocity of the three carts?

A. −0.35 m/s   **C.** −0.87 m/s

B. −0.28 m/s   **D.** 0.35 m/s   **E.** 0.15 m/s

10. A 480 kg car is moving at 14.4 m/s when it collides with another car that is moving at 13.3 m/s in the same direction. If the second car has a mass of 570 kg and a new velocity of 17.9 m/s after the collision, what is the velocity of the first car after the collision?

A. 19 m/s   **B.** −9 m/s   **C.** 9 m/s   **D.** 14 m/s   **E.** −14 m/s

11. An 8 g bullet is shot into a 4 kg block at rest on a frictionless horizontal surface. The bullet remains lodged in the block. The block moves into a spring and compresses it by 8.9 cm. After the block comes to a stop, the spring fully decompresses and sends the block in the opposite direction. What is the magnitude of the impulse of the block (including the bullet), due to the spring, during the entire time interval in which the block and spring are in contact? (Use the spring constant = 1,400 N/m)

A. 11 N·s   **B.** 8.3 N·s   **C.** 6.4 N·s   **D.** 12 N·s   **E.** 13 N·s

12. An ice skater performs a fast spin by pulling in her outstretched arms close to her body. What happens to her rotational kinetic energy about the axis of rotation?

A. Decreases   **C.** Increases

B. Remains the same   **D.** It changes, but it depends on her body mass

     E. It decreases in proportion to $\sqrt{}$(length of her arms)

13. A toy car is traveling in a circular path. If the velocity of the object is doubled without changing the path, what is the force required to maintain the object's motion?

A. $2F$ **B.** F **C.** $\frac{1}{2}F$ **D.** $4F$ **E.** $\sqrt{2}F$

14. Which of the following is units of momentum?

   A. kg·m/s^2 **B.** J·s/m   **C.** N·m   **D.** kg·s   **E.** kg·m^2/s^2

15. The impulse on an apple hitting the ground depends on:

      I. the speed of the apple just before it hits
      II. whether or not the apple bounces
      III. the time of impact with the ground

   A. I only   **B.** II only   **C.** III only   **D.** I and III only   **E.** I, II and III

16. A 55 kg girl throws a 0.8 kg ball against a wall. The ball strikes the wall horizontally with a speed of 25 m/s and bounces back with the same speed. The ball is in contact with the wall for 0.05 s. What is the average force exerted on the wall by the ball?

   A. 27,500 N   **B.** 55,000 N   **C.** 400 N   **D.** 800 N   **E.** 13,750 N

17. Three objects are moving along a straight line as shown. If the positive direction is to the right, what is the total momentum of this system?

   A. −70 kg·m/s   **C.** +86 kg·m/s

   B. +70 kg·m/s   **D.** −86 kg·m/s   **E.** 0 kg·m/s

6 m/s   3 m/s   2 m/s

7 kg   12 kg   4 kg

Questions **18-19** are based on the following:

Two ice skaters, Vladimir (60 kg) and Olga (40 kg) collide in midair. Just before the collision, Vladimir was going North at 0.5 m/s and Olga was going West at 1 m/s. Right after the collision and well before they land on the ground, they stick together. Assume they have no vertical velocity.

18. What is the magnitude of their velocity just after the collision?

   A. 0.1 m/s   **B.** 1.8 m/s   **C.** 0.9 m/s   **D.** 1.5 m/s   **E.** 0.5 m/s

19. What is the magnitude of the total momentum just after the collision?

   A. 25 kg·m/s   **C.** 65 kg·m/s

   B. 50 kg·m/s   **D.** 80 kg·m/s   **E.** 40 kg·m/s

20. A horse is running in a straight line. If both the mass and the speed of the horse are doubled, by what factor does its momentum increase?

   A. $\sqrt{2}$ **B.** 2   **C.** 4   **D.** 8   **E.** 16

---

21. The mass of box P is greater than the mass of box Q. Both boxes are on a frictionless horizontal surface and connected by a light cord. A horizontal force F is applied to box Q, accelerating the boxes to the right. What is the magnitude of the force exerted by the connecting cord on box P?

A. equal to F **C.** zero

B. equal to $2F$ **D.** less than F but > 0 **E.** equal to $3F$

22. Which of the following is true when Melissa and her friend Samantha are riding on a merry-go-round, as viewed from above?

A. They have the same speed, but different angular velocity

B. They have different speeds, but the same angular velocity

C. They have the same speed and the same angular velocity

D. They have different speeds and different angular velocities

E. Requires the radius of the merry-go-round

23. The relationship between impulse and impact force involves the:

A. time the force acts   **C.** difference between acceleration and velocity

B. distance the force acts   **D.** mass and its effect on resisting a change in velocity

      E. difference between acceleration and speed

24. Angular momentum cannot be conserved if the:

A. moment of inertia changes   **C.** angular velocity changes

B. system is experiencing a net force   **D.** angular displacement changes

      E. system has a net torque

25. A 6.8 kg block of mass m is moving on a frictionless surface with a speed of $v_i = 5.4$ m/s and makes a perfectly elastic collision with a stationary block of mass M. After the collision, the 6.8 kg block recoils with a speed of $v_f = 3.2$ m/s. What is the magnitude of the average force on the 6.8 kg block while the two blocks are in contact for 2 s?

A. 4.4 N   **B.** 47.6 N   **C.** 32.6 N   **D.** 29.2 N   **E.** 18.4 N

Questions **26-27** are based on the following:

A 4 kg rifle imparts a high velocity to a small 10 g bullet by exploding a charge that causes the bullet to leave the barrel at 300 m/s. Take the system as the combination of the rifle and bullet. Normally, the rifle is fired with the butt of the gun pressed against the shooter's shoulder. Ignore the force of the shoulder on the rifle.

26. What is the momentum of the system just after the bullet leaves the barrel?

A. 0 kg·m/s   **B.** 3 kg·m/s   **C.** 9 kg·m/s   **D.** 30 kg·m/s   **E.** 120 kg·m/s

27. What is the recoil velocity of the rifle (i.e. the velocity of the rifle just after firing)?

A. 23 m/s   **B.** 1.5 m/s   **C.** 5.6 m/s   **D.** 12.4 m/s   **E.** 0.75 m/s

28. A ball thrown horizontally from a point 24 m above the ground strikes the ground after traveling horizontally a distance of 18 m. With what speed was it thrown, assuming negligible air resistance? (Use acceleration due to gravity $g = 9.8$ m/s²)

A. 6.8 m/s   **B.** 7.5 m/s   **C.** 8.2 m/s   **D.** 8.6 m/s **E.** 9.7 m/s

29. An object is moving in a circle at constant speed. Its acceleration vector is directed:

A. toward the center of the circle
B. away from the center of the circle
C. tangent to the circle and in the direction of the motion
D. behind the normal and toward the center of the circle
E. ahead of the normal and toward the center of the circle

30. Impulse is equal to the:

I. force multiplied by the distance over which the force acts
II. change in momentum
III. momentum

A. I only   **B.** II only   **C.** III only   **D.** I and II only   **E.** I and III only

31. A 4 kg object is at a height of 10 m above the Earth's surface. Ignoring air resistance, what is its kinetic energy immediately before impacting the ground if it is thrown straight downward with an initial speed of 20 m/s? (Use acceleration due to gravity $g = 10$ m/s²)

A. 150 J   **B.** 300 J   **C.** 1,200 J   **D.** 900 J   **E.** 600 J

32. A car traveling along the highway needs a certain amount of force exerted on it to stop. More stopping force may be required when the car has:

I. less stopping distance   II. more momentum   III. more mass

A. I only   **B.** II only   **C.** III only   **D.** I and III only   **E.** I, II and III

33. A table tennis ball moving East at a speed of 4 m/s collides with a stationary bowling ball. The table tennis ball bounces back to the West, and the bowling ball moves very slowly to the East. Which ball experiences the greater magnitude of impulse during the collision?

A. Bowling ball

B. Table tennis ball

C. Neither because both experience the same magnitude of impulse

D. It is not possible to determine since the velocities after the collision are unknown

E. It is not possible to determine since the masses of the objects are unknown

34. Assume that a massless bar of 5 m is suspended from a rope and that the rope is attached to the bar at a distance *x* from the bar's left end. If a 30 kg mass hangs from the right side of the bar and a 6 kg mass hangs from the left side of the bar, what value of *x* results in equilibrium? (Use acceleration due to gravity $g = 9.8$ m/s^2)

A. 2.8 m   **B.** 4.2 m   **C.** 3.2 m   **D.** 1.6 m   **E.** 4.5 m

35. A block of mass *m* sits at rest on a rough inclined ramp that makes an angle θ with the horizontal. What must be true about the force of static friction (*f*) on the block?

A. $f > mg \sin \theta$

B. $f = mg \cos \theta$

C. $f = mg$

D. $f < mg \cos \theta$

E. $f = mg \sin \theta$

36. A 30 kg block is pushed in a straight line across a horizontal surface. What is the coefficient of kinetic friction μ_k between the block and the surface if a constant force of 45 N must be applied to the block in order to maintain a constant velocity of 3 m/s? (Use acceleration due to gravity $g = 10$ m/s^2)

A. 0.1   **B.** 0.33   **C.** 0.15   **D.** 0.5   **E.** 0.66

37. The impulse-momentum relationship is a direct result of:

I. Newton's First Law   II. Newton's Second Law   III. Newton's Third Law

A. I only   **B.** II only   **C.** III only   **D.** I and II only   **E.** I and III only

---

Questions **38-40** are based on the following:

A 0.5 m by 0.6 m rectangular piece of metal is hinged ($\otimes$) (as shown) in the upper left corner, hanging so that the long edge is vertical. A 25 N force (Y) acts to the left at the lower left corner. A 15 N force (X) acts down at the lower right corner. A 30 N force (Z) acts to the right at the upper right corner. Each force vector is in the plane of the metal. Use counterclockwise as the positive direction.

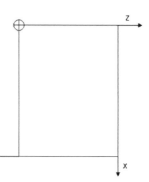

38. What is the torque of force X about the pivot?

    A. 5 N·m   **B.** 3 N·m   **C.** −7.5 N·m   **D.** 0 N·m   **E.** −5 N·m

39. What is the torque of force Z about the pivot?

    A. −10 N·m   **B.** −4.5 N·m   **C.** 4.5 N·m   **D.** 10 N·m   **E.** 0 N·m

40. What is the torque of force Y about the pivot?

    A. −15 N·m   **B.** −3 N·m   **C.** 0 N·m   **D.** 3 N·m   **E.** 7.5 N·m

41. A 50 g weight is tied to the end of a string and whirled at 20 m/s in a horizontal circle with a radius of 2 m. Ignoring the force of gravity, what is the tension in the string?

    A. 5 N   **B.** 10 N   **C.** 50 N   **D.** 150 N   **E.** 20 N

42. A small car collides with a large truck in a head-on collision. Which of the following statements concerning the magnitude of the average force during the collision is correct?

    A. The small car and the truck experience the same average force
    B. The force experienced by each one is inversely proportional to its velocity
    C. The truck experiences the greater average force
    D. The small car experiences the greater average force
    E. The force experienced by each one is directly proportional to its velocity

43. A 10 kg bar that is 2 m long extends perpendicularly from a vertical wall. The free end of the bar is attached to a point on the wall by a light cable, which makes an angle of 30° with the bar. What is the tension in the cable? (Use acceleration due to gravity $g = 10$ m/s^2)

    A. 75 N   **B.** 150 N   **C.** 100 N   **D.** 125 N   **E.** 50 N

44. Object A has the same size and shape as object B, but is twice as heavy. When objects A and B are dropped simultaneously from a tower, they reach the ground at the same time. Object A has greater:

    I. speed   II. momentum   III. acceleration

    A. I only   **B.** II only   **C.** III only   **D.** I and II only   **E.** I and III only

45. Two vehicles approach a right angle intersection and then collide. After the collision, they become entangled. If their mass ratio was 1 : 4 and their respective speeds as they approached were both 12 m/s, what is the magnitude of the velocity immediately following the collision?

    A. 16.4 m/s   **B.** 11.9 m/s   **C.** 13.4 m/s   **D.** 9.9 m/s   **E.** 8.5 m/s

46. A fisherman is on a boat that is stationary on the water. He throws the anchor off his boat at an angle of 5° above the horizontal. With reference to the water, if the anchor weighs twice as much as he does and the boat reacts by moving with a speed of 2.9 m/s during the throw, how fast did he throw the anchor? (Assume the mass of the boat is negligible)

    A. 2.2 m/s   **B.** 0.2 m/s   **C.** 1.5 m/s   **D.** 0.8 m/s   **E.** 3.1 m/s

47. Ignoring the forces of friction, what horizontal force must be applied to an object with a weight of 98 N to give it a horizontal acceleration of 10 m/s^2? (Use acceleration due to gravity $g = 9.8$ m/s^2)

    A. 9.8 N   **B.** 100 N   **C.** 79 N   **D.** 125 N   **E.** 4.9 N

48. Consider a winch that pulls a cart at constant speed up an incline. Point A is at the bottom of the incline and point B is at the top. Which of the following statements is/are true from point A to B?

    I. The KE of the cart is conserved
    II. The PE of the cart is conserved
    III. The sum of the KE and PE of the cart is conserved

    A. I only   **B.** II only   **C.** III only   **D.** I and II only   **E.** I, II and III

49. A high speed dart is shot from ground level with a speed of 140 m/s at an angle of 35° above the horizontal. What is the vertical component of its velocity after 4 s if air resistance is ignored? (Use acceleration due to gravity $g = 9.8$ m/s^2)

    A. 59 m/s   **B.** 75 m/s   **C.** 34 m/s   **D.** 41 m/s   **E.** 38 m/s

50. What does the area under the curve of a force vs. time graph represent for a diver as she leaves the platform during her approach to the water below?

    A. Work   **B.** Momentum   **C.** Impulse   **D.** Displacement   **E.** Force

51. A rifle of mass 2 kg is suspended by strings. The rifle fires a bullet of mass 0.01 kg at a speed of 220 m/s. What is the recoil velocity of the rifle?

    A. 0.001 m/s   **B.** 0.01 m/s   **C.** 0.1 m/s   **D.** 1.1 m/s   **E.** 10.1 m/s

52. How do automobile air bags reduce injury during a collision?

    A. They reduce the kinetic energy transferred to the passenger
    B. They reduce the momentum exerted upon the passenger
    C. They reduce the acceleration of the automobile
    D. They reduce the forces exerted upon the passenger
    E. All of the above

Questions **53-55** are based on the following:

Tim nails a meter stick to a board at the meter stick's 0 m mark. Force I acts at the 0.5 m mark perpendicular to the meter stick with a force of 10 N, as shown in the figure. Force II acts at the end of the meter stick with a force of 5 N, making a 35° angle. Force III acts at the same point with a force of 20 N, providing tension but no sheer stress. Use counterclockwise as the positive direction.

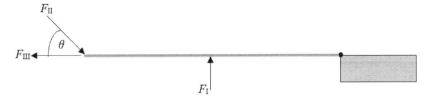

53. What is the torque of Force I about the fixed point?

　A. –5 N·m　　**B.** 0 N·m　　**C.** 5 N·m　　　**D.** 10 N·m　　**E.** –10 N·m

54. What is the torque of Force II about the fixed point?

　A. –4.8 N·m　**B.** –2.9 N·m　　**C.** 4.8 N·m　　**D.** 6.6 N·m　　**E.** 2.9 N·m

55. What is the torque of Force III about the fixed point?

　A. –20 N·m　**B.** 0 N·m　　**C.** 10 N·m　　　**D.** 20 N·m　　**E.** –10 N·m

56. Two equal mass balls (one yellow and the other red) are dropped from the same height, and rebound off the floor. The yellow ball rebounds to a higher position. Which ball is subjected to the greater magnitude of impulse during its collision with the floor?

　A. Both balls were subjected to the same magnitude of impulse
　B. Red ball
　C. Yellow ball
　D. Requires the time intervals and forces
　E. Requires the mass of each ball

57. Calculate the impulse associated with a force of 4.5 N that lasts for 1.4 s:

　A. 5.4 kg·m/s　**B.** 6.8 kg·m/s　　**C.** 4.6 kg·m/s　　**D.** 6.3 kg·m/s　　**E.** 6 kg·m/s

58. A heavy truck and a small truck roll down a hill. Ignoring friction, at the bottom of the hill, the heavy truck has greater:

　　　I. momentum　　　　II. acceleration　　　III. speed

　A. I only　　**B.** II only　　**C.** III only　　**D.** I and II only　　**E.** I and III only

59. A 78 g steel ball is released from rest and falls vertically onto a rigid surface. The ball strikes the surface and is in contact with it for 0.5 ms. The ball rebounds elastically, and returns to its original height during a round trip of 4 s. Assume that the surface does not deform during contact. What is the maximum elastic energy stored by the ball? (Use acceleration due to gravity $g = 9.8$ m/s^2)

    A. 23 J   **B.** 43 J   **C.** 11 J   **D.** 32 J   **E.** 15 J

60. Cart A is 5 kg and cart B is 10 kg, and they are initially stationary on a frictionless horizontal surface. A force of 3 N to the right acts on cart A for 2 s. Subsequently, it hits cart B and the two carts stick together. What is the final velocity of the two carts?

    A. 1 m/s   **B.** 0.4 m/s   **C.** 1.2 m/s   **D.** 1.8 m/s   **E.** 2.4 m/s

Equilibrium & Momentum – Answer Key

1: A	13: D	25: D	37: B	49: D
2: D	14: B	26: A	38: C	50: C
3: E	15: E	27: E	39: E	51: D
4: C	16: D	28: C	40: A	52: D
5: E	17: B	29: A	41: B	53: A
6: B	18: E	30: B	42: A	54: E
7: D	19: B	31: C	43: C	55: B
8: A	20: C	32: E	44: B	56: C
9: B	21: D	33: C	45: D	57: D
10: C	22: B	34: B	46: C	58: A
11: E	23: A	35: E	47: B	59: E
12: C	24: E	36: C	48: A	60: B

Work and Energy

1. Consider the following ways that a girl might throw a stone from a bridge. The speed of the stone as it leaves her hand is the same in each of the three cases.

    I. Thrown straight up
    II. Thrown straight down
    III. Thrown straight out horizontally

Ignoring air resistance, in which case is the vertical speed of the stone the greatest when it hits the water below?

    A. I only
    C. III only
    B. II only
    D. I and II only
    E. II and III only

2. A package is being pulled along the ground by a 5 N force F directed 45° above the horizontal. Approximately how much work is exerted when the force pulls the package 10 m?

    A. 14 J   **B.** 35 J   **C.** 70 J   **D.** 46 J   **E.** 64 J

3. Which quantity has the greatest influence on the amount of kinetic energy that a large truck has while moving down the highway?

    A. Velocity
    C. Density
    B. Mass
    D. Direction
    E. Acceleration

4. No work is done by gravity on a bowling ball that rolls along the floor of a bowling alley because:

    A. no potential energy is being converted to kinetic energy
    B. the force on the ball is at a right angle to the ball's motion
    C. its velocity is constant
    D. the total force on the ball is zero
    E. its kinetic energy remains constant

5. A 5 kg toy car is rolling along level ground. At a given time, it is traveling at a speed of 2 m/s and accelerating at 3 m/s^2. What is the cart's kinetic energy at this time?

    A. 20 J   **B.** 8 J   **C.** 12 J   **D.** 4 J   **E.** 10 J

6. A tree house is 8 m above the ground. If Peter does 360 J of work while pulling a box from the ground up to his tree house with a rope, what is the mass of a box? (Use acceleration due to gravity $g = 10$ m/s^2)

    A. 4.5 kg   **B.** 3.5 kg   **C.** 5.8 kg   **D.** 2.5 kg   **E.** 1.4 kg

7. For an ideal elastic spring, what does the slope of the curve represent for a displacement (x) vs. applied force (F) graph?

A. The acceleration of gravity

B. The square root of the spring constant

C. The spring constant

D. The reciprocal of the spring constant

E. The square of the spring constant

8. A spring with a spring constant of 22 N/m is stretched from equilibrium to 3 m. How much work is done in the process?

A. 33 J   **B.** 66 J   **C.** 99 J   **D.** 198 J   **E.** 242 J

9. A baseball is thrown straight up. Compare the sign of the work done by gravity while the ball goes up with the sign of the work done by gravity while it goes down:

A. negative on the way up and positive on the way down

B. negative on the way up and negative on the way down

C. positive on the way up and positive on the way down

D. positive on the way up and negative on the way down

E. requires information about the mass of the baseball

10. Let A_1 represent the magnitude of the work done by gravity as mass A's gravitational energy increases by 400 J. Let B_1 represent the total amount of work necessary to increase mass B's kinetic energy by 400 J. How do A_1 and B_1 compare?

A. $A_1 > B_1$

B. $A_1 = B_1$

C. $A_1 < B_1$

D. $A_1 = 400 B_1$

E. $400 A_1 = B_1$

11. According to the definition of work, pushing on a rock accomplishes no work unless there is:

A. an applied force equal to the rock's weight

B. movement perpendicular to the force

C. an applied force greater than the rock's weight

D. movement parallel to the force

E. force perpendicular to the movement

12. A job is done slowly, while an identical job is done quickly. Both jobs require the same amount of work, but different amounts of:

I. energy   II. power   III. torque

A. I only   **B.** II only   **C.** I and II only   **D.** I and III only   **E.** none are true

13. On a force (F) vs. distance (d) graph, what represents the work done by the force F?

A. The area under the curve

B. A line connecting two points on the curve

C. The slope of the curve

D. The length of the curve

E. The maximum F × the maximum d

14. A 3 kg cat leaps from a tree to the ground, which is a distance of 4 m. What is its kinetic energy just before the cat reaches the ground? (Use acceleration due to gravity $g = 10$ m/s^2)

A. 0 J   **B.** 9 J   **C.** 120 J   **D.** 60 J   **E.** 36 J

15. A book is resting on a plank of wood. Jackie pushes the plank and accelerates it in such a way that the book is stationary with respect to the plank. The work done by static friction is:

A. zero

B. positive

C. negative

D. parallel to the surface

E. perpendicular to the surface

16. 350 J of work are required to fully drive a stake into the ground. If the average resistive force on the stake by the ground is 900 N, how long is the stake?

A. 2.3 m   **B.** 0.23 m   **C.** 3 m   **D.** 0.39 m   **E.** 0.46 m

17. A lightweight object and a very heavy object are sliding with equal speeds along a level, frictionless surface. They both slide up the same frictionless hill with no air resistance. Which object rises to a greater height?

A. The lightweight object, because the force of gravity on it is less

B. The heavy object, because it has more kinetic energy to carry it up the hill

C. The heavy object, because it has greater potential energy

D. The lightweight object, because it has more kinetic energy to carry it up the hill

E. They both slide to exactly the same height

18. If Investigator II does 3 times the work of Investigator I in one third the time, the power output of Investigator II is:

A. 9 times greater

B. 3 times greater

C. 1/3 times greater

D. the same

E. √3 times greater

19. A diver who weighs 450 N steps off a diving board that is 9 m above the water. What is the kinetic energy when the diver strikes the water? (Use acceleration due to gravity $g = 10$ m/s^2)

A. 160 J   **B.** 540 J   **C.** 45 J   **D.** 4,050 J   **E.** 5,400 J

20. A vertical, hanging spring stretches by 23 cm when a 160 N object is attached. What is the weight of a hanging plant that stretches the spring by 34 cm?

    A. 237 N   **B.** 167 N   **C.** 158 N   **D.** 309 N   **E.** 249 N

21. A mule pulls with a horizontal force *F* on a covered wagon of mass *M*. The mule and covered wagon are traveling at a constant speed *v* on level ground. How much work is done by the mule on the covered wagon during time Δ*t*? (Use acceleration due to gravity $g = 10$ m/s^2)

    A. $-Fv\Delta t$ **B.** $Fv\Delta t$ **C.** 0 J   **D.** $-F\sqrt{v}\Delta t$ **E.** $-Fv/\Delta t$

22. Jane pulls on the strap of a sled at an angle of 32° above the horizontal. If 540 J of work are done by the strap while moving the suitcase a horizontal distance of 18 m, what is the tension in the strap?

    A. 86 N   **B.** 112 N   **C.** 24 N   **D.** 35 N   **E.** 69 N

23. A spring stretches 6 cm when a 120 g mass is attached to one of its ends. If an additional 120 g mass is added to the spring, what is the potential energy of the spring?

    A. the same   **C.** 2 times greater

    B. 4 times greater   **D.** $\sqrt{2}$ times greater   **E.** 3 times greater

24. A Ferrari, Maserati and Lamborghini are moving with the same speed and each driver slams on his brakes. The most massive is the Ferrari, and the least massive is the Lamborghini. If the tires of all three cars have identical coefficients of kinetic friction with the road surface, which car experiences the greatest amount of work done by friction?

    A. Maserati   **C.** Ferrari

    B. Lamborghini   **D.** The amount is the same   **E.** Requires more information

25. A hammer does the work of driving a nail into a wooden board. Compared to the moment before the hammer strikes the nail, after it impacts the nail, the hammer's mechanical energy is:

    A. the same

    B. less, because work has been done on the hammer

    C. greater, because the hammer has done work

    D. greater, because work has been done on the hammer

    E. less, because the hammer has done work

26. A 1,500 kg car is traveling at 25 m/s on a level road and the driver slams on the brakes. The skid marks are 10 m long. What is the work done by the road on the car?

    A. -4.7×10^5 J   **C.** 2×10^5 J

    B. 0 J   **D.** 3.5×10^5 J   **E.** -3.5×10^5 J

27. A 1,000 kg car is traveling at 4.72 m/s. If a 2,000 kg truck has 20 times the kinetic energy of the car, how fast is the truck traveling?

    A. 23.6 m/s   **B.** 47.2 m/s   **C.** 94.4 m/s   **D.** 14.9 m/s   **E.** 9.71 m/s

28. A 1,500 kg car is traveling at 25 m/s on a level road and the driver slams on the brakes. The skid marks are 30 m long. What forces are acting on the car while it is coming to a stop?

    A. Gravity down, normal force up, and a frictional force forwards

    B. Gravity down, normal force up, and the engine force forwards

    C. Gravity down, normal force forward, and a frictional force backwards

    D. Gravity down, normal force forward, and the engine force backwards

    E. Gravity down, normal force up, and a frictional force backwards

29. A 6,000 N piano is being raised via a pulley. For every 1 m that the rope is pulled down, the piano rises 0.15 m. In this pulley system, what is the force needed to lift the piano?

    A. 60 N   **B.** 900 N   **C.** 600 N   **D.** 300 N   **E.** 6 N

30. What does the area under the curve on a force vs. position graph represent?

    A. Kinetic energy   **B.** Momentum   **C.** Work   **D.** Displacement   **E.** Friction

31. What is the form in which most energy comes to and leaves the Earth?

    A. Kinetic   **B.** Radiant   **C.** Chemical   **D.** Light   **E.** Heat

32. A driver abruptly slams on the brakes in her car, and the car skids a certain distance on a straight level road. If she had been traveling twice as fast, what distance would the car have skid, under the same conditions?

    A. 1.4 times farther   **C.** 4 times farther

    B. ½ as far   **D.** 2 times farther   **E.** 8 times farther

33. A crane hoists an object weighing 2,000 N to the top of a building. The crane raises the object straight upward at a constant rate. Ignoring the forces of friction, at what rate is energy consumed by the electric motor of the crane if it takes 60 s to lift the mass 320 m?

A. 2.5 kW   **B.** 6.9 kW   **C.** 3.50 kW   **D.** 10.7 kW   **E.** 16.3 kW

34. A barbell with a mass of 25 kg is raised 3 m in 3 s before it reaches constant velocity. What is the power expended in this time? (Use acceleration due to gravity $g = 9.8$ m/s^2)

A. 138 J   **B.** 34 J   **C.** 67 J   **D.** 98 J   **E.** 262 J

35. Susan carried a 6.5 kg bag of groceries 1.4 m above the ground at constant velocity for 2.4 m across the kitchen. How much work did Susan do on the bag in the process? (Use acceleration due to gravity $g = 10$ m/s^2)

A. 52 J   **B.** 0 J   **C.** 164 J   **D.** 138 J   **E.** 172 J

36. A 1,000 kg car experiences a net force of 9,600 N while decelerating from 30 m/s to 22 m/s. How far does it travel while slowing down?

A. 17 m   **B.** 22 m   **C.** 12 m   **D.** 34 m   **E.** 26 m

37. What is the power output in relation to the work W if a person exerts 100 J in 50 s?

A. ¼ W   **B.** ½ W   **C.** 2 W   **D.** 4 W   **E.** √2 W

38. If a ball is released from a cliff ledge 58 m above the ground, how fast is the ball traveling when it reaches the ground? (Use acceleration due to gravity $g = 10$ m/s^2)

A. 68 m/s   **B.** 16 m/s   **C.** 44 m/s   **D.** 34 m/s   **E.** 53 m/s

39. A stone is held at a height h above the ground. A second stone with four times the mass is held at the same height. What is the gravitational potential energy of the second stone compared to that of the first stone?

A. Twice as much   **C.** One fourth as much

B. The same   **D.** One half as much   **E.** Four times as much

40. A 1.3 kg coconut falls off a coconut tree, landing on the ground 600 cm below. How much work is done on the coconut by the gravitational force? (Use acceleration due to gravity $g = 10$ m/s^2)

A. 6 J   **B.** 78 J   **C.** 168 J   **D.** 340 J   **E.** 236 J

41. Potential energy of an object is due to its:

    A. location   **B.** momentum   **C.** acceleration   **D.** kinetic energy   **E.** velocity

42. A spring has a spring constant of 65 N/m. One end of the spring is fixed at point P, while the other end is connected to a 7 kg mass m. The fixed end and the mass sit on a horizontal, frictionless surface, so that the mass and the spring are able to rotate about P. The mass moves in a circle of radius $r = 4$ m, and the centripetal force of the mass is 15 N. What is the potential energy stored in the spring?

    A. 1.7 J   **B.** 2.8 J   **C.** 3.7 J   **D.** 7.5 J   **E.** 11.2 J

43. If electricity costs 8.16 cents/kW·h, how much would it cost you to run a 120 W stereo system 3.5 hours per day for 5 weeks?

    A. $1.11   **B.** $1.46   **C.** $1.20   **D.** $0.34   **E.** $0.49

44. A boy does 120 J of work to pull his sister back on a swing that has a 5.1 m chain, until the swing makes an angle of 32° with the vertical. What is the mass of his sister? (Use acceleration due to gravity $g = 9.8$ m/s^2)

    A. 18 kg   **B.** 16.4 kg   **C.** 13.6 kg   **D.** 11.8 kg   **E.** 15.8 kg

45. What is the value of the spring constant if 111 J of work are needed to stretch a spring from 1.4 m to 2.9 m, if the spring starts at equilibrium?

    A. 58 N/m   **B.** 53 N/m   **C.** 67 N/m   **D.** 34 N/m   **E.** 41 N/m

46. The metric unit of a joule (J) is a unit of:

    I. potential energy   II. kinetic energy   III. work

    A. I only   **B.** II only   **C.** III only   **D.** I and III only   **E.** I, II and III

47. A horizontal spring-mass system oscillates on a frictionless table. Find the maximum extension of the spring if the ratio of the mass to the spring constant is 0.038 kg·m/N, and the maximum speed of the mass is 18 m/s?

    A. 3.4 m   **B.** 0.67 m   **C.** 3.4 cm   **D.** 67 cm   **E.** 34 cm

48. A truck weighs twice as much as a car, and is moving at twice the speed of the car. Which statement is true about the truck's kinetic energy compared to that of the car?

    A. The truck has 8 times the KE   **C.** The truck has $\sqrt{2}$ times the KE

    B. The truck has twice the KE   **D.** The truck has 4 times the KE

                                         E. The truck has $\sqrt{8}$ times the KE

49. When a car brakes to a stop, its kinetic energy is transformed into:

A. energy of rest   **C.** potential energy

B. energy of momentum   **D.** stopping energy   **E.** heat

50. A 30 kg block hangs from a spring with a spring constant of 900 N/m. How far does the spring stretch from its equilibrium position? (Use acceleration due to gravity $g = 10$ m/s^2)

A. 12 cm   **B.** 33 cm   **C.** 50 cm   **D.** 0.5 cm   **E.** 5 cm

51. What is the kinetic energy of a 0.33 kg baseball thrown at a velocity of 40 m/s?

A. 426 J   **B.** 574 J   **C.** 318 J   **D.** 264 J   **E.** 138 J

52. An object is acted upon by a force as represented by the force vs. position graph below. What is the work done as the object moves from 0 m to 4 m?

A. 10 J   **C.** 20 J

B. 50 J   **D.** 30 J   **E.** 60 J

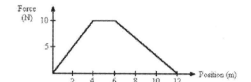

53. James and Bob throw identical balls vertically upward. James throws his ball with an initial speed twice that of Bob's. Assuming no air resistance, what is the maximum height of James's ball compared with that of Bob's ball?

A. Equal   **C.** Four times

B. Eight times   **D.** Two times   **E.** $\sqrt{2}$ times

54. The graphs show the magnitude of the force (F) exerted by a spring as a function of the distance (x) the spring has been stretched. Which of the graphs shows a spring that obeys Hooke's Law?

A.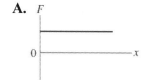

C.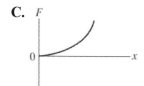

B.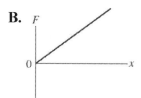

D.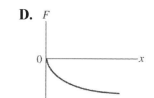

E.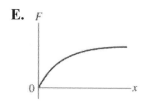

55. If a rocket travels through the air, it loses some of its kinetic energy due to air resistance. Some of this transferred energy:

    A. decreases the temperature of the air around the rocket

    B. is found in increased KE of the rocket

    C. is found in increased KE of the air molecules

    D. decreases the temperature of the rocket

    E. is found in increased PE of the air molecules

56. A car moves four times as fast as an identical car. Compared to the slower car, the faster car has how much more kinetic energy?

    A. 4 times   **B.** 8 times   **C.** $\sqrt{2}$ times   **D.** 16 times   **E.** 2 times

57. A massless, ideal spring with spring constant k is connected to a wall on one end and to a massless plate on the other end. A mass m is sitting on a frictionless floor. The mass m is slid against the plate and pushed back a distance x. After release, it achieves a maximum speed v_1. In a second experiment, the same mass is pushed back a distance $4x$. After its release, it reaches a maximum speed v_2. How does v_2 compare with v_1?

    A. $v_2 = v_1$ **B.** $v_2 = 2v_1$ **C.** $v_2 = 4v_1$ **D.** $v_2 = 16v_1$ **E.** $v_2 = v_1 / 4$

58. A N·m/s is a unit of:

    I. work   II. force   III. power

    A. I only   **B.** II only   **C.** III only   **D.** I and II only   **E.** I and III only

59. For the work energy theorem, which statement is accurate regarding the net work done?

    A. The net work done minus the initial KE is the final KE

    B. Final KE plus the net work done is the initial KE

    C. The net work done minus the final KE is the initial KE

    D. The net work done is equal to the initial KE plus the final KE

    E. The net work done plus the initial KE is the final KE

60. A 1,320 kg car climbs a 5° slope at a constant velocity of 70 km/h. Ignoring air resistance, at what rate must the engine deliver energy to drive the car? (Use acceleration due to gravity $g = 9.8$ m/s^2)

    A. 45.1 kW   **B.** 18.7 kW   **C.** 38.3 kW   **D.** 22.6 kW   **E.** 32.2 kW

Our guarantee – the highest quality preparation materials.

We expect our books to have the highest quality content and be error-free.

Be the first to report an error, typo or inaccuracy and receive a
$10 reward for a content error or
$5 reward for a typo or grammatical mistake.

info@sterling-prep.com

Work & Energy – Answer Key

1: D	11: D	21: B	31: B	41: A	51: D
2: B	12: B	22: D	32: C	42: A	52: C
3: A	13: A	23: B	33: D	43: C	53: C
4: B	14: C	24: C	34: E	44: E	54: B
5: E	15: B	25: E	35: B	45: D	55: C
6: A	16: D	26: A	36: B	46: E	56: D
7: D	17: E	27: D	37: C	47: A	57: C
8: C	18: A	28: E	38: D	48: A	58: C
9: A	19: D	29: B	39: E	49: E	59: E
10: B	20: A	30: C	40: B	50: B	60: D

Waves and Periodic Motion

1. A simple harmonic oscillator oscillates with frequency f when its amplitude is A. What is the new frequency if the amplitude is doubled to 2A?

    A. $f/2$ **B.** f **C.** $4f$ **D.** $2f$ **E.** $f/4$

2. Springs A and B are attached in series with the free end of spring B attached to a wall. Spring A, which has a spring constant k_A, is then pulled a distance L_A from its rest position. If the connection point between Spring A and Spring B is pulled a distance L_B from its rest position by Spring A, what is the expression for the spring constant k_B of Spring B?

    A. L_B/k_A **B.** $k_A{}^2$ **C.** $k_A L_B$ **D.** $(k_A L_A)/L_B$ **E.** $2k_A$

3. What is the source of all wave motion?

    A. Regions of variable high and low pressure   **C.** Harmonic particles
    B. Vibrating particles   **D.** Wave patterns
                                                       E. Sound sources

4. If a wave has a wavelength of 25 cm and a frequency of 1.68 kHz, what is its speed?

    A. 44 m/s   **B.** 160 m/s   **C.** 420 m/s   **D.** 314 m/s   **E.** 16 m/s

5. The total energy stored in simple harmonic motion (SHM) is proportional to the:

    A. amplitude^2 **C.** spring constant^2
    B. $\sqrt{\text{amplitude}}$ **D.** amplitude   **E.** $\sqrt{\lambda}$

6. A 11 kg mass m is attached to a spring and allowed to hang in the Earth's gravitational field. The spring stretches 3 cm before reaching its equilibrium position. If the spring were allowed to oscillate, what would be its frequency? (Use acceleration due to gravity $g = 9.8$ m/s^2)

    A. 0.7 Hz   **B.** 1.8 Hz   **C.** 4.1 Hz   **D.** 0.6×10^{-3} Hz   **E.** 2.9 Hz

7. The time required for one cycle of any repeating event is the:

    A. amplitude   **C.** period
    B. frequency   **D.** rotation   **E.** second

8. A pendulum of length L is suspended from the ceiling of an elevator. When the elevator is at rest, the period of the pendulum is T. How does T change when the elevator moves upward with a constant velocity?

  A. Decreases only if the upward acceleration is less than ½g
  B. Decreases
  C. Increases
  D. Remains the same
  E. Increases only if the upward acceleration is more than ½g

9. What is the period of a transverse wave with a frequency of 100 Hz?

  A. 0.01 s   **B.** 0.05 s   **C.** 0.2 s   **D.** 20 s   **E.** 50 s

10. Two radio antennae are located on a seacoast 10 km apart on a North-South axis. The antennas broadcast identical in-phase AM radio waves at a frequency of 4.7 MHz. 200 km offshore, a steamship travels North at 15 km/h passing East of the antennae with a radio tuned to the broadcast frequency. From the moment of the maximum reception of the radio signal on the ship, what is the time interval until the next occurrence of maximum reception? (Use the speed of radio waves equals the speed of light $c = 3 \times 10^8$ m/s and the path difference = 1 λ)

  A. 7.7 min   **B.** 6.4 min   **C.** 3.8 min   **D.** 8.9 min   **E.** 5.1 min

11. A 2.31 kg rope is stretched between supports 10.4 m apart. If one end of the rope is tweaked, how long will it take for the resulting disturbance to reach the other end? Assume that the tension in the rope is 74.4 N.

  A. 0.33 s   **B.** 0.74 s   **C.** 0.65 s   **D.** 0.57 s   **E.** 0.42 s

12. Simple pendulum A swings back and forth at twice the frequency of simple pendulum B. Which statement is correct?

  A. Pendulum B is ¼ as long as A   **C.** Pendulum A is ½ as long as B
  B. Pendulum A is twice as massive as B   **D.** Pendulum B is twice as massive as A
                                       E. Pendulum A is ¼ as long as B

13. A weight attached to the free end of an anchored spring is allowed to slide back and forth in simple harmonic motion on a frictionless table. How many times greater is the spring's restoring force at $x = 5$ cm compared to $x = 1$ cm (measured from equilibrium)?

  A. 2.5   **B.** 5   **C.** 7.5   **D.** 15   **E.** √2.5

14. A massless, ideal spring projects horizontally from a wall and is connected to a 1 kg mass. The mass is oscillating in one dimension, such that it moves 0.5 m from one end of its oscillation to the other. It undergoes 10 complete oscillations in 60 s. What is the period of the oscillation?

   A. 9 s   **B.** 3 s   **C.** 6 s   **D.** 12 s   **E.** 0.6 s

15. The total mechanical energy of a simple harmonic oscillating system is:

   A. always zero, which is why it is oscillating
   B. maximum when it reaches the maximum displacement
   C. zero when it reaches the maximum displacement
   D. zero as it passes the equilibrium point
   E. a nonzero constant

16. What is the frequency of the oscillations when a vibrating spring moves from its position of maximum elongation to its position of maximum compression in 1 s?

   A. 0.75 Hz   **B.** 0.5 Hz   **C.** 1 Hz   **D.** 2.5 Hz   **E.** 4 Hz

17. Which of the following is not a transverse wave?

   I. Radio   II. Light   III. Sound

   A. I only   **B.** II only   **C.** III only   **D.** I and II only   **E.** I and III only

18. If a wave has a speed of 362 m/s and a period of 4 ms, its wavelength is closest to:

   A. 8.6 m   **B.** 5.2 m   **C.** 0.86 m   **D.** 15 m   **E.** 1.5 m

19. Simple harmonic motion is characterized by:

   A. acceleration that is proportional to negative displacement
   B. acceleration that is proportional to velocity
   C. constant positive acceleration
   D. acceleration that is inversely proportional to negative displacement
   E. acceleration that is inversely proportional to velocity

20. If the frequency of a harmonic oscillator doubles, by what factor does the maximum value of acceleration change?

   A. $2/\pi$ **B.** $\sqrt{2}$ **C.** 2   **D.** 4   **E.** ½

21. An object that hangs from the ceiling of a stationary elevator by an ideal spring oscillates with a period T. If the elevator were to accelerate upwards with an acceleration of 2g, what is the period of oscillation of the object?

    A. T/2   **B.** T   **C.** 2T   **D.** 4T   **E.** T/4

22. Which of the following changes made to a transverse wave must result in an increase in wavelength?

    A. An increase in frequency and a decrease in speed
    B. The wavelength is only affected by a change in amplitude
    C. An increase in frequency and an increase in speed
    D. A decrease in frequency and a decrease in speed
    E. A decrease in frequency and an increase in speed

23. If a wave travels 30 m in 1 s, making 60 vibrations per second, what are its frequency and speed, respectively?

    A. 30 Hz and 60 m/s   **C.** 30 Hz and 30 m/s
    B. 60 Hz and 30 m/s   **D.** 60 Hz and 15 m/s   **E.** 15 Hz and 30 m/s

24. Transverse waves propagate at 40 m/s in a string that is subjected to a tension of 60 N. If the string is 16 m long, what is its mass?

    A. 0.6 kg   **B.** 0.9 kg   **C.** 0.2 kg   **D.** 9 kg   **E.** 2 kg

25. Doubling only the amplitude of a vibrating mass-on-spring system, changes the system frequency by what factor?

    A. Increases by 3   **C.** Increases by 5
    B. Increases by 2   **D.** Increases by 4   **E.** Remains the same

26. A leaky faucet drips 60 times in 40 s. What is the frequency of the dripping?

    A. 0.75 Hz   **B.** 0.67 Hz   **C.** 1.5 Hz   **D.** 12 Hz   **E.** 0.3 Hz

27. Particles of a material that move up and down perpendicular to the direction that the wave is moving are in what type of wave?

    A. torsional   **C.** longitudinal
    B. mechanical   **D.** transverse   **E.** surface

28. The figure shows a graph of the velocity *v* as a function of time *t* for a system undergoing simple harmonic motion. Which one of the following graphs represents the acceleration of this system as a function of time?

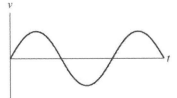

A.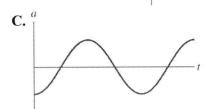

C.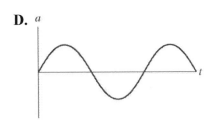

B.

D.

E. None of these

29. When compared, a transverse wave and a longitudinal wave are found to have amplitudes of equal magnitude. Which statement is true about their speeds?

    A. The waves have the same speeds

    B. The transverse wave has exactly twice the speed of the longitudinal wave

    C. The transverse wave has a slower speed

    D. The longitudinal wave has a slower speed

    E. The speeds of the two waves are unrelated to their amplitudes

30. What is the frequency when a weight on the end of a spring bobs up and down and completes one cycle every 2 s?

    A. 0.5 Hz   **B.** 1 Hz   **C.** 2 Hz   **D.** 2.5 Hz   **E.** Depends on the mass

31. The velocity of a given longitudinal sound wave in an ideal gas is $v = 340$ m/s at constant pressure and constant volume. Assuming an ideal gas, what is the wavelength for a 2,100 Hz sound wave?

    A. 0.08 m   **B.** 0.16 m   **C.** 1.6 m   **D.** 7.3 m   **E.** 0.73 m

32. When the mass of a simple pendulum is quadrupled, how does the time *t* required for one complete oscillation change?

    A. Decreases to ¼*t*   **C.** Increases to 4*t*

    B. Decreases to ¾*t*   **D.** Remains the same   **E.** Decreases to ½*t*

33. An object undergoing simple harmonic motion has an amplitude of 2.5 m. If the maximum velocity of the object is 15 m/s, what is the object's angular frequency (ω)?

 A. 0.17 rad/s   **B.** 3.6 rad/s   **C.** 37.5 rad/s   **D.** 8.8 rad/s   **E.** 6.0 rad/s

34. Unpolarized light is incident upon two polarization filters that do not have their transmission axes aligned. If 14% of the light passes through, what is the measure of the angle between the transmission axes of the filters?

 A. 73°   **B.** 81°   **C.** 43°   **D.** 58°   **E.** 64°

35. A mass on a spring undergoes simple harmonic motion. Which of the statements is true when the mass is at its maximum distance from the equilibrium position?

 A. KE is nonzero
 B. Acceleration is at a minimum
 C. Speed is zero
 D. Speed is maximum
 E. Total mechanical energy = KE

36. What is the frequency if the speed of a sound wave is 240 m/s and its wavelength is 10 cm?

 A. 2.4 Hz   **B.** 24 Hz   **C.** 240 Hz   **D.** 2,400 Hz   **E.** 0.24 Hz

37. Unlike a transverse wave, a longitudinal wave has no:

 A. wavelength
 B. crests or troughs
 C. amplitude
 D. frequency
 E. all of the above

38. The density of aluminum is 2,700 kg/m³. If transverse waves propagate at 36 m/s in a 9.2 mm diameter aluminum wire, what is the tension in the wire?

 A. 43 N   **B.** 68 N   **C.** 58 N   **D.** 35 N   **E.** 72 N

39. When a wave obliquely crosses a boundary into another medium, it is:

 A. always slowed down
 B. reflected
 C. diffracted
 D. refracted
 E. always sped up

40. A floating leaf oscillates up and down two complete cycles each second as a water wave passes by. What is the wave's frequency?

 A. 0.5 Hz   **B.** 1 Hz   **C.** 2 Hz   **D.** 3 Hz   **E.** 6 Hz

41. A higher pitch for a sound wave means the wave has a greater:

    A. frequency   **C.** amplitude

    B. wavelength   **D.** period   **E.** acceleration

42. An object is attached to a vertical spring and bobs up and down between points A and B. Where is the object located when its kinetic energy is at a maximum?

    A. One fourth of the way between A and B   **C.** Midway between A and B

    B. One third of the way between A and B   **D.** At either A or B

    E. At none of the above points

43. A pendulum consists of a 0.5 kg mass attached to the end of a 1 m rod of negligible mass. What is the magnitude of the torque τ about the pivot when the rod makes an angle θ of 60º with the vertical? (Use acceleration due to gravity $g = 10$ m/s^2)

    A. 2.7 N·m   **B.** 4.4 N·m   **C.** 5.2 N·m   **D.** 10.6 N·m   **E.** 12.7 N·m

44. The Doppler effect is characteristic of:

    I. light waves   II. sound waves   III. water waves

    A. I only   **B.** II only   **C.** III only   **D.** I and III only   **E.** I, II and III

45. A crane lifts a 2,500 kg cement block using a steel cable which has a mass per unit length of 0.65 kg/m. What is the speed of the transverse waves on this cable? (Use acceleration due to gravity $g = 10$ m/s^2)

    A. 196 m/s   **B.** 1,162 m/s   **C.** 322 m/s   **D.** 558 m/s   **E.** 1,420 m/s

46. A simple pendulum consists of a mass M attached to a weightless string of length L. Which statement about the frequency f is accurate for this system when it experiences small oscillations?

    A. The f is directly proportional to the period

    B. The f is independent of the mass M

    C. The f is inversely proportional to the amplitude

    D. The f is independent of the length L

    E. The f is dependent on the mass M

47. A child on a swing set swings back and forth. If the length of the supporting cables for the swing is 3.3 m, what is the period of oscillation? (Use acceleration due to gravity $g = 10$ m/s^2)

    A. 3.6 s   **B.** 5.9 s   **C.** 4.3 s   **D.** 2.7 s   **E.** 5 s

48. A massless, ideal spring projects horizontally from a wall and is connected to a 0.3 kg mass. The mass is oscillating in one dimension, such that it moves 0.4 m from one end of its oscillation to the other. It undergoes 15 complete oscillations in 60 s. How does the frequency change if the spring constant is increased by a factor of 2?

A. Increases by 200%   **C.** Increases by 41%

B. Decreases by 59%   **D.** Decreases by 41%

                                E. Increases by 59%

49. A ball swinging at the end of a massless string undergoes simple harmonic motion. At what point(s) is the instantaneous acceleration of the ball the greatest?

A. A   **C.** C

B. B   **D.** A and D

          E. B and C

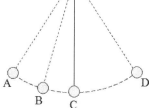

50. A simple pendulum, consisting of a 2 kg weight connected to a 10 m massless rod, is brought to an angle of 90° from the vertical, and then released. What is the speed of the weight at its lowest point? (Use acceleration due to gravity $g = 10$ m/s^2)

A. 14 m/s   **B.** 10 m/s   **C.** 20 m/s   **D.** 25 m/s   **E.** 7 m/s

51. A sound source of high frequency emits a wave with a high:

          I. pitch   II. amplitude   III. speed

A. I only   **B.** II only   **C.** III only   **D.** I, II and III   **E.** I and III only

52. Find the wavelength of a train whistle that is heard by a fixed observer as the train moves toward him with a velocity of 50 m/s. A wind blows at 5 m/s from the observer to the train. The whistle has a natural frequency of 500 Hz. (Use v of sound = 340 m/s)

A. 0.75 m   **B.** 0.43 m   **C.** 0.58 m   **D.** 7.5 m   **E.** 5.5 m

53. Considering a vibrating mass on a spring, what effect on the system's mechanical energy is caused by doubling of the amplitude only?

A. Increases by a factor of two   **C.** Increases by a factor of three

B. Increases by a factor of four   **D.** Produces no change

                                        E. Increases by a factor of $\sqrt{2}$

54. Which of the following is an accurate statement?

    A. Tensile stress is measured in N·m
    B. Stress is a measure of external forces on a body
    C. Stress is inversely proportional to strain
    D. Tensile strain is measured in meters
    E. The ratio stress/strain is called the elastic modulus

55. An efficient transfer of energy that takes place at a natural frequency is known as:

    A. reverberation   **C.** beats
    B. the Doppler effect   **D.** resonance   **E.** the standing wave phenomenon

56. A simple pendulum and a mass oscillating on an ideal spring both have period T in an elevator at rest. If the elevator now accelerates downward uniformly at 2 m/s^2, what is true about the periods of these two systems?

    A. The period of the pendulum increases, but the period of the spring remains the same
    B. The period of the pendulum increases and the period of the spring decreases
    C. The period of the pendulum decreases, but the period of the spring remains the same
    D. The periods of the pendulum and of the spring both increase
    E. The periods of the pendulum and of the spring both decrease

57. All of the following is true of a pendulum that has swung to the top of its arc and has not yet reversed its direction, EXCEPT:

    A. The PE of the pendulum is at a maximum
    B. The displacement of the pendulum from its equilibrium position is at a maximum
    C. The KE of the pendulum equals zero
    D. The velocity of the pendulum equals zero
    E. The acceleration of the pendulum equals zero

58. The Doppler effect occurs when a source of sound moves:

    I. toward the observer
    II. away from the observer
    III. with the observer

    A. I only   **B.** II only   **C.** III only   **D.** I and II only   **E.** I and III only

59. Consider the wave shown in the figure. The amplitude is: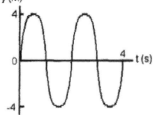

    A. 1 m

    B. 2 m

    C. 4 m

    D. 8 m

    E. √2 m

60. Increasing the mass m of a mass-and-spring system causes what kind of change on the resonant frequency f of the system?

    A. The f decreases

    B. There is no change in the f

    C. The f decreases only if the ratio k / m is < 1

    D. The f increases

    E. The f decreases only if the ratio k / m is > 1

Waves & Periodic Motion – Answer Key

1: B	11: D	21: B	31: B	41: A	51: A
2: D	12: A	22: E	32: D	42: C	52: C
3: B	13: B	23: B	33: E	43: B	53: B
4: C	14: C	24: A	34: D	44: E	54: E
5: A	15: E	25: E	35: C	45: A	55: D
6: E	16: B	26: C	36: D	46: B	56: A
7: C	17: C	27: D	37: B	47: A	57: E
8: D	18: E	28: B	38: C	48: C	58: D
9: A	19: A	29: E	39: D	49: D	59: C
10: E	20: D	30: A	40: C	50: A	60: A

Sound

1. A 20 decibel (dB) noise is heard from a cricket 30 m away. How loud would it sound if the cricket were 3 m away?

    A. 30 dB   **B.** 40 dB   **C.** $20 \times \sqrt{2}$ dB   **D.** 80 dB   **E.** 60 dB

2. A thunder clap occurs at a distance of 6 km from a stationary person. How soon does the person hear it? (Use speed of sound in air $v = 340$ m/s)

    A. 18 s   **B.** 30 s   **C.** 48 s   **D.** 56 s   **E.** 96 s

3. Enrico Caruso, a famous opera singer, is said to have made a crystal chandelier shatter with his voice. This is a demonstration of:

    A. ideal frequency   **C.** a standing wave

    B. resonance   **D.** sound refraction   **E.** interference

4. A taut 2 m string is fixed at both ends and plucked. What is the wavelength corresponding to the third harmonic?

    A. 2/3 m   **B.** 1 m   **C.** 4/3 m   **D.** 3 m   **E.** 4 m

5. High-pitched sound has a high:

    I. number of partial tones   II. frequency   III. speed

    A. I only   **B.** II only   **C.** III only   **D.** I and II only   **E.** I and III only

6. A light ray in air strikes a medium whose index of refraction is 1.5. If the angle of incidence is 60°, which of the following expressions gives the angle of refraction?
(Use $n_{air} = 1$)

    A. $\sin^{-1}(1.5 \sin 60°)$ **C.** $\sin^{-1}(1.5 \sin 30°)$

    B. $\sin^{-1}(1.5 \cos 60°)$ **D.** $\sin^{-1}(0.67 \sin 30°)$ **E.** $\sin^{-1}(0.67 \sin 60°)$

7. A string, 2 m in length, is fixed at both ends and tightened until the wave speed is 92 m/s. What is the frequency of the standing wave shown?

    A. 46 Hz   **B.** 33 Hz   **C.** 240 Hz   **D.** 138 Hz   **E.** 184 Hz

8. A 0.6 m uniform bar of metal, with a diameter of 2 cm, has a mass of 2.5 kg. A 1.5 MHz longitudinal wave is propagated along the length of the bar. A wave compression traverses the length of the bar in 0.14 ms. What is the wavelength of the longitudinal wave in the metal?

    A. 2.9 mm   **B.** 1.8 mm   **C.** 3.2 mm   **D.** 4.6 mm   **E.** 3.8 mm

---

Questions **9-12** are based on the following:

The velocity of a wave on a wire or string is not dependent (to a close approximation) on frequency or amplitude and is given by $v^2 = T / \rho_L$. T is the tension is the wire. The linear mass density ρ_L (rho) is the mass per unit length of wire. Therefore ρ_L is the product of the mass density and the cross-sectional area (A).

A sine wave is traveling to the right with frequency 250 Hz. Wire A is composed of steel and has a circular cross-section diameter of 0.6 mm and a tension of 2,000 N. Wire B is under the same tension and is made of the same material as wire A, but has a circular cross-section diameter of 0.3 mm. Wire C has the same tension as wire A and is made of a composite material. (Use density of steel wire $\rho = 7$ g/cm^3 and density of the composite material $\rho = 3$ g/cm^3)

9. By how much does the tension need to be increased to increase the wave velocity on a wire by 30%?

    A. 37%   **B.** 60%   **C.** 69%   **D.** 81%   **E.** 74%

10. What is the linear mass density of wire B compared to wire A?

    A. $\sqrt{2}$ times   **B.** 2 times   **C.** 1/8   **D.** 1/4   **E.** 4 times

11. What must the diameter of wire C be to have the same wave velocity as wire A?

    A. 0.41 mm   **B.** 0.92 mm   **C.** 0.83 mm   **D.** 3.2 mm   **E.** 0.2 mm

12. How does the cross-sectional area change if the diameter increases by a factor of 4?

    A. Increases by a factor of 16   **C.** Increases by a factor of 2
    B. Increases by a factor of 4   **D.** Decreases by a factor of 4
                                            E. Increases by a factor of $\sqrt{2}$

13. A bird, emitting sounds with a frequency of 60 kHz, is moving at a speed of 10 m/s toward a stationary observer. What is the frequency of the sound waves detected by the observer? (Use speed of sound in air $v = 340$ m/s)

    A. 55 kHz   **B.** 46 kHz   **C.** 68 kHz   **D.** 76 kHz   **E.** 62 kHz

14. What is observed for a frequency heard by a stationary person when a sound source is approaching?

    A. Equal to zero

    B. The same as the source

    C. Higher than the source

    D. Lower than the source

    E. Requires more information

15. Which of the following is a false statement?

    A. The transverse waves on a vibrating string are different from sound waves

    B. Sound travels much slower than light

    C. Sound waves are longitudinal pressure waves

    D. Sound can travel through a vacuum

    E. Musical pitch and frequency have approximately the same meaning

16. Which of the following is a real-life example of the Doppler effect?

    A. London police whistle, which uses two short pipes to produce a three-note sound

    B. Radio signal transmission

    C. Sound becomes quieter as the observer moves away from the source

    D. Human hearing is most acute at 2,500 Hz

    E. Changing pitch of the siren as an ambulance passes by the observer

17. Two sound waves have the same frequency and amplitudes of 0.4 Pa and 0.6 Pa, respectively. When they arrive at point X, what is the range of possible amplitudes for sound at point X?

    A. 0 – 0.4 Pa

    B. 0.4 – 0.6 Pa

    C. 0.2 – 1.0 Pa

    D. 0.4 – 0.8 Pa

    E. 0.2 – 0.6 Pa

18. The intensity of the waves from a point source at a distance *d* from the source is I. What is the intensity at a distance 2*d* from the source?

    A. I/2   **B.** I/4   **C.** 4I   **D.** 2I   **E.** I/$\sqrt{2}$

19. Sound would be expected to travel most slowly in a medium that exhibited:

    A. low resistance to compression and high density

    B. high resistance to compression and low density

    C. low resistance to compression and low density

    D. high resistance to compression and high density

    E. equal resistance to compression and density

20. Which is true for a resonating pipe that is open at both ends?

   A. Displacement node at one end and a displacement antinode at the other end

   B. Displacement antinodes at each end

   C. Displacement nodes at each end

   D. Displacement node at one end and a one-fourth antinode at the other end

   E. Displacement antinode at one end and a one-fourth node at the other end

21. In a pipe of length L that is open at both ends, the lowest tone to resonate is 200 Hz. Which of the following frequencies does not resonate in this pipe?

   A. 400 Hz   **B.** 600 Hz   **C.** 1,200 Hz   **D.** 800 Hz   **E.** 500 Hz

22. In general, sound is conducted fastest through:

   A. vacuum   **B.** gases   **C.** liquids   **D.** solids   **E.** warm air

23. If an electric charge is shaken up and down:

   A. electron excitation occurs   **C.** sound is emitted

   B. a magnetic field is created   **D.** light is emitted   **E.** its mass decreases

24. What is the wavelength of a sound wave of frequency 620 Hz in steel, given that the speed of sound in steel is 5,000 m/s?

   A. 1.8 m   **B.** 6.2 m   **C.** 8.1 m   **D.** 2.6 m   **E.** 5.7 m

25. If the sound from a constant sound source is radiating equally in all directions, as the distance doubles, by what amount is the intensity of the sound reduced?

   A. 1/8   **B.** 1/16   **C.** $1/\sqrt{2}$ **D.** ½   **E.** ¼

26. Why does the intensity of waves from a sound source decrease with the square of the distance from the source?

   A. The medium through which the waves travel absorbs the energy of the waves

   B. The waves speed up as they travel away from the source

   C. The waves lose energy as they travel

   D. The waves spread out as they travel

   E. The frequency of the waves decreases as they get farther from the source

Questions **27-30** are based on the following:

Steven is preparing a mailing tube that is 1.5 m long and 4 cm in diameter. The tube is open at one end and sealed at the other. Before he inserted his documents, the mailing tube fell to the floor and produced a note. (Use the speed of sound in air $v = 340$ m/s)

27. What is the wavelength of the fundamental?

  A. 0.04 m   **B.** 6 m   **C.** 0.75 m   **D.** 1.5 m   **E.** 9 m

28. If the tube was filled with helium, in which sound travels at 960 m/s, what would be the frequency of the fundamental?

  A. 160 Hz   **B.** 320 Hz   **C.** 80 Hz   **D.** 640 Hz   **E.** 590 Hz

29. What is the wavelength of the fifth harmonic?

  A. 3.2 m   **B.** 0.6 m   **C.** 2.4 m   **D.** 1.5 m   **E.** 1.2 m

30. What is the frequency of the note that Steven heard?

  A. 57 Hz   **B.** 85 Hz   **C.** 30 Hz   **D.** 120 Hz   **E.** 25 Hz

31. A 4 g string, 0.34 m long, is under tension. The string vibrates in the third harmonic. What is the wavelength of the standing wave in the string? (Use the speed of sound in air = 344 m/s)

  A. 0.56 m   **B.** 0.33 m   **C.** 0.23 m   **D.** 0.61 m   **E.** 0.87 m

32. Two pure tones are sounded together and a particular beat frequency is heard. What happens to the beat frequency if the frequency of one of the tones is increased?

  A. Increases   **C.** Remains the same
  B. Decreases   **D.** Either increase or decrease
                                   E. Increases logarithmically

33. Consider a closed pipe of length L. What are the wavelengths of the three lowest tones produced by this pipe?

  A. $4L$, $4/3L$, $4/5L$ **C.** $2L$, L, ½L
  B. $2L$, L, $2/3L$ **D.** $4L$, $2L$, L **E.** $4L$, $4/3L$, L

34. Mary hears the barely perceptible buzz of a mosquito one meter away from her ear in a quiet room. How much energy does a mosquito produce in 200 s? (Note: an almost inaudible sound has a threshold value of 9.8×10^{-12} W/m^2)

    A. 6.1×10^{-8} J   **C.** 6.4×10^{-10} J

    B. 1.3×10^{-8} J   **D.** 3.6×10^{-10} J   **E.** 2.5×10^{-8} J

35. How long does it take for a light wave to travel 1 km through water with a refractive index of 1.33? (Use the speed of light $c = 3 \times 10^8$ m/s)

    A. 4.4×10^{-6} s   **C.** 2.8×10^{-9} s

    B. 4.4×10^{-9} s   **D.** 2.8×10^{-12} s   **E.** 3.4×10^{-9} s

36. In designing a music hall, an acoustical engineer deals mainly with:

    A. beats   **C.** forced vibrations

    B. resonance   **D.** modulation   **E.** wave interference

37. Which curve in the figure represents the variation of wave speed (v) as a function of tension (T) for transverse waves on a stretched string?

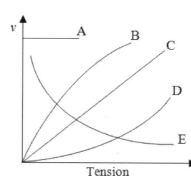

    A. A

    B. B

    C. C

    D. D

    E. E

38. A string, 4 meters in length, is fixed at both ends and tightened until the wave speed is 20 m/s. What is the frequency of the standing wave shown?

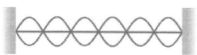

    A. 13 Hz   **B.** 8.1 Hz   **C.** 5.4 Hz   **D.** 15.4 Hz   **E.** 7.8 Hz

39. Compared to the velocity of a 600 Hz sound, the velocity of a 300 Hz sound through air is:

    A. one-half as great   **C.** twice as great

    B. one-fourth as great   **D.** four times as great   **E.** the same

40. Consider a string having linear mass density of 0.40 g/m stretched to a length of 0.50 m by a tension of 75 N, vibrating at the 6th harmonic. It excites an open pipe into the second overtone. What is the length of the pipe?

A. 0.25 m **B.** 0.1 m **C.** 0.20 m **D.** 0.6 m **E.** 0.32 m

41. A string of length L is under tension, and the speed of a wave in the string is v. What is the speed of a wave in the string if the length increases to $2L$ with no change in tension or mass?

A. $v\sqrt2$ **B.** $2v$ **C.** $v/2$ **D.** $v/\sqrt2$ **E.** $4v$

42. If a guitar string has a fundamental frequency of 500 Hz, which one of the following frequencies can set the string into resonant vibration?

A. 450 Hz **B.** 760 Hz **C.** 1,500 Hz **D.** 2,250 Hz **E.** 1,250 Hz

43. When a light wave is passing from a medium with lower refractive index to a medium with higher refractive index, some of the incident light is refracted, while some is reflected. What is the angle of refraction?

A. Greater than the angle of incidence and less than the angle of reflection
B. Less than the angle of incidence and greater than the angle of reflection
C. Greater than the angles of incidence and reflection
D. Less than the angles of incidence and reflection
E. Equal to the angles of incidence and reflection

44. The speed of a sound wave in air depends on:

     I. the air temperature   II. its wavelength   III. its frequency

A. I only **B.** II only **C.** III only **D.** I and II only **E.** I and III only

45. Which of the following statements is false?

A. The speed of a wave and the speed of the vibrating particles that constitute the wave are different entities
B. Waves transport energy and matter from one region to another
C. In a transverse wave, the particle motion is perpendicular to the velocity vector of the wave
D. Not all waves are mechanical in nature
E. A wave in which particles move back and forth in the same direction that the wave is moving is referred to as a longitudinal wave

---

46. A 2.5 g string, 0.75 m long, is under tension. The string produces a 700 Hz tone when it vibrates in the third harmonic. What is the wavelength of the tone in air? (Use the speed of sound in air $v = 344$ m/s)

    A. 0.65 m   **B.** 0.57 m   **C.** 0.33 m   **D.** 0.4 m   **E.** 0.5 m

47. Suppose that a source of sound is emitting waves uniformly in all directions. If an observer moves to a point twice as far away from the source, what is the frequency of the sound?

    A. $\sqrt{2}$ as large   **C.** Unchanged

    B. Twice as large   **D.** Half as large   **E.** One-fourth as large

48. A 2.5 kg rope is stretched between supports 8 m apart. If one end of the rope is tweaked, how long will it take for the resulting disturbance to reach the other end? Assume that the tension in the rope is 40 N.

    A. 0.71 s   **B.** 0.62 s   **C.** 0.58 s   **D.** 0.47 s   **E.** 0.84 s

49. An office machine is making a rattling sound with an intensity of 10^{-5} W/m² when perceived by an office worker that is sitting 3 m away. What is the sound level in decibels for the sound of the machine? (Use threshold of hearing $I_0 = 10^{-12}$ W/m²)

    A. 10 dB   **B.** 35 dB   **C.** 70 dB   **D.** 95 dB   **E.** 45 dB

50. A taut 1 m string is plucked. Point B is midway between both ends and a finger is placed on point B such that a waveform exists with a node at B. What is the lowest frequency that can be heard? (Use the speed of waves on the string $v = 3.8 \times 10^4$ m/s)

    A. 4.8×10^5 Hz   **C.** 9.7×10^3 Hz

    B. 2.3×10^4 Hz   **D.** 7.4×10^3 Hz   **E.** 3.8×10^4 Hz

51. For a light wave travelling in a vacuum, which of the following properties is true?

    A. Increased f results in increased amplitude

    B. Increased f results in decreased speed

    C. Increased f results in increased wavelength

    D. Increased f results in decreased wavelength

    E. Increased f results in decreased amplitude

52. Which wave is a different classification than the others (i.e. does not belong to the same grouping)?

    A. Shock waves   **C.** Ultrasonic waves

    B. Radio waves   **D.** Infrasonic waves   **E.** Longitudinal waves

53. Two speakers are placed 2 m apart and both produce a sound wave (in phase) with wavelength 0.8 m. A microphone is placed between the speakers to determine the intensity of the sound at various points. What point is precisely halfway between the two speakers? (Use the speed of sound $v = 340$ m/s)

   A. Both an antinode and a node

   B. Neither an antinode nor a node

   C. A node

   D. An antinode

   E. Need information about the frequency

54. The siren of an ambulance blares at 1,200 Hz when the ambulance is stationary. What frequency does a stationary observer hear after this ambulance passes her while traveling at 30 m/s? (Use the speed of sound $v = 342$ m/s)

   A. 1,240 Hz   **B.** 1,128 Hz   **C.** 1,103 Hz   **D.** 1,427 Hz   **E.** 1,182 Hz

55. Compared to the wavelength of a 600 Hz sound, the wavelength of a 300 Hz sound in air is:

   A. one-half as long

   B. the same

   C. one-fourth as long

   D. four times as long

   E. twice as long

56. An organ pipe that is open at both ends is tuned to a given frequency. A second pipe with both ends open resonates with twice this frequency. What is the ratio of the length of the first pipe to the second pipe?

   A. 0.5   **B.** 1   **C.** 2   **D.** 2.5   **E.** 5

57. The frequency of the third harmonic of the C_4 string of a piano is 783.7 Hz. The fundamental frequency of the G_5 string is 782.4 Hz. When the key for C_4 is held down so that the string can vibrate, and the G_5 key is stricken loudly, the third harmonic of the C_4 string is excited. Then, when striking the G_5 key again more softly, the volume of the two strings are matched. What phenomenon is demonstrated when the G_5 string is used to excite the vibration of the C_4 string?

   A. Resonance

   B. Dispersion

   C. Beats

   D. Interference

   E. Doppler effect

58. Crests of an ocean wave pass a pier every 10 s. If the waves are moving at 4.5 m/s, what is the wavelength of the ocean waves?

   A. 38 m   **B.** 16 m   **C.** 45 m   **D.** 25 m   **E.** 32 m

59. Which statement explains why sound travels faster in water than in air?

   A. Sound shifts to increased frequency

   B. Sound shifts to decreased density

   C. Density of water increases more quickly than its resistance to compression

   D. Density of water increases more slowly than its resistance to compression

   E. Sound shifts to increased density

60. When visible light is incident upon clear glass, atoms in the glass:

   I. convert the light energy into internal energy

   II. resonate

   III. vibrate

   A. I only   **B.** II only   **C.** III only   **D.** I and II only   **E.** I and III only

Sound – Answer Key

1: B	11: B	21: E	31: C	41: A	51: D
2: A	12: A	22: D	32: D	42: C	52: B
3: B	13: E	23: B	33: A	43: D	53: D
4: C	14: C	24: C	34: E	44: A	54: C
5: B	15: D	25: E	35: A	45: B	55: E
6: E	16: E	26: D	36: E	46: E	56: C
7: D	17: C	27: B	37: B	47: C	57: A
8: A	18: B	28: A	38: D	48: A	58: C
9: C	19: A	29: E	39: E	49: C	59: D
10: D	20: B	30: A	40: C	50: E	60: C

Electrostatics and Electromagnetism

1. How many excess electrons are present for an object that has a charge of -1 Coulomb? (Use Coulomb's constant $k = 9 \times 10^9$ N·m^2/C^2 and charge of an electron $e = -1.6 \times 10^{-19}$ C)

    A. 3.1×10^{19} electrons   **C.** 6.3×10^{18} electrons

    B. 6.3×10^{19} electrons   **D.** 1.6×10^{19} electrons   **E.** 6.5×10^{17} electrons

2. A flat disk 1 m in diameter is oriented so that the area vector of the disk makes an angle of $\pi/6$ radians with a uniform electric field. What is the electric flux through the surface if the field strength is 740 N/C?

    A. 196π N·m^2/C   **C.** 644π N·m^2/C

    B. $250/\pi$ N·m^2/C   **D.** 160π N·m^2/C   **E.** $10/\pi$ N·m^2/C

3. A positive charge $Q = 1.3 \times 10^{-9}$ C is located along the x-axis at $x = -10^{-3}$ m, and a negative charge of the same magnitude is located at the origin. What is the magnitude and direction of the electric field at the point along the x-axis where $x = 10^{-3}$ m? (Use Coulomb's constant $k = 9 \times 10^9$ N·m^2/C^2 and to the right as the positive direction)

    A. 8.8×10^6 N/C to the left   **C.** 5.5×10^7 N/C to the right

    B. 3.25×10^7 N/C to the right   **D.** 2.75×10^6 N/C to the right

                                                  E. 8.5×10^7 N/C to the left

4. Two charges $Q_1 = 2.4 \times 10^{-10}$ C and $Q_2 = 9.2 \times 10^{-10}$ C are near each other, and charge Q_1 exerts a force F_1 on Q_2. How does F_1 change if the distance between Q_1 and Q_2 is increased by a factor of 4?

    A. Decreases by a factor of 4   **C.** Decreases by a factor of 16

    B. Increases by a factor of 16   **D.** Increases by a factor of 4

                                                  E. Remains the same

5. A proton is located at ($x = 1$ nm, $y = 0$ nm) and an electron is located at ($x = 0$ nm, $y = 4$ nm). Find the attractive Coulomb force between them. (Use Coulomb's constant $k = 9 \times 10^9$ N·m^2/C^2 and the charge of an electron $e = -1.6 \times 10^{-19}$ C)

    A. 5.3×10^8 N   **C.** 9.3×10^4 N

    B. 1.9×10^{-15} N   **D.** 2.6×10^{-18} N   **E.** 1.4×10^{-11} N

6. Which form of electromagnetic radiation has photons with the highest energy?

    A. Gamma rays   **C.** Microwaves

    B. Visible light   **D.** Ultraviolet radiation   **E.** Infrared radiation

7. A 54,000 kg asteroid carrying a negative charge of 15 μC is 180 m from another 51,000 kg asteroid carrying a negative charge of 11 μC. What is the net force the asteroids exert upon each other? (Use gravitational constant $G = 6.673 \times 10^{-11}$ N·m²/kg² and Coulomb's constant $k = 9 \times 10^9$ N·m²/C²)

A. 400,000 N
B. 5,700 N

C. -8.2×10^{-5} N
D. -4×10^{-5} N

E. 5.7×10^{-5} N

8. Two small beads are 30 cm apart with no other charges or fields present. Bead A has 20 μC of charge and bead B has 5 μC. Which of the following statements is true about the electric forces on these beads?

A. The force on A is 120 times the force on B
B. The force on A is exactly equal to the force on B
C. The force on B is 4 times the force on A
D. The force on A is 20 times the force on B
E. The force on B is 120 times the force on A

Questions **9-10** are based on the following:

Two parallel metal plates separated by 0.01 m are charged to create a uniform electric field of 3.5×10^4 N/C between them, which points down. A small, stationary 0.008 kg plastic ball m is located between the plates and has a small charge Q on it. The only forces acting on it are the force of gravity and of the electric field. (Use Coulomb's constant $k = 9 \times 10^9$ N·m²/C², charge of an electron $= -1.6 \times 10^{-19}$ C, charge of a proton $= 1.6 \times 10^{-19}$ C, mass of a proton $= 1.67 \times 10^{-27}$ kg, mass of an electron $= 9.11 \times 10^{-31}$ kg and acceleration due to gravity $g = 9.8$ m/s²)

9. What is the charge on the ball?

A. -250 C
B. 250 C

C. 3.8×10^{-6} C
D. -2.2×10^{-6} C

E. 2.5×10^{-3} C

10. How would the acceleration of an electron between the plates compare to the acceleration of a proton between the plates?

A. One thousand eight hundred thirty times as large, and in the opposite direction
B. The square root times as large, and in the opposite direction
C. Twice as large, and in the opposite direction
D. The same magnitude, but in the opposite direction
E. One hundred times as large, and in the opposite direction

11. A positive charge $Q = 2.3 \times 10^{-11}$ C is 10^{-2} m away from a negative charge of equal magnitude. Point P is located equidistant between them. What is the magnitude of the electric field at point P? (Use Coulomb's constant $k = 9 \times 10^9$ N·m²/C²)

A. 9×10^3 N/C   **C.** 3×10^4 N/C

B. 4×10^3 N/C   **D.** 1.7×10^4 N/C   **E.** 6×10^5 N/C

12. A point charge $Q = -10$ μC. What is the number of excess electrons on charge Q? (Use charge of an electron $e = -1.6 \times 10^{-19}$ C)

A. 4.5×10^{13} electrons   **C.** 9×10^{13} electrons

B. 1.6×10^{13} electrons   **D.** 8×10^{13} electrons   **E.** 6.3×10^{13} electrons

13. An electron and a proton are separated by a distance of 3 m. What happens to the magnitude of the force on the proton if the electron is moved 1.5 m closer to the proton?

A. It increases to twice its original value

B. It decreases to one-fourth its original value

C. It increases to four times its original value

D. It decreases to one-half its original value

E. It remains the same

14. How will the magnitude of the electrostatic force between two objects be affected, if the distance between them and both of their charges are doubled?

A. It will increase by a factor of 4   **C.** It will decrease by a factor of 2

B. It will increase by a factor of 2   **D.** It will increase by a factor of √2

                                                        E. It will be unchanged

15. Which statement is true for an H nucleus, which has a charge $+e$ that is situated to the left of a C nucleus, which has a charge $+6e$?

A. The electrical force experienced by the H nucleus is to the right, and the magnitude is equal to the force exerted on the C nucleus

B. The electrical force experienced by the H nucleus is to the right, and the magnitude is less than the force exerted on the C nucleus

C. The electrical force experienced by the H nucleus is to the left, and the magnitude is greater than the force exerted on the C nucleus

D. The electrical force experienced by the H nucleus is to the left, and the magnitude is equal to the force exerted on the C nucleus

E. The electrical force experienced by the H nucleus is to the right, and the magnitude is greater than the force exerted on the C nucleus

16. Two oppositely charged particles are slowly separated from each other. What happens to the force as the particles are slowly moved apart?

   A. attractive and decreasing

   B. repulsive and decreasing

   C. attractive and increasing

   D. repulsive and increasing

   E. none of the above

17. Electrons move in an electrical circuit:

   A. because the wires are so thin

   B. by interacting with an established electric field

   C. by colliding with each other

   D. by being repelled by protons

   E. by interacting with an established gravitational field

18. If the number of turns on the secondary coil of a transformer are less than those on the primary, the result is a:

   A. 240 V transformer

   B. 110 V transformer

   C. step-up transformer

   D. step-down transformer

   E. impedance transformer

19. Two charges $Q_1 = 3 \times 10^{-8}$ C and $Q_2 = 9 \times 10^{-8}$ C are near each other, and charge Q_1 exerts a force F_1 on Q_2. What is F_2, the force that charge Q_2 exerts on charge Q_1?

   A. $F_1 / 3$ **B.** F_1 **C.** $3F_1$ **D.** $2F_1$ **E.** $F_1 / 2$

20. Two electrons are passing 30 mm apart. What is the electric repulsive force that they exert on each other? (Use Coulomb's constant $k = 9 \times 10^9$ N·m^2/C^2 and charge of an electron $= -1.6 \times 10^{-19}$ C)

   A. 1.3×10^{-25} N

   B. 3.4×10^{-27} N

   C. 1.3×10^{27} N

   D. 3.4×10^{10} N

   E. 2.56×10^{-25} N

21. A light bulb is connected in a circuit and has a wire leading to it in a loop. What happens when a strong magnet is quickly through the loop?

   A. The brightness of the light bulb dims or gets brighter due to an induced emf produced by the magnet

   B. The light bulb's brightness remains the same although current decreases

   C. The light bulb gets brighter because more energy is being added to the system by the magnet inside the coil

   D. The light bulb gets brighter because there is an induced emf that drives more current through the light bulb

   E. This does not affect the light bulb's brightness because the coil does not shift the magnitude of the current through the light bulb

22. Suppose a van de Graaff generator builds a negative static charge, and a grounded conductor is placed near enough to it so that a 8 μC of negative charge arcs to the conductor. What is the number of electrons that are transferred? (Use charge of an electron $e = -1.6 \times 10^{-19}$ C)

   A. 1.8×10^{14} electrons   **C.** 5×10^{13} electrons

   B. 48 electrons   **D.** 74 electrons   **E.** 5×10^{20} electrons

23. Which statement must be true if two objects are electrically attracted to each other?

   A. One of the objects could be electrically neutral

   B. One object must be negatively charged and the other must be positively charged

   C. At least one of the objects must be positively charged

   D. At least one of the objects must be negatively charged

   E. None of the above statements are true

24. An amp is a unit of electrical:

   A. capacity   **B.** current   **C.** potential difference   **D.** charge   **E.** pressure

25. A loop of wire is rotated about a diameter (which is perpendicular to a given magnetic field). In one revolution, the induced current in the loop reverses direction how many times?

   A. 2   **B.** 1   **C.** 0   **D.** 4   **E.** 3

26. Two charges ($Q_1 = 2.3 \times 10^{-8}$ C and $Q_2 = 2.5 \times 10^{-9}$ C) are a distance 0.1 m apart. How much energy is required to bring them to a distance 0.01 m apart? (Use Coulomb's constant $k = 9 \times 10^9$ N·m^2/C^2)

   A. 2.2×10^{-4} J   **C.** 1.7×10^{-5} J

   B. 8.9×10^{-5} J   **D.** 4.7×10^{-5} J   **E.** 6.2×10^{-5} J

27. A solid aluminum cube rests on a wooden table in a region where a uniform external electric field is directed straight upward. What can be concluded regarding the charge on the top surface of the cube?

   A. The top surface is neutral

   B. The top surface is charged negatively

   C. The top surface fluctuates between being charged neutral and positively

   D. The top surface's charge cannot be determined without further information

   E. The top surface is charged positively

28. A point charge of $+Q$ is placed at the center of an equilateral triangle, as shown. When a second charge of $+Q$ is placed at one of the triangle's vertices, an electrostatic force of 5 N acts on it. What is the magnitude of the force that acts on the center charge when a third charge of $+Q$ is placed at one of the other vertices?

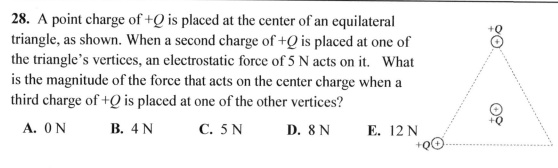

    A. 0 N   **B.** 4 N   **C.** 5 N   **D.** 8 N   **E.** 12 N

29. In the figure below, the charge in the middle is fixed and $Q = -7.5$ nC. For what fixed, positive charge q_1 will non-stationary, negative charge q_2 be in static equilibrium?

    A. 53 nC   **C.** 15 nC

    B. 7.5 nC   **D.** 30 nC   **E.** 12.8 nC

30. Which form of electromagnetic radiation has the highest frequency?

    A. Gamma radiation   **C.** Visible light

    B. Ultraviolet radiation   **D.** Radio waves   **E.** Infrared radiation

31. All of the following affect the electrostatic field strength at a point at a distance from a source charge, EXCEPT:

    A. the sign of the source charge

    B. the distance from the source charge

    C. the magnitude of the source charge

    D. the nature of the medium surrounding the source charge

    E. the electric force on the source charge

32. A charged particle is observed traveling in a circular path in a uniform magnetic field. If the particle had been traveling twice as fast, the radius of the circular path would be:

    A. three times the original radius   **C.** one-half of the original radius

    B. twice the original radius   **D.** four times the original radius

                                       E. one-third of the original radius

33. Two charges separated by 1 m exert a 1 N force on each other. If the magnitude of each charge is doubled, the force on each charge is:

    A. 1 N   **B.** 2 N   **C.** 4 N   **D.** 6 N   **E.** 10 N

34. In a water solution of NaCl, the NaCl dissociates into ions surrounded by water molecules. Consider a water molecule near a Na^+ ion. What tends to be the orientation of the water molecule?

    A. The hydrogen atoms are nearer the Na^+ ion because of their positive charge

    B. The hydrogen atoms are nearer the Na^+ ion because of their negative charge

    C. The oxygen atom is nearer the Na^+ ion because of the oxygen's positive charge

    D. The oxygen atom is nearer the Na^+ ion because of the oxygen's negative charge

    E. The hydrogen and oxygen atom center themselves on either side of the Na^+ ion
       because an atom itself has no charge

35. A metal sphere is insulated electrically and is given a charge. If 30 electrons are added to the sphere in giving a charge, how many Coulombs are added to the sphere? (Use Coulomb's constant $k = 9 \times 10^9$ N·m²/C² and charge of an electron $e = -1.6 \times 10^{-19}$ C)

    A. -2.4 C   **B.** -30 C   **C.** -4.8×10^{-18} C   **D.** -4.8×10^{-16} C   **E.** -13 C

36. What happens to the cyclotron frequency of a charged particle if its speed doubles?

    A. It is ¼ as large   **C.** It doubles

    B. It is ½ as large   **D.** It is $\sqrt{2}$ times as large   **E.** It remains the same

37. A positive test charge q is released near a positive fixed charge Q. As q moves away from Q, it experiences:

    A. increasing acceleration   **C.** constant velocity

    B. decreasing acceleration   **D.** decreasing velocity   **E.** constant momentum

38. If a value has SI units kg·m²/s² C, this value can be:

    A. electric potential difference   **C.** electric field strength

    B. resistance   **D.** Newton's forces   **E.** electric potential energy

39. A Coulomb is a unit of electrical:

    A. capacity   **C.** charge

    B. resistance   **D.** potential difference   **E.** pressure

40. To say that electric charge is conserved means that no case has ever been found where the:

    A. net charge has been created or destroyed

    B. total charge on an object has increased

    C. net negative charge on an object is unbalanced by a positive charge on another object

    D. total charge on an object has changed by a significant amount

    E. total charge on an object has decreased

41. Two charges $Q_1 = 1.7 \times 10^{-10}$ C and $Q_2 = 6.8 \times 10^{-10}$ C are near each other. How would F change if the charges were both doubled, but the distance between them remained the same?

    A. F increases by a factor of 2   **C.** F decreases by a factor of $\sqrt{2}$

    B. F increases by a factor of 4   **D.** F decreases by a factor of 4

                                      E. F increases by a factor of $\sqrt{2}$

42. Two like charges of the same magnitude are 10 mm apart. If the force of repulsion they exert upon each other is 4 N, what is the magnitude of each charge? (Use Coulomb's constant $k = 9 \times 10^9$ N·m²/C²)

    A. 6×10^{-5} C   **C.** 2×10^{-7} C

    B. 6×10^5 C   **D.** 1.5×10^{-7} C   **E.** 6×10^{-7} C

43. A circular loop of wire is rotated about an axis whose direction at constant angular speed can be varied. In a region where a uniform magnetic field points straight down, what must be the orientation of the loop's axis of rotation if the induced emf is zero?

    A. It must be vertical

    B. It must make an angle of 45° to the direction South

    C. Any horizontal orientation is equivalent

    D. It must make an angle of 45° to the vertical

    E. It must make an angle of 90° to the direction South

44. Two identical small charged spheres are a certain distance apart, and each initially experiences an electrostatic force of magnitude F due to the other. With time, charge gradually diminishes on both spheres. What is the magnitude of the electrostatic force when each of the spheres has lost half its initial charge?

    A. 1/16 F **B.** 1/8 F **C.** 1/4 F **D.** 2 F **E.** F

45. A proton, moving in a uniform magnetic field, moves in a circle perpendicular to the field lines and takes time T for each circle. If the proton's speed tripled, what would now be its time to go around each circle?

    A. T   **B.** T/3   **C.** 6T   **D.** 3T   **E.** T/6

46. As measurements of the electrostatic field strength are taken at points that progressively approach a negatively-charged particle, the field vectors will point:

    A. away from the particle and have constant magnitude

    B. away from the particle and have progressively decreasing magnitude

    C. towards the particle and have progressively increasing magnitude

    D. towards the particle and have progressively decreasing magnitude

    E. towards the particle and have constant magnitude

47. Every proton in the universe is surrounded by its own:

      I. electric field   II. gravitational field   III. magnetic field

    A. I only   **B.** II only   **C.** III only   **D.** I and III only   **E.** I, II and III

48. A charge $Q = 3.1 \times 10^{-5}$ C is fixed in space while another charge $q = -10^{-6}$ C is 6 m away. Charge q is slowly moved 4 m in a straight line directly toward the charge Q. How much work is required to move charge q? (Use Coulomb's constant $k = 9 \times 10^9$ N·m^2/C^2)

    A. −0.09 J   **B.** −0.03 J   **C.** 0.16 J   **D.** 0.08 J   **E.** 0.8 J

49. A point charge $Q = -600$ nC. What is the number of excess electrons in charge Q? (Use the charge of an electron $e = -1.6 \times 10^{-19}$ C)

    A. 5.6×10^{12} electrons   **C.** 2.8×10^{11} electrons

    B. 2.1×10^{10} electrons   **D.** 3.8×10^{12} electrons   **E.** 4.3×10^{8} electrons

50. In electricity, what quantity is analogous to acceleration of gravity, g (i.e. a force per unit mass)?

    A. Electric charge   **C.** Electric field

    B. Electric current   **D.** Electromagnetic force   **E.** Electric dipole

51. Which type of electromagnetic (EM) wave travels through space the slowest?

    A. Visible light   **C.** Gamma rays

    B. Ultraviolet light   **D.** Radio waves   **E.** All EM waves travel at the same speed

52. As a proton moves in the direction of the electric field lines, it is moving from:

    A. high potential to low potential and losing electric potential energy

    B. high potential to low potential and gaining electric potential energy

    C. low potential to high potential and gaining electric potential energy

    D. low potential to high potential and retaining electric potential energy

    E. high potential to low potential and retaining electric potential energy

53. Which of the following requires a measure of time?

    A. Joule   **B.** Watt   **C.** Volt   **D.** Coulomb   **E.** Ohm

54. If an object is characterized as electrically polarized:

    A. its internal electric field is zero   **C.** it is electrically charged

    B. it is a strong insulator   **D.** its charges have been rearranged

                                      E. it is a weak insulator

55. Two positive charges Q_1 and $Q_2 = 3.4 \times 10^{-10}$ C are located 10^{-3} m away from each other, and point P is exactly between them. What is the magnitude of the electric field at point P?

A. 0 N/C

B. 10^{-10} N/C

C. 6.8×10^{-7} N/C

D. 1.7×10^{-5} N/C

E. 1.2×10^{-9} N/C

56. Two equally-charged spheres of mass 1 g are placed 2 cm apart. When released, they begin to accelerate at 440 m/s². What is the magnitude of the charge on each sphere? (Use Coulomb's constant $k = 9 \times 10^9$ N·m²/C²)

A. 80 nC
B. 65 nC
C. 115 nC
D. 100 nC
E. 140 nC

57. Which of the following is an accurate statement?

A. A conductor cannot carry a net charge

B. The electric field at the surface of a conductor is not necessarily parallel to the surface

C. If a solid metal sphere carries a net charge, the charge distributes uniformly throughout

D. If a solid metal sphere carries a net charge, the charge will move to the sphere surface

E. If a solid metal sphere carries a net charge, the charge congregates in the center of the sphere

58. Two equal and opposite charges a certain distance apart are called an electric 'dipole'. A positive test charge +q is placed as shown, equidistant from the two charges.

Which diagram below gives the direction of the net force on the test charge?

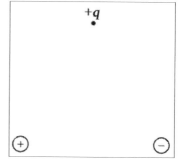

A. ←

B. →

C. ↑

D. ↓

E. ↕

59. A charged particle moves and experiences no magnetic force. What can be concluded?

A. Either no magnetic field exists or the particle is moving parallel to the field

B. No magnetic field exists in that region of space

C. The particle is moving at right angles to the magnetic field

D. The particle is moving parallel to the magnetic field

E. The particle must be massive

60. Find the magnitude of the electrostatic force between a +3 C point charge and a –12 C point charge if they are separated by 50 cm of empty space.
(Use Coulomb's constant $k = 9 \times 10^9$ N·m²/C²)

A. 9.2×10^{12} N

B. 1.3×10^{12} N

C. 7.7×10^{12} N

D. 4.8×10^{12} N

E. 2.7×10^{12} N

Electrostatics & Electromagnetism – Answer Key

1: C	11: D	21: A	31: A	41: B	51: E
2: D	12: E	22: C	32: B	42: C	52: A
3: A	13: C	23: A	33: C	43: A	53: B
4: C	14: E	24: B	34: D	44: C	54: D
5: E	15: D	25: A	35: C	45: B	55: A
6: A	16: A	26: D	36: E	46: C	56: E
7: D	17: B	27: E	37: B	47: E	57: D
8: B	18: D	28: C	38: A	48: A	58: B
9: D	19: B	29: D	39: C	49: D	59: A
10: A	20: E	30: A	40: A	50: C	60: B

Circuit Elements and DC Circuits

1. What is the new resistance of a wire if the length of a certain wire is doubled and its radius is also doubled?

   A. It is $\sqrt{2}$ times as large   **C.** It stays the same

   B. It is ½ as large   **D.** It is 2 times as large   **E.** It is ¼ as large

2. A 6 Ω resistor is connected across the terminals of a 12 V battery. If 0.6 A of current flows, what is the internal resistance of the battery?

   A. 2 Ω   **B.** 26 Ω   **C.** 20 Ω   **D.** 14 Ω   **E.** 3.6 Ω

3. Three 8 V batteries are connected in series in order to power light bulbs A and B. The resistance of light bulb A is 60 Ω and the resistance of light bulb B is 30 Ω. How does the current through light bulb A compare with the current through light bulb B?

   A. The current through light bulb A is less

   B. The current through light bulb A is greater

   C. The current through light bulb A is the same

   D. The current through light bulb A is exactly doubled that through light bulb B

   E. None are true

4. A sphere with radius 2 mm carries a 1 μC charge. What is the potential difference, $V_B - V_A$, between point B 3.5 m from the center of the sphere and point A 8 m from the center of the sphere? (Use Coulomb's constant $k = 9 \times 10^9$ N·m²/C²)

   A. −485 V   **B.** 1,140 V   **C.** −140 V   **D.** 1,446 V   **E.** 2,457 V

5. Which of the following affect(s) capacitance of capacitors?

      I. material between the conductors

      II. distance between the conductors

      III. geometry of the conductors

   A. I only   **B.** II only   **C.** III only   **D.** I and III only   **E.** I, II and III

6. A proton with an initial speed of 1.5×10^5 m/s falls through a potential difference of 100 volts, gaining speed. What is the speed reached? (Use the mass of a proton $= 1.67 \times 10^{-27}$ kg and the charge of a proton $= 1.6 \times 10^{-19}$ C)

   A. 2×10^5 m/s   **C.** 8.6×10^5 m/s

   B. 4×10^5 m/s   **D.** 7.6×10^5 m/s   **E.** 6.6×10^5 m/s

---

7. The current flowing through a circuit of constant resistance is doubled. What is the effect on the power dissipated by that circuit?

A. Decreases to one-half its original value

B. Decreases to one-fourth its original value

C. Quadruples its original value

D. Doubles its original value

E. Decreases to one-eighth its original value

8. A positively-charged particle is at rest in an unknown medium. What is the magnitude of the magnetic field generated by this particle?

A. Constant everywhere and dependent only on the mass of the medium

B. Less at points near to the particle compared to a distant point

C. Greater at points near to the particle compared to a distant point

D. Equal to zero

E. Constant everywhere and dependent only on the density of the medium

9. The heating element of a toaster is a long wire of some metal, often a metal alloy, which heats up when a 120 V potential difference is applied across it. Consider a 300 W toaster connected to a wall outlet. Which statement would result in an increase in the rate by which heat is produced?

A. Use a longer wire

B. Use a thicker wire

C. Use a thicker and longer wire

D. Use a thinner and longer wire

E. Use a thinner wire of the same length

10. A 4 μC point charge and an 8 μC point charge are initially infinitely far apart. How much work is required to bring the 4 μC point charge to ($x = 2$ mm, $y = 0$ mm), and the 8 μC point charge to ($x = -2$ mm, $y = 0$ mm)? (Use Coulomb's constant $k = 9 \times 10^9$ N·m^2/C^2)

A. 32.6 J   **B.** 9.8 J   **C.** 47 J   **D.** 81 J   **E.** 72 J

11. What current flows when a 400 Ω resistor is connected across a 220 V circuit?

A. 0.55 A   **B.** 1.8 A   **C.** 5.5 A   **D.** 0.18 A   **E.** 18 A

12. Which statement is accurate for when different resistors are connected in parallel across an ideal battery?

A. Power dissipated in each is the same

B. Their equivalent resistance is greater than the resistance of any one of the individual resistors

C. Current flowing in each is the same

D. Their equivalent resistance is equal to the average of the individual resistances

E. Potential difference across each is the same

13. An electron was accelerated from rest through a potential difference of 990 V. What is its speed? (Use mass of an electron = 9.11×10^{-31} kg, mass of a proton = 1.67×10^{-27} kg and charge of a proton = 1.6×10^{-19} C)

A. 0.8×10^7 m/s   **C.** 7.4×10^7 m/s

B. 3.7×10^7 m/s   **D.** 1.9×10^7 m/s   **E.** 6.9×10^7 m/s

14. A circular conducting loop with a radius of 0.5 m and a small gap filled with a 12 Ω resistor is oriented in the *xy*-plane. If a magnetic field of 1 T, making an angle of 30° with the *z*-axis, increases to 12 T, in 5 s, what is the magnitude of the current flowing in the conductor?

A. 0.33 A   **B.** 0.13 A   **C.** 0.88 A   **D.** 1.5 A   **E.** 4.5 A

15. For an electric motor with a resistance of 35 Ω that draws 10 A of current, what is the voltage drop?

A. 3.5 V   **B.** 25 V   **C.** 350 V   **D.** 3,500 V   **E.** 0.3 V

16. A charged parallel-plate capacitor has an electric field E_0 between its plates. The bare nuclei of a stationary ^{1}H and ^{4}He are between the plates. Ignoring the force of gravity, how does the magnitude of the acceleration of the hydrogen nucleus a_H compare with the magnitude of the acceleration of the helium nucleus a_{He}? (Use mass of an electron = 9×10^{-31} kg, mass of a proton = 1.67×10^{-27} kg, mass of a neutron = 1.67×10^{-27} kg and charge of a proton = 1.6×10^{-19} C)

A. $a_H = 2a_{He}$ **B.** $a_H = 4a_{He}$ **C.** $a_H = \frac{1}{4}a_{He}$ **D.** $a_H = a_{He}$ **E.** $a_H = \frac{1}{2}a_{He}$

17. Identical light bulbs are attached to identical batteries in three different ways (A, B, or C), as shown in the figure. What is the ranking (from lowest to highest) of the total power produced by the battery?

A. C, B, A   **C.** A, C, B

B. B, A, C   **D.** A, B, C

                        E. C, A, B

18. A parallel-plate capacitor consists of two parallel, square plates that have dimensions 1 cm by 1 cm. If the plates are separated by 1 mm, and the space between them is filled with Teflon, what is the capacitance? (Use dielectric constant *k* for Teflon = 2.1 and electric permittivity $\varepsilon_0 = 8.854 \times 10^{-12}$ F/m)

A. 0.83 pF   **B.** 2.2 pF   **C.** 0.46 pF   **D.** 1.9 pF   **E.** 0.11 pF

19. The resistor R has a variable resistance. Which statement is true when R is decreased?

A. I_1 decreases, I_2 increases
B. I_1 increases, I_2 remains the same
C. I_1 remains the same, I_2 increases
D. I_1 remains the same, I_2 decreases
E. I_1 increases, I_2 increases

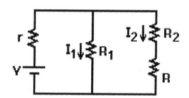

20. What physical quantity does the slope of the graph represent?

A. 1 / Current
B. Voltage
C. Current
D. Resistivity
E. 1 / Voltage

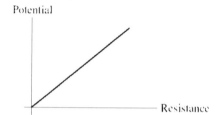

21. An alternating current is supplied to an electronic component with a rating that it be used only for voltages below 12 V. What is the highest V_{rms} that can be supplied to this component while staying below the voltage limit?

A. 6 V　　　B. 12 V　　　C. $3\sqrt{2}$ V　　　D. $12\sqrt{2}$ V　　　E. $6\sqrt{2}$ V

22. A generator produces alternating current electricity with a frequency of 40 cycles per second. What is the maximum potential difference created by the generator, if the rms voltage is 150 V?

A. 54 V　　　B. 91 V　　　C. 212 V　　　D. 141 V　　E. 223 V

23. Kirchhoff's junction rule is a statement of:

A. Law of conservation of energy　　　C. Law of conservation of momentum
B. Law of conservation of angular momentum　　D. Law of conservation of charge
　　　　　　　　　　　　　　　　　　　　　　E. Newton's Second Law

24. Four identical capacitors are connected in parallel to a battery. If a total charge of Q flows from the battery, how much charge does each capacitor carry?

A. $Q/4$　　　B. Q　　　C. $4Q$　　　D. $16Q$　　　E. $Q/16$

25. Which statement is correct for two conductors that are joined by a long copper wire?

    A. The electric field at the surface of each conductor is the same

    B. Each conductor must be at the same potential

    C. Each conductor must have the same resistivity

    D. A free charge must be present on either conductor

    E. The potential of the wire is the average of the potential of each conductor

26. Electromagnetic induction occurs in a coil when there is a change in the:

    A. coil's charge   **C.** magnetic field intensity in the coil

    B. current in the coil   **D.** electric field intensity in the coil

                                         E. electromagnetic polarity

27. When unequal resistors are connected in series across an ideal battery, the:

    A. current flowing in each is the same

    B. equivalent resistance of the circuit is less than that of the greatest resistor

    C. power dissipated in each turn is the same

    D. potential difference across each is the same

    E. current is still unequal in the two resistors

28. Electric current flows only from a point of:

    A. equal potential

    B. high pressure to a point of lower pressure

    C. low pressure to a point of higher pressure

    D. high potential to a point of lower potential

    E. low potential to a point of higher potential

29. Consider the group of charges in this figure. All three charges have $Q = 3.8$ nC. What is their electric potential energy? (Use Coulomb's constant $k = 9 \times 10^9$ N·m^2/C^2)

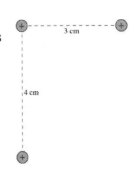

    A. 1.9×10^{-6} J   **C.** 8.8×10^{-6} J

    B. 7.4×10^{-5} J   **D.** 9.7×10^{-6} J

                                     E. 1×10^{-5} J

30. A positively-charged and negatively-charged particle are traveling on the same path perpendicular to a constant magnetic field. How do the forces experienced by the two particles differ, if the magnitudes of the charges are equal?

    A. Differ in direction, but not in magnitude

    B. Differ in magnitude, but not in direction

    C. No difference in magnitude or direction

    D. Differ in both magnitude and direction

    E. Cannot be predicted

31. Potential energy of an electron moving in a direction opposite to the electric field:

    A. decreases and the electron's electric potential decreases

    B. increases while the electron's electric potential remains constant

    C. decreases while the electron's electric potential increases

    D. remains constant while the electron's electric potential increases

    E. remains constant and the electron's electric potential remain constant

32. What is the name of a device that transforms electrical energy into mechanical energy?

    A. Magnet   **C.** Turbine

    B. Transformer   **D.** Generator   **E.** Motor

33. A hydrogen atom consists of a proton and an electron. If the orbital radius of the electron increases, the absolute magnitude of the potential energy of the electron:

    A. remains the same   **C.** increases

    B. decreases   **D.** depends on the potential of the electron

                          E. is independent of the orbital radius

34. Copper wire A has a length L and a radius r. Copper wire B has a length $2L$ and a radius $2r$. Which of the following is true regarding the resistances across the ends of the wires?

    A. The resistance of wire A is one-half that of wire B

    B. The resistance of wire A is four times higher than that of wire B

    C. The resistance of wire A is twice as high as that of wire B

    D. The resistance of wire A is equal to that of wire B

    E. The resistance of wire A is one-fourth that of wire B

35. When a negative charge is free, it tries to move:

    A. toward infinity   **C.** from high potential to low potential

    B. away from infinity   **D.** from low potential to high potential

                           E. in the direction of the electric field

36. Four 6 V batteries (in a linear sequence of A → B → C → D) are connected in series in order to power lights A and B. The resistance of light A is 50 Ω and the resistance of light B is 25 Ω. What is the potential difference at a point between battery C and battery D?

A. 4 volts   **B.** 12 volts   **C.** 18 volts   **D.** 26 volts   **E.** 30 volts

37. By what factor does the dielectric constant change when a material is introduced between the plates of a parallel-plate capacitor, if the capacitance increases by a factor of 4?

A. ½   **B.** 4   **C.** 0.4   **D.** ¼   **E.** 2

38. Two isolated copper plates, each of area 0.4 m², carry opposite charges of magnitude 6.8×10^{-10} C. They are placed opposite each other in parallel alignment. What is the potential difference between the plates when their spacing is 4 cm? (Use the dielectric constant $k = 1$ in air and electric permittivity $\varepsilon_0 = 8.854 \times 10^{-12}$ F/m)

A. 1.4 V   **B.** 4.1 V   **C.** 5.8 V   **D.** 3.2 V   **E.** 7.7 V

39. The force on an electron moving in a magnetic field is largest when its direction is:

A. perpendicular to the magnetic field direction
B. at any angle greater than 90° to the magnetic field direction
C. at any angle less than 90° to the magnetic field direction
D. exactly opposite to the magnetic field direction
E. parallel to the magnetic field direction

40. What is the quantity that is calculated in units of A·s?

A. Passivity   **B.** Capacitance   **C.** Potential   **D.** Current   **E.** Charge

41. A proton with a speed of 1.7×10^5 m/s falls through a potential difference V and thereby increases its speed to 3.2×10^5 m/s. Through what potential difference did the proton fall? (Use the mass of a proton = 1.67×10^{-27} kg and the charge of a proton = 1.6×10^{-19} C)

A. 880 V   **B.** 1,020 V   **C.** 384 V   **D.** 430 V   **E.** 130 V

42. Three capacitors are connected to a battery as shown. The capacitances are: $C_1 = 2C_2$ and $C_1 = 3C_3$. Which of the three capacitors stores the smallest amount of charge?

A. C_1
B. C_1 or C_3
C. C_2
D. C_3
E. The amount of charge is the same in all three capacitors

43. Two isolated copper plates, each of area 0.6 m², carry opposite charges of magnitude 7.08 × 10⁻¹⁰ C. They are placed opposite each other in parallel alignment, with a spacing of 2 mm. What will be the potential difference between the plates when their spacing is increased to 6 cm? (Use the dielectric constant k = 1 in air and electric permittivity ε_0 = 8.854 × 10⁻¹² F/m)

   A. 8 V   **B.** 3.1 V   **C.** 4.3 V   **D.** 7.2 V   **E.** 0.9 V

44. Electric current can only flow:

   A. in a region of negligible resistance   **C.** in a perfect conductor
   B. through a potential difference   **D.** in the absence of resistance
                                       E. in a semi-perfect conductor

45. The metal detectors used to screen passengers at airports operate via:

   A. Newton's Laws   **C.** Faraday's Law
   B. Bragg's Law   **D.** Ohm's Law   **E.** Ampere's Law

46. A 7 µC negative charge is attracted to a large, well-anchored, positive charge. How much kinetic energy does the negatively-charged object gain if the potential difference through which it moves is 3.5 mV?

   A. 0.86 J   **B.** 6.7 µJ   **C.** 36.7 µJ   **D.** 0.5 kJ   **E.** 24.5 nJ

47. A wire of resistivity ρ is replaced in a circuit by a wire of the same material but four times as long. If the total resistance remains the same, the diameter of the new wire must be:

   A. one-fourth the original diameter   **C.** the same as the original diameter
   B. two times the original diameter   **D.** one-half the original diameter
                                       E. four times the original diameter

48. The addition of resistors in series to a resistor in an existing circuit, while voltage remains constant, would result in [   ] in the original resistor.

   A. an increase in current   **C.** an increase in resistance
   B. a decrease in resistance   **D.** a decrease in current   **E.** no change

49. In an experiment, a battery is connected to a variable resistor R, where resistance can be adjusted by turning a knob. The potential difference across the resistor and the current through it are recorded for different settings of the resistor knob. The battery is an ideal potential source in series with an internal resistor. The emf of the potential source is 9 V and the internal resistance is 0.1 Ω. What is the current if the variable resistor is set at 0.5 Ω?

   A. 15 A   **B.** 0.9 A   **C.** 4.5 A   **D.** 45 A   **E.** 9 A

50. Two parallel plates that are initially uncharged are separated by 1.6 mm. What charge must be transferred from one plate to the other if 10 kJ of energy is to be stored in the plates? The area of each plate is 24 mm^2. (Use dielectric constant $k = 1$ in air and electric permittivity $\mathcal{E}_0 = 8.854 \times 10^{-12}$ F/m)

    A. 78 μC   **B.** 15 mC   **C.** 52 μC   **D.** 29 μC   **E.** 66 mC

51. When a proton is moving in the direction of the electric field, its potential energy U [   ] and its electric potential V [   ]. (Use dielectric constant $k = 1$ in air and electric permittivity $\mathcal{E}_0 = 8.854 \times 10^{-12}$ F/m)

    A. increases ... increases   **C.** increases ... decreases

    B. decreases ... decreases   **D.** decreases ... remains the same

                                      E. remains the same ... decreases

52. Each plate of a parallel-plate air capacitor has an area of 0.004 m^2, and the separation of the plates is 0.02 mm. An electric field of 8.6×10^6 V/m is present between the plates. What is the energy density between the plates? (Use the electric permittivity $\mathcal{E}_0 = 8.854 \times 10^{-12}$ F/m)

    A. 100 J/m^3 **B.** 400 J/m^3 **C.** 220 J/m^3 **D.** 330 J/m^3 **E.** 510 J/m^3

53. What is the quantity that is calculated with units of kg·m^2/s·C^2?

    A. Resistance   **C.** Potential

    B. Capacitance   **D.** Resistivity   **E.** Current

54. At a constant voltage, an increase in the resistance of a circuit results in:

    A. no change in I or V   **C.** an increase in power

    B. an increase in I **D.** constant power   **E.** a decrease in I

55. A charge $+Q$ is located at one of the corners of a square. The absolute potential at the center of a square is 3 V. If a second charge $-Q$ is placed at one of the other three corners, what is the absolute potential at the square's center?

    A. –6 V   **B.** 12 V   **C.** 6 V   **D.** 0 V   **E.** –12 V

56. A uniform electric field has a strength of 6 N/C. What is the electric energy density of the field? (Use electric permittivity $\mathcal{E}_0 = 8.854 \times 10^{-12}$ F/m)

    A. 1.5×10^{12} J/m^3 **C.** 2.3×10^{12} J/m^3

    B. 1.6×10^{-10} J/m^3 **D.** 2.7×10^{-11} J/m^3 **E.** 1.5×10^{-10} J/m^3

57. Which change to a circuit will always result in an increase in the current?

    A. Increased voltage and decreased resistance

    B. Decreased voltage and increased resistance

    C. Increased voltage and increased resistance

    D. Only a decrease in resistance, the voltage has no effect on current

    E. Only an increase in voltage, the resistance has no effect on current

58. Three capacitors are arranged as shown. C_1 has a capacitance of 9 pF, C_2 has a capacitance of 18 pF, and C_3 has a capacitance of 24 pF. What is the voltage drop across the entire system if the voltage drop across C_2 is 240 V?

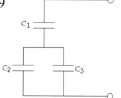

    A. 430 V   **C.** 1,200 V

    B. 870 V   **D.** 1,350 V   **E.** 1,750 V

59. Doubling the capacitance of a capacitor that is holding a constant charge causes the energy stored in that capacitor to:

    A. decrease to one-half   **C.** quadruple

    B. decrease to one-fourth   **D.** double   **E.** remain the same

60. When three resistors are added in series to a resistor in a circuit, the original resistor's voltage [   ] and its current [   ].

    A. decreases ... increases   **C.** decrease ... decreases

    B. increases ... increases   **D.** decreases ... remains the same

                                    E. remains the same ... decreases

Circuit Elements & DC Circuits – Answer Key

1: B	11: A	21: E	31: C	41: C	51: B
2: D	12: E	22: C	32: E	42: E	52: D
3: C	13: D	23: D	33: B	43: A	53: A
4: D	14: B	24: A	34: C	44: B	54: E
5: E	15: C	25: B	35: D	45: C	55: D
6: A	16: A	26: C	36: C	46: E	56: B
7: C	17: B	27: A	37: B	47: B	57: A
8: D	18: D	28: D	38: E	48: D	58: D
9: B	19: A	29: E	39: A	49: A	59: A
10: E	20: C	30: A	40: E	50: C	60: C

Light and Optics

1. What is the minimum thickness of a soap film that reflects a given wavelength of light?

   A. ¼ the wavelength

   B. ½ the wavelength

   C. One wavelength

   D. Two wavelengths

   E. There is no minimum thickness

2. As the angle of an incident ray of light increases, the angle of the reflected ray:

   A. increases

   B. decreases

   C. stays the same

   D. increases or decreases

   E. requires more information

3. At what distance from a concave spherical mirror (with a focal length of 100 cm) must a woman stand in order to see an upright image of herself that is twice her actual height?

   A. 100 cm   **B.** 50 cm   **C.** 300 cm   **D.** 25 cm   **E.** 150 cm

4. If a person's eyeball is too long from front to back, what is the name of the condition that the person likely suffers?

   A. Hyperopia

   B. Astigmatism

   C. Presbyopia

   D. Myopia

   E. Diplopia

5. According to the relationship between frequency and energy of light ($E = hf$), which color of light has more energy?

   A. Red   **B.** Yellow   **C.** Green   **D.** Orange   **E.** Blue

6. A candle 18 cm tall sits 4 m away from a diverging lens with a focal length of 3 m. What is the size of the image?

   A. 6.3 cm   **B.** 7.7 cm   **C.** 2.9 cm   **D.** 13.5 cm   **E.** 18 cm

---

Questions **7-8** are based on the following:

A tank holds a layer of oil 1.58 m thick that floats on a layer of syrup that is 0.66 m thick. Both liquids are clear and do not intermix. A ray, which originates at the bottom of the tank on a vertical axis (see figure), crosses the oil-syrup interface at a point 0.9 m to the right of the vertical axis. The ray continues and arrives at the oil-air interface, 2 m from the axis and at the critical angle. (Use the refractive index $n = 1$ for air)

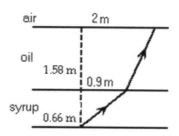

7. The index of refraction of the oil is closest to:

A. 1.39   B. 1.56   C. 1.75   D. 1.82   E. 1.94

8. What is the index of refraction of the syrup?

A. 1.53   B. 1.46   C. 1.17   D. 1.24   E. 1.33

9. Which of the following cannot be explained with the wave theory of light?

A. Photoelectric effect   C. Polarization
B. Interference   D. Diffusion   E. All of the above

10. The use of wave fronts and rays to describe optical phenomena is known as:

A. dispersive optics   C. wave optics
B. reflector optics   D. geometrical optics   E. array optics

11. In the investigation of a new type of optical fiber (index of refraction $n = 1.26$), a laser beam is incident on the flat end of a straight fiber in air, as shown in the figure below. What is the maximum angle of incidence (θ_1) if the beam is not to escape from the fiber?

A. 36°   C. 58°
B. 43°   D. 50°   E. 28°

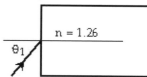

12. An object is placed at a distance of 0.5 m from a converging lens with a power of 10 diopters. At what distance from the lens does the image appear?

A. 0.13 m   B. 0.47 m   C. 0.7 m   D. 1.5 m   E. 1.8 m

13. A virtual image is:

    I. produced by light rays
    II. the brain's interpretations of light rays
    III. found only on a concave mirror

A. I only   B. II only   C. III only   D. I and II only   E. I and III only

14. If Karen stands in front of a convex mirror, at the same distance from it as its radius of curvature:

    A. Karen does not see her image because it's focused at a different distance

    B. Karen sees her image and she appears the same size

    C. Karen does not see her image and she is not within its range

    D. Karen sees her image and she appears larger

    E. Karen sees her image and she appears smaller

15. An object is viewed at various distances using a mirror with a focal length of 10 m. If the object is 20 m away from the mirror, what best characterizes the image?

    A. Inverted and real

    B. Inverted and virtual

    C. Upright and real

    D. Upright and virtual

    E. Real, but it cannot be determined if it is inverted or upright

16. If an object is placed at a position beyond $2f$ of the focal point of a converging lens, the image is:

    A. real, upright and enlarged

    B. virtual, inverted and enlarged

    C. virtual, upright and reduced

    D. real, inverted and enlarged

    E. real, inverted and reduced

17. Which form of electromagnetic radiation has photons with the lowest energy?

    A. X-rays

    B. Ultraviolet radiation

    C. Radio waves

    D. Microwaves

    E. Infrared radiation

18. If the index of refraction of diamond is 2.43, a given wavelength of light travels:

    A. 2.43 times faster in diamond than it does in air

    B. 2.43 times faster in a vacuum than it does in diamond

    C. 2.43 times faster in diamond than it does in a vacuum

    D. 2.43 times faster in air than it does in diamond

    E. 2.43 times faster in air than it does in a vacuum

19. An object is placed 15 cm to the left of a double-convex lens of focal length 20 cm. Where is the image of this object located?

    A. 15 cm to the left of the lens

    B. 30 cm to the left of the lens

    C. 60 cm to the right of the lens

    D. 60 cm to the left of the lens

    E. 30 cm to the right of the lens

20. A sheet of red paper appears black when it is illuminated with:

A. orange light
B. cyan light

C. red light
D. yellow light

E. violet light

21. Where is an object if the image produced by a lens appears very close to its focal point?

A. near the center of curvature of the lens
B. far from the lens

C. near the lens
D. near the focal point
E. requires more information

22. A light with the frequency 4.9×10^{14} Hz is produced by a source located 6 m from a converging lens with a focal length of 3 m. For a different frequency of light, the focal length of the lens is different than 3 m. This phenomenon is called:

A. Diffusion
B. Incidence

C. Interference
D. Refraction

E. Dispersion

23. If an image appears at the same distance from a mirror as the object, the size of the image is:

A. exactly quadruple the size of the object
B. exactly ¼ the size of the object

C. the same size as the object
D. exactly twice the size of the object
E. exactly ½ the size of the object

24. When viewed straight down (90° to the surface), an incident light ray moving from water to air is refracted:

A. 37° away from the normal
B. 37° toward the normal

C. 28° toward the normal
D. 28° away from the normal

E. 0°

25. Suppose that a beachgoer uses two lenses from a pair of disassembled polarized sunglasses and places one on top of the other. What would he observe if he rotates one lens 90° with respect to the normal position of the other lens and looks directly at the sun overhead?

A. Light with an intensity reduced to about 50% of what it would be with one lens
B. Light with an intensity that is the same of what it would be with one lens
C. Complete darkness, since no light would be transmitted
D. Light with an intensity reduced to about 25% of what it would be with one lens
E. Light with an intensity increased to about 150% of what it would be with one lens

26. A glass plate with an index of refraction of 1.45 is immersed in a liquid. The liquid is an oil with an index of refraction of 1.35. The surface of the glass is inclined at an angle of 54° with the vertical. A horizontal ray in the glass is incident on the interface of glass and liquid. The incident horizontal ray refracts at the interface. The angle that the refracted ray in the oil makes with the horizontal is closest to:

A. 8.3°   **B.** 14°   **C.** 6°   **D.** 12°   **E.** 17°

27. Two plane mirrors make an angle of 30°. A light ray enters the system and is reflected once off each mirror. Through what angle is the ray turned?

A. 60°   **B.** 90°   **C.** 120°   **D.** 160°   **E.** 180°

28. Which of the statements about light is FALSE?

A. A packet of light energy is known as a photon
B. Color can be used to determine the approximate energy of visible light
C. Light travels through space at a speed of 3.0×10^8 m/s
D. Ultraviolet light cannot be seen with the unaided eye
E. All statements are true

29. The angle of incidence:

A. may be greater than, less than, or equal to the angle of refraction
B. is always less than the angle of refraction
C. must equal the angle of refraction
D. is always greater than the angle of refraction
E. is independent of the angle of refraction

30. As a person walks away from a plane mirror on a wall, her image:

A. is always a real image, no matter how far she is from the mirror
B. changes from being upright to being inverted as she passes the focal point
C. gets smaller
D. may or may not get smaller, depending on where she is positioned
E. is always the same size

31. If a spherical concave mirror has a radius of curvature R, its focal length is:

A. $2R$ **B.** R **C.** $R/2$ **D.** $R/4$ **E.** $4R$

32. Let n_1 be the index of refraction of the incident medium, and let n_2 be the index of refraction of the refracting medium. Which of the following must be true if the angle that the refracted ray makes with the boundary (not with the normal) is less than the angle that the incident ray makes with the boundary?

A. $n_1 < n_2$ **B.** $n_1 > n_2$ **C.** $n_1 < 1$ **D.** $n_2 < 1$ **E.** $n_1 = n_2$

33. If a person's eyeball is too short from front to back, the person is likely to suffer from:

A. nearsightedness   **C.** presbyopia

B. farsightedness   **D.** astigmatism   **E.** diplopia

34. The shimmering that is observed over a hot surface is:

A. changing refraction from the mixing of warm and cool air
B. a mirage
C. heat rays
D. reflections from evaporating water vapor
E. reflections from condensing water vapor

35. When two parallel white rays pass through the outer edges of a converging glass lens, chromatic aberrations cause colors to appear on the screen in what order, from the top down?

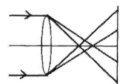

A. blue, blue, red, red   **C.** blue, red, blue, red

B. red, blue, blue, red   **D.** red, red, blue, blue   **E.** blue, red, red, blue

36. Two thin converging lenses are near each other, so that the lens on the left has a focal length of 2 m and the one on the right has a focal length of 4 m. What is the focal length of the combination?

A. 1/4 m   **B.** 4/3 m   **C.** 3/4 m   **D.** 4 m   **E.** 8 m

37. A cylindrical tank is 50 ft deep, 37.5 ft in diameter, and filled to the top with water. A flashlight shines into the tank from above. What is the minimum angle θ that its beam can make with the water surface if the beam is to illuminate part of the bottom? (Use the index of refraction $n = 1.33$ for water)

A. 25°   **B.** 31°   **C.** 37°   **D.** 53°   **E.** 18°

38. Which color of the visible spectrum has the shortest wavelength (400 nm)?

A. Violet   **B.** Green   **C.** Orange   **D.** Blue   **E.** Yellow

39. An object is placed at a distance *d* in front of a plane mirror. The size of the image is:

 A. dependent on where the observer is positioned when looking at the image
 B. twice the size of the object
 C. half the size of the object
 D. dependent on the distance *d*
 E. the same as the object, independent of the position of the observer or distance *d*

40. If a single lens forms a virtual image of an object, then the:

 A. image must be inverted
 B. lens could be either a diverging or a converging lens
 C. lens must be a converging lens
 D. lens must be a diverging lens
 E. image must be upright

41. When neon light passes through a prism, what is observed?

 A. White light   **C.** The same neon light
 B. Bright spots or lines **D.** Continuous spectrum   **E.** Both A and B

42. The law of reflection holds for:

   I. plane mirrors II. curved mirrors III. spherical mirrors

 A. I only **B.** II only **C.** III only **D.** I and III only **E.** I, II and III

43. The image formed by a single concave lens:

 A. can be real or virtual, but is always real when the object is placed at the focal point
 B. can be real or virtual, depending on the object's distance compared to the focal length
 C. is always virtual
 D. is always real
 E. is always inverted

44. A lens forms a virtual image of an object. Which of the following must be true of the image?

 A. It is inverted   **C.** It is larger than the object and upright
 B. It is upright   **D.** It is smaller than the object and inverted
           E. It is the same size as the object and upright

45. Light with the lowest frequency (longest wavelength) detected by your eyes is perceived as:

 A. violet **B.** green **C.** yellow   **D.** orange   **E.** red

46. A 0.1 m tall candle is observed through a converging lens that is 3 m away and has a focal length of 6 m. The resulting image is:

    A. 3 m from the lens on the opposite side of the object

    B. 6 m from the lens on the opposite side of the object

    C. 3 m from the lens on the same side as the object

    D. 6 m from the lens on the same side as the object

    E. 0.5 m from the lens on the opposite side of the object

47. Which statement about thin lenses is correct when considering only a single lens?

    A. A diverging lens always produces a virtual erect image

    B. A diverging lens always produces a real erect image

    C. A diverging lens always produces a virtual inverted image

    D. A diverging lens always produces a real inverted image

    E. A converging lens always produces a real inverted image

48. A double-concave lens has equal radii of curvature of 15 cm. An object placed 14 cm from the lens forms a virtual image 5 cm from the lens. What is the index of refraction of the lens material?

    A. 0.8   **B.** 1.4   **C.** 2   **D.** 2.6   **E.** 2.8

49. The magnification m for an object reflected from a mirror is the ratio of what characteristic of the image to the object?

    A. Center of curvature   **C.** Orientation

    B. Focal distances   **D.** Angular size   **E.** Distance

50. Suppose Mike places his face in front of a concave mirror. Which of the following statements is correct?

    A. Mike's image is diminished in size

    B. Mike's image is always inverted

    C. No matter where Mike places himself, a virtual image is formed

    D. If Mike positions himself between the center of curvature and the focal point of the mirror, he will not be able to see his image

    E. Mike's image is enlarged in size

51. Single-concave spherical mirrors produce images that:

A. are always smaller than the actual object

B. are always the same size as the actual object

C. are always larger than the actual object

D. could be smaller than, larger than, or the same size as the actual object, depending on the placement of the object

E. are always upright

52. When two converging lenses of equal focal lengths are used together, the effective combined focal length is less than the focal length of either one of the individual lens. The combined power of the two lenses used together is:

A. greater than the power of either individual lens

B. the same as the power of either individual lens

C. less than the power of either individual lens

D. greater than the sum of the powers of both individual lens

E. exactly the sum of the powers of both individual lens

53. The index of refraction is based on the ratio of the speed of light in:

A. water to the speed of light in the transparent material

B. a vacuum to the speed of light in the transparent material

C. two different transparent materials

D. air to the speed of light in the transparent material

E. a solid to the speed of light in the transparent material

54. An object is located 2.2 m in front of a plane mirror. The image formed by the mirror appears:

A. 4.4 m behind the mirror's surface   **C.** 4.4 m in front of the mirror's surface

B. 2.2 m in front of the mirror's surface   **D.** on the mirror's surface

                                                 E. 2.2 m behind the mirror's surface

55. An upright object is 40 cm from a concave mirror with a radius of 50 cm. The image is:

A. virtual and inverted   **C.** real and inverted

B. virtual and upright   **D.** real and upright   **E.** real or virtual

56. In the figure a ray in glass arrives at the glass-water interface at an angle of 48° with the normal. The refracted ray makes an angle of 68° with the normal. If another ray in the glass makes an angle of 29° with the normal, what is the angle of refraction in the water? (Use the index of refraction of water $n = 1.33$)

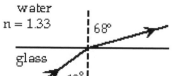

A. 29°   C. 31°

B. 37°   D. 46°

E. 41°

57. In a compound microscope:

A. the magnification is $m_1 + M_2$, where m_1 is the lateral magnification of the objective and M_2 is the angular magnification of the eyepiece

B. magnification is provided by the objective and not by the eyepiece. The eyepiece merely increases the brightness of the image viewed

C. magnification is provided by the objective and not by the eyepiece. The eyepiece merely increases the resolution of the image viewed

D. both the objective and the eyepiece form real images

E. the image of the objective serves as the object for the eyepiece

58. Except for air, the refractive index of all transparent materials is:

A. equal to 1   C. less than 1

B. less than or equal to 1   D. greater than 1   E. greater than or equal to 1

59. The radius of curvature of the curved side of a convex lens made of glass is 33 cm. What is the focal length of the lens? (Use index of refraction for glass $n = 1.64$)

A. –28 cm   B. 28 cm   C. 38 cm   D. 52 cm   E. 16 cm

60. The part of the electromagnetic spectrum most absorbed by water is:

A. lower frequencies in the visible   C. infrared

B. higher frequencies in the visible   D. ultraviolet

E. none of the above

Light & Optics – Answer Key

1: A	11: D	21: B	31: C	41: B	51: D
2: A	12: A	22: E	32: B	42: E	52: A
3: B	13: D	23: C	33: B	43: C	53: B
4: D	14: E	24: E	34: A	44: B	54: E
5: E	15: A	25: C	35: E	45: E	55: C
6: B	16: E	26: C	36: B	46: D	56: B
7: C	17: C	27: A	37: C	47: A	57: E
8: D	18: B	28: E	38: A	48: C	58: D
9: A	19: D	29: A	39: E	49: E	59: D
10: D	20: B	30: E	40: B	50: D	60: C

Heat and Thermodynamics

1. Compared to the initial value, what is the resulting pressure for an ideal gas that is compressed isothermally to one-third of its initial volume?

   A. Equal   **C.** Larger, but less than three times larger
   B. Three times larger   **D.** More than three times larger
                           E. Requires more information

2. A uniform hole in a brass plate has a diameter of 1.2 cm at 25 °C. What is the diameter of the hole when the plate is heated to 225 °C? (Use the coefficient of linear thermal expansion for brass = 19×10^{-6} K^{-1})

   A. 2.2 cm   **B.** 2.8 cm   **C.** 1.2 cm   **D.** 1.6 cm   **E.** 0.8 cm

3. A student heats 90 g of water using 50 W of power, with 100% efficiency. How long does it take to raise the temperature of the water from 10 °C to 30 °C? (Use specific heat of water $c = 4.186$ J/g·°C)

   A. 232 s   **B.** 81 s   **C.** 59 s   **D.** 151 s   **E.** 102 s

4. A runner generates 1,260 W of thermal energy. If her heat is to be dissipated only by evaporation, how much water does she shed in 15 minutes of running? (Use the latent heat of vaporization of water $L_v = 22.6 \times 10^5$ J/kg)

   A. 500 g   **B.** 35 g   **C.** 350 g   **D.** 50 g   **E.** 40 g

5. Phase changes occur as temperature:

     I. decreases   II. increases   III. remains the same

   A. I only   **B.** II only   **C.** III only   **D.** I and II only   **E.** I and III only

6. How much heat is needed to melt a 55 kg sample of ice that is at 0 °C? (Use latent heat of fusion for water $L_f = 334$ kJ/kg and latent heat of vaporization $L_v = 2{,}257$ kJ/kg)

   A. 0 kJ   **C.** 3×10^5 kJ
   B. 2.6×10^5 kJ   **D.** 4.6×10^6 kJ   **E.** 1.8×10^4 kJ

7. Metals are both good heat conductors and good electrical conductors because of the:

A. relatively high densities of metals

B. high elasticity of metals

C. similarity between thermal and electrical conductive properties

D. looseness of outer electrons in metal atoms

E. ability of metals to transfer energy easily

8. Solar houses are designed to retain the heat absorbed during the day so that the stored heat can be released during the night. A botanist produces steam at 100 °C during the day, and then allows the steam to cool to 0 °C and freeze during the night. How many kilograms of water are needed to store 200 kJ of energy for this process? (Use latent heat of vaporization of water $L_v = 22.6 \times 10^5$ J/kg, latent heat of fusion of water $L_f = 33.5 \times 10^4$ J/kg, and specific heat capacity of water $c = 4{,}186$ J/kg·K)

A. 0.066 kg   B. 0.103 kg   C. 0.482 kg   D. 1.18 kg   E. 3.66 kg

9. The heat required to change a substance from the solid to the liquid state is referred to as the heat of:

A. condensation   C. fusion

B. freezing   D. vaporization   E. sublimation

10. A rigid container holds 0.20 g of hydrogen gas. How much heat is needed to change the temperature of the gas from 250 K to 280 K? (Use specific heat of hydrogen gas = 14.3 J/g·K)

A. 46 J   B. 72 J   C. 56 J   D. 35 J   E. 86 J

11. An aluminum electric tea kettle with a mass of 500 g is heated with a 500 W heating coil. How many minutes are required to heat 1 kg of water from 18 °C to 98 °C in the tea kettle? (Use specific heat of aluminum = 900 J/kg·K and specific heat of water = 4,186 J/kg·K)

A. 16 min   B. 12 min   C. 8 min   D. 4 min   E. 10 min

12. Heat is added at a constant rate to a pure substance in a closed container. The temperature of the substance as a function of time is shown in the graph. If L_f = latent heat of fusion and L_v = latent heat of vaporization, what is the value of the ratio L_v / L_f for this substance?

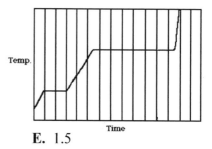

A. 3.5   B. 7.2   C. 4.5   D. 5.0   E. 1.5

13. The moderate temperatures of islands throughout the world have much to do with water's:

A. high evaporation rate

B. high specific heat capacity

C. vast supply of thermal energy

D. poor conductivity

E. absorption of solar energy

14. A 4.5 g lead BB moving at 46 m/s penetrates a wood block and comes to rest inside the block. If half of the kinetic energy is absorbed by the BB, what is the change in the temperature of the BB? (Use specific heat of lead = 128 J/kg·K)

A. 2.8 K   **B.** 3.6 K   **C.** 1.6 K   **D.** 0.8 K   **E.** 4.1 K

15. The heat required to change a substance from the liquid to the vapor state is referred to as the heat of:

A. melting

B. condensation

C. vaporization

D. fusion

E. sublimation

16. A Carnot engine operating between a reservoir of liquid mercury at its melting point and a colder reservoir extracts 18 J of heat from the mercury and does 5 J of work during each cycle. What is the temperature of the colder reservoir? (Use melting temperature of mercury = 233 K)

A. 168 K   **B.** 66 K   **C.** 57 K   **D.** 82 K   **E.** 94 K

17. A 920 g empty iron pan is put on a stove. How much heat in joules must the iron pan absorb to raise its temperature from 18 °C to 96 °C? (Use specific heat for iron = 113 cal/kg·°C and 1 cal = 4.186 J)

A. 50,180 J   **B.** 81,010 J   **C.** 63,420 J   **D.** 33,940 J   **E.** 26,500 J

18. When a solid melts, what change occurs in the substance?

A. Heat energy dissipates

B. Heat energy enters

C. Temperature increases

D. Temperature decreases

E. Kinetic energy increases

19. Which of the following is an accurate statement about the work done for a cyclic process carried out in a gas? (Use P for pressure and V for volume on the graph)

A. It is equal to the area under *ab* minus the area under *dc*

B. It is equal to the area under the curve *adc*

C. It is equal to the area under the curve *abc*

D. It equals zero

E. It is equal to the area enclosed by the cyclic process

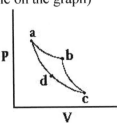

20. Substance A has a higher specific heat than substance B. With all other factors equal, which substance requires more energy to be heated to the same temperature?

A. Substance A
B. Substance B
C. Both require the same amount of heat
D. Depends on the density of each substance
E. Depends on the volume of each substance

21. A 6.5 g meteor hits the Earth at a speed of 300 m/s. If the meteor's kinetic energy is entirely converted to heat, by how much does its temperature rise? (Use specific heat of the meteor = 120 cal/kg·°C and conversion of 1 cal = 4.186 J)

A. 134 °C   B. 68 °C   C. 120 °C   D. 90 °C   E. 44 °C

22. When a liquid freezes, what change occurs in the substance?

A. Heat energy dissipates   C. Temperature increases
B. Heat energy enters   D. Temperature decreases
                                     E. Kinetic energy increases

23. A monatomic ideal gas (C_v = 3/2 R) undergoes an isothermal expansion at 300 K, as the volume increases from 0.05 m^3 to 0.2 m^3. The final pressure is 130 kPa. What is the heat transfer of the gas? (Use ideal gas constant R = 8.314 J/mol·K)

A. −14 kJ   B. 36 kJ   C. 14 kJ   D. −21 kJ   E. 0 kJ

24. What is the maximum temperature rise expected for a waterfall with a vertical drop of 30 m? (Use acceleration due to gravity g = 9.8 m/s^2 and specific heat of water = 4,186 J/kg·K)

A. 0.1 °C   B. 0.06 °C   C. 0.15 °C   D. 0.07 °C   E. 0.03 °C

25. When 0.75 kg of water at 0 °C freezes, what is the change in entropy of the water? (Use latent heat of fusion of water L_f = 33,400 J/kg)

A. −92 J/K   B. −18 J/K   C. 44 J/K   D. 80 J/K   E. −60 J/K

26. When a bimetallic bar made of a copper and iron strip is heated, the copper part of the bar bends toward the iron strip. The reason for this is:

A. copper expands more than iron   C. iron gets hotter before copper
B. iron expands more than copper   D. copper gets hotter before iron
                                         E. both copper and iron expand at the same rate

27. In a flask, 110 g of water is heated using 60 W of power, with perfect efficiency. How long does it take to raise the temperature of the water from 20 °C to 30 °C? (Use specific heat of water c = 4,186 J/kg·K)

A. 132 s   **B.** 57 s   **C.** 9.6 s   **D.** 77 s   **E.** 41 s

28. When a liquid evaporates, what change occurs in the substance?

    A. Heat energy dissipates   **C.** Temperature increases
    B. Heat energy enters   **D.** Temperature decreases
          E. Kinetic energy increases

29. A flask of liquid nitrogen is at a temperature of –243 °C. If the nitrogen is heated until the average energy of the particles is doubled, what is the new temperature?

    A. 356 °C   **B.** –356 °C   **C.** –134 °C   **D.** 134 °C   **E.** –213 °C

30. If a researcher is attempting to determine how much the temperature of a particular piece of material would rise when a known amount of heat is added to it, knowing which of the following quantities would be most helpful?

    A. density   **C.** initial temperature
    B. coefficient of linear expansion   **D.** specific heat   **E.** thermal conductivity

31. A substance has a density of 1,800 kg/m^3 in the liquid state. At atmospheric pressure, the substance has a boiling point of 170 °C. The vapor has a density of 6 kg/m^3 at the boiling point at atmospheric pressure. What is the change in the internal energy of 1 kg of the substance, as it vaporizes at atmospheric pressure? (Use heat of vaporization L_v= 1.7 × 10^5 J/kg)

    A. 180 kJ   **B.** 170 kJ   **C.** 6 kJ   **D.** 12 kJ   **E.** 200 kJ

32. If an aluminum rod that is at 5 °C is heated until it has twice the thermal energy, its temperature is:

    A. 10 °C   **B.** 56 °C   **C.** 278 °C   **D.** 283 °C   **E.** 556 °C

33. A thermally isolated system is made up of a hot piece of aluminum and a cold piece of copper, with the aluminum and the copper in thermal contact. The specific heat capacity of aluminum is more than double that of copper. Which object experiences the greater temperature change during the time the system takes to reach thermal equilibrium?

    A. Both experience the same magnitude of temperature change
    B. The volume of each is required   **D.** The aluminum
    C. The copper   **E.** The mass of each is required

34. In liquid water of a given temperature, the water molecules are moving randomly with different speeds. Electrostatic forces of cohesion tend to hold them together. However, occasionally one molecule gains enough energy through multiple collisions to pull away from the others and escape from the liquid. Which of the following is an illustration of this phenomenon?

    A. When a large steel suspension bridge is built, gaps are left between the girders
    B. When Kevin steps out of a swimming pool and stands in the wind, he feels colder than if he was not exposed to the wind
    C. Increasing the atmospheric pressure over a liquid causes the boiling temperature to decrease
    D. If snow begins to fall when Mary is skiing, she feels colder than before it started to snow
    E. A hot water bottle is more effective in keeping a person warm than would a rock of the same mass heated to the same temperature

35. A 2,200 kg sample of water at 0 °C is cooled to –30 °C, and freezes in the process. Approximately how much heat is liberated during this process? (Use heat of fusion for water $L_f = 334$ kJ/kg, heat of vaporization $L_v = 2,257$ kJ/kg and specific heat for ice = 2,050 J/kg·K)

    A. 328,600 kJ   **C.** 637,200 kJ
    B. 190,040 kJ   **D.** 870,100 kJ   **E.** 768,200 kJ

36. Object 1 has three times the specific heat capacity and four times the mass of Object 2. The same amount of heat is given to the two objects. If the temperature of Object 1 changes by an amount of ΔT, what is the change in temperature of Object 2?

    A. $(4/3)\Delta T$ **B.** $3\Delta T$ **C.** ΔT **D.** $(3/4)\Delta T$ **E.** $\Delta T/12$

37. The process whereby heat flows by means of molecular collisions is known as:

    A. radiation   **C.** conduction
    B. inversion   **D.** convection   **E.** evaporation

38. The graph shows a PV diagram for 5.1 g of oxygen gas in a sealed container. The temperature of T_1 is 20 °C. What are the values for temperatures of T_3 and T_4, respectively? (Use the gas constant R= 8.314 J/mol·K)

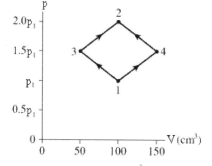

    A. –53 °C and 387 °C   **C.** 210 °C and 640 °C
    B. –14 °C and 34 °C   **D.** 12 °C and 58 °C
                           E. 29 °C and 171 °C

39. On a cold day, a piece of steel feels much colder to the touch than a piece of plastic. This is due to the difference in which one of the following physical properties of these materials?

A. Emissivity   **C.** Density
B. Thermal conductivity   **D.** Specific heat   **E.** Mass

40. What is the term for a process when a gas is allowed to expand as heat is added to it at constant pressure?

A. Isochoric   **B.** Isobaric   **C.** Adiabatic   **D.** Isothermal   **E.** Isentropic

41. A Carnot engine is used as an air conditioner to cool a house in the summer. The air conditioner removes 20 kJ of heat per second from the house, and maintains the inside temperature at 293 K, while the outside temperature is 307 K. What is the power required for the air conditioner?

A. 2.3 kW   **B.** 3.22 kW   **C.** 1.6 kW   **D.** 4.88 kW   **E.** 0.96 kW

42. Heat energy is measured in units of:

I. Joules   II. calories   III. work

A. I only   **B.** II only   **C.** I and II only   **D.** III only   **E.** I, II and III

43. The process in which heat flows by the mass movement of molecules from one place to another is known as:

I. conduction   II. convection   III. radiation

A. I only   **B.** II only   **C.** III only   **D.** I and II only   **E.** I and III only

44. The process whereby heat flows in the absence of any medium is known as:

A. radiation   **C.** conduction
B. inversion   **D.** convection   **E.** evaporation

45. The figure shows 0.008 mol of gas that undergoes the process $1 \rightarrow 2 \rightarrow 3$. What is the volume of V_3?

(Use ideal gas constant R = 8.314 J/mol·K and 1 atm = 101,325 Pa)

A. 435 cm³   **C.** 656 cm³
B. 568 cm³   **D.** 800 cm³
                            E. 940 cm³

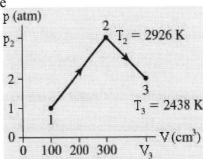

46. When a gas expands adiabatically:

A. it does no work

B. work is done on the gas

C. the internal (thermal) energy of the gas decreases

D. the internal (thermal) energy of the gas increases

E. the temperature of the gas remains constant

47. Why is it that when a swimmer gets out of a swimming pool and stands in a breeze dripping wet, he feels much colder compared to after he dries off?

A. This is a physiological effect resulting from the skin's sensory nerves

B. The water on his skin is colder than the surrounding air

C. The moisture on his skin has good thermal conductivity

D. Water has a relatively small specific heat

E. To evaporate a gram of water from his skin requires heat and most of this heat flows out of his body

48. Which method of heat flow requires the movement of energy through solid matter to a new location?

I. Conduction   II. Convection   III. Radiation

A. I only   B. II only   C. III only   D. I and II only   E. I and III only

49. An ideal gas is compressed via an isobaric process to one-third of its initial volume. Compared to the initial pressure, the resulting pressure is:

A. more than three times greater

B. nine times greater

C. three times greater

D. the same

E. requires more information

50. Which of the following would be the best radiator of thermal energy?

A. A metallic surface

B. A black surface

C. A white surface

D. A shiny surface

E. Styrofoam

51. A brass rod is 59.1 cm long and an aluminum rod is 39.3 cm long when both rods are at an initial temperature of 0 °C. The rods are placed with a distance of 1.1 cm between them. The distance between the far ends of the rods is maintained at 99.5 cm. The temperature is raised until the two rods are barely in contact. In the figure, what is the temperature at which contact of the rods barely occurs? (Use coefficient of linear expansion of brass = $2 \times 10^{-5} \text{ K}^{-1}$ and coefficient of linear expansion of aluminum = $2.4 \times 10^{-5} \text{ K}^{-1}$)

A. 424 °C   C. 483 °C

B. 588 °C   D. 363 °C   E. 517 °C

←—99.5 cm—→

brass   aluminum
59.1 cm   39.3 cm

52. At room temperature, a person loses energy to the surroundings at the rate of 60 W. If this energy loss is compensated by an equivalent food intake, how many kilocalories does he need to consume every 24 hours? (Use conversion of 1 cal = 4.186 J)

    A. 1,240 kcal   **B.** 1,660 kcal   **C.** 600 kcal   **D.** 880 kcal   **E.** 1,920 kcal

53. By what primary heat transfer mechanism does one end of an iron bar become hot when the other end is placed in a flame?

    A. Convection   **C.** Radiation

    B. Forced convection   **D.** Conduction   **E.** Diffusion

---

Questions **54-55** are based on the following:

Two experiments are performed to determine the calorimetric properties of an alcohol which has a melting point of –10 °C. In the first trial, a 220 g cube of frozen alcohol, at the melting point, is added to 350 g of water at 26 °C in a Styrofoam container. When thermal equilibrium is reached, the alcohol-water solution is at a temperature of 5 °C. In the second trial, an identical cube of alcohol is added to 400 g of water at 30 °C, and the temperature at thermal equilibrium is 10 °C. (Use specific heat of water = 4,190 J/kg·K and assume no heat exchange between the Styrofoam container and the surroundings).

54. What is the specific heat capacity of the alcohol?

    A. 2,150 J/kg·K   **C.** 1,175 J/kg·K

    B. 2,475 J/kg·K   **D.** 1,820 J/kg·K   **E.** 2,730 J/kg·K

55. What is the heat of fusion of the alcohol?

    A. 7.2×10^3 J/kg   **C.** 5.2×10^4 J/kg

    B. 1.9×10^5 J/kg   **D.** 10.3×10^4 J/kg   **E.** 3.3×10^4 J/kg

56. The silver coating on the glass surface of a Thermos bottle reduces energy that is transferred by:

I. conduction   II. convection   III. radiation

    A. I only   **B.** II only   **C.** III only   **D.** I and II only   **E.** I and III only

57. A person consumes a snack containing 16 kcal. What is the power this food produces if it is to be expended during exercise in 5 hours? (Use the conversion 1 cal = 4.186 J)

    A. 0.6 W   **B.** 11.2 W   **C.** 9.7 W   **D.** 96.3 W   **E.** 3.7 W

---

58. If 50 kcal of heat is added to 5 kg of water, what is the resulting temperature change? (Use specific heat of water = 1 kcal/kg·°C)

    A. 10 °C   **B.** 20 °C   **C.** 5 °C   **D.** 40 °C   **E.** 0.5 °C

59. How much heat is needed to melt it a 30 kg sample of ice that is at 0 °C? (Use latent heat of fusion for water L_f = 334 kJ/kg and latent heat of vaporization for water L_v = 2,257 kJ/kg)

    A. 0 kJ   **B.** 5.6×10^4 kJ   **C.** 1×10^4 kJ   **D.** 2.4×10^6 kJ   **E.** 6.3×10^3 kJ

60. A 6 kg aluminum rod is originally at 12 °C. If 160 kJ of heat is added to the rod, what is its final temperature? (Use specific heat capacity of aluminum = 910 J/kg·K)

    A. 32 °C   **B.** 41 °C   **C.** 54 °C   **D.** 23 °C   **E.** 66 °C

Heat & Thermodynamics – Answer Key

1: B	13: B	25: A	37: C	49: D
2: C	14: E	26: A	38: A	50: B
3: D	15: C	27: D	39: B	51: E
4: A	16: A	28: B	40: B	52: A
5: C	17: D	29: E	41: E	53: D
6: E	18: B	30: D	42: C	54: B
7: D	19: E	31: B	43: B	55: D
8: A	20: A	32: D	44: A	56: C
9: C	21: D	33: E	45: D	57: E
10: E	22: A	34: B	46: C	58: A
11: B	23: B	35: D	47: E	59: C
12: A	24: D	36: E	48: A	60: B

Atomic and Nuclear Structure

1. Which statement(s) about alpha particles is/are FALSE?

      I. They are a harmless form of radiation
      II. They have low penetrating power
      III. They have high ionization power

  A. I only   **B.** II only   **C.** III only   **D.** I and II only   **E.** I and III only

2. What is the term for nuclear radiation that is identical to an electron?

  A. Positron   **C.** Beta minus particle
  B. Gamma ray   **D.** Alpha particle   **E.** Beta plus particle

3. Protons are being accelerated in a particle accelerator. When the speed of the protons is doubled, by what factor does their de Broglie wavelength change? Note: consider this situation non-relativistic.

  A. Increases by $\sqrt{2}$ **C.** Increases by 2
  B. Decreases by $\sqrt{2}$ **D.** Increases by 4   **E.** Decreases by 2

4. The Bohr model of the atom was able to explain the Balmer series because:

  A. electrons were allowed to exist only in specific orbits and nowhere else
  B. differences between the energy levels of the orbits matched the differences between the energy levels of the line spectra
  C. smaller orbits require electrons to have more negative energy to match the angular momentum
  D. differences between the energy levels of the orbits were exactly half the differences between the energy levels of the line spectra
  E. none of the above

5. Radioactivity is the tendency for an element to:

  A. become ionized easily   **C.** emit radiation
  B. be dangerous to living things   **D.** emit protons   **E.** radiate heat

6. Which is the missing species in the nuclear equation: $^{100}_{44}\text{Ru} + ^{0}_{-1}\text{e}^{-} \rightarrow$ ___?

  A. $^{100}_{45}\text{Ru}$ **B.** $^{100}_{43}\text{Ru}$ **C.** $^{101}_{44}\text{Ru}$ **D.** $^{100}_{43}\text{Tc}$ **E.** $^{101}_{43}\text{Tc}$

---

7. The term nucleon refers to:

   A. the nucleus of a specific isotope
   B. both protons and neutrons
   C. positrons that are emitted from an atom that undergoes nuclear decay
   D. electrons that are emitted from a nucleus in a nuclear reaction
   E. neutrons that are emitted from a nucleus in a nuclear reaction

8. An isolated ^{9}Be atom spontaneously decays into two alpha particles. What can be concluded about the mass of the ^{9}Be atom?

   A. The mass is less than twice the mass of the ^{4}He atom, but not equal to the mass of ^{4}He
   B. No conclusions can be made about the mass
   C. The mass is exactly twice the mass of the ^{4}He atom
   D. The mass is equal to the mass of the ^{4}He atom
   E. The mass is greater than twice the mass of the ^{4}He atom

9. Which of the following isotopes contains the most neutrons?

   A. $^{178}_{84}$Po   B. $^{178}_{87}$Fr   C. $^{181}_{86}$Rn   D. $^{170}_{83}$Bi   E. $^{177}_{86}$Rn

10. Which of the following statements regarding a nucleon is true in regards to nuclear reactions?

   A. A nucleon has high energy inside a nucleus and releases the energy when it undergoes nuclear reactions
   B. A nucleon outside a nucleus has a lower mass than a nucleon inside a nucleus
   C. A nucleon inside a nucleus has a lower mass than a nucleon outside a nucleus
   D. The number of nucleons changes during a nuclear reaction and therefore the mass changes
   E. A nucleon inside a nucleus has the same mass as a nucleon outside a nucleus

11. What is the frequency of the light emitted by atomic hydrogen according to Balmer's formula where n = 12? (Use Balmer series constant B = 3.6×10^{-7} m and speed of light c = 3×10^8 m/s)

   A. 5.3×10^6 Hz   C. 5.9×10^{13} Hz
   B. 9.8 Hz   D. 1.2×10^{11} Hz   E. 8.1×10^{14} Hz

12. Gamma rays require the heaviest shielding of all the common types of nuclear radiation because gamma rays have the:

   A. heaviest particles   C. most intense color
   B. lowest energy   D. highest energy   E. lowest frequency

13. In making a transition from state n = 1 to state n = 2, the hydrogen atom must [   ] a photon of [   ]. (Use Planck's constant $h = 4.14 \times 10^{-15}$ eV·s, speed of light $c = 3 \times 10^8$ m/s and Rydberg constant $R = 1.097 \times 10^7$ m^{-1})

A. absorb … 10.2 Ev

B. absorb … 8.6 eV

C. emit … 8.6 eV

D. emit … 10.2 eV

E. absorb … 4.3 eV

14. Rubidium $^{87}_{37}$Rb is a naturally-occurring nuclide which undergoes β$^-$ decay. What is the resultant nuclide from this decay?

A. $^{86}_{36}$Rb

B. $^{87}_{38}$Kr

C. $^{87}_{38}$Sr

D. $^{87}_{36}$Kr

E. $^{86}_{37}$Rb

15. Which of the following statements best describes the role of neutrons in the nucleus?

A. The neutrons stabilize the nucleus by attracting protons

B. The neutrons stabilize the nucleus by balancing charge

C. The neutrons stabilize the nucleus by attracting other nucleons

D. The neutrons stabilize the nucleus by forming bonds with other nucleons

E. The neutrons stabilize the nucleus by attracting electrons

16. A Geiger–Muller counter detects radioactivity by:

A. ionizing argon gas in a chamber which produces an electrical signal

B. analyzing the mass and velocity of each particle

C. developing film which is exposed by radioactive particles

D. slowing the neutrons using a moderator and then counting the secondary charges produced

E. converting electrical charges from a chemical reaction into light

17. What percentage of the radionuclides in a given sample remains after three half-lives?

A. 25%

B. 12.5%

C. 6.25%

D. 33.3%

E. 50%

18. The Lyman series is formed by electron transitions in hydrogen that:

A. begin on the n = 2 shell

B. end on the n = 2 shell

C. begin on the n = 1 shell

D. end on the n = 1 shell

E. are between the n = 1 and n = 3 shells

19. Most of the volume of an atom is occupied by:

A. neutrons

B. empty space

C. electrons

D. protons

E. interface with protons

20. Alpha and beta minus particles are deflected in opposite directions in a magnetic field because:

      I. they have opposite charges
      II. alpha particles contain nucleons and beta minus particles do not
      III. they spin in opposite directions

    A. I only   **B.** II only   **C.** III only   **D.** I and II only   **E.** I and III only

21. The conversion of mass to energy is measureable only in:

    A. chemiluminescent transformations   **C.** endothermic reactions
    B. spontaneous chemical reactions   **D.** exothermic reactions
                                           E. nuclear reactions

22. What is the term given to the amount of a radioactive substance that undergoes 3.7×10^{10} disintegrations per second?

    A. Rem   **B.** Rad   **C.** Curie   **D.** Roentgen   **E.** Sievert

23. An isolated ^{235}U atom spontaneously undergoes fission into two approximately equal-sized fragments. What is missing from the product side of the reaction:

$$^{235}\text{U} \rightarrow {}^{141}\text{Ba} + {}^{92}\text{Kr} + \underline{\quad}?$$

    A. A neutron   **C.** Two protons and two neutrons
    B. Two neutrons   **D.** Two protons and a neutron
                                   E. A proton and two neutrons

24. How many protons and neutrons are in $^{34}_{16}\text{S}$?

    A. 18 neutrons and 34 protons   **C.** 16 protons and 34 neutrons
    B. 16 neutrons and 18 protons   **D.** 16 protons and 18 neutrons
                                   E. 34 neutrons and 18 protons

25. The radioactive isotope Z has a half-life of 12 hours. What is the fraction of the original amount remaining after 2 days?

    A. 1/16   **B.** 1/8   **C.** 1/4   **D.** 1/2   **E.** 1/3

26. Which of the following nuclear equations correctly describes alpha emission?

    A. $^{238}_{92}\text{U} \rightarrow {}^{242}_{94}\text{Pu} + {}^{4}_{2}\text{He}$ **C.** $^{238}_{92}\text{U} \rightarrow {}^{234}_{90}\text{Th} + {}^{4}_{2}\text{He}$

    B. $^{238}_{92}\text{U} \rightarrow {}^{4}_{2}\text{He}$ **D.** $^{238}_{92}\text{U} \rightarrow {}^{235}_{90}\text{Th} + {}^{4}_{2}\text{He}$ **E.** None of the above

27. A hydrogen atom makes a downward transition from the n = 20 state to the n = 5 state. Find the wavelength of the emitted photon. (Use Planck's constant $h = 4.14 \times 10^{-15}$ eV·s, speed of light $c = 3 \times 10^8$ m/s and the Rydberg constant R = $1.097 \times 10^7\,\text{m}^{-1}$)

    A. 1.93 µm   **B.** 2.82 µm   **C.** 1.54 µm   **D.** 1.38 µm   **E.** 2.43 µm

28. A nuclear equation is balanced when the:

    A. same elements are found on both sides of the equation

    B. sums of the atomic numbers of the particles and atoms are the same on both sides of the equation

    C. sum of the mass numbers of the particles and the sum of atoms are the same on both sides of the equation

    D. sum of the mass numbers and the sum of the atomic numbers of the particles and atoms are the same on both sides of the equation

    E. charges of the particles and atoms are the same on both sides of the equation

29. A blackbody is an ideal system that:

    A. absorbs 50% of the light incident upon it, and emits 50% of the radiation it generates

    B. absorbs 0% of the light incident upon it, and emits 100% of the radiation it generates

    C. absorbs 100% of the light incident upon it, and emits 100% of the radiation it generates

    D. emits 100% of the light it generates, and absorbs 50% of the radiation incident upon it

    E. absorbs 50% of the light incident upon it, and emits 100% of the radiation it generates

30. Recent nuclear bomb tests have created an extra-high level of atmospheric ^{14}C. When future archaeologists date samples, without knowing of these nuclear tests, will the dates they calculate be correct?

    A. Correct, because biological materials do not gather ^{14}C from bomb tests

    B. Correct, since the ^{14}C decays within the atmosphere at the natural rate

    C. Incorrect, they would appear too old

    D. Incorrect, they would appear too young

    E. Incorrect, since there is more ^{14}C than there should be

31. When an isotope releases gamma radiation, the atomic number:

    A. and the mass number remain the same

    B. and the mass number decrease by one

    C. and the mass number increase by one

    D. remains the same and the mass number increases by one

    E. remains the same and the mass number decreases by one

32. If ^{14}Carbon is a beta emitter, what is the likely product of radioactive decay?

   A. ^{22}Silicon   **C.** ^{14}Nitrogen

   B. ^{13}Boron   **D.** ^{12}Carbon   **E.** None of the above

33. In a nuclear equation, the:

      I. sum of the mass numbers on both sides must be equal

      II. sum of the atomic numbers on both sides must be equal

      III. daughter nuclide appears on the right side of the arrow

   A. I only   **B.** II only   **C.** III only   **D.** I and III only   **E.** I, II and III

34. What is the term for the number that characterizes an element and indicates the number of protons found in the nucleus of the atom?

   A. Mass number   **C.** Atomic mass

   B. Atomic number   **D.** Neutron number   **E.** None of the above

35. Hydrogen atoms can emit four spectral lines with visible colors from red to violet. These four visible lines emitted by hydrogen atoms are produced by electrons that:

   A. end in the ground state   **C.** end in the $n = 2$ level

   B. end in the $n = 3$ level   **D.** start in the ground state   **E.** start in the $n = 3$ level

36. The electron was discovered through experiments with:

   A. quarks   **B.** foil   **C.** light   **D.** electricity   **E.** magnets

Questions **37-39** are based on the following:

The image shows a beam of radiation passing between two electrically-charged plates.

     I. a

     II. b

     III. c

37. Which of the beams is due to an energetic light wave?

   A. I only   **B.** II only   **C.** III only   **D.** I and II only   **E.** None

38. Which of the beams is/are composed of particles?

   A. I only   **B.** II only   **C.** III only   **D.** I and III only   **E.** I, II and III

39. Which of the beams is due to a positively-charged helium nucleus?

   A. I only   **B.** II only   **C.** III only   **D.** I, II and III   **E.** None of the above

40. Lithium atoms are able to absorb photons transitioning from the ground state (at –5.37 eV) to an excited state. When one electron is completely removed from the atom, it corresponds to the zero energy state. What is the wavelength of light associated with this transition? (Use Planck's constant $h = 4.14 \times 10^{-15}$ eV·s and speed of light $c = 3 \times 10^8$ m/s)

   A. 6.6×10^{-6} m   **C.** 3.6×10^6 m

   B. 2.3×10^{-7} m   **D.** 4.2×10^5 m   **E.** 2.6×10^{-6} m

41. All of the elements with atomic numbers of 84 and higher are radioactive because:

   A. strong attractions between their nucleons make them unstable

   B. their atomic numbers are larger than their mass numbers

   C. strong repulsions between their electrons make them unstable

   D. strong repulsions between their protons make their nuclei unstable

   E. strong repulsions between their neutrons make their nuclei unstable

42. Which of the following statements about β particles is FALSE?

   A. They have a smaller mass than α particles

   B. They have high energy and a charge

   C. They are created when neutrons become protons and vise versa

   D. They can be positively or negatively charged

   E. They are a harmless form of radioactivity

43. Which of the following is a FALSE statement regarding the nuclear force?

   A. For two protons in close proximity, the nuclear force and the electromagnetic force have comparable magnitudes

   B. The nuclear force is stronger than the electromagnetic force

   C. The nuclear force has a short range, of the order of nuclear dimensions

   D. The nuclear force is created between nucleons by the exchange of meson particles

   E. The nuclear force favors binding of pairs of protons or neutrons with opposite spin angular momenta

44. Which statement regarding Planck's constant is true?

   A. It relates mass to the amount of energy that can be emitted

   B. It sets a lower limit to the amount of energy that can be absorbed or emitted

   C. It sets an upper limit to the amount of energy that can be absorbed

   D. It sets an upper limit to the amount of energy that can be absorbed or emitted

   E. It relates mass to the amount of energy that can be absorbed or emitted

45. The decay rate of a radioactive isotope will NOT be increased by increasing the:

   I. surface area   II. pressure   III. temperature

   A. I only   **B.** II only   **C.** III only   **D.** I and III only   **E.** I, II and III

46. Why are some smaller nuclei such as ^{14}Carbon often radioactive?

   I. The attractive force of the nucleons has a limited range

   II. The neutron to proton ratio is too large or too small

   III. Most smaller nuclei are not stable

   A. I only   **B.** II only   **C.** III only   **D.** II and III only   **E.** I and III only

47. Scandium ^{44}Sc decays by emitting a positron. What is the resultant nuclide which is produced by this decay?

   A. $^{43}_{21}$Sc   **B.** $^{45}_{21}$Sc   **C.** $^{44}_{20}$Ca   **D.** $^{43}_{20}$Ca   **E.** $^{45}_{22}$Ti

48. A scintillation counter detects radioactivity by:

   A. analyzing the mass and velocity of each electron

   B. ionizing argon gas in a chamber which produces an electrical signal

   C. emitting light from a NaI crystal when radioactivity passes through the crystal

   D. developing film which is exposed by radioactive particles

   E. slowing the neutrons using a moderator and then counting the secondary charges produced

49. Which of the following is indicated by each detection sound by a Geiger counter?

   A. One half-life   **C.** One neutron being emitted

   B. One nucleus decaying   **D.** One positron being emitted

                                     E. None of the above

50. According to the Pauli Exclusion Principle, how many electrons in an atom may have a particular set of quantum numbers?

   A. 1   **B.** 2   **C.** 3   **D.** 4   **E.** 5

51. The atomic number of an atom identifies the number of:

A. excited states   **C.** neutrons

B. electron orbits   **D.** protons   **E.** valence electrons

52. Which of the following correctly characterizes gamma radiation?

A. High penetrating power; charge $= -1$; mass $= 0$ amu

B. Low penetrating power; charge $= -1$; mass $= 0$ amu

C. Low penetrating power; charge $= 0$; mass $= 4$ amu

D. High penetrating power; charge $= 0$; mass $= 4$ amu

E. High penetrating power; charge $= 0$; mass $= 0$ amu

53. The rest mass of a proton is 1.0072764669 amu and that of a neutron is 1.0086649156 amu. The ^{4}He nucleus weighs 4.002602 amu. What is the total binding energy of the nucleus? (Use speed of light $c = 3 \times 10^8$ m/s and 1 amu $= 1.6606 \times 10^{-27}$ kg)

A. 2.7×10^{-11} J   **C.** 1.6×10^{-7} J

B. 4.4×10^{-12} J   **D.** 2.6×10^{-12} J   **E.** 4.4×10^{-10} J

54. Which is the correct electron configuration for ground state boron ($Z = 5$)?

A. $1s^2 1p^2 2s$ **C.** $1s^2 2p^3$

B. $1s^2 2p^2 3s$ **D.** $1s^2 2s^2 3p^2$ **E.** $1s^2 2s^2 2p$

55. The Sun produces 3.85×10^{26} J each second. How much mass does it lose per second from nuclear processes alone? (Use speed of light $c = 3 \times 10^8$ m/s)

A. 9.8×10^1 kg   **C.** 4.3×10^9 kg

B. 2.4×10^9 kg   **D.** 1.1×10^8 kg   **E.** 4.6×10^6 kg

56. The damaging effects of radiation on the body are a result of:

A. extensive damage to nerve cells

B. transmutation reactions in the body

C. the formation of radioactive particles in the body

D. the formation of unstable ions or radicals in the body

E. the production of radioactive uranium ions in the body

57. How does the emission of a gamma ray affect the radioactive atom?

     I. The atomic mass increases

     II. The atom has a smaller amount of energy

     III. The atom gains energy for further radioactive particle emission

A. I only   **B.** II only   **C.** III only   **D.** I and II only   **E.** I and III only

58. The nuclear particle, which is described by the symbol $_{0}^{1}n$, is a(n):

    A. neutron   **B.** gamma ray   **C.** beta particle   **D.** electron   **E.** proton

59. Heisenberg's uncertainty principle states that:

    A. at times a photon appears to be a particle and at other times it appears to be a wave

    B. whether a photon is a wave or a particle cannot be determined with certainty

    C. the position and the momentum of a particle cannot be simultaneously known with absolute certainty

    D. the properties of an electron cannot be known with absolute certainty

    E. the charge on an electron can never be known with absolute accuracy

60. The material used in nuclear bombs is ^{239}Pu, with a half-life of about 20,000 years. What is the approximate amount of time that must elapse for a buried stockpile of this substance to decay to 3% of its original ^{239}Pu mass?

    A. 0.8 thousand years   **C.** 90 thousand years

    B. 65 thousand years   **D.** 101 thousand years   **E.** 184 thousand years

Atomic & Nuclear Structure – Answer Key

1: A	11: E	21: E	31: A	41: D	51: D
2: C	12: D	22: C	32: C	42: E	52: E
3: E	13: A	23: B	33: E	43: A	53: B
4: B	14: C	24: D	34: B	44: B	54: E
5: C	15: C	25: A	35: C	45: E	55: C
6: D	16: A	26: C	36: D	46: B	56: D
7: B	17: B	27: E	37: B	47: C	57: B
8: E	18: D	28: D	38: E	48: C	58: A
9: C	19: B	29: C	39: C	49: B	59: C
10: C	20: A	30: D	40: B	50: A	60: D

Diagnostic Tests

Explanations

Diagnostic Test #1 – Explanations

1. A is correct.

An object's resistance to change in its state of motion is characterized by its inertia.

Inertia is not a physical property but is directly related to an object's mass. Thus, mass determines resistance to change in motion.

2. E is correct.

The three forces are in equilibrium, so the net force $F_{net} = 0$

$$F_{net} = F_1 + F_2 + F_3$$

$$0 = F_1 + F_2 + F_3$$

Since the forces F_1 and F_2 are mirror images of each other along the x-axis, their net force in the y direction is zero. Therefore, F_3 is also zero in the y direction.

The net force along the x direction must add to zero, so set the sum of the x components to zero.

The angles for F_1 and F_2 are equal and measured with respect to the x-axis, so θ_1 and θ_2 are both 20°.

Since F_3 has no y component, $\theta_3 = 0°$. Note that force components to the left are set negative in this answer and components to the right are set positive.

$$0 = F_{1x} + F_{2x} + F_{3x}$$

$$0 = F_1 \cos \theta_1 + F_2 \cos \theta_2 + F_3 \cos \theta_3$$

$$0 = (-4.6 \text{ N} \cos 20°) + (-4.6 \text{ N} \cos 20°) + (F_3 \cos 0°)$$

Since $\cos 0° = 1$:

$$0 = (-4.3 \text{ N}) + (-4.3 \text{ N}) + F_3$$

$$-F_3 = -8.6 \text{ N}$$

$$F_3 = 8.6 \text{ N, to the right}$$

3. C is correct.

Heat transfer between two materials occurs until both materials reach the same temperature, so the amount of heat lost by the hotter material is gained by the colder material.

4. B is correct.

$$W = Fd$$

$$W = (20 \text{ N}) \cdot (3.5 \text{ m})$$

$$W = 70 \text{ J}$$

5. E is correct.

Constructive interference occurs when two or more waves of equal frequency and phase produce a single amplitude wave that is the sum of amplitudes of the individual waves.

If there is any phase difference the interference will not be the sum total of the amplitude of each individual wave.

If the phase difference is 180° there will be total destructive interference.

6. B is correct.

The expression for the Doppler shift is:

$$f = f_s[(c + v_o) / (c + v_s)]$$

where f is the frequency heard by the observer, f_s is the frequency of the source, c is the speed of sound, v_o is the velocity of the observer, v_s is the velocity of the source

The velocity of the source v_s is positive when the source is moving away from the observer and negative when it is moving toward the observer

Since the train is traveling away, once it passes the velocity of the source (i.e. train) is positive.

Kevin is standing still, so the velocity of the observer is zero.

$$f = f_s[(c + v_o) / (c + v_s)]$$
$$f = (420 \text{ Hz}) \cdot [(350 \text{ m/s} + 0 \text{ m/s}) / (350 \text{ m/s} + 50 \text{ m/s})]$$
$$f = (420 \text{ Hz}) \cdot [(350 \text{ m/s}) / (400 \text{ m/s})]$$
$$f = (147,000 \text{ Hz·m/s}) / (400 \text{ m/s})$$
$$f = 368 \text{ Hz}$$

7. C is correct.

Momentum is the product of mass and velocity.

$$p_0 = mv_0$$

If velocity doubles:

$$p = m(2v_0)$$
$$p = 2mv_0$$
$$p = 2p_0$$

Therefore momentum doubles.

8. A is correct.

A moving charge experiences a magnetic force from a magnetic field, but the force is perpendicular to the velocity (as well as the magnetic field), so the speed does not change.

$$F_B = qvB \sin \theta \qquad F_B \text{ is perpendicular to both } v \text{ and } B$$

9. D is correct.

If one mass is halved, then the gravitational attraction between them is halved.

For equilibrium, the electrostatic repulsion must also be halved.

$F_e = F_g$

$F_e = kQ_1Q_2 / r^2$

$F_g = Gm_1m_2 / r^2$

$kQ_1Q_2 / r^2 = Gm_1m_2 / r^2$

$kQ_1Q_2 = Gm_1m_2$, k and G are constants and cannot be manipulated.

If the mass of object 1 is halved, while equilibrium is maintained:

$G(m_1 / 2)m_2 = (Gm_1m_2) / 2$

If the electrostatic force is halved, the charge of one of the objects must be halved:

$(kQ_1Q_2) / 2 = kQ_1(Q_2 / 2)$

10. E is correct. Calculate the focal length:

$1 / f = 1 / d_i + 1 / d_o$

where f is focal length d_o is distance to the object and d_i is distance to the image

$1 / f = 1 / 2 \text{ m} + 1 / 4 \text{ m}$

$1 / f = 2 / 4 \text{ m} + 1 / 4 \text{ m}$

$1 / f = 3 / 4 \text{ m}$

$f = 4 / 3 \text{ m}$

11. B is correct.

$$_Z^A n + e^- \rightarrow {}_{Z-1}^A (n - 1) + v_e$$

An inner electron is captured by a proton of the same atom, and both transform into a neutron. Therefore the atomic number Z decreases by 1 because the nucleus contains one less proton. The $(n-1)$ signifies the new element name (since the atomic number changed), and v_e is the release of an electron neutrino.

12. B is correct.

To balance the torques due to the weight, the fulcrum must be placed 4 times farther from the son than from the man, because the father weighs 4 times more.

Since the total length of the seesaw is 10 m, the fulcrum must be placed 8 m from the son and 2 m from the father who is on the heavier end.

$x + 4x = 10 \text{ m}$

$5x = 10 \text{ m}$

$x = 2 \text{ m}$

Another method to solve the problem:

$$\frac{200\ \text{N}}{10-x} \qquad \Delta \qquad \frac{800\ \text{N}}{x}$$

$$(200\ \text{N}) \cdot (10-x) = (800\ \text{N})x$$

$$x = 2\ \text{m}$$

13. E is correct.

The energy before release and at the top of each bounce equals gravitational PE:

PE = *mgh*

Gravitational potential energy is proportional to height, and mass and *g* stay constant.

Multiply by 0.8 (80%) to determine the height after a bounce if 20% of the energy is lost.

$h_{\text{initial}} = 250\ \text{cm}$

250 cm × (0.8 × 0.8 × 0.8), equals *h* after 3 bounces

$h_3 = (250\ \text{cm}) \cdot (0.8)^3$

$h_3 = 128\ \text{cm}$

14. A is correct.

$T = 1/f$

$T = 1/(10\ \text{Hz})$

$T = 0.1\ \text{s}$

15. A is correct.

$f = v/\lambda$

$f = (1{,}600\ \text{m/s})/(2.5\ \text{m})$

$f = 640\ \text{Hz}$

16. B is correct. $_0^0\gamma$ is a gamma particle, so the atomic mass and atomic number do not change.

Alpha decay: during alpha decay, the parent nuclide sheds two protons and two neutrons which is identical to the nucleus of ^{4}He.

$$_Z^A\text{X} \rightarrow\ _{Z-2}^{A-4}\text{Y} +\ _2^4\alpha$$

Beta Decay (minus): during beta minus decay, the parent nuclide sheds an electron and electron antineutrino. However, in the process a neutron converts to a proton so the mass number remains the same but the atomic number increases by 1.

$$_Z^A\text{X} \rightarrow\ _{Z+1}^A\text{Y} +\ _{-1}^0\text{e}^- +\ _0^0\text{v}_{\text{e}}$$

Beta Decay (plus): during beta plus decay, the parent nuclide sheds a positron and neutrino. However, in the process a proton converts to a neutron so the mass number remains the same but the atomic number decreases by 1.

$$_Z^A X \rightarrow {}_{Z-1}^A Y + {}_{+1}^0 e^+ + {}_0^0 v_e$$

17. C is correct.

18. A is correct.

Find Capacitive Reactance:

$$X_c = 1 / 2\pi C f$$

$$X_c = 1 / (2\pi)\cdot(26 \times 10^{-6} \text{ F})\cdot(60 \text{ Hz})$$

$$X_c = 102 \ \Omega$$

Find peak current:

$$I = V_{rms} / X_c$$

$$I = 120 \text{ V} / 102 \ \Omega$$

$$I = 1.2 \text{ A}$$

19. C is correct.

Snell's Law:

$$n_g / n_w = (\sin \phi) / (\sin \theta)$$

Find the index of refraction for glass:

$$n_g / 1.33 = (\sin 61°) / (\sin 48°)$$

$$n_g / 1.33 = (0.875) / (0.743)$$

$$n_g / 1.33 = 1.18$$

$$n_g = (1.18)\cdot(1.33)$$

$$n_g = 1.57$$

Solve for the new angle of refraction after the angle of incidence has changed:

$$1.57 / 1.33 = (\sin \phi) / (\sin 25°)$$

$$1.18 = (\sin \phi) / (0.423)$$

$$(1.18)\cdot(0.423) = \sin \phi$$

$$\sin \phi = 0.5$$

$$\phi = 30°$$

20. A is correct.

Gamma radiation is high energy electromagnetic rays and not particles. As such its notation contains zero in the subscript and zero in the superscript.

21. B is correct.

Enthalpy of fusion

As a solid undergoes a phase change, the temperature will always stay constant until the phase change is complete.

To calculate the amount of heat absorbed to completely melt the solid, multiply the heat of fusion by the mass undergoing the phase change.

Heat needed to melt a solid:

$$q = m\Delta H_f$$

22. E is correct.

$$a = g \sin \theta$$

An object's acceleration down a frictionless ramp (with an incline angle) is constant.

23. D is correct.

Sound cannot travel through a vacuum because there is no medium to propagate the wave.

In air, sound waves travel through gas, in the ocean they travel through liquid, and in the Earth they travel through solids. These are all mediums in which sound waves can propagate.

However, vacuums are devoid of matter; there is no medium, and the wave cannot pass.

24. D is correct.

Newton's Second Law for each block:

$ma = F_{net}$ acting on the object.

The tension and acceleration on each block are equal in magnitude, but act in different directions.

The only nonzero net forces will be in the horizontal direction for the 15 kg block and in the vertical direction for the 60 kg block.

For the 15 kg block:

ma = tension acting to the right

$$(15 \text{ kg})a = F_T$$

For the 60 kg block:

ma = (weight acting downward) – (tension acting upward)

$$(60 \text{ kg})a = (60 \text{ kg}) \cdot (10 \text{ m/s}^2) - F_T$$

Substitute F_T from the first equation into the second:

$(60 \text{ kg})a = (60 \text{ kg}) \cdot (10 \text{ m/s}^2) - (15 \text{ kg})a$

$(60 \text{ kg})a + (15 \text{ kg})a = (60 \text{ kg}) \cdot (10 \text{ m/s}^2)$

$(75 \text{ kg})a = (60 \text{ kg}) \cdot (10 \text{ m/s}^2)$

$a = [(60 \text{ kg}) \cdot (10 \text{ m/s}^2)] / (75 \text{ kg})$

$a = 8 \text{ m/s}^2$

25. B is correct. By Newton's Third Law, F_1 and F_2 form an *action–reaction* pair. The ratio of their magnitudes equals 1.

26. E is correct.

$P = IV$

$P = (2 \text{ A}) \cdot (120 \text{ V})$

$P = 240 \text{ W}$

An ampere (A) is a rate of electric charge flowing in a circuit in coulombs per second (C/s), where 1 A = 1 C/s. The volt (V) measures the difference in electric potential between two points, where 1 V is defined as the electric potential difference when 1 ampere consumes 1 watt (W) of power.

Power is a measure of energy per unit time:

$1 \text{ W} = 1 \text{ A} \cdot \text{V}$

$1 \text{ W} = 1 \text{ J} / \text{s}$

$1 \text{ W} = 1 \text{ N} \cdot \text{m/s}$

$1 \text{ W} = 1 \text{ kg} \cdot \text{m}^2/\text{s}^3$

27. A is correct. When an atom absorbs energy their valence electrons move to higher "orbits". As the electrons fall back to their original (ground state), they emit the absorbed energy as light.

28. A is correct. Sievert (Sv) is the standard SI unit that measures a low radiation dose and is equivalent to the biological effect of one joule of x-rays per kilogram of recipient mass. The average person receives about 0.002-0.003 sieverts per year from naturally occurring radiation in the environment.

29. B is correct.

$d = \frac{1}{2}gt^2$

$t^2 = 2d / g$

$t^2 = 2(42 \text{ m}) / 10 \text{ m/s}^2$

$t^2 = 8.4 \text{ s}^2 \approx 2.9 \text{ s}$

30. D is correct.

$$F = ma$$
$$W = mg$$
$$m = W / g$$
$$F = (W / g)a$$
$$a = F / m$$

The $F_{\text{friction}} = 8.8$ N, and the mass is known from the box's weight.

$$8.8 \text{ N} = (40 \text{ N} / 10 \text{ m/s}^2)a$$
$$a = (8.8 \text{ N}) / (4 \text{ N/m/s}^2)$$
$$a = 2.2 \text{ m/s}^2$$

Since the box moves at constant velocity when force F is applied, F = force due to kinetic friction.

Once the force F is removed, the net force that causes its deceleration is the frictional force.

31. B is correct.

A longer barrel gives the propellant a longer time to impart a force upon a bullet and thus a higher velocity. This is characterized by impulse.

$$J = F\Delta t$$

32. A is correct.

$$KE_{\text{final}} = 0 \text{ since } v_f = 0$$

The length of the skid marks are irrelevant.

$$\Delta \text{Energy} = KE_{\text{final}} - KE_{\text{initial}}$$
$$\Delta E = \tfrac{1}{2}mv_f^2 - \tfrac{1}{2}mv_i^2$$
$$\Delta E = 0 \text{ J} - \tfrac{1}{2}(1,000 \text{ kg}) \cdot (30 \text{ m/s})^2$$
$$\Delta E = -4.5 \times 10^5 \text{ J}$$

33. B is correct.

The position of an object in simple harmonic motion (SHM) is represented as a function of time using sine or cosine:

$$x = A \sin (\omega t - \theta)$$

where x = position, A = amplitude (i.e. max displacement of object from equilibrium position), ω = angular velocity in radians/sec (or degrees/sec), t = time elapsed, θ = phase

Here, $\theta = 0$ since the graph matches the phase of the standard sine graph, so there is no need for a phase correction. $A = 1$ is used for simplicity.

$$x = \sin (\omega t)$$

The object's velocity in SHM is represented by the derivative of the position function:

$$v = \omega \cos(\omega t)$$

The object's acceleration in SHM is represented by the derivative of the velocity function:

$$a = -\omega^2 \sin(\omega t)$$

Therefore, the acceleration of objects in SHM is represented as the opposite value of position, multiplied by the square of angular velocity.

ω is constant, so the graphs keep the same wavelengths.

34. D is correct.

$$KE_{avg} = (3/2)kT$$

$$KE_{avg} = (3/2) \cdot (1.38 \times 10^{-23} \text{ J/K}) \cdot (740 \text{ K})$$

$$KE_{avg} = 1.5 \times 10^{-20} \text{ J}$$

35. B is correct.

The power of the combination is:

$$P = P_1 + P_2$$

Since power is the reciprocal of the focal length (in meters),

$$f_1 = 10 \text{ cm} = 1 / 10 \text{ m}$$

$$P_1 = 1 / f_1$$

$$P_1 = 1 / (1 / 10 \text{ m})$$

$$P_1 = 10 \text{ D}$$

$$f_2 = 20 \text{ cm} = 1 / 5 \text{ m}$$

$$P_2 = 1 / f_2$$

$$P_2 = 1 / (1 / 5 \text{ m})$$

$$P_2 = 5 \text{ D}$$

$$P = P_1 + P_2$$

$$P = 10 \text{ D} + 5 \text{ D} = 15 \text{ D}$$

36. E is correct.

$$C = 1 / (2\pi Rf)$$

$$C = 1 / (2\pi \times 4{,}000 \ \Omega \times 600 \text{ Hz})$$

$$C = 6.6 \times 10^{-8} \text{ F}$$

Because the answers are in the micro-Faradays, divide by 10^{-6} to find proper units (μFaradays)

$$C = 6.6 \times 10^{-8} \text{ F} / (10^{-6})$$

$$C = 0.066 \ \mu\text{F}$$

37. C is correct.

If the voltage drop across the 3 Ω resistor is 2 V, the current through the 3 Ω resistor is:

$I = V / R$

$I = 2 \text{ V} / 3 \text{ Ω}$

$I = 2/3 \text{ amp}$

Since the 1.5 Ω resistor is connected in parallel with the 3 Ω resistor, voltage drop = 2 V (parallel resistors always share the same voltage drop).

The current through the 1.5 Ω resistor is:

$I = 2 \text{ V} / 1.5 \text{ Ω}$

$I = 4/3 \text{ amps}$

Then, sum the currents:

$I_{total} = 2/3 \text{ amp} + 4/3 \text{ amps}$

$I_{total} = 2 \text{ amps}$

38. C is correct.

$y = v_i t + \frac{1}{2} a t^2$

$50 \text{ m} = 0 + \frac{1}{2}(10 \text{ m/s}^2) t^2$

$50 \text{ m} = \frac{1}{2}(10 \text{ m/s}^2) t^2$

$t^2 = 50 \text{ m} / 5 \text{ m/s}^2$

$t^2 = 10 \text{ s}^2$

$t = 3.2 \text{ s}$

Solve for speed:

$v_f = v_i + at$

$v_f = 0 + (10 \text{ m/s}^2) \cdot (3.2 \text{ s})$

$v_f = 32 \text{ m/s}$

39. D is correct.

Sound is a travelling acoustic pressure wave that is propagated through vibrations of particles such as air or water.

In a vacuum no particles exist so the wave cannot propagate and no sound is heard.

Thus sound can refract in air or water but not in a vacuum.

40. E is correct.

$\lambda = vt$

$\lambda = (4.6 \text{ m/s}) \cdot (10 \text{ s})$

$\lambda = 46 \text{ m}$

41. D is correct.

$W = Fd \cos \theta$

$W = (20 \text{ N}) \cdot (2 \text{ m})$

$W = 40 \text{ J}$

42. C is correct.

Total momentum of the system is always conserved. Before the ball was thrown the momentum was zero because all mass on the canoe was stationary.

After the ball is thrown and caught on the canoe the momentum must still be equal to zero so the canoe must remain stationary.

$p = mv$

43. D is correct.

According to Newton's First Law: an object at rest tends to stay at rest and an object in motion tends to stay in motion unless acted upon by an outside force.

Lisa fell backwards because the truck accelerated to increase its velocity and Lisa's body tended to stay in its original motion.

44. C is correct.

45. D is correct. For materials with a positive coefficient of thermal expansion, a hole drilled in the material expands as temperature increases. Regardless of the surrounding metal's expansion, the hole's diameter always increases with higher temperature.

46. C is correct.

The kinetic energy of a falling object is directly proportional to height from which it falls. This is because mass and gravity are constants so only the height varies the kinetic energy of a dropped object.

$\text{KE} = \text{PE}$

$\frac{1}{2}mv^2 = mgh$

47. B is correct.

If the two sound sources are in phase then there is no destructive interference.

The point can be related to the wavelength of the sound wave.

$0.5 \text{ m} = x\lambda$

$0.5 \text{ m} = x(1 \text{ m})$

$x = \frac{1}{2}$

One half of a wavelength is a node.

48. C is correct.

An object becomes electrostatically charged when a charge imbalance exists.

Charge can only be transferred by electrons because protons are not mobile, thus electron transfer creates electrostatic charge.

49. A is correct.

Car mirrors are convex because they offer a wider field of view than plane mirrors.

Convex mirrors compress images to create this wider field of view. Thus the image on the mirror looks smaller than what a plane mirror would show. Because of this, the objects in a car mirror are closer than what the small image would lead the viewer to believe.

50. D is correct.

Velocity is in the direction of the current:

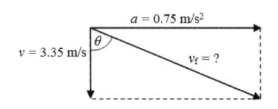

$$v_c = at$$

$$v_c = (0.75 \text{ m/s}^2) \cdot (33.5 \text{ s})$$

$$v_c = 25 \text{ m/s}$$

Final velocity:

$$v_f^2 = v^2 + v_c^2$$

$$v_f^2 = (3.35 \text{ m/s})^2 + (25 \text{ m/s})^2$$

$$v_f^2 = 636.2 \text{ m}^2/\text{s}^2$$

$$v_f = 25 \text{ m/s}$$

The angle of motion with respect to the initial velocity:

$$\theta = \tan^{-1} (v_c / v)$$

$$\theta = \tan^{-1} [(25 \text{ m/s}) / (3.35 \text{ m/s})]$$

$$\theta = \tan^{-1} 7.5$$

$$\theta = 82.4°$$

51. D is correct.

Divide the problem into three parts: initial acceleration, constant velocity, final deceleration stage.

1) Initial acceleration: determine α, then solve for the displacement during the acceleration. The initial velocity is zero.

Convert the displacement in radians to revolutions.

$$\alpha = (\omega_f - \omega_i) / t$$

$$\alpha = (58 \text{ radians/s} - 0) / 10 \text{ s}$$

$$\alpha = 5.8 \text{ radians/s}^2$$

$$\theta = \tfrac{1}{2}\alpha t^2$$

$$\theta = \tfrac{1}{2}(5.8 \text{ radians/s}^2)\cdot(10 \text{ s})^2$$

$$\theta = 290 \text{ radians}$$

$$Rev = \theta \,/\, 2\pi$$

$$Rev = 290 \text{ radians} \,/\, 2\pi$$

$$Rev = 46 \text{ revolutions}$$

2) Constant velocity: solve θ using constant angular velocity.

Convert radians to revolutions.

$$\theta = \omega t$$

$$\theta = (58 \text{ radians/s})\cdot(30 \text{ s})$$

$$\theta = 1{,}740 \text{ radians}$$

$$Rev = \theta \,/\, 2\pi$$

$$Rev = 1{,}740 \text{ radians} \,/\, 2\pi$$

$$Rev = 277 \text{ revolutions}$$

3) Final deceleration: determine t for the period of deceleration using the final velocity as zero.

Solve for the displacement during this constant deceleration and convert to revolutions.

$$\alpha = (\omega_f - \omega_i) \,/\, t$$

$$t = (\omega_f - \omega_i) \,/\, \alpha$$

$$t = (0 - 58 \text{ radians/s}) \,/\, (-1.4 \text{ radians/s}^2)$$

$$t = 41 \text{ s}$$

$$\theta = \omega_i t + \tfrac{1}{2}\alpha t^2$$

$$\theta = [(58 \text{ radians/s})\cdot(41 \text{ s})] + [\tfrac{1}{2}(-1.4 \text{ radians/s}^2)\cdot(41 \text{ s})^2]$$

$$\theta = 1{,}201 \text{ radians}$$

$$Rev = 1{,}201 \text{ radians} \,/\, 2\pi$$

$$Rev = 191 \text{ revolutions}$$

Add the revolutions:

$$Rev_{total} = 46 \text{ rev} + 277 \text{ rev} + 191 \text{ rev}$$

$$Rev_{total} = 514 \approx 510 \text{ revolutions}$$

52. E is correct.

The wave has to travel for 4 amplitudes of distance in 1 cycle.

Simple harmonic motion can be represented by a wave of one cycle:

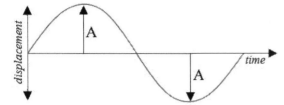

In one half cycle the object travels from zero displacement to A back to zero giving a total displacement of zero but a total distance of 2A. Thus in one complete cycle the object travels 4A.

53. E is correct.

54. E is correct.

Capacitance:

$C = Q / V$

$Q = CV$

$V = IR$

$Q = C \times (IR)$

$Q = (12 \times 10^{-6}\,F) \cdot (33 \times 10^{-6}\,A) \cdot (8.5 \times 10^{6}\,\Omega)$

$Q = 0.0034$ C

Divide by 10^{-6} to determine micro-coulombs:

$Q = (0.0034\ C) / 10^{-6}$

$Q = 3{,}400\ \mu C$

55. D is correct.

An alpha particle is composed of two neutrons and two protons and can be represented by a helium nucleus:

$^{4}_{2}\text{He}$

Diagnostic Test #2 – Explanations

1. C is correct.

Distance is direction independent

Displacement is direction dependent

Distance = (16 m North + 12 m South) = 28 m

Displacement = (16 m – 12 m) = 4 m

2. B is correct.

The angle the board makes before the pot slides is dependent upon the static friction coefficient as static friction influences the force of friction before the pot slides. Kinetic friction only occurs after movement of the pot.

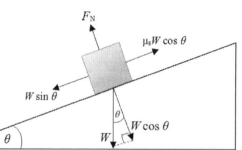

3. E is correct.

$Q = mc\Delta T$, where ΔT is constant

If m = 4 times increase and c = 3 times increase

$Q = (4)\cdot(3)\Delta T$

$Q = (12)\Delta T$

$Q_1 / 12 = \Delta T$

4. C is correct.

Ignoring air resistance, energy is conserved. The loss in PE = the gain in KE.

$KE = \frac{1}{2}mv^2$

$KE = \frac{1}{2}(20 \text{ kg})\cdot(30 \text{ m/s})^2$

$KE = 9,000 \text{ J}$

This equals the amount of PE that is lost (i.e. converted into KE).

5. C is correct.

velocity = frequency × wavelength

$v = f\lambda$

$\lambda = v / f$

$f = 1 / T$

$\lambda = v \times T$

$\lambda = 360 \text{ m/s} \times 4.2 \text{ s}$

$\lambda \approx 1,512 \text{ m}$

6. B is correct.

$$PE = \tfrac{1}{2}kx^2$$
$$PE = \tfrac{1}{2}k(2x)^2$$
$$PE = 4(\tfrac{1}{2}kx^2)$$

7. C is correct.

Efficiency is defined as $KE_{final}/KE_{initial}$.

Kinetic energy:

$$KE = \tfrac{1}{2}mv^2$$
$$KE = p^2/2m$$

Note that momentum is always conserved in a collision:

$$p_{initial} = p_{final} = p$$

Therefore:

$$Efficiency = KE_{final}/KE_{initial}$$
$$Efficiency = (p^2/2m_1) \,/\, (p^2/2m_2)$$
$$Efficiency = m_2 \,/\, m_1$$
$$Efficiency = (2.0 \text{ kg}) \,/\, (2.5 \text{ kg})$$
$$Efficiency = 0.8 \times 100\% = 80\%$$

8. D is correct.

From Coulomb's Law, the electrostatic force is *inversely proportional* to the square of the distance between the charges.

$$F = kq_1q_2 / r^2$$

If the distance increases by a factor of 2, then the force decreases by a factor of $2^2 = 4$.

9. C is correct.

$$P = IV$$
$$I = P / V$$
$$I = (1 \times 10^{-3} \text{ W}) / (9 \text{ V})$$
$$P = 0.00011 \text{ A} = 0.11 \text{ mA}$$

10. C is correct. The plane mirror is double the distance from an object, so ½*h* is required for the minimum length.

Law of reflection: $\theta_1 = \theta_2$

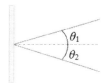

$$h = 2x$$

$$x = \tfrac{1}{2}h$$

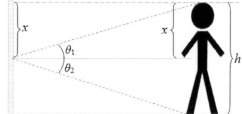

11. C is correct.

Fission occurs when an atom with a larger atomic number is struck by a free neutron and splits.

For example:

$$^{235}_{92}U + {}^{1}_{0}n \rightarrow {}^{92}_{36}Kr + {}^{141}_{56}Ba + 3{}^{1}_{0}n$$

12. B is correct.

Momentum is conserved

$$m_1v_1 + m_2v_2 = m_3v_3$$

momentum before = momentum after

$$p_i = p_f$$

$$p_{\text{total}} = m_1v_1 + m_2v_2$$

$$p_{\text{total}} = (1 \text{ kg})\cdot(1 \text{ m/s}) + (6 \text{ kg})\cdot(0 \text{ m/s})$$

$$p_{\text{total}} = 1 \text{ kg·m/s}$$

13. C is correct.

The work done by the force can be related to kinetic energy.

6 kg mass:

$$KE = W$$

$$\tfrac{1}{2}(6 \text{ kg})\cdot(2 \text{ m/s})^2 = Fd_1$$

$$d_1 = 12 / F$$

3 kg mass:

$$KE = W$$

$$\tfrac{1}{2}(3 \text{ kg})\cdot(4 \text{ m/s})^2 = Fd_2$$

$$d_2 = 24 / F$$

$$d_2 = 2(12 / F)$$

Therefore:

$$2d_1 = d_2$$

14. A is correct.

Separation between maxima in a double slit interference pattern is given by:

$$\Delta y = \lambda D / d$$

where y = maximum separation, λ = wavelength, D = distance from slit to diffraction pattern and d = slit separation.

Red light has the highest value wavelength and has the largest maximum separation.

15. B is correct.

The λ of a stretched string of length L that is fixed at both ends is:

$$\lambda = 2L / n$$

where n = 1 for the fundamental frequency.

Therefore, if the fundamental frequency (f_1) is 860 Hz, then:

$$\lambda = 2(0.25 \text{ m})$$

$$\lambda = 0.5 \text{ m}$$

$$v = f\lambda$$

$$v = (860 \text{ Hz}) \cdot (0.5 \text{ m})$$

$$v = 430 \text{ m/s}$$

16. B is correct.

The nucleus of an atom consists of protons and neutrons held together by the strong nuclear force. This force counteracts the electrostatic force of repulsion between the protons in the nucleus.

The gravitational and weak nuclear forces are negligible when discussing the nucleus and the force acting within it.

17. E is correct.

18. C is correct.

When two conductors are joined by a copper wire they must have the same potential because the wire allows for charge to flow. Any potential difference is neutralized by charge flow.

19. C is correct.

$$d = 130 \text{ m}$$

$$f = 3.6 \text{ MHz}$$

$$\theta = ?$$

velocity = frequency × wavelength

$$\lambda = c / f$$

$\lambda = (3 \times 10^8 \text{ m/s}) / (3.6 \times 10^6 \text{ Hz})$

$\lambda = 83.3 \text{ m}$

$\lambda = d \cos \theta$

$\theta = \cos^{-1} (\lambda / d)$

$\theta = \cos^{-1} (83.3 \text{ m} / 130 \text{ m})$

$\theta = 50°$

20. A is correct.

The magnetic quantum number is an interval from $-\ell$ to $+\ell$ (includes zero and an allowable value). The total amount of magnetic quantum numbers possible is:

$2(\ell) + 1$

For example:

$\ell = 2$

$m_\ell = -2, -1, 0, 1, 2$

$m_{\ell \text{ total possible}} = 2(2) + 1 = 5$

In the range from $-\ell$ to $+\ell$, there are 5 possible magnetic quantum numbers.

Verification through the equation:

$m_{\ell \text{ tot possible}} = 2(\ell) + 1$

21. A is correct.

Conduction occurs through microscopic diffusion and collision of particles with a material. It transfers energy from molecule to molecule through their collision. Example: a spoon that gets warmer from being submerged into a cup of hot coffee.

Convection is the concerted, collective movement of groups of molecules within fluids (e.g. liquids and gases). It does not occur in solids because neither bulk current flows nor significant diffusion can occur. Example: heat leaves a hot cup of coffee as the current of steam and air rise.

Radiation uses electromagnetic waves that transport energy through space. Example: the interior of a car gets hot when sitting in direct sunlight.

22. E is correct.

velocity = acceleration × time

$a = \Delta v / \Delta t$

If $\Delta v = 0$, then $a = 0$

23. B is correct. Sound intensity is defined as power per unit area and is usually expressed as W/m^2. Thus, sound intensity is directly proportional to power.

24. A is correct.

Horizontal velocity has no effect on the pebble's downward trajectory, so it is effectively in free fall like the second pebble.

25. D is correct.

$$E = F / q$$

$$F = Eq_{proton}$$

$$F = (4 \times 10^4 \text{ N/C}) \cdot (1.6 \times 10^{-19} \text{ C})$$

$$F = 6.4 \times 10^{-15} \text{ N}$$

26. D is correct.

Ohm's law:

$$V = IR$$

$$R = V / I$$

27. A is correct.

Optical density is related to the index of refraction of a material and describes how electromagnetic waves travel in a medium.

The optical density of a material is not related to its mass (physical) density.

28. B is correct.

Beta radiation is more powerful than alpha radiation, but less powerful than gamma rays.

Beta radiation can penetrate skin, paper or even a light layer of clothing.

29. E is correct.

The inertia of an object is its resistance to change in motion and is dependent on its mass which has units of kilograms.

30. D is correct.

$$T = W \pm ma$$

$$F = W \pm ma$$

Positive (add) if body is moving upward and negative (subtract) if moving downward.

$$T = mg + ma$$

$$T = m(g + a)$$

$$T = (900 \text{ kg}) \cdot (9.8 \text{ m/s}^2 + 0.6 \text{ m/s}^2)$$

$$T = 9,360 \text{ N}$$

31. B is correct.

Check if KE is conserved:

$KE_{before} = KE_{after}$ if collision is elastic

Before:

$(½)·(4 \text{ kg})·(1.8 \text{ m/s})^2 + (½)·(6 \text{ kg})·(0.2 \text{ m/s})^2 = KE_{before}$

$KE_{before} = 6.6 \text{ J}$

After:

$(½)·(4 \text{ kg})·(0.6 \text{ m/s})^2 + (½)·(6 \text{ kg})·(1.4 \text{ m/s})^2 = KE_{after}$

$KE_{after} = 6.6 \text{ J}$

Therefore:

$KE_{before} = KE_{after}$

The collision was completely elastic because kinetic energy was conserved.

32. B is correct.

Work is the dot product of *force* and *distance*, so:

Work = Force × distance × cos θ

$W = F × d × cos θ$

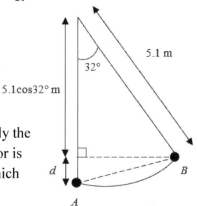

5.1 m

32°

5.1cos32° m

d

B

A

In this equation for work, the *cos θ* is to ensure that only the component of distance that is parallel to the force vector is multiplied. In the figure, the force vector is gravity, which points downward, and the distance vector is *AB*.

However, the distance component is calculated without actually using the distance vector *AB*.

The component of *AB* parallel to the force of gravity is labelled *d*.

d is calculated by using the length of the swing's chain, the angle that the swing is raised through, and the right triangle drawn in the figure above:

$d = 5.1 \text{ m} – (5.1 \text{ m cos } 32°)$

$d = 0.775 \text{ m}$

Since the force of gravity on Amanda is equal to *mg*, write an equation for work using the known value of 174 J. Note that the work is calculated as essentially the gravitational potential energy that Steve is adding to the system.

$W = Fd$

$F = ma$

$F = mg$ (where *a* is due to gravity)

$W = (mg)d$

$m = W / gd$

$174 \text{ J} = m(9.8 \text{ m/s}^2)·(0.775 \text{ m})$

$$m = (174 \text{ J}) / [(9.8 \text{ m/s}^2)\cdot(0.775 \text{ m})]$$
$$m = (174 \text{ J}) / (7.595 \text{ m}^2/\text{s}^2)$$
$$m = 22.9 \text{ kg}$$

33. A is correct.

It takes 2 s for the object to travel from one end of its displacement to the other (½ a cycle).

The time for a complete cycle is 2 s + 2 s = 4 s.

$$f = 1 / T$$
$$f = 1 / (4 \text{ s})$$
$$f = 0.25 \text{ s}^{-1} = 0.25 \text{ Hz}$$

34. D is correct.

$$2 (10 \text{ cm aluminum rods}) + 5 (8 \text{ cm steel rods}) = 20 \text{ cm} + 40 \text{ cm} = 60 \text{ cm}$$

$\Delta L = L\alpha\Delta T$, where α is the coefficient of linear expansion

$$\Delta L_{alum} = (20 \text{ cm})(2.4 \times 10^{-5} \text{ K}^{-1})(80 \text{ °C} - 5 \text{ °C})$$
$$\Delta L_{alum} = 3.6 \times 10^{-2} \text{ cm} = 0.36 \text{ mm}$$
$$\Delta L_{steel} = (40 \text{ cm})(1.2 \times 10^{-5} \text{ K}^{-1})(80 \text{ °C} - 5 \text{ °C})$$
$$\Delta L_{steel} = 3.6 \times 10^{-2} \text{ cm} = 0.36 \text{ mm}$$

The change in length of the composite rod is the sum of these: 0.72 mm

35. D is correct.

Diverging mirrors (i.e. convex mirrors) are curved outward toward the light source and therefore have a focal point *behind* the mirror, so the focal length f is a negative value.

Using the equation for focal length:

$$1 / f = 1 / d_o + 1 / d_i$$

where d_o is the distance to the light source and d_i is the distance to the image.

$$-1 / 6 \text{ m} = 1 / 12 \text{ m} + 1 / d_i$$
$$1 / d_i = -1 / 4 \text{ m}$$
$$d_i = -4 \text{ m}$$

36. D is correct.

$$P = IV$$
$$P = (2 \text{ A})\cdot(120 \text{ V})$$
$$P = 240 \text{ W}$$

37. C is correct.

$V = IR$

$I = V / R$

$I = (120 \text{ V}) / 12 \text{ } \Omega$

$I = 10 \text{ A}$

38. C is correct.

$\Delta d = v \Delta t$

$\Delta d = (-3 \text{ m/s}) \cdot (4 \text{ s})$

$\Delta d = -12 \text{ m}$

$d - d_0 = -12 \text{ m}$

$d - 4 \text{ m} = -12 \text{ m}$

$d = -8 \text{ m}$

39. C is correct. The source is stationary and the detector is traveling towards the source at $v_d = 50$ m/s. Since they are moving toward each other, the velocity of the detector is positive and the detected frequency will be higher than the emitted frequency.

For the frequency perceived when the source of noises is approaching; the Doppler calculation takes the form:

$f_{observed} = f_{source} (v + v_{observer}) / (v - v_{source})$

$f_{observed} = (420 \text{ Hz}) \times [(350 \text{ m/s} + 50 \text{ m/s}) / (350 \text{ m/s} - 0 \text{ m/s})]$

$f_{observed} = 420 \text{ Hz} \times 1.14$

$f_{observed} = 480 \text{ Hz}$

40. A is correct. Beats are observed when two sound waves of different frequency approach and the alternating constructive/destructive causes the sound to be soft and loud.

$f_{beat} = |f_1 - f_2|$

41. B is correct. The extension x beyond the resting length is given by:

$x = F_{spring} / k$

spring force $\leftarrow$ M $\rightarrow$ centripetal force

$F_{spring} = F_{centripetal}$

$x = (12 \text{ N}) / (40 \text{ N/m})$

$x = 0.3 \text{ m}$

Since the radius of the circle of revolution is 2 m and the spring is pulling, the resting length of the spring is (2 m − 0.3 m) = 1.7 m.

42. E is correct. The acceleration of a point on a rotating circle is the centripetal acceleration:

$a_c = v^2 / r$

where $r = 7.2$ cm $= 0.072$ m

Convert rpm to rps:

(2,640 rotation/min)·(1 min / 60 s) = 44 rps

The speed of a point on the edge of the motor is:

$v = C / T,$

where C is the circumference and T is the period of revolution.

Calculate the circumference:

$C = 2\pi r$

$C = 2\pi(0.072$ m$) = 0.45$ m

Calculate the speed:

$v = (0.45$ m$) / (1$ s $/ 44$ rps$)$

$v = 19.81$ m/s

$a = v^2 / r$

$a = (19.81$ m/s$)^2 / (0.072$ m$)$

$a = 5,451$ m/s^2

43. D is correct.

$x = x_0 + v_0t + \frac{1}{2}at^2$

where $t = 0.51$ s

$x = 0 + 0 + \frac{1}{2}at^2$

$x = \frac{1}{2}at^2$

$2x / t^2 = a$

$2(1$ m$) / (0.51$ s$)^2 = a$

$a = 2$ m $/ 0.26$ s^2

$a = 7.7$ m/s^2

$(m_1 + m_2)a = m_1g - m_2g$

$m_1a + m_2a = m_1g - m_2g$

$m_2(a + g) = m_1(g - a)$

$m_2 = [m_1(g - a)] / (a + g)$

$m_2 = [(100$ kg$)·(9.8$ m/s$^2 - 7.7$ m/s$^2)] / (7.7$ m/s$^2 + 9.8$ m/s$^2)$

$m_2 = [(100$ kg$)·(2.1$ m/s$^2)] / (17.5$ m/s$^2)$

$m_2 = 12$ kg

44. A is correct. In projectile motion, the projectile is always experiencing a net force downward due to gravity, which is why it accelerates when traveling downward and decelerates when traveling upward. Since deceleration upward is equivalent to acceleration downward, the rock is always accelerating downward.

45. C is correct.

46. E is correct.

The object has constant velocity upward and the force necessary to propel the object is also constant and upward.

> Power = Watts / time
>
> $W = Fd$
>
> $P = Fd / t$
>
> $d / t = v$
>
> $P = Fv$
>
> $P = (50 \text{ N}) \cdot (10 \text{ m/s})$
>
> $P = 500 \text{ W}$

47. D is correct.

For a pipe closed at one end, the harmonic frequencies are odd multiples of the fundamental frequency, so n = 1, 3, 5….

The harmonic frequency has a wavelength $\lambda_n = 4L / n$

The wavelength of the fundamental frequency is:

> $\lambda_1 = 4L / 1$
>
> $\lambda_1 = 4L$

Since the wavelength is four times greater than the length of the pipe, the pipe accommodates ¼λ, and therefore it has a displacement node at the closed end and an antinode at the open end.

48. A is correct. Charged objects always interact with other charged objects.

If electric charge is conserved, by definition charge cannot be created or destroyed.

Electrons and protons are the fundamental particles that carry charge.

Therefore the charge of any object is a whole-number multiple of an electron ($Q = ne^-$).

The electric charge of an object can be infinitely large, so there are infinite whole-number multiples of an electron's charge.

Because charge is a whole-number multiple of an electron's charge, it cannot have a value that is not a whole-number multiple, and therefore it occurs in restricted quantities.

49. E is correct.

The velocity of light in a medium is:

$$v = c / n$$

where c is the speed of light in a vacuum and n is the refractive index.

Thus, light travels slower in glass because its refraction index is higher than that of air.

50. B is correct.

Area under a curve is the same as taking the integral of velocity with respect to time.

The integral of velocity with respect to time gives displacement.

51. E is correct.

Momentum is conserved in the collision, so it neither increases nor decreases.

Kinetic energy is also conserved in the collision since the collision is elastic; the pucks are made of rubber and, due to the frictionless surface, bounce off each other without losing any speed.

If these pucks have identical masses and travel towards each other with identical speeds, each puck will have a final velocity that is equal in magnitude but opposite in direction to its initial velocity.

52. D is correct.

$$c = \lambda f$$
$$\lambda = c / f$$
$$\lambda = (3 \times 10^8 \text{ m/s}) / (2.4 \times 10^{20} \text{ Hz})$$
$$\lambda = 1.25 \times 10^{-12} \text{ m}$$
$$r = 5 \times 10^{-13} \text{ cm} = 5 \times 10^{-15} \text{ m}$$
$$\lambda / r = (1.25 \times 10^{-12} \text{ m}) / (5 \times 10^{-15} \text{ m})$$
$$\lambda / r = 250$$

53. E is correct. The Carnot cycle is an idealized thermodynamic cycle consisting of two isothermal processes and two adiabatic processes. It is the most efficient heat engine operating between two temperatures.

54. D is correct.

Series: $R_{tot} = R_1 + R_2 + R_3$

Parallel: $1 / R_{tot} = 1 / R_1 + 1 / R_2 + 1 / R_3$

55. D is correct.

In the photoelectric effect, photons from a light source are absorbed by electrons on a metal surface and cause them to be ejected. The energy of the ejected electrons is only dependent upon photon frequency and is found by:

$$KE = hf - \phi$$

where h = Planck's constant, f = frequency and ϕ = stopping potential

Increasing the intensity of the light only increases the number of photons incident upon the metal and thus the number of ejected electrons but their KE does not change.

We want to hear from you

Your feedback is important to us because we strive to provide the highest quality prep materials. If you have any questions, comments or suggestions, email us, so we can incorporate your feedback into future editions.

Customer Satisfaction Guarantee

If you have any concerns about this book, including printing issues, contact us and we will resolve any issues to your satisfaction.

info@sterling-prep.com

Diagnostic Test #3 – Explanations

1. D is correct. There is no acceleration in the horizontal direction, so velocity is constant.

$v_{0x} = v_x$

$d = v_x \times t$

$d = (30 \text{ m/s}){\cdot}(75 \text{ s})$

$d = 2{,}250 \text{ m}$

2. A is correct.

$F_{\text{friction}} = \mu_k N$

3. D is correct. The rate of heat transfer:

$Q / t = k A \Delta T / d$

where k is the thermal conductivity of the wall material, A is the surface area of the wall, d is the wall's thickness and ΔT is the temperature difference on either side.

Therefore, if thickness d is doubled, the rate is halved.

4. E is correct. Energy can exist as work, PE, KE, heat, waves, etc.

The statement ability to do work describes PE

The other statements describe work which is a form of energy.

5. E is correct. The displacement of the tines of a tuning fork from their resting positions is a measure of the amplitude of the resulting sound wave.

6. D is correct. $I \text{ (dB)} = 10 \log_{10}(I / I_o)$

7. B is correct. The forces on the block (with bullet) are gravity and the tension of the string. The tension is perpendicular to the direction of travel, so the tension does no work. This problem is solved using conservation of energy, assuming a full transfer of KE into gravitational PE.

KE (block with bullet at bottom) = PE (block with bullet at top)

$\frac{1}{2}mv^2 = mgh$, cancel m from both sides of the expression

$\frac{1}{2}v^2 = gh$

$\frac{1}{2}(2 \text{ m/s})^2 = (9.8 \text{ m/s}^2)h$

$\frac{1}{2}(4 \text{ m}^2/\text{s}^2) = (9.8 \text{ m/s}^2)h$

$(2 \text{ m}^2/\text{s}^2) = (9.8 \text{ m/s}^2)h$

$$h = (2\ m^2/s^2)\ /\ (9.8\ m/s^2)$$
$$h = 0.20\ m = 20\ cm$$

8. B is correct. Voltage results in a current but not vice versa.

Voltage is a potential difference across a circuit but does not flow through it.

9. C is correct.

voltage = current × resistance

$$V = IR$$
$$V = (10\ A)\cdot(5\ \Omega)$$
$$V = 55\ V$$

10. C is correct. Ultraviolet radiation has the highest frequency among the choices.

Energy is related to frequency by:

$$E = hf$$

Thus ultraviolet light has the most energy per photon because it has the highest frequency which is directly proportional to energy.

11. E is correct.

This is an example of a β^- decay.

A neutron converts to a proton and an electron (e^-) along with an electron neutrino (v_e).

12. C is correct. Moment of inertia I is defined as the ratio of the angular momentum L of a system to its angular velocity ω around a principal axis.

Moment of inertia:

$$I = L\ /\ \omega$$

Angular acceleration around a fixed axis:

$$\tau = \alpha I$$

Mass moment of inertia of a thin disk:

$$I = \tfrac{1}{2}mr^2$$
$$\tau = \alpha(\tfrac{1}{2}mr^2)$$
$$m = (2\tau)\ /\ \alpha r^2$$
$$m = [(2)\cdot(14\ N\cdot m)]\ /\ [(5.3\ rad/s^2)\cdot(0.6\ m)^2]$$
$$m = 14.7\ kg$$

13. C is correct.

$$v = v_0 + at$$

$$29 \text{ m/s} = 0 + (10 \text{ m/s}^2)t$$

$$v = at$$

$$t = v \,/\, a$$

$$t = (29 \text{ m/s}) \,/\, (10 \text{ m/s}^2)$$

$$t = 2.9 \text{ s}$$

$$y = \tfrac{1}{2}at^2$$

$$y = \tfrac{1}{2}(10 \text{ m/s}^2){\cdot}(2.9 \text{ s})^2 + 1 \text{ m}$$

$$y = \tfrac{1}{2}(10 \text{ m/s}^2){\cdot}(8.41 \text{ s}^2) + 1 \text{ m}$$

$$y = 42 \text{ m} + 1 \text{ m}$$

$$y = 43 \text{ m}$$

14. B is correct. Resonant frequency of a spring mass system:

$$\omega = \sqrt{(k \,/\, m)}$$

Increasing the spring constant k results in a higher resonant frequency.

15. C is correct. Sound velocity in an ideal gas:

$$v_{\text{sound}} = \sqrt{(yRT \,/\, M)}$$

where y = adiabatic constant, R = gas constant, T = temperature and M = molecular mass of gas. Increasing the temperature increases the velocity of sound in air.

16. E is correct. Photon energy:

$$E = hf$$

$$f = c \,/\, \lambda$$

$$f = (3 \times 10^8 \text{ m/s}) \,/\, (6.5 \times 10^{-6} \text{ µm})$$

$$f = 4.6 \times 10^{13} \text{ Hz}$$

$$E = (4.136 \times 10^{-15} \text{ eV·s}){\cdot}(4.6 \times 10^{13} \text{ Hz})$$

$$E = 0.19 \text{ eV}$$

17. E is correct. The Earth's magnetic field is thought to be created by circulating electric currents in the Earth's mantle (liquid portion). These charges move slowly due to the convection currents in the mantle and create the magnetic field through the large number of charges present.

18. B is correct. Polarity switches twice per wavelength.

There are 60 λ per second.

$2 \times f = $ # polarity switches

$2 \times 60 = 120$ times/s

19. B is correct. A blue object illuminated with yellow light appears black because it absorbs the yellow light and reflects none.

20. C is correct.

$${}^{A}_{Z}X \rightarrow {}^{A-4}_{Z-2}Y + {}^{4}_{2}\alpha$$

Alpha decay: the parent nuclide ejects two protons and two neutrons as ${}^{4}_{2}He$ (essentially a helium nucleus). The daughter nucleus has an atomic number of two less than the parent nucleus and an atomic weight of four less than the parent nucleus.

21. E is correct. From the Second Law of Thermodynamics: it is not possible to extract heat from a hot reservoir and convert it all into useful work.

The maximum efficiency is that of a Carnot cycle given as:

$$\eta = (Q_H - Q_C) / Q_H$$

22. C is correct. Centripetal acceleration:

$F_c = (m) \cdot (v^2 / r)$

$F_c = (1{,}200 \text{ kg}) \cdot [(3.5 \text{ m/s})^2 / 4 \text{ m}]$

$F_c = (1{,}200 \text{ kg}) \cdot [(12.25 \text{ m}^2/\text{s}^2) / 4 \text{ m}]$

$F_c = (1{,}200 \text{ kg}) \cdot (3 \text{ m/s}^2)$

$F_c = 3{,}600 \text{ N}$

23. D is correct. Frequency, length, and velocity are related by:

$f = v / 2L$

$v = f \times 2L$

$v = (440 \text{ Hz}) \cdot (2 \times 0.14 \text{ m})$

$v = 123.2 \text{ m/s} \approx 123 \text{ m/s}$

$L = v / 2f$

$L = (123 \text{ m/s}) / (2) \cdot (520 \text{ Hz})$

$L = 0.118 \text{ m}$

$\Delta L = 0.14 \text{ m} - 0.118 \text{ m}$

$\Delta L = 0.022 \text{ m} = 2.2 \text{ cm}$

24. C is correct.

$F_{tot} = F_{gravity} + F_{friction}$

$ma_{tot} = mg \sin \theta + \mu_k mg \cos \theta$, cancel m from both sides

$a_{tot} = g(\sin \theta + \mu_k \cos \theta)$

$a_{tot} = -9.8 \text{ m/s}^2(\sin 30^o + 0.3 \cos 30^o)$

$a_{tot} = -7.44 \text{ m/s}^2$

Find time taken to reach 0 m/s:

$v_f = v_0 + at$

$0 \text{ m/s} = 14 \text{ m/s} + (-7.44 \text{ m/s}^2)t$

$t = 1.88 \text{ s}$

$x = x_0 + v_0 t + \frac{1}{2}at^2$

$x = 0 \text{ m} + (14 \text{ m/s}) \cdot (1.88 \text{ s}) + \frac{1}{2}(-7.44 \text{ m/s}^2) \cdot (1.88 \text{ s})^2$

$x = 13.2 \text{ m}$

Find vertical component of x:

$y = x \sin \theta$

$y = (13.2 \text{ m}) \sin 30°$

$y = 6.6 \text{ m}$

25. B is correct. Magnetic moment of a circular loop:

$\mu = IA$

$A = (\pi r^2)$

$\mu = I(\pi r^2)$

If r is doubled:

$\mu = I\pi(2r)^2$

$\mu = I\pi(4r^2)$

The magnetic moment increases by a factor of 4.

26. C is correct. First, find the total resistance of each set of resistors in parallel:

Resistors in parallel:

$1 / R_{total} = 1 / R_1 + 1 / R_2 \ldots + 1 / R_n$

$1 / R_{total} = 1 / 600 \text{ } \Omega + 1 / 600 \text{ } \Omega$

$R_{total} = 300 \text{ } \Omega$

The two sets of parallel resistors are in series. Resistors in series:

$$R_{total} = R_1 + R_2 \ldots + R_n$$
$$R_{total} = 300\ \Omega + 300\ \Omega$$
$$R_{total} = 600\ \Omega$$

27. E is correct.

28. B is correct. De Broglie equation:

$$\lambda = h / mv$$

If velocity increases then λ decreases because they are inversely proportional.

29. C is correct. The slope of the line is the derivative of the position vs. time graph.

The derivative of a position graph gives velocity. Thus, at a single point along the line, the instantaneous velocity is given.

30. B is correct.

Newton's Third Law: for every action there is an equal and opposite reaction force

31. E is correct.

$$F = ma$$
$$m = F / a$$
$$m_1 = (69\ N) / (9.8\ m/s^2)$$
$$m_1 = 7.04\ kg$$
$$m_2 = (94\ N) / (9.8\ m/s^2)$$
$$m_2 = 9.59\ kg$$
$$m_1 r_1 = m_2 r_2$$
$$m_1 / m_2 = r_2 / r_1$$
$$m_1 / m_2 = (7.04\ kg) / (9.59\ kg)$$
$$m_1 / m_2 = 0.734$$
$$r_2 / r_1 = 0.734$$
$$r_2 + r_1 = 10\ m$$

Two equations, two unknowns:

Eq$_1$: $r_2 + r_1 = 10\ m$

Eq$_2$: $r_2 - (0.734) \cdot (r_1) = 0$

Multiply Eq$_2$ by -1 and add to Eq$_1$:

$$(1.734)r_1 = 10\ m$$
$$r_1 = 5.8\ m$$

32. A is correct. The potential energy of a system can be zero because potential energy is defined against an arbitrary reference point. In a gravitational potential problem, if the reference point is ground level and the object is below ground level, it will have a negative potential energy relative to the reference point.

33. D is correct.

$\lambda = 2$ m and T = 1 s

$f = 1 / T$

$f = 1 / 1$ s

$f = 1$ Hz

$v = f\lambda$

$v = (1$ Hz$)\cdot(2$ m$)$

$v = 2$ m/s

34. C is correct.

$\Delta E = E_2 - E_1$

$\Delta E = 110$ J $- 40$ J

$\Delta E = 70$ J

35. D is correct. A plane mirror has a magnification of m = 1.

$m = -d_i / d_o$

$m = h_i / h_o$

$1 = -d_i / d_o$

$1 = h_i / h_o$

$-d_i = d_o$

$h_i = h_o$

The negative image distance indicates that the image is virtual and the positive image height indicates that the image is erect.

36. A is correct.

Current through 8 Ω resistor:

$V = IR$

$V = 8\ \Omega \times 0.8$ A

$V = 6.4$

$I = 6.4$ V $/ 16\ \Omega$

$I = 0.4$ A

$I_{total} = 0.4$ A + 0.8 A

$I_{total} = 1.2$ A

Voltage drop across 20 Ω resistor:

$V = IR$

$V = (1.2$ A$)\cdot(20$ Ω$)$

$V = 24$ V

$V_{total} = 6.4$ V + 24 V

$V_{total} = 30.4$ V

Voltage is the same in parallel, thus 30.4 V goes across the 6 Ω and 2 Ω resistors:

$I = V / R$

$I = (30.4$ V$) / (2$ Ω$)$

$I = 15.2$ A

37. B is correct. Force exerted on a particle of charge q:

$F = qE$

Work is being done on the proton because it is speeding up. The acceleration of the proton is to the right so the force is also to the right. Therefore, the electric field must be to the right.

38. B is correct. First determine how long it takes the ball to drop 50 m:

PE = KE

$mgh = \frac{1}{2}mv_{yf}^2$, cancel m from both sides of the expression

$gh = \frac{1}{2}v_{yf}^2$

$v_{yf}^2 = 2gh$

$v_{yf}^2 = (2)\cdot(10$ m/s$^2)\cdot(50$ m$)$

$v_{yf}^2 = 1{,}000$ m^2/s^2

$v_{yf} \approx 32$ m/s

$t = (v_{yf} - v_{yi}) / a$

$t = (32$ m/s $- 0) / (10$ m/s$^2)$

$t = 3.2$ s

Calculate the distance traveled horizontally in 3.2 s:

$d_x = v_x \times t$

$d_x = (5$ m/s$)\cdot(3.2$ s$)$

$d_x = 16$ m

39. A is correct.

Simple harmonic motion equation:

position: $y = A \sin \omega t$

acceleration: $a = -\omega^2 A \sin \omega t$

$a = -\omega^2 y$

From the position and acceleration equations of motion, acceleration is directly proportional to position.

40. B is correct.

Period of a pendulum:

$T = 2\pi\sqrt{(L / g)}$

The period does not depend on mass, so changes to M do not affect the period.

41. A is correct.

Work equation:

$W = Fd$

$W = (70 \text{ N}) \cdot (45 \text{ m})$

$W = 3{,}150 \text{ J}$

Power equation:

$P = W / t$

$P = (3{,}150 \text{ J}) / (60 \times 30 \text{ s})$

$P = (3{,}150 \text{ J}) / (180 \text{ s})$

$P = 18 \text{ W}$

42. C is correct.

Balance the counterclockwise (CCW) torque with the sum of the two clockwise (CW) torques.

The CCW torque due to the weight of the man is:

$\tau = r_1 F_1$

$F = mg$

where g = acceleration due to gravity

$\tau = r_1(m_1 g)$

$\tau = 5.5 \text{ m} \times 105 \text{ kg} \times g$

$\tau = 578 \, g$

The total CW torque due to the weight of the two children is:

$$\tau = r_2F_2 + r_3F_3$$

$$\tau = r_2mg + r_3mg$$

$$\tau = (r_2 \times m_2 \times g) + (r_3 \times m_3 \times g)$$

$$\tau = (r_2 \times 20 \times g) + (10 \times 20 \times g)$$

$$\tau = (20r_2 \times g) + (200 \times g)$$

$$\tau = g(20r_2 + 200)$$

Set the two expressions equal to each other,

$578\ g = g(20r_2 + 200)$, cancel g from both sides of the expression

$$578 = 20r_2 + 200$$

$$378 = 20r_2$$

$$r_2 = 378 / 20$$

$$r_2 = 19\ m$$

43. E is correct.

In a circular path, the object's direction of motion is always changing.

Therefore, the velocity is not constant.

The acceleration (i.e. centripetal force) points toward the center of the circular path.

44. A is correct.

$$v_y = 3.13 \sin 30°$$

$$v_y = 1.6\ m/s$$

$$v_f = v_o + at$$

$$0 = (1.6\ m/s) + (-9.8\ m/s^2)t$$

$$(9.8\ m/s^2)t = (1.6\ m/s)$$

$$t = (1.6\ m/s) / (9.8\ m/s^2)$$

$$t = 0.16\ s$$

$v_i = 3.13$ m/s, v_y, $30°$, v_x

45. B is correct.

Boltzmann's constant (k) relates energy at the individual particle level to temperature. $k =$ gas constant (R) divided by Avogadro's constant (N_A).

$$k_B = R / N_A$$

where $k_B = 1.381 \times 10^{-23}$ J/K

Boltzmann's constant has the same dimensions as entropy (energy / temperature)

46. A is correct.

Before it is released, the hammer has zero velocity and a gravitational PE of *mgh*. This PE is converted completely into KE when it reaches the ground.

PE (top) = KE (bottom)

$mgh_0 = \frac{1}{2}m(v_0^2)$, cancel *m* from both sides of the expression

$v_0 = \sqrt{(2gh_0)}$

If h_0 increases by a factor of 2, substitute $2h_0$ for h_0

$v = \sqrt{[2g(2h_0)]}$

$v = \sqrt{2} \times \sqrt{2gh_0}$

$v = \sqrt{2} \times (v_0)$

The new velocity is $\sqrt{2}$ times faster.

47. D is correct.

Perceived color of light depends on frequency and wavelength which are related to each other through the speed of light:

$c = f\lambda$

48. A is correct.

An electric current measures the amount of charge passing a point in the circuit per unit of time. In a flow of water, the analogous parameter is the volume (i.e. amount) of water passing a point per unit of time (i.e. volume flow rate).

By analogy, the current is the same for resistors in series, and the volume flow rate is constant (absent any branching) along a flow, which is not true of flow velocity.

49. E is correct.

$v = c\,/\,n$

$v = 3 \times 10^8 \text{ m/s} \,/\, 2$

$v = 1.5 \times 10^8 \text{ m/s}$

50. A is correct.

For constant acceleration, the velocity increases with time. If velocity increases with time, the position vs. time line of the graph is curved over each time interval.

51. C is correct.

Use conservation of momentum for momenta in the *x* coordinate to solve for the *x* component of the second ball's final velocity.

Use *m* as the mass for the first ball and 1.4*m* as mass of the second ball.

$p_{before} = p_{after}$

$m(4 \text{ m/s}) \cos 60° = 1.4mv_x$

$v_x = (4 \text{ m/s}) \cdot (\cos 60°) / 1.4$

$v_x = (4 \text{ m/s}) \cdot (0.5) / 1.4$

$v_x = 1.4 \text{ m/s}$

52. A is correct. In a longitudinal wave, the particle displacement is parallel to the direction of the wave, resulting in a distribution of compressions and rarefactions.

Rarefaction is the decrease in an item's density and it is the opposite of compression. Like compression, which can travel in waves (e.g. sound waves), rarefaction waves also exist in nature. A common example of rarefaction is the area of low relative pressure following a shock wave.

Compression is the increase in an items density.

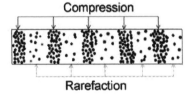

53. A is correct.

$Q = c_p m \Delta T$

$c_{p1} m_w \Delta T = c_{p2} m \Delta T$

$c_{p2} = (c_{p1} m_w \Delta T_w) / (m_2 \Delta T_2)$

$c_{p2} = (1 \text{ kcal/kg} \cdot °C) \cdot (0.2 \text{ kg}) \cdot (40 \text{ °C}) / (0.06 \text{ kg}) \cdot (60 \text{ °C})$

$c_{p2} = 2.2 \text{ kcal/kg} \cdot °C$

54. A is correct. The magnetic force on a charged particle can change the velocity and direction of the particle but cannot change its speed.

Kinetic energy is calculated using the square of speed:

$KE = \frac{1}{2}mv^2$

Thus if speed does not change the energy of the charge does not change.

55. B is correct.

Beta (β^-) decay: the parent nuclide ejects an electron and electron antineutrino. However, in the process a neutron converts to a proton so the mass number remains the same but the atomic number increases by 1.

$$^A_Z X \rightarrow {}^{A}_{Z+1} Y + {}^{0}_{-1}e^- + {}^{0}_{0}v_e$$

Diagnostic Test #4 – Explanations

1. E is correct.

$$v_f^2 = v_0^2 + 2ad$$

where $v_0 = 0$

$$v_f^2 = 0 + 2ad$$

$$v_f^2 = 2ad$$

Since a is constant, d is proportional to v_f^2

If v_f increases by a factor of 4, then d increases by a factor of $4^2 = 16$.

2. B is correct.

The period of a satellite is found through Kepler's Third Law:

$$T = 2\pi\sqrt{(r^3 / GM)}$$

where T = period, r = distance from Earth's center, G = gravitational constant and M = mass of Earth

The period does not depend on the mass of the satellite so the period remains the same.

3. B is correct.

Heat conduction follows the equation:

$$\Delta Q / \Delta t = kA\Delta T / d$$

Assuming all other values are constant the equation can be written as:

$$\Delta Q / \Delta t = (1 / d)x$$

where x is a constant

The rate of heat loss is inversely proportional to the thickness, so by increasing d, the slope of the curve is negative.

4. B is correct.

The arrows experience the same stopping force when they impart the hay bales.

The kinetic energy can be related to the work done by the force:

Arrow 1: $KE_1 = W$

              $KE_1 = Fd_1$

              $d_1 = KE_1 / F$

Arrow 2: $KE_2 = 2KE_1$

              $2KE_1 = W$

              $2KE_1 = Fd_2$

              $d_2 = 2KE_1 / F$

              $d_2 = 2d_1$

---

5. E is correct.

The period of a pendulum:

$$T = 2\pi\sqrt{(L / g)}$$

where L is the length of the pendulum and g is acceleration due to gravity.

Use $g / 6$ for g.

$$T = 2\pi\sqrt{(L / (g / 6))}$$

$$T = 2\pi\sqrt{(6L / g)}$$

$$T = 2\pi\sqrt{(L / g)} \times \sqrt{6}$$

New period = $T\sqrt{6}$

6. D is correct.

Decibels use a logarithmic scale.

$$\text{Intensity (dB)} = 10\log_{10}[I / I_0]$$

Where I_0 is the intensity at the threshold of hearing (10^{-12} W/m^2)

$$I = 10\log_{10}[10^{-7} \text{ W/m}^2 / 10^{-12} \text{ W/m}^2]$$

$$I = 10\log_{10}[10^5]$$

$$I = 50 \text{ dB}$$

7. B is correct.

Find the amount of time it takes the ball to fall 1 m from the apex:

$$\Delta x = v_0 t + \tfrac{1}{2}at^2$$

$$1 \text{ m} = (0 \text{ m/s})t + \tfrac{1}{2}(9.8 \text{ m/s}^2)t^2$$

$$1 \text{ m} = \tfrac{1}{2}(9.8 \text{ m/s}^2)t^2$$

$$1 \text{ m} = 4.9 \text{ m/s}^2 t^2$$

$$t = \sqrt{(1 \text{ m} / 4.9 \text{ m/s}^2)}$$

$$t = 0.452 \text{ s}$$

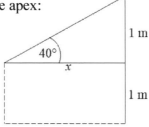

Find initial upward velocity of the ball:

$$v^2 = v_0^2 + 2a\Delta x$$

$$0 \text{ m/s} = v_0^2 + 2(-9.8 \text{ m/s}^2)\cdot(1 \text{ m})$$

$$0 \text{ m/s} = v_0^2 + (-19.6 \text{ m}^2/\text{s}^2)$$

$$19.6 \text{ m}^2/\text{s}^2 = v_0^2$$

$$v_0 = \sqrt{(19.6 \text{ m}^2/\text{s}^2)}$$

$$v_0 = 4.427 \text{ m/s}$$

Calculate the horizontal velocity:

$$\tan(40°) = (4.427 \text{ m/s}) / v_h$$

$$0.839 = (4.427 \text{ m/s}) / v_h$$

$$v_h = (4.427 \text{ m/s}) / 0.839$$

$$v_h = 5.277 \text{ m/s}$$

Calculate the distance from fence using elapsed time and horizontal velocity:

$$d = v_h t$$

$$d = 5.277 \text{ m/s} \times 0.452 \text{ s}$$

$$d = 2.39 \text{ m} \approx 2.4 \text{ m}$$

8. D is correct.

Acceleration is always positive and away from charge Q.

Therefore, velocity increases (no opposing force of friction).

The energy of the system starts as electrical PE.

$$PE_{elec} = (kQq) / r$$

where r is the initial distance between the point charges.

Electrical PE is the energy required to bring a system together from the charges starting at infinity.

After charge Q has moved very far away, the energy of the system is only $KE = \frac{1}{2}mv^2$

v has a limit because KE cannot exceed kQq / r

9. C is correct.

Resistance in series experience equal current because there is only one path for the current to travel.

10. B is correct. For the critical angle, the refracted angle is 90°

$$n_{water} \sin \theta_{crit} = n_{air} \sin 90°$$

$$\sin \theta_{crit} = (n_{air} / n_{water}) \sin 90°$$

$$\theta_{crit} = \sin^{-1} [(1 / 1.33) \cdot (1)]$$

$$\theta_{crit} = \sin^{-1} (3/4)$$

11. C is correct.

Energy needed to change hydrogen from one state to another:

$$E = -13.6 \text{ eV}[(1 / n_1^2) - (1 / n_2^2)]$$

To ionize hydrogen, the electron must be removed to the n = ∞ state.

Energy needed to change from ground state:

$$E = -13.6[(1 / 1) - (1 / \infty)]$$

$$E = -13.6 \text{ eV}$$

Energy is expressed as a negative number to indicate that this much energy is needed to be input to the atom.

12. D is correct.

Find the perimeter (i.e. circumference) of the carousel: distance traveled in one revolution.

$$\text{Perimeter} = \pi \times d$$

$$\text{Perimeter} = \pi \times 18 \text{ m}$$

$$\text{Perimeter} = 56.5 \text{ m}$$

Convert to rev/min, to rev/s

$$v = (5 \text{ rev/min}) \cdot (1 \text{ min/60 s})$$

$$v = 0.083 \text{ rev/s}$$

Convert rev/s to m/s:

where 1 rev = 56.5 m

$$v = (0.083 \text{ rev/s}) \cdot (56.5 \text{ m/1 rev})$$

$$v = 4.7 \text{ m/s}$$

13. A is correct.

$$\text{Power} = \text{work} / \text{time}$$

$$\text{Power} = (\text{force} \times \text{distance}) / \text{time}$$

Newton's First Law: no force is required to keep the object moving with constant velocity.

The projectile maintains horizontal v since no forces are acting on the horizontal axis.

The vertical forces must also be balanced since it maintains its elevation (only moving horizontally).

Since there is no net force, no work is done, and therefore no power is required.

14. D is correct. Solve for spring constant k:

$$\text{PE} = \tfrac{1}{2}kx^2$$

$$k = 2(\text{PE}) / x^2$$

where x is the amplitude (maximum distance traveled from rest).

$$k = 2(10 \text{ J}) / (0.2 \text{ m})^2$$

$$k = 500 \text{ N/m}$$

Solve for the period

$$T = 2\pi[\sqrt{(m / k)}]$$

$$T = 2\pi[\sqrt{(0.4 \text{ kg} / 500 \text{ N/m})}]$$

$$T = 0.18 \text{ s}$$

Convert the period to frequency:

$$f = 1 / T$$

$$f = 1 / (0.18 \text{ s})$$

$$f = 5.6 \text{ Hz}$$

15. E is correct.

Electromagnetic waves propagate at the speed of light oscillations of electric and magnetic fields that propagate at the speed of light.

The oscillations of the two fields form a transverse wave perpendicular to each other and perpendicular to the direction of energy and wave propagation.

16. E is correct.

During beta minus decay, the parent nuclide ejects an electron and electron antineutrino. However, in the process a neutron converts to a proton so the mass number remains the same but the atomic number increases by 1.

$$^A_Z X \rightarrow \,^A_{Z+1} Y + \,^0_{-1} e^- + \,^0_0 v_e$$

17. B is correct.
When the switch is closed, current in the solenoid flows from positive to negative and the magnetic field points toward the right (by the solenoid right-hand rule).

When the switch is open, the magnetic field dissipates creating a changing magnetic flux.

According to Lenz's Law, an induced emf is produced in the second solenoid to oppose the change in magnetic flux and to keep the magnetic field constant.

By the right-hand solenoid rule, the current must flow from right to left to create a temporary magnetic field in the same direction as the original magnetic field.

18. A is correct.

Resistance in a wire:

$$R = (\rho L) / A$$

where ρ = resistivity, L = length of wire and A = cross-sectional area of wire

Cross-sectional area of a wire:

$$A = \pi r^2$$

$$A = \pi D^2 / 4$$

If D is doubled:

$$A = \pi(2D)^2 / 4$$
$$A = \pi(4D^2) / 4$$

The area is increased by a factor of 4.

The new resistance if D is doubled and L is doubled:

$$R = (\rho \times 2L) / (4A)$$
$$R = \tfrac{1}{2}(\rho L / A)$$

19. A is correct.

$$m = -d_i / d_o$$
$$m = -(-10 \text{ m}) / (5 \text{ m})$$
$$m = 2$$

The image is upright because the magnification is positive.

20. C is correct.

21. A is correct.

Kelvin is calculated as 273 more than the temperature in Celsius.

$$1 \text{ K} = 273 \text{ °C}$$

Kelvin is measured in Kelvin so there is no ° symbol as in °C

22. C is correct.

Forces in each axis must be equal.

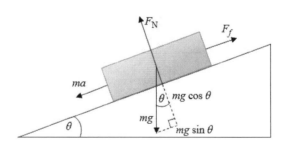

$$F_N = mg \cos \theta$$
$$F_f = \mu_f F_N$$
$$F_f = \mu_k mg \cos \theta$$

Forces along the incline:

$$ma = mg \sin \theta - F_f$$

Using the expression for F_N:

$ma = mg \sin \theta - \mu_f mg \cos \theta$, cancel m from both sides of the expression

$$a = g \sin \theta - \mu_f g \cos \theta$$
$$a = [(9.8 \text{ m/s}^2) \sin 40°] - [(0.19)\cdot(9.8 \text{ m/s}^2) \cos 40°]$$
$$a = (6.3 \text{ m/s}^2) - (1.4 \text{ m/s}^2)$$
$$a = 4.9 \text{ m/s}^2$$

23. E is correct.

The difference in intensity between a shout and a whisper is given by:

90 dB – 20 dB = 70 dB

A change of 10 decibels corresponds to a factor change of 10 in the intensity I in W/m^2.

An increase of 70 dB corresponds to an intensity increase of seven factors of 10, which equals a 10^7 or a ten million-fold increase in the intensity of the sound.

24. D is correct.

Objects in orbit around Earth still experience the force of gravity. The reason the astronauts feel weightless in space is because they are in free fall and cannot feel the force of gravity.

25. B is correct. Magnetics are materials that produce magnetic fields and can therefore exert a magnetic force. The field surrounds the magnet as shown:

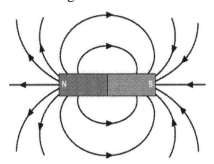

26. C is correct.

V = IR

Resistivity is the measure of resistance along the length of a given material:

$R = \rho L / A$

where ρ is resistivity

$\rho = RA / L$

$\rho = (\Omega) \cdot (m^2) / (m)$

$\rho = \Omega \cdot m$

27. D is correct.

The magnification:

m = $-d_i / d_o$

m = –3 m / 6 m

m = –½, where the negative sign indicates that the image is inverted

28. D is correct.

Uranium decays because the electromagnetic repulsion of the protons overcomes the strong nuclear force due to its limited range and the massive size of the uranium nucleus.

29. E is correct.

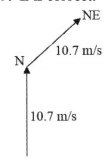

Find the horizontal component of the NE drift:

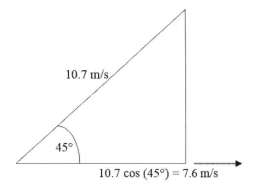

Find the horizontal component of the NW acceleration:

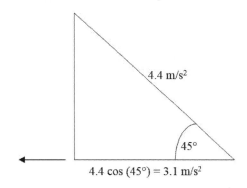

The drift is fully corrected when there is 0 horizontal velocity.

$$v_f = v_i + a_x t$$

$$0 = (7.6 \text{ m/s}) + (3.1 \text{ m/s}^2)(t)$$

$$t = (7.6 \text{ m/s}) / (3.1 \text{ m/s}^2)$$

$$t = 2.4 \text{ s}$$

30. A is correct.

$d = x_i + v_i t + \frac{1}{2} a t^2$

where $x_i = 0$ and $v_i = 0$

$d = \frac{1}{2} a t^2$

$a = \Delta v / t$

$a = (v_f - v_i) / t$

$d = \frac{1}{2} [(v_f - v_i) / t] \cdot (t^2)$

$d = \frac{1}{2} (v_f - v_i) t$

$d = \frac{1}{2} (20 \text{ m/s} - 0 \text{ m/s}) \cdot (10 \text{ s})$

$d = 100 \text{ m}$

31. B is correct. Proportionality: find the change in height that doubles the speed of impact

$PE = KE$

$mgh = mv^2$, cancel m from both sides of the expression

$gh = v^2$

h is proportional to v^2

To double v, h increases by $2^2 = 4$.

32. E is correct. There are two forces on the ball: tension and the force of gravity. When the ball is at the bottom of its circular path, tension points up and the force of gravity points down.

The tension at the bottom is related to the net force on the ball and the force of gravity:

$F_{net} = T - F_{gravity}$

$F_{net} = T - mg$

or

$T = F_{net} + mg$

The ball will be executing circular motion, but its speed will be changing. Consider the speed to be approximately constant if observed for short intervals of time, so the motion is uniform circular motion during a short interval.

For any object executing uniform circular motion the net force is the centripetal force:

$F_{net} = F_{centripetal}$

$F_{net} = mv^2/r$

Putting this into the previous equation:

$T = mv^2/r + mg$

The velocity at the bottom can be related to the initial height using conservation of energy:

$KE_{final} = PE_{initial}$

$$\tfrac{1}{2}\,mv^2 = mgh$$

The height change is equal to twice the radius:

$$\tfrac{1}{2}\,mv^2 = mg(2r)$$

Therefore:

$$mv^2 = 4mgr$$

Putting this into the equation for the tension:

$$T = (4mgr)/r + mg$$

$$T = 5mg$$

$$T = 5(4 \text{ kg}) \cdot (9.8 \text{ m/s}^2)$$

$$T = 196.0 \text{ N}$$

33. C is correct.

$$T = 12 \text{ s}$$

$$f = 1 \, / \, T$$

$$f = (1 \, / \, 12 \text{ s})$$

$$f = 0.083 \text{ Hz}$$

$$\lambda = v \, / f$$

$$\lambda = (4.5 \text{ m/s} \, / \, 0.083 \text{ Hz})$$

$$\lambda = 54 \text{ m}$$

34. C is correct. Although an iceberg has a much lower temperature than hot coffee it contains far more thermal energy due to its much greater mass.

For example, assume coffee at 90 °C goes to 80 °C:

$$Q = mc\Delta T$$

$$Q = (1 \text{ kg}) \cdot (4.2 \text{ kJ/kg} \cdot \text{K}) \cdot (90 \text{ °C} - 80 \text{ °C})$$

where specific heat for water = 4.2 kJ/kg·K

Q = 42 kJ were released during temperature change

If a 10,000 kg iceberg (very small iceberg) were to go from 0 °C to –10 °C:

$$Q = mc\Delta T$$

$$Q = (10{,}000 \text{ kg}) \cdot (2.05 \text{ kJ/kg} \cdot \text{K}) \cdot (0 \text{ °C} - (-10 \text{ °C}))$$

where specific heat for ice = 2.05 kJ/kg·K

Q = 205,000 kJ were released during temperature change

Therefore, even a small iceberg at a much lower temperature contains more thermal energy due to its far greater mass.

35. B is correct.

The equation for focal length is:

$1/f = 1/d_o + 1/d_i$

where d_o is object distance and d_i is image distance

$1/f = 1/d_o + 1/d_i$

$1/f = 1/24 \text{ cm} + 1/3 \text{ cm}$

$1/f = 1/24 \text{ cm} + 8/24 \text{ cm}$

$1/f = 0.375 \text{ cm}$

$f = 2.7 \text{ cm}$

36. A is correct.

B and C only have circuit elements in series.

In D, the resistor is in series with one of the batteries.

A correctly has the resistor and capacitor in parallel, which is between the two batteries.

37. B is correct.

The equation for the magnetic field of an infinitely long straight wire is given as:

$B = \mu I / 2\pi r$

Where μ = permittivity of free space, I = current and r is radial distance from the wire

When r doubles, B decreases by a factor of ½.

38. B is correct. According to Newton's First Law: every object remains at rest or in motion in a straight line unless acted upon by an unbalanced force. Thus if the object's motion changes an unbalanced force is being applied.

39. A is correct.

Intensity related to decibels may be expressed as:

$I(\text{dB}) = 10\log_{10}(I / I_0)$

If intensity is increased by 100:

$I(\text{dB}) = 10\log_{10}(100 / 1)$

$I(\text{dB}) = 20$

40. D is correct.

Velocity in a wire:

$v = \sqrt{[T / (m / L)]}$

$T = v^2(m / L)$

volume = $A_{\text{cross-section}} \times$ length

$V = (\pi D^2 / 4)\cdot(L)$

$m = V\rho$

$m = (\rho)\cdot(\pi D^2 / 4)\cdot(L)$

Rewrite tension formula with mass:

$T = v^2[(\rho)\cdot(\pi\rho^2 / 4)\cdot(L) / (L)]$

$T = v^2(\rho\pi\rho^2 / 4)$

$T = (42 \text{ m/s})^2 \times (\pi / 4)\cdot(2{,}600 \text{ kg/m}^3)\cdot(0.0044 \text{ m})^2$

$T = (1{,}764 \text{ m}^2/\text{s}^2)\cdot(\pi / 4)\cdot(2{,}600 \text{ kg/m}^3)\cdot(0.000019 \text{ m}^2)$

$T = 68 \text{ N}$

41. C is correct.

Force along the incline:

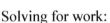

$F = mg \sin \theta$

$F = (5 \text{ kg})\cdot(9.8 \text{ m/s}^2) \sin 30°$

$F = (5 \text{ kg})\cdot(9.8 \text{ m/s}^2)\cdot(0.5)$

$F = 24.5 \text{ N}$

Solving for work:

Work = force × distance

$W = (24.5 \text{ N})\cdot(10 \text{ m})$

$W = 245 \text{ J}$

42. C is correct.

Momentum is:

$p = mv$

$v = 400 \text{ m} / 50 \text{ s}$

$v = 8 \text{ m/s}$

$p = (65 \text{ kg})\cdot(8 \text{ m/s})$

$p = 520 \text{ kg}\cdot\text{m/s}$

43. B is correct.

$F = $ mass × acceleration

$a = F / m$

$a = 40 \text{ N} / 10 \text{ kg}$

$a = 4 \text{ m/s}^2$

44. E is correct.

$$\Delta v = at$$

$$a = \Delta v \,/\, t$$

$$a = (v_f - v_i) \,/\, t$$

$$(v_f - v_i) = at$$

$$v_f = at + v_i$$

$$v_f = (2 \text{ m/s}^2) \cdot (6 \text{ s}) + (5 \text{ m/s})$$

$$v_f = 17 \text{ m/s}$$

45. A is correct.

$$KE = \tfrac{1}{2}mv^2$$

$$KE = \tfrac{1}{2}(0.83 \text{ kg}) \cdot (1{,}250 \text{ m/s})^2$$

$$KE = 6.48 \times 10^5 \text{ J}$$

Convert to calories:

$$\text{calories} = (6.48 \times 10^5 \text{ J}/1) \cdot (1 \text{ cal}/4.186 \text{ J})$$

$$\text{calories} = 1.55 \times 10^5 \text{ cal}$$

Calculate ΔT:

$$Q = cm\Delta T$$

$$\Delta T = Q \,/\, cm$$

$$\Delta T = (1.55 \times 10^5 \text{ cal}) \,/\, [(108 \text{ cal/kg} \cdot {}^\circ\text{C}) \cdot (0.83 \text{ kg})]$$

$$\Delta T = 1{,}728 \text{ }^\circ\text{C}$$

46. D is correct.

Relate KE to PE:

$$KE_B = PE_B$$

$$\tfrac{1}{2}mv_B^2 = mgh_B, \text{ cancel } m \text{ from both sides of the expression}$$

$$\tfrac{1}{2}v_B^2 = gh_B$$

$$h_B = v_B^2 \,/\, 2g$$

$$\text{If } v_M = 2v_B$$

$$h_M = (2v_B)^2 \,/\, 2g$$

$$h_M = 4v_B^2 \,/\, 2g$$

$$h_M = 4h_B$$

Mary's ball travels four times as high as Brittany's ball.

47. D is correct.

For tubes open at both ends:

$\lambda = 2L / n$

where n = 1 is the fundamental

$\lambda = 2 (0.2 \text{ m}) / 1$

$\lambda = 0.4 \text{ m}$

48. B is correct.

According to the Lorentz force law for a charged particle in a magnetic field, the magnetic force on a particle acts in a direction given by the right-hand rule.

For particles with velocity perpendicular to the field (as in this case), the magnitude of the force is:

$F_B = qvB$

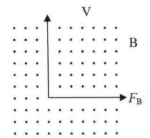

The centripetal force F_C on the proton is the magnetic force F_B:

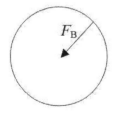

$F_B = F_C$

$qvB = (mv^2) / r$

Therefore:

$r = (mv) / (qB)$

The values for m, q and B are fixed. If the speed is increased by a factor of three, so is the radius.

Thus, the time needed to complete one circular path is:

$t = 2\pi(3r) / 3v$

$t = 2\pi r / v$, unchanged from the original time.

49. B is correct.

$$1 / f = 1 / d_i + 1 / d_o$$

$$1 / 2 \text{ m} = 1 / d_i + 1 / 6 \text{ m}$$

$$1 / 3 \text{ m} = 1 / d_i$$

$$d_i = 3 \text{ m}$$

$$m = -d_i / d_o$$

$$m = h_i / h_o$$

$$-3 \text{ m} / 6 \text{ m} = h_i / h_o$$

$$-\tfrac{1}{2} = h_i / h_o$$

For a converging lens, a positive image distance indicates a real image.

The image is inverted because $h_i / h_o = -\tfrac{1}{2}$ and h_o cannot be negative so h_i must be negative.

A negative image height indicates an inverted image.

50. D is correct.

$$F = m_0 a_0$$

$$a_0 = F / m_0$$

If m_0 is doubled:

$$a = F / (2m_0)$$

$$a = (\tfrac{1}{2})F / m_0$$

$$a = (\tfrac{1}{2})a_0$$

If the mass is doubled then the acceleration is halved.

51. C is correct.

Conservation of energy states that Δp before and after the collision is consistent.

$$p_i = p_f$$

$$p = mv$$

$$m_1 v_1 = m_2 v_2$$

$$m_1 \Delta v_1 = m_2 \Delta v_2$$

$$(6 \text{ kg}) \cdot (v_f - v_i)_1 = (8 \text{ kg}) \cdot (v_f - v_i)_2$$

$$(v_f - v_i)_1 \text{ must be larger}$$

52. B is correct.

The period of a pendulum is:

$$T = 2\pi \sqrt{(L / g)}$$

If the elevator is accelerating upwards then the constant acceleration adds to gravity and the period decreases.

$$g < g + a$$

The period decreases as the gravitational acceleration increases.

53. D is correct.

A larger coefficient of thermal expansion causes a greater size increase compared to materials with smaller coefficients of thermal expansion. If the pin were removed easily while hot it did not expand as much as material X and must have a smaller coefficient.

54. B is correct.

The magnetic force on an object changes the direction of the charge and thus the velocity. However the speed does not change. Kinetic energy is calculated using speed thus if the magnetic force does not change the speed it does not change its kinetic energy.

55. C is correct.

Heavy nuclides with atomic numbers greater than 83 almost always undergo alpha decay to reduce the number of neutrons and protons in the nucleus.

Topical
Practice Questions

Explanations

Kinematics and Dynamics – Explanations

1. D is correct.

$t = (v_f - v_i) / a$

$t = (60 \text{ mi/h} - 0 \text{ mi/h}) / (13.1 \text{ mi/h·s})$

$t = 4.6 \text{ s}$

Acceleration is in mi/h·s, so miles and hours cancel and the answer is in units of seconds.

2. B is correct. At the top of the parabolic trajectory, the vertical velocity $v_{yf} = 0$

The initial upward velocity is the vertical component of the initial velocity:

$v_{yi} = v \sin \theta$

$v_{yi} = (20 \text{ m/s}) \sin 30°$

$v_{yi} = (20 \text{ m/s})·(0.5)$

$v_{yi} = 10 \text{ m/s}$

$t = (v_{yf} - v_{yi}) / a$

$t = (0 - 10 \text{ m/s}) / (-10 \text{ m/s}^2)$

$t = (-10 \text{ m/s}) / (-10 \text{ m/s}^2)$

$t = 1 \text{ s}$

3. B is correct.

$\Delta d = 31.5 \text{ km} = 31,500 \text{ m}$

$1.25 \text{ hr} \times 60 \text{ min/hr} = 75 \text{ min}$

$\Delta t = 75 \text{ min} \times 60 \text{ s/min} = 4,500 \text{ s}$

$v_{avg} = \Delta d / \Delta t$

$v_{avg} = 31,500 \text{ m} / 4,500 \text{ s}$

$v_{avg} = 7 \text{ m/s}$

4. A is correct. Instantaneous speed is the scalar magnitude of velocity. It can only be positive or zero (because magnitudes cannot be negative).

5. C is correct.

$d = (v_f^2 - v_i^2) / 2a$

$d = [(21 \text{ m/s})^2 - (5 \text{ m/s})^2] / [2(3 \text{ m/s}^2)]$

$d = (441 \text{ m}^2/\text{s}^2 - 25 \text{ m}^2/\text{s}^2) / 6 \text{ m/s}^2$

$d = (416 \text{ m}^2/\text{s}^2) / 6 \text{ m/s}^2$

$d = 69 \text{ m}$

6. E is correct.

$$a = (v_f - v_i) / t$$

$$a = [0 - (-30 \text{ m/s})] / 0.15 \text{ s}$$

$$a = (30 \text{ m/s}) / 0.15 \text{ s}$$

$$a = 200 \text{ m/s}^2$$

To represent the acceleration in terms of *g*, divide *a* by 9.8 m/s²:

$$\# \text{ of } g = (200 \text{ m/s}^2) / 9.8 \text{ m/s}^2$$

$$\# \text{ of } g = 20 \, g$$

The initial velocity (v_i) is negative due to the acceleration of the car being a positive value. Since the car is decelerating, its acceleration is opposite of its initial velocity.

7. D is correct.

When a bullet is fired it is in projectile motion. The only force in projectile motion (if air resistance is ignored) is the force of gravity.

8. B is correct.

When a car is slowing down, it is decelerating, which is equivalent to acceleration in the opposite direction.

9. A is correct

Uniform acceleration:

$$a = \text{change in velocity} / \text{change in time}$$

$$a = \Delta v / \Delta t$$

$$\Delta v = a \Delta t$$

$$\Delta v = (20 \text{ m/s}^2) \cdot (1 \text{ s})$$

$$\Delta v = 20 \text{ m/s}$$

10. B is correct.

Uniform acceleration:

$$a = \text{change in velocity} / \text{change in time}$$

$$a = \Delta v / \Delta t$$

$$a = (40 \text{ m/s} - 15 \text{ m/s}) / 10 \text{ s}$$

$$a = (25 \text{ m/s}) / 10 \text{ s}$$

$$a = 2.5 \text{ m/s}^2$$

11. C is correct.

$$t = d / v$$
$$t = (540 \text{ mi}) / (65 \text{ mi/h})$$
$$t = 8.3 \text{ h}$$

The time she can stop is the difference between her total allowed time and the time t that it takes to make the trip:

$$t_{stop} = 9.8 \text{ h} - 8.3 \text{ h}$$
$$t_{stop} = 1.5 \text{ h}$$

12. B is correct. Velocity is the change in position with respect to time:

$$v = \Delta x / \Delta t$$

After one lap, the racecar's final position is the same as its initial position.

Thus $x = 0$, which implies the average velocity of 0 m/s.

13. A is correct.

$$d = v_i \Delta t + \tfrac{1}{2} a \Delta t^2$$
$$d = (0.2 \text{ m/s}) \cdot (5 \text{ s}) + \tfrac{1}{2} (-0.05 \text{ m/s}^2) \cdot (5 \text{ s})^2$$
$$d = 1 \text{ m} + \tfrac{1}{2} (-0.05 \text{ m/s}^2) \cdot (25 \text{ s}^2)$$
$$d = 1 \text{ m} + (-0.625 \text{ m})$$
$$d = 0.375 \text{ m} \approx 0.4 \text{ m}$$

Decelerating is set to negative.

The net displacement is the difference between the final and initial positions after 5 s.

14. C is correct.

$$a = \text{change in velocity} / \text{change in time}$$
$$a = \Delta v / \Delta t$$

15. B is correct. Convert the final speed from km/h to m/s:

$$v_f = (210 \text{ km/h}) \times [(1{,}000 \text{ m/1 km})] \times [(1 \text{ h/3,600 s})]$$
$$v_f = 58.33 \text{ m/s}$$

Calculate the acceleration necessary to reach this speed:

$$a = (v_f^2 - v_i^2) / 2d$$
$$a = [(58.33 \text{ m/s})^2 - (0 \text{ m/s})^2] / 2(1{,}800 \text{ m})$$
$$a = (3{,}402.39 \text{ m}^2/\text{s}^2) / (3{,}600 \text{ m})$$
$$a = 0.95 \text{ m/s}^2$$

16. D is correct.

The distance the rocket travels during its acceleration upward is calculated by:

$$d_1 = \tfrac{1}{2}at^2$$

$$d_1 = \tfrac{1}{2}(22 \text{ m/s}^2)\cdot(4 \text{ s})^2$$

$$d_1 = 176 \text{ m}$$

The distance from when the motor shuts off to when the rocket reaches maximum height can be calculated using the conservation of energy:

$$mgd_2 = \tfrac{1}{2}mv^2, \text{ cancel } m \text{ from both sides of the expression}$$

$$gd_2 = \tfrac{1}{2}v^2$$

where $v = at$

$$gd_2 = \tfrac{1}{2}(at)^2$$

$$d_2 = \tfrac{1}{2}(at)^2 / g$$

$$d_2 = \tfrac{1}{2}[(22 \text{ m/s}^2)\cdot(4 \text{ s})]^2 / (10 \text{ m/s}^2)$$

Magnitudes are not vectors but scalars, so no direction is needed

$$d_2 = 387 \text{ m}$$

For the maximum elevation, add the two distances:

$$h = d_1 + d_2$$

$$h = 176 \text{ m} + 387 \text{ m}$$

$$h = 563 \text{ m}$$

17. E is correct.

Speed is a scalar (i.e. one-dimensional physical property), while velocity is a vector (i.e. has both magnitude and direction).

18. B is correct.

Acceleration due to gravity is constant and independent of mass.

19. D is correct.

As an object falls its acceleration is constant due to gravity. However, the magnitude of the velocity increases due to the acceleration of gravity and the displacement increases because the object is going further away from its starting point.

20. C is correct.

The suitcase is not sitting on a surface, so there is no normal force. Jack is pushing upward, but (since the suitcase is moving at constant speed in a straight line) he is not pushing forward.

21. E is correct. Horizontal velocity (v_x):

$$v_x = d_x / t$$

$$v_x = (44 \text{ m}) / (2.9 \text{ s})$$

$$v_x = 15.2 \text{ m/s}$$

The x component of a vector is calculated by:

$$v_x = v \cos \theta$$

Rearrange the equation to determine the initial velocity of the ball:

$$v = v_x / \cos \theta$$

$$v = (15.2 \text{ m/s}) / (\cos 45°)$$

$$v = (15.2 \text{ m/s}) / 0.7$$

$$v = 21.4 \text{ m/s}$$

22. A is correct. Conservation of energy:

$mgh = \frac{1}{2}mv_f^2$, cancel m from both sides of the expression

$$gh = \frac{1}{2}v_f^2$$

$$(10 \text{ m/s}^2)h = \frac{1}{2}(14 \text{ m/s})^2$$

$$(10 \text{ m/s}^2)h = \frac{1}{2}(196 \text{ m}^2/\text{s}^2)$$

$$h = (98 \text{ m}^2/\text{s}^2) / (10 \text{ m/s}^2)$$

$$h = 9.8 \text{ m} \approx 10 \text{ m}$$

23. B is correct.

$$d = v_i t + \frac{1}{2}at^2$$

$$d = (20 \text{ m/s}) \cdot (7 \text{ s}) + \frac{1}{2}(1.4 \text{ m/s}^2) \cdot (7 \text{ s})^2$$

$$d = (140 \text{ m}) + \frac{1}{2}(1.4 \text{ m/s}^2) \cdot (49 \text{ s}^2)$$

$$d = 174.3 \text{ m} \approx 174 \text{ m}$$

24. D is correct. Force is not a scalar because it has a magnitude and direction.

25. B is correct.

$$d = \frac{1}{2}at^2$$

$$d_A = \frac{1}{2}at^2$$

$$d_B = \frac{1}{2}a(2t)^2$$

$$d_B = \frac{1}{2}a(4t^2)$$

$$d_B = 4 \times \frac{1}{2}at^2$$

$$d_B = 4d_A$$

26. E is correct.

$$d = v_{average} \times \Delta t$$

$$d = \tfrac{1}{2}(v_i + v_f)\Delta t$$

$$d = \tfrac{1}{2}(5 \text{ m/s} + 30 \text{ m/s}) \cdot (10 \text{ s})$$

$$d = 175 \text{ m}$$

27. C is correct.

If there is no acceleration, then velocity is constant.

28. D is correct.

The gravitational force between two objects in space, each having masses of m_1 and m_2, is:

$$F_G = Gm_1m_2 / r^2$$

where G is the gravitational constant and r is the distance between the two objects.

Doubling the distance between the two objects:

$$F_{G2} = Gm_1m_2 / (2r)^2$$

$$F_{G2} = Gm_1m_2 / (4r^2)$$

$$F_{G2} = \tfrac{1}{4}Gm_1m_2 / r^2$$

$$F_{G2} = \tfrac{1}{4}Gm_1m_2 / r^2$$

$$F_{G2} = \tfrac{1}{4}F_G$$

Therefore, when the distance between the objects is doubled, the force (F_G) is one fourth as much.

29. D is correct.

I: If the velocity is constant, the instantaneous velocity is always equal to the average velocity.

II and III: If the velocity is increasing, the average value of velocity over an interval must lie between the initial velocity and the final velocity. In going from its initial value to its final value, the instantaneous velocity must cross the average value at one point, regardless of whether or not the velocity is changing at a constant rate, or changing irregularly.

30. E is correct.

$$\text{velocity} = \text{acceleration} \times \text{time}$$

$$v = at$$

$$v = (10 \text{ m/s}^2) \cdot (10 \text{ s})$$

$$v = 100 \text{ m/s}$$

31. B is correct.

velocity = distance / time

$v = d / t$

d is constant, while t decreases by a factor of 3

32. C is correct. The equation for distance, given a constant acceleration and both the initial and final velocity, is:

$d = (v_i^2 + v_f^2) / 2a$

Since the car is coming to rest, $v_f = 0$

$d = v_i^2 / 2a$

If the initial velocity is doubled while acceleration and final velocity remain unchanged, the new distance traveled is:

$d_2 = (2v_i)^2 / 2a$

$d_2 = 4(v_i^2 / 2a)$

$d_2 = 4d_1$

Another method to solve this problem:

$d_1 = (29 \text{ mi/h})^2 / 2a$

$d_2 = (59 \text{ mi/h})^2 / 2a$

$d_2 / d_1 = [(59 \text{ mi/h})^2 / 2a] / [(29 \text{ mi/h})^2 / 2a]$

$d_2 / d_1 = (59 \text{ mi/h})^2 / (29 \text{ mi/h})^2$

$d_2 / d_1 = (3{,}481) / (841)$

$d_2 / d_1 = 4$

33. D is correct.

$speed_{average}$ = total distance / time

speed = (400 m) / (20 s) = 20 m/s

If this were velocity, it would be 0.

34. E is correct.

$\Delta v = a\Delta t$

$(v_f - v_i) = a\Delta t$, where $v_f = 0$ m/s (when the car stops)

$a = -0.1$ m/s^2 (negative because deceleration), $\Delta t = 5$ s

$v_i = v_f - a\Delta t$

$v_i = [(0 \text{ m/s}) - (-0.1 \text{ m/s}^2)] \cdot (5 \text{ s})$

$v_i = (0.1 \text{ m/s}^2) \cdot (5 \text{ s}) = 0.5$ m/s

35. C is correct.

If acceleration is constant then the velocity vs. time graph is linear and the average velocity is the average of the final and initial velocity.

$$v_{average} = v_f - v_i / \Delta t$$

If acceleration is not constant then the velocity vs. time graph is nonlinear.

$$v_{average} \neq v_f - v_i / \Delta t$$

36. E is correct.

Find velocity of thrown rock:

$$v_{f1}^2 - v_i^2 = 2ad$$

$$v_{f1}^2 = v_i^2 + 2ad$$

$$v_{f1}^2 = (10 \text{ m/s})^2 + [2(9.8 \text{ m/s}^2) \cdot (300 \text{ m})]$$

$$v_{f1}^2 = 100 \text{ m}^2/\text{s}^2 + 5,880 \text{ m}^2/\text{s}^2$$

$$v_{f1}^2 = 5,980 \text{ m}^2/\text{s}^2$$

$$v_{f1} = 77.33 \text{ m/s}$$

$$t_1 = (v_f - v_i) / a$$

$$t_1 = (77.33 \text{ m/s} - 10 \text{ m/s}) / 9.8 \text{ m/s}^2$$

$$t_1 = (67.33 \text{ m/s}) / (9.8 \text{ m/s}^2)$$

$$t_1 = 6.87 \text{ s}$$

Find velocity of dropped rock:

$$v_{f2} = \sqrt{2ad}$$

$$v_{f2} = \sqrt{[(2) \cdot (9.8 \text{ m/s}^2) \cdot (300 \text{ m})]}$$

$$v_{f2} = 76.7 \text{ m/s}$$

$$t_2 = (76.7 \text{ m/s}) / (9.8 \text{ m/s}^2)$$

$$t_2 = 7.82 \text{ s}$$

$$\Delta t = (7.82 \text{ s} - 6.87 \text{ s})$$

$$\Delta t = 0.95 \text{ s}$$

37. D is correct.

$$F = ma$$

Force and acceleration are directly proportional so doubling force doubles acceleration.

38. B is correct.

Velocity is defined as having a speed and direction. If either, or both, of these change then the object is experiencing acceleration.

39. E is correct. The acceleration is negative because it acts to slow the car down against the $+y$ direction.

It is unclear if the acceleration decreases in magnitude from the data provided.

40. E is correct. Total distance is represented by the area under the velocity-time curve with respect to the x-axis.

This graph can be broken up into sections; calculate the area under the curve.

$$d_{total} = d_A + d_B + d_C + d_D$$

$$d_A = \frac{1}{2}(4 \text{ m/s}) \cdot (2 \text{ s}) = 4 \text{ m}$$

$$d_B = \frac{1}{2}(4 \text{ m/s} + 2 \text{ m/s}) \cdot (2 \text{ s}) = 6 \text{ m}$$

$$d_C = (2 \text{ m/s}) \cdot (4 \text{ s}) = 8 \text{ m}$$

Since the total distance traveled needs to be calculated, the area under the curve when the velocity is negative is calculated as a positive value. Distance is a scalar quantity and therefore has no direction.

$$d_D = \frac{1}{2}(2 \text{ m/s}) \cdot (1 \text{ s}) + \frac{1}{2}(2 \text{ m/s}) \cdot (1 \text{ s}) = 2 \text{ m}$$

$$d_{total} = 4 \text{ m} + 6 \text{ m} + 8 \text{ m} + 2 \text{ m}$$

$$d_{total} = 20 \text{ m}$$

If the question was asking to find the displacement, the velocity under the curve would be calculated as negative and the answer would be 18 m.

41. C is correct.

The two bullets have different velocities when hitting the water, but they both only experience the force due to gravity. Thus the acceleration due to gravity is the same for each bullet.

42. A is correct.

$$v_f = v_i + at$$

$$v_f = 0 + (2.5 \text{ m/s}^2) \cdot (9 \text{ s})$$

$$v_f = 22.5 \text{ m/s}$$

43. E is correct. The equation for impulse is used for contact between two objects over a specified time period:

$$F\Delta t = m\Delta v$$

$$ma\Delta t = m(v_f - v_i), \text{ cancel } m \text{ from both sides of the expression}$$

$$a\Delta t = (v_f - v_i)$$

$$a = (v_f - v_i) / \Delta t$$

$a = (-2v - v) / (0.45 \text{ s})$

$a = (-3v) / (0.45 \text{ s})$

$a = (-6.7 \text{ s}^{-1})v$

Ratio $a : v = -6.7 \text{ s}^{-1} : 1$

44. B is correct. The time for the round trip is 4 s.

The weight reaches the top of its path in ½ time:

$½(4 \text{ s}) = 2 \text{ s}$, where $v = 0$

$a = \Delta v / t$ for the first half of the trip

$a = (v_f - v_i) / t$

$a = (0 - 3.2 \text{ m/s}) / 2 \text{ s}$

$a = -1.6 \text{ m/s}^2$

$|a| = 1.6 \text{ m/s}^2$

Acceleration is a vector and the negative direction only indicates direction.

45. A is correct.

$\Delta v = a\Delta t$

$\Delta v = (0.3 \text{ m/s}^2) \cdot (3 \text{ s})$

$\Delta v = 0.9 \text{ m/s}$

46. D is correct.

47. E is correct.

$d = d_0 + (v_i^2 + v_f^2) / 2a$

$d = 64 \text{ m} + (0 + 60 \text{ m/s})^2 / 2(9.8 \text{ m/s}^2)$

$d = 64 \text{ m} + (3{,}600 \text{ m}^2/\text{s}^2) / (19.6 \text{ m/s}^2)$

$d = 64 \text{ m} + 184 \text{ m}$

$d = 248 \text{ m}$

48. C is correct.

$a = (v_f^2 + v_i^2) / 2d$

$a = [(60 \text{ m/s})^2 + (0 \text{ m/s})^2] / 2(64 \text{ m})$

$a = (3{,}600 \text{ m}^2/\text{s}^2) / 128 \text{ m}$

$a = 28 \text{ m/s}^2$

49. D is correct. Expression for the time interval during constant acceleration upward:

$$d = \tfrac{1}{2}at^2$$

Solving for acceleration:

$$a = (v_f^2 + v_i^2) / 2d$$
$$a = [(60 \text{ m/s})^2 + (0 \text{ m/s})^2] / 2(64 \text{ m})$$
$$a = (3{,}600 \text{ m}^2/\text{s}^2) / (128 \text{ m})$$
$$a = 28.1 \text{ m/s}^2$$

Solving for time:

$$t^2 = 2d / a$$
$$t^2 = 2(64 \text{ m}) / 28.1 \text{ m/s}^2$$
$$t^2 = 4.5 \text{ s}^2$$
$$t = 2.1 \text{ s}$$

50. E is correct. $d = (v_i^2 + v_f^2) / 2a$, where $v_i = 0$

$$d = v_f^2 / 2a$$

For half the final velocity:

$$d_2 = (v_f / 2)^2 / 2a$$
$$d_2 = \tfrac{1}{4}v_f^2 / 2a$$
$$d_2 \approx \tfrac{1}{4}d$$

51. A is correct. $v_{\text{average}} = \Delta d / \Delta t$

52. A is correct. Use an equation that relates v, d and t:

$$d = v \times t$$
$$v = d / t$$

If v increases by a factor of 3, then t decreases by a factor of 3.

Another method to solve this problem:

$$d = vt, \; t = \text{original time and } t_N = \text{new time}$$
$$d = 3vt_N$$
$$vt = d = 3vt_N$$
$$vt = 3vt_N$$
$$t = 3t_N$$
$$t / 3 = t_N$$

Thus, if v increases by a factor of 3, then the original time decreases by a factor of 3.

53. E is correct.

$$v_f = v_i + at$$

$$t = (v_f - v_i) / a$$

Since the ball is thrown straight up, its initial speed upward equals its final speed downward (just before hitting the ground): $v_f = -v_i$

$$t = [39 \text{ m/s} - (-39 \text{ m/s})] / 9.8 \text{ m/s}^2$$

$$t = (78 \text{ m/s}) / 9.8 \text{ m/s}^2$$

$$t = 8 \text{ s}$$

54. D is correct. Since the speed is changing, the velocity is changing, and therefore there *is* an acceleration.

Since the speed is *decreasing*, the acceleration must be *in the reverse direction* (i.e. opposite to the direction of travel).

Since the particle is moving to the right, the acceleration vector points to the left.

If the speed were increasing, the acceleration is in the *same* direction as the direction of travel, and the acceleration vector points to the right.

55. A is correct.

$$W = Fd \cos \theta$$

$$F = ma$$

$$W = ma \times d \times \cos \theta$$

Larry's force is perpendicular to the direction of the package's motion ($\theta = 90°$).

Since $\cos 90° = 0$, W = 0

Work done = 0 J

56. A is correct.

The slope of a tangent line on a velocity vs. time graph is the acceleration at that time point. Thus is equivalent to taking the derivative of the velocity with respect to time to find the instantaneous acceleration.

57. C is correct. Since the car is initially traveling North, let North be the positive direction and South be the negative direction:

$$a = (v_f - v_i) / t$$

$$a = (14.1 \text{ m/s} - 17.7 \text{ m/s}) / 12 \text{ s}$$

$$a = (-3.6 \text{ m/s}) / 12 \text{ s}$$

$$a = -0.3 \text{ m/s}^2$$

$$a = 0.3 \text{ m/s}^2 \text{ South}$$

58. C is correct.

Speed is represented by the magnitude of the slope of a position vs. time plot.

A steeper slope equates to a higher speed.

59. E is correct.

If the object has not reached terminal velocity it continues to accelerate until it does and thus speed is increasing.

60. D is correct.

Let d_1 be the distance the car travels during the initial acceleration, d_2 be the distance during constant speed and d_3 be the distance as the car slows down.

$d_1 = \frac{1}{2}at^2$

$d_1 = \frac{1}{2}(2 \text{ m/s}^2) \cdot (10 \text{ s})^2$

$d_1 = 100 \text{ m}$

$d_2 = vt$

$d_2 = (at)t$

$d_2 = at^2$

$d_2 = (2 \text{ m/s}^2) \cdot (10 \text{ s})^2$

$d_2 = 200 \text{ m}$

$d_3 = (v_i^2 + v_f^2) / 2a$

$d_3 = [(20 \text{ m/s})^2 + (0 \text{ m/s})^2] / 2(2 \text{ m/s}^2)$

$d_3 = (400 \text{ m}^2/\text{s}^2) / (4 \text{ m/s}^2)$

$d_3 = 100 \text{ m}$

The total distance traveled is the sum of d_1, d_2 and d_3:

$d_{\text{total}} = 100 \text{ m} + 200 \text{ m} + 100 \text{ m}$

$d_{\text{total}} = 400 \text{ m}$

We want to hear from you

Your feedback is important to us because we strive to provide the highest quality prep materials. If you have any questions, comments or suggestions, email us, so we can incorporate your feedback into future editions.

Customer Satisfaction Guarantee

If you have any concerns about this book, including printing issues, contact us and we will resolve any issues to your satisfaction.

info@sterling-prep.com

Force, Motion, Gravitation – Explanations

1. B is correct. The tension of the string keeps the weight traveling in a circular path, otherwise it would move linearly on a tangent path to the circle.

2. E is correct. The vertical force on the garment bag from the left side of the clothesline is:

$$T_{y,\text{left}} = T \cos \theta$$

Similarly, for the right side:

$$T_{y,\text{right}} = T \cos \theta$$

where $T = 10$ N (tension) and $\theta = 60°$.

Since the garment bag is at rest, its acceleration is zero. Therefore, according to Newton's second law:

$$T_{y,\text{left}} + T_{y,\text{right}} - mg = 0 = 2T (\cos \theta) - mg$$

Or: $\quad 2T (\cos \theta) = mg$

$$m = 2T (\cos \theta) / g$$

$$m = 2(10 \text{ N}) \cdot (\cos 60°) / (10.0 \text{ m/s}^2)$$

$$m = 2(10 \text{ N}) \cdot (0.5) / (10.0 \text{ m/s}^2)$$

$$m = 1 \text{ kg}$$

3. A is correct.

An object's inertia is its resistance to change in motion.

4. C is correct.

$$(F_{\text{net}})_y = F_N - F_g$$

The car is not moving up or down, so $a_y = 0$:

$$(F_{\text{net}})_y = 0$$

$$0 = F_N - F_g$$

$$F_N = F_g$$

$$F_N = F_g \cos \theta$$

$$F_N = mg \cos \theta$$

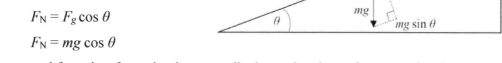

The normal force is a force that is perpendicular to the plane of contact (the slope).

5. E is correct.

$$F = ma$$
$$F = (27 \text{ kg}) \cdot (1.7 \text{ m/s}^2)$$
$$F = 46 \text{ N}$$

6. D is correct. The mass on the table causes a tension force in the string that acts against the force of gravity.

7. A is correct. Although the net force acting on the object is decreasing with time and the magnitude of the object's acceleration is decreasing there exists a positive acceleration. Therefore, the object's speed continues to increase.

8. E is correct. Objects moving at constant velocity experience zero net force on them.

9. A is correct. The sine of an angle is equal to the opposite side over the hypotenuse:

$$\sin \theta = \text{opposite} / \text{hypotenuse}$$
$$\sin \theta = h / L$$
$$h = L \sin \theta$$

10. C is correct. A car accelerating horizontally does not rely on the force of gravity to move it. Since mass does not depend on gravity, a car on Earth and a car on the Moon that experience the same horizontal acceleration also experience the same force.

11. A is correct.

$$a = (v_f - v_i) / t$$
$$a = (3.5 \text{ m/s} - 1.5 \text{ m/s}) / (3 \text{ s})$$
$$a = (2 \text{ m/s}) / (3 \text{ s})$$
$$a = 0.67 \text{ m/s}^2$$

12. E is correct. An object with uniform circular motion (i.e. constant angular velocity) only experiences centripetal acceleration directed toward the center of the circle.

13. B is correct. $F = ma$, so zero force means zero acceleration in any direction.

14. C is correct. $F = ma$

$$a = F / m$$
$$a = 9 \text{ N} / 9 \text{ kg}$$
$$a = 1 \text{ m/s}^2$$

15. E is correct.

The only force acting on a projectile in motion is the force due to gravity. Since that force always acts downward, there is always only a downward acceleration.

16. A is correct.

$$F_{net} = ma$$

If an object moves with constant v, its $a = 0$, so:

$$F_{net} = 0$$

Since gravity pulls down on the can with a force of mg:

$$F_g = mg$$
$$F_g = (10 \text{ kg}) \cdot (10 \text{ m/s}^2)$$
$$F_g = 100 \text{ N}$$

The rope pulls *up* on the can with the same magnitude of force, so the tension is 100 N, for a net force = 0.

17. D is correct.

$$F = ma$$
$$F = (1,000 \text{ kg}) \cdot (2 \text{ m/s}^2)$$
$$F = 2,000 \text{ N}$$

18. C is correct.

$$a_{cent} = v^2 / r$$
$$a_{cent} = (4 \text{ m/s})^2 / (4 \text{ m})$$
$$a_{cent} = (16 \text{ m}^2/\text{s}^2) / (4 \text{ m})$$
$$a_{cent} = 4 \text{ m/s}^2$$

19. E is correct.

Solve for m_1:

$$F_{net} = 0$$
$$m_2 g = F_T$$
$$m_1 g \sin \theta + F_f = F_T$$
$$m_1 g \sin \theta + \mu_s m_1 g \cos \theta = m_2 g$$

cancel g from both sides

$$m_1(\sin \theta + \mu_s \cos \theta) = m_2$$
$$m_1 = m_2 / (\sin \theta + \mu_s \cos \theta)$$
$$m_1 = 2 \text{ kg} / [\sin 20° + (0.55) \cos 20°]$$

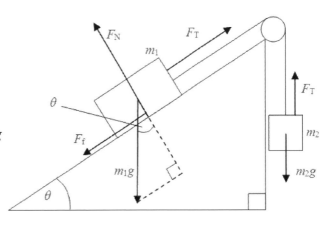

$m_1 = 2 \text{ kg} / 0.86$

$m_1 = 2.3 \text{ kg}$

Kinetic friction is only used when the mass is in motion.

20. B is correct.

Force only depends on mass and acceleration. Therefore, since the masses are identical and the acceleration is gravity for both masses, they have a net force of zero, and therefore remain stationary.

21. B is correct.

Newton's Third Law states that for every action there is an equal and opposite reaction.

22. A is correct.

Newton's Third Law states that for every action there is an equal and opposite reaction.

23. C is correct.

If w denotes the magnitude of the box's weight, then the component of this force that is parallel to the inclined plane is $w \sin \theta$, where θ is the incline angle.

If θ is less than 90°, then $\sin \theta$ is less than 1.

The component of w parallel to the inclined plane is less than w.

24. E is correct.

The package experiences projectile motion upon leaving the truck, so it experiences no horizontal forces and its initial velocity of 30 m/s remains unchanged.

25. D is correct.

f = revolutions / unit of time

Each revolution represents a length of $2\pi r$.

Velocity is the total distance / time:

$v = 2\pi r / t$

$v = 2\pi r f$

If f doubles, then v doubles.

26. A is correct.

$$F = ma$$

$$m = F \,/\, a$$

$$m = 4{,}500 \text{ N} \,/\, 5 \text{ m/s}^2$$

$$m = 900 \text{ kg}$$

27. E is correct.

Newton's First Law states that every object will remain at rest or in uniform motion unless acted upon by an outside force.

In this case, Steve and the bus are in uniform constant motion until the bus stops due to sudden deceleration (the ground exerts no frictional force on Steve). There is no force acting upon Steve. However, his inertia carries him forward because he is still in uniform motion while the bus comes to a stop.

28. D is correct.

The ball is in a state of rest, so $F_{net} = 0$

$$F_{down} = F_{up}$$

$$F_{external} + F_w = F_{buoyant}$$

$$F_{external} = F_{buoyant} - F_w$$

$$F_{external} = 8.4 \text{ N} - 4.4 \text{ N}$$

$F_{external} = 4$ N, in the same direction as the weight

29. A is correct.

The luggage and the train move at the same speed, so when the luggage moves forward with respect to the train, it means the train has slowed down while the luggage is continuing to move at the train's original speed.

30. D is correct.

The mass does not change by changing the object's location.

Since the object is outside of Earth's atmosphere, the object's weight is represented by the equation:

$$F_g = GmM_{Earth} \,/\, R^2$$

If the altitude is $2R_{Earth}$, then the distance from the center of the Earth is $3R_{Earth}$.

The gravitational acceleration decreases by a factor of $3^2 = 9$ ($g = GmM \,/\, R^2$).

Weight decreases by a factor of 9.

$$\text{New weight} = 360 \text{ N} \,/\, 9 = 40 \text{ N}$$

31. C is correct.

The rock experiences the same horizontal velocity as the truck, so as a projectile falls, it travels forward at the same velocity as the truck.

32. E is correct.

The acceleration of Jason due to thrust is:

$$F_{net} = ma_1$$

$$ma_1 = F_{ski} - \mu_k mg$$

$$a_1 = (F_{ski} - \mu_k mg) / m$$

$$a_1 = [200 \text{ N} - (0.1) \cdot (75 \text{ kg}) \cdot (9.8 \text{ m/s}^2)] / 75 \text{ kg}$$

$$a_1 = (126.5 \text{ N}) / 75 \text{ kg}$$

$$a_1 = 1.69 \text{ m/s}^2$$

The distance traveled during the acceleration stage is:

$$d_1 = \tfrac{1}{2}a_1 t^2$$

$$d_1 = \tfrac{1}{2}(1.69 \text{ m/s}^2) \cdot (67 \text{ s})^2$$

$$d_1 = 3,793 \text{ m}$$

The distance traveled after the skis run out of fuel is:

$$d_2 = (v_f^2 - v_i^2) / 2a_2$$

a_2 is Jason's acceleration after the fuel runs out:

$$F_{net} = ma_2$$

$ma_2 = -\mu_k mg$, cancel m from both sides of the expression

$$a_2 = -\mu_k g$$

$$a_2 = -(0.1) \cdot (9.8 \text{ m/s}^2)$$

$$a_2 = -0.98 \text{ m/s}^2$$

The acceleration is negative since the frictional force opposes the direction of motion.

v_i is the velocity at the moment when the fuel runs out:

$$v_i = a_1 t$$

$$v_i = (1.69 \text{ m/s}^2) \cdot (67 \text{ s})$$

$$v_i = 113.2 \text{ m/s}$$

Substitute a_2 and v_i into the equation for d_2:

$$d_2 = [(0 \text{ m/s})^2 - (113.2 \text{ m/s})^2] / 2(-0.98 \text{ m/s}^2)$$

$$d_2 = (-12,814.2 \text{ m}^2/\text{s}^2) / -1.96 \text{ m/s}^2$$

$$d_2 = 6,538 \text{ m}$$

The total distance Jason traveled is:

$d_{total} = d_1 + d_2$

$d_{total} = 3{,}793 \text{ m} + 6{,}538 \text{ m}$

$d_{total} = 10{,}331 \text{ m}$

33. D is correct.

Using energy to solve the problem:

$KE = PE + W_f$

$\frac{1}{2}mv^2 = mgd \sin \theta + \mu_k mgd \cos \theta$, cancel m from the expression

$\frac{1}{2}v^2 = gd \sin \theta + \mu_k gd \cos \theta$

$\frac{1}{2}v^2 = d(g \sin \theta + \mu_k g \cos \theta)$

$d = v^2 \,/\, [2g(\sin \theta + \mu_k \cos \theta)]$

$d = (63 \text{ m/s})^2 \,/\, [(2){\cdot}(9.8 \text{ m/s}^2){\cdot}(\sin 30° + 0.3 \times \cos 30°)]$

$d = 267 \text{ m}$

$h = d \sin \theta$

$h = (267 \text{ m}) \sin 30°$

$h = 130 \text{ m}$

Another method using balancing the forces (an alternative method but several more steps):

$F_{net} = F_g + F_{fk}$

$F_g = mg \sin \theta$

$F_g = (0.2 \text{ kg}){\cdot}(-9.8 \text{ m/s}^2) \sin 30°$

$F_g = (0.2 \text{ kg}){\cdot}(-9.8 \text{ m/s}^2){\cdot}(1/2)$

$F_g = -1 \text{ N}$

$F_{fk} = \mu_k F_N$

$F_{fk} = \mu_k mg \cos \theta$

$F_{fk} = (0.3){\cdot}(0.2 \text{ kg}){\cdot}(-9.8 \text{ m/s}^2) \cos 30°$

$F_{fk} = (0.3){\cdot}(0.2 \text{ kg}){\cdot}(-9.8 \text{ m/s}^2){\cdot}(0.866)$

$F_{fk} = -0.5 \text{ N}$

$F_{net} = -1 \text{ N} + (-0.5 \text{ N})$

$F_{net} = -1.5 \text{ N}$

$a = F_{net} \,/\, m$

$a = -1.5 \text{ N} \,/\, 0.2 \text{ kg}$

$a = -7.5 \text{ m/s}^2$

The distance it travels until it reaches a velocity of 0 at its maximum height:

$$d = (v_\mathrm{f}^2 - v_\mathrm{i}^2) / 2a$$

$$d = [(0 \text{ m/s})^2 - (63 \text{ m/s})^2] / 2(-7.5 \text{ m/s}^2)$$

$$d = (-4{,}000 \text{ m}^2/\text{s}^2) / (-15 \text{ m/s}^2)$$

$$d = 267 \text{ m}$$

The vertical height is:

$$h = d \sin \theta$$

$$h = (267 \text{ m}) \sin 30°$$

$$h = (267 \text{ m}) \cdot (0.5)$$

$$h = 130 \text{ m}$$

34. A is correct.

$$F = ma$$

$$a = F / m$$

$$a_1 = F / 4 \text{ kg}$$

$$a_2 = F / 10 \text{ kg}$$

$$4a_1 = 10a_2$$

$$a_1 = 2.5a_2$$

35. D is correct.

Mass is independent of gravity, however weight is not; as a person moves farther away from any stars or planets, the gravitational pull decreases and, therefore, her weight decreases.

36. A is correct.

Newton's Third Law states that for every action there is an equal and opposite reaction.

37. D is correct.

$$m = F / a_\mathrm{Earth}$$

$$m = 20 \text{ N} / 3 \text{ m/s}^2$$

$$m = 6.67 \text{ kg}$$

$$F_\mathrm{Moon} = mg_\mathrm{Moon}$$

$$F_\mathrm{Moon} = (6.67 \text{ kg}) \cdot (1.62 \text{ m/s}^2)$$

$$F_\mathrm{Moon} = 11 \text{ N}$$

38. B is correct.

weight = mass × gravity

$w = (0.4 \text{ kg}) \cdot (9.8 \text{ m/s}^2)$

$w \approx 4 \text{ N}$

39. B is correct.

Need an expression which connects time and mass.

Given information for F, v_1, and d:

$a = F / m$

$d = v_1 t + \frac{1}{2}at^2$

Combine the expressions and set $v_i = 0$ m/s because initial velocity is zero:

$d = \frac{1}{2}at^2$

$a = F / m$

$d = \frac{1}{2}(F / m)t^2$

$t^2 = 2dm / F$

$t = \sqrt{(2dm / F)}$

If m increases by a factor of 4, t increases by a factor of $\sqrt{4} = 2$

40. C is correct.

$a = (v_f^2 - v_i^2) / 2d$

$a = [(0 \text{ m/s})^2 - (27 \text{ m/s})^2] / 2(578 \text{ m})$

$a = (-729 \text{ m}^2/\text{s}^2) / 1{,}056 \text{ m}$

$a = -0.63 \text{ m/s}^2$

$F = ma$

$F = (1{,}100 \text{ kg}) \cdot (-0.63 \text{ m/s}^2)$

$F = -690 \text{ N}$

The car is decelerating, so the acceleration (and therefore the force) is negative.

41. A is correct.

Constant speed upward means no net force.

Tension = weight (equals Mg)

42. C is correct.

Weight $= mg$

$75 \text{ N} = mg$

$m = 75 \text{ N} / 9.8 \text{ m/s}^2$

$m = 7.65$ kg

$F_{net} = F_{right} - F_{left}$

$F_{net} = 50$ N $- 30$ N

$F_{net} = 20$ N

$F_{net} = ma$

$a = F_{net} / m$

$a = 20$ N $/ 7.65$ kg

$a = 2.6$ m/s^2

43. B is correct.

The string was traveling at the same velocity as the plane with respect to the ground outside. When the plane began accelerating backward (decelerating), the string continued to move forward at its original velocity and appeared to go towards the front of the plane.

Since the string is attached to the ceiling at one end, only the bottom of the string moved.

44. C is correct.

If the object slides down the ramp with a constant speed, velocity is constant.

Acceleration and the net force $= 0$

$F_{net} = F_{grav\ down\ ramp} - F_{friction}$

$F_{net} = mg \sin \theta - \mu_k mg \cos \theta$

$F_{net} = 0$

$mg \sin \theta - \mu_k mg \cos \theta = 0$

$mg \sin \theta = \mu_k mg \cos \theta$

$\mu_k = \sin \theta / \cos \theta$

45. A is correct.

The net force on an object in free fall is equal to its weight.

46. C is correct.

$a = \Delta v / \Delta t$

$a = (v_f - v_i) / t$

$a = (20$ m/s $- 0$ m/s$) / (10$ s$)$

$a = (20$ m/s$) / (10$ s$)$

$a = 2$ m/s^2

47. E is correct. Since the object does not move, it is in a state of equilibrium, so there are

forces acting on it that equal and oppose the force *F* that Yania applies to the object.

48. E is correct.

Newton's Third Law states that for every action there is an equal and opposite reaction.

49. C is correct.

$$F = mg$$

$$m = F / g$$

$$m = 685 \text{ N} / 9.8 \text{ m/s}^2$$

$$m = 69.9 \text{ kg} \approx 70 \text{ kg}$$

50. A is correct.

$$m_{\text{Bob}} = 4m_{\text{Sarah}}$$

Conservation of momentum:

$$m_{\text{Bob}}v_{\text{Bob}} = m_{\text{Sarah}}v_{\text{Sarah}}$$

$$4mv_{\text{Bob}} = m(4v_{\text{Sarah}})$$

51. C is correct. For most surfaces, the coefficient of static friction is greater than the coefficient of kinetic friction. Thus, the force needed to overcome static friction and start the object's motion is greater than the amount of force needed to overcome kinetic friction and keep the object moving at a constant velocity.

52. B is correct.

Weight on Jupiter:

$$W = mg$$

$$W = m(3g)$$

$$W = (100 \text{ kg}) \cdot (3 \times 10 \text{ m/s}^2)$$

$$W = 3,000 \text{ N}$$

53. D is correct.

Neither Joe nor Bill is moving, so the net force is zero:

$$F_{\text{net}} = F_{\text{Joe}} - F_{\text{T}}$$

$$0 = F_{\text{Joe}} - F_{\text{T}}$$

$$F_{\text{Joe}} = F_{\text{T}}$$

$$F_{\text{T}} = 200 \text{ N}$$

54. E is correct.

Tension in the rope is always equal to F_T.

The net force on block A to the right is:

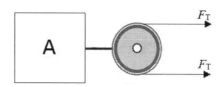

$$F_{right} = m_A a_A = 2F_T$$

The net force of block B downward is:

$$F_{down} = m_B a_B = m_B g - F_T$$

Since block A is connected to both the pulley at the end of the table and the wall, it uses twice the amount of rope length to travel the same distance as block B. Therefore, the distance block A moves is half that of block B, the velocity of block A is half the velocity of block B, and the acceleration of block A is half the acceleration of block B:

$$a_A = a_B / 2$$

$$F_{right} = m_A(a_B / 2)$$

$$m_A(a_B / 2) = 2F_T$$

$$m_A a_B = 4F_T$$

$$F_T = \tfrac{1}{4} m_A a_B$$

$$m_B a_B = m_B g - \tfrac{1}{4} m_A a_B$$

$$m_B a_B + \tfrac{1}{4} m_A a_B = m_B g$$

$$a_B[m_B + \tfrac{1}{4} m_A] = m_B g$$

$$a_B = m_B g / [m_B + \tfrac{1}{4} m_A]$$

$$a_B = (5 \text{ kg}) \cdot (9.8 \text{ m/s}^2) / [5 \text{ kg} + \tfrac{1}{4}(4 \text{ kg})]$$

$$a_B = 49 \text{ N} / 6 \text{ kg}$$

$$a_B = 8.2 \text{ m/s}^2$$

$$a_A = a_B / 2$$

$$a_A = (8.2 \text{ m/s}^2) / 2$$

$$a_A = 4.1 \text{ m/s}^2$$

55. B is correct. The force exerted by one surface on another has a perpendicular component (i.e. normal force) and a parallel component (i.e. friction force).

The force of kinetic friction on an object acts opposite to the direction of its velocity.

56. D is correct.

Before slowing down, the elevator rises at a constant velocity, so there is no net force and the scale reads the person's normal weight.

$$F = ma$$

$$600 \text{ N} = m(9.8 \text{ m/s}^2)$$

$$m = 61 \text{ kg}$$

Because the elevator is slowing down the weight will be lower.

$$F_{net} = m(g - a)$$
$$F_{net} = (61 \text{ kg}) \cdot (9.8 \text{ m/s}^2 - 6 \text{ m/s}^2)$$
$$F_{net} = 231 \text{ N}$$

57. B is correct.

Newton's Third Law states that for every action there is an equal and opposite reaction.

58. D is correct.

Since the crate can only move in the horizontal direction, only consider the horizontal component of the applied force when computing the acceleration.

$$F_x = F \cos \theta$$
$$F_x = (140 \text{ N})\cos 30°$$
$$F_x = (140 \text{ N}) \cdot (0.866)$$
$$F_x = 121 \text{ N}$$
$$a = F_x / m$$
$$a = 121 \text{ N} / 40 \text{ kg}$$
$$a = 3 \text{ m/s}^2$$

59. C is correct.

Vectors indicate magnitude and direction, while scalars only indicate magnitude.

60. B is correct.

The gravitational force and the direction of travel are perpendicular:

$$W = Fd \cos \theta$$
$$\cos \theta = 0$$

61. E is correct.

$$\text{Work} = \text{Force} \times \text{distance}$$
$$W_{rope} = Fd_x$$
$$W_{rope} = Fd \cos \theta$$
$$d = vt$$
$$d = (2.5 \text{ m/s}) \cdot (4 \text{ s})$$
$$W_{rope} = (30 \text{ N}) \cdot (10 \text{ m})\cos 30°$$
$$W_{rope} = 260 \text{ J}$$

Our guarantee – the highest quality preparation materials.

We expect our books to have the highest quality content and be error-free.

Be the first to report an error, typo or inaccuracy and receive a
$10 reward for a content error or
$5 reward for a typo or grammatical mistake.

info@sterling-prep.com

Equilibrium and Momentum – Explanations

1. A is correct.

Torque can be written as:

$\tau = I\alpha$

where I = moment of inertia and α = angular acceleration

Thus if no torque acts on the system then the average angular acceleration is zero.

Angular acceleration can be written as:

$\alpha = \Delta\omega / \Delta t$

where ω = angular speed

Angular momentum can be written as:

$L = I\omega$

If angular acceleration is zero then there is no change in angular velocity so it must be constant. Therefore, angular momentum is constant because the moment of inertia does not change.

2. D is correct.

If the velocity is 7 m/s down the mountain, the horizontal component v_x is:

$v_x = v \cos\theta$

$1.8 \text{ m/s} = (7 \text{ m/s}) \cos\theta$

$\cos\theta = 0.26$

$\theta \approx 75°$

3. E is correct.

The hill exerts a normal force on the sled. However, this force is *perpendicular* to the surface of the hill. There is no parallel force that the hill exerts because it is frictionless.

4. C is correct.

Assuming that the water flow is tangent to the wheel, it is perpendicular to the radius vector at the point of contact.

The torque around the center of the wheel is:

$\tau = rF$

$\tau = (10 \text{ m}) \cdot (300 \text{ N})$

$\tau = 3,000 \text{ N·m}$

5. E is correct.

> 1 revolution = 360°, 1 min = 60 s
>
> 33 rpm = 33 revs/min
>
> (33 revs/min)·(360°/rev) = 11,880°/min
>
> (11,880°/min)·(1 min/60 s) = 198°/s

Degrees per second is a *rate*:

> rate × time = total degrees
>
> (198°/s)·(0.32 s) ≈ 63°

6. B is correct.

> momentum = mass × velocity
>
> $p = mv$

Since momentum is directly proportional to mass, doubling the mass doubles the momentum.

7. D is correct.

The total momentum before the collision is:

> $p_{total} = m_I v_I + m_{II} v_{II} + m_{III} v_{III}$
>
> p_{before} = (1 kg)·(0.5 m/s) + (1.5 kg)·(–0.3 m/s) + (3.5 kg)·(–0.5 m/s)
>
> p_{before} = (0.5 kg·m/s) + (–0.45 kg·m/s) + (–1.75 kg·m/s)
>
> p_{before} = –1.7 kg·m/s

8. A is correct.

The collision of I and II does not affect the momentum of the system:

> $p_{before} = p_{after}$
>
> $p_{I\ \&\ II}$ = (1 kg)·(0.5 m/s) + (1.5 kg)·(–0.3 m/s)
>
> $p_{I\ \&\ II}$ = (0.5 kg·m/s) – (0.45 kg·m/s)
>
> $p_{I\ \&\ II}$ = 0.05 kg·m/s
>
> p_{III} = (3.5 kg)·(–0.5 m/s)
>
> p_{III} = –1.75 kg·m/s
>
> $p_{net} = p_{I\ and\ II} + p_{III}$
>
> p_{net} = (0.05 kg·m/s) + (–1.75 kg·m/s)
>
> p_{net} = –1.7 kg·m/s

Momentum is conserved at all times.

9. B is correct.

Set the initial momentum equal to the final momentum after all the collisions have occurred.

$p_{before} = p_{after}$

$p_{before} = (m_I + m_{II} + m_{III})v_f$

$-1.7 \text{ kg·m/s} = (1 \text{ kg} + 1.5 \text{ kg} + 3.5 \text{ kg})v_f$

$v_f = (-1.7 \text{ kg·m/s}) / (6 \text{ kg})$

$v_f = -0.28 \text{ m/s}$

10. C is correct.

Momentum is conserved in this system. The momentum of each car is given by mv, and the sum of the momenta before the collision must equal the sum of the momenta after the collision:

$p_{before} = p_{after}$

Solve for the velocity of the first car after the collision. Each car is traveling in the same direction before and after the collision, so each velocity value has the same sign.

$m_1v_{i1} + m_2v_{i2} = m_1v_{f1} + m_2v_{f2}$

$(480 \text{ kg})·(14.4 \text{ m/s}) + (570 \text{ kg})·(13.3 \text{ m/s}) = (480 \text{ kg})·(v_{f2}) + (570 \text{ kg})·(17.9 \text{ m/s})$

$(480 \text{ kg})·(v_{f2}) = (480 \text{ kg})·(14.4 \text{ m/s}) + (570 \text{ kg})·(13.3 \text{ m/s}) - (570 \text{ kg})·(17.9 \text{ m/s})$

$v_{f2} = [(480 \text{ kg})·(14.4 \text{ m/s}) + (570 \text{ kg})·(13.3 \text{ m/s}) - (570 \text{ kg})·(17.9 \text{ m/s})] / (480 \text{ kg})$

$v_{f2} = 8.9 \text{ m/s} \approx 9 \text{ m/s}$

11. E is correct.

Impulse is a force acting over a period of time:

$J = F\Delta t$

An impulse changes a system's momentum, so:

$F\Delta t = \Delta p_{system}$

The moving block with the lodged bullet comes to a stop when it compresses the spring, losing all momentum.

The initial velocity of the block and bullet separately can be determined by conservation of energy. The two values of interest are the KE of the block and bullet and the PE of the spring.

$(KE + PE)_{before} = (KE + PE)_{after}$

$\frac{1}{2}mv^2 + 0 = 0 + \frac{1}{2}kx^2$

x = distance of compression of the spring

k = spring constant

$$\tfrac{1}{2}(4 \text{ kg} + 0.008 \text{ kg})v^2 = \tfrac{1}{2}(1{,}400 \text{ N/m})\cdot(0.089 \text{ m})^2$$

$$v^2 = (1{,}400 \text{ N/m})\cdot(0.089 \text{ m})^2 \,/\, (4.008 \text{ kg})$$

$$v^2 = 2.76 \text{ m}^2/\text{s}^2$$

$$v = 1.66 \text{ m/s}$$

Thus, the block with the lodged bullet hits the spring with an initial velocity of 1.66 m/s.

Since there is no friction, the block is sent in the opposite direction with the same speed of 1.66 m/s when the spring decompresses. Calculate the momentum, with initial momentum toward the spring and final momentum away from the spring.

$$\Delta p = p_{\text{final}} - p_{\text{initial}}$$

$$\Delta p = (4.008 \text{ kg})\cdot(-1.66 \text{ m/s}) - (4.008 \text{ kg})\cdot(1.66 \text{ m/s})$$

$$\Delta p = (-6.65 \text{ kg}\cdot\text{m/s}) - (6.65 \text{ kg}\cdot\text{m/s})$$

$$\Delta p \approx -13 \text{ kg}\cdot\text{m/s}$$

$$\Delta p \approx -13 \text{ N}\cdot\text{s}$$

Since $F\Delta t = \Delta p$, the impulse is also -13 kg·m/s $= -13$ N·s

The negative sign signifies the coordinate system chosen in this calculation: toward the spring is the positive direction, and away from the spring is the negative direction.

12. C is correct.

Angular momentum is conserved:

$$L = I\omega$$

where I = moment of inertia and ω = angular velocity

$$L = (\tfrac{1}{2}mr^2)\omega$$

If r (radius of arm out from body) decreases, ω increases to conserve angular momentum.

$$L_1 = L_2$$

$$I_1\omega_1 = I_2\omega_2$$

$$I_1 > I_2$$

$$\omega_1 < \omega_2$$

Thus when the skater brings in her arms the moment of inertia and angular velocity change in proportion to each other.

$$KE_R = \tfrac{1}{2}I\omega^2$$

$$KE_1 < KE_2$$

However, rotational KE increases because I is constant and ω is squared. Thus the resulting KE is greater because it has a greater ω. The increase in KE comes from the work performed by the skater when retracting her arms.

13. D is correct.

The centripetal force is the net force required to maintain an object in uniform circular motion.

$F_{\text{centripetal}} = mv^2/r$

where r is the radius of the circular path

Since m is constant and r remains unchanged, the centripetal force is proportional to v^2.

$2^2 = 4$

Thus, if v is doubled, then $F_{\text{centripetal}}$ is quadrupled.

14. B is correct.

$1 \text{ J} = \text{kg·m}^2/\text{s}^2$

$p = mv = \text{kg·m/s}$

$\text{J·s/m} = (\text{kg·m}^2/\text{s}^2)·(\text{s/m})$

$\text{J·s/m} = \text{kg·m/s}$

$\text{kg·m/s} = p$

$\text{J·s/m} = p$

15. E is correct.

Impulse is a change in momentum.

$J = \Delta p$

$J = m\Delta v$

Impulse is also the product of average force and time.

$J = F\Delta t$

$F\Delta t = m\Delta v$

$ma\Delta t = m\Delta v$, cancel m from both sides of the expression

$a\Delta t = \Delta v$

Because acceleration g is constant impulse depends only upon time and velocity.

The speed of the apple affects the impulse as this is included in the Δv term.

Bouncing results in a change in direction. This means a greater change in velocity (the Δv term), so the impulse is greater.

The time of impulse changes the impulse as it is included in the Δt term.

16. D is correct.

$$F\Delta t = m\Delta v$$

$$F = m\Delta v \,/\, \Delta t$$

Choosing toward the wall as the positive direction, the initial velocity is 25 m/s and the final velocity is –25 m/s:

$$F = m(v_f - v_i) \,/\, \Delta t$$

$$F = (0.8 \text{ kg}) \cdot (-25 \text{ m/s} - 25 \text{ m/s}) \,/\, (0.05 \text{ s})$$

$$F = -800 \text{ N}$$

Thus, the wall exerts an average force of 800 N on the ball in the negative direction. From Newton's Third Law, the ball exerts a force of 800 N on the wall in the opposite direction.

17. B is correct.

$$p = mv$$

Sum momentum:

$$p_{total} = m_1 v_1 + m_2 v_2 + m_3 v_3$$

All objects moving to the left have negative velocity.

$$p_{total} = (7 \text{ kg}) \cdot (6 \text{ m/s}) + (12 \text{ kg}) \cdot (3 \text{ m/s}) + (4 \text{ kg}) \cdot (-2 \text{ m/s})$$

$$p_{total} = (42 \text{ kg} \cdot \text{m/s}) + (36 \text{ kg} \cdot \text{m/s}) + (-8 \text{ kg} \cdot \text{m/s})$$

$$p_{total} = 70 \text{ kg} \cdot \text{m/s}$$

18. E is correct.

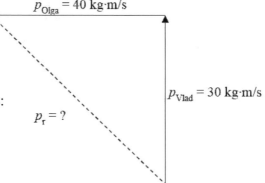

Use conservation of momentum to determine the momentum after the collision. Since they stick together, treat it as a perfectly inelastic collision.

Before the collision, Vladimir's momentum is: (60 kg)·(0.5 m/s) = 30 kg·m/s pointing North

Before the collision, Olga's momentum is:

(40 kg)·(1 m/s) = 40 kg·m/s pointing West

Write two expressions: one for conservation of momentum on the *y*-axis (North-South) and one for conservation of momentum on the *x*-axis (East-West). They do not interact since they are perpendicular to each other. Since Olga and Vladimir stick together, the final mass is the sum of their masses.

Simply use the Pythagorean Theorem:

$$a^2 + b^2 = c^2$$

$$(30 \text{ kg} \cdot \text{m/s})^2 + (40 \text{ kg} \cdot \text{m/s})^2 = p^2$$

$$900 \text{ (kg} \cdot \text{m/s)}^2 + 1{,}600 \text{ (kg} \cdot \text{m/s)}^2 = p^2$$

$$2,500(\text{kg·m/s})^2 = p^2$$

$$p = 50 \text{ kg·m/s}$$

Use this to solve for velocity:

$$p = mv$$

$$50 \text{ kg·m/s} = (100 \text{ kg})v$$

$$v = 50 \text{ kg·m/s} / 100 \text{ kg}$$

$$v = 0.5 \text{ m/s}$$

Also, this problem can be solved algebraically:

$$p_{\text{before}} = p_{\text{after}}$$

$$p = mv$$

On the y coordinate:

$$(60 \text{ kg})·(0.5 \text{ m/s}) = (60 \text{ kg} + 40 \text{ kg})v_y$$

$$v_y = (30 \text{ kg·m/s}) / (100 \text{ kg})$$

$$v_y = 0.3 \text{ m/s}$$

On the x coordinate:

$$(40 \text{ kg})·(1 \text{ m/s}) = (60 \text{ kg} + 40 \text{ kg})v_x$$

$$v_x = (40 \text{ kg·m/s}) / (100 \text{ kg})$$

$$v_x = 0.4 \text{ m/s}$$

Combine these final velocity components using the Pythagorean Theorem since they are perpendicular.

$$v^2 = v_x{}^2 + v_y{}^2$$

$$v^2 = (0.4 \text{ m/s})^2 + (0.3 \text{ m/s})^2$$

$$v = 0.5 \text{ m/s}$$

19. B is correct.

Use conservation of momentum to determine the momentum after the collision. Since they stick together, treat it as a perfectly inelastic collision.

Before collision, Vladimir's momentum is $(60 \text{ kg})·(0.5 \text{ m/s}) = 30$ kg·m/s pointing North

Before collision, Olga's momentum is $(40 \text{ kg})·(1 \text{ m/s}) = 40$ kg·m/s pointing West

Write two expressions: one for conservation of momentum on the y coordinate (North-South) and one for conservation of momentum on the x coordinate (East-West). They do not interact since they are perpendicular to each other. Since they stick together, the final mass is the sum of their masses.

Simply use the Pythagorean Theorem:

$$a^2 + b^2 = c^2$$

$$(30 \text{ kg·m/s})^2 + (40 \text{ kg·m/s})^2 = p^2$$

$$900(\text{kg·m/s})^2 + 1,600(\text{kg·m/s})^2 = p^2$$

$$2,500(\text{kg·m/s})^2 = p^2$$

$$p = 50 \text{ kg·m/s}$$

This problem can also be solved algebraically:

$$p_{\text{before}} = p_{\text{after}}$$

$$p = mv$$

On the y coordinate:

$$(60 \text{ kg})·(0.5 \text{ m/s}) = (60 \text{ kg} + 40 \text{ kg})v_y$$

$$v_y = (30 \text{ kg·m/s}) / (100 \text{ kg})$$

$$v_y = 0.3 \text{ m/s}$$

On the x coordinate:

$$(40 \text{ kg})·(1 \text{ m/s}) = (60 \text{ kg} + 40 \text{ kg})v_x$$

$$v_x = (40 \text{ kg·m/s}) / (100 \text{ kg})$$

$$v_x = 0.4 \text{ m/s}$$

Combine these final velocity components using the Pythagorean Theorem since they are perpendicular:

$$v^2 = v_x^2 + v_y^2$$

$$v^2 = (0.4 \text{ m/s})^2 + (0.3 \text{ m/s})^2$$

$$v = 0.5 \text{ m/s}$$

Use the final weight and final velocity to find the final momentum directly after the collision:

$$p = mv$$

$$p = (60 \text{ kg} + 40 \text{ kg})·(0.5 \text{ m/s})$$

$$p = 50 \text{ kg·m/s}$$

20. C is correct.

$$p_0 = mv$$

If m and v are doubled:

$$p = (2m)·(2v)$$

$$p = 4mv$$

$$p = 4p_0$$

The momentum increases by a factor of 4.

21. D is correct. Balance forces on box Q to solve for tension on box P cable:

$m_Q a = F - T_P$

$T_P = F - m_Q a$

$0 < T_P < F$

Thus the tension on the cable connected to box P is less than F because it is equal to the difference of F and $m_Q a$ but is not equal because the boxes are accelerating.

22. B is correct. At all points on a rotating body the angular velocity is equal. The speed at different points along a rotating body is directly proportional to the radius.

$v = \omega r$

where v = speed, ω = angular velocity and r = radius

Thus Melissa and her friend have different speeds due to their different radial locations.

A is correct. Impulse is directly proportional to force and change in time:

$J = F \Delta t$

Increasing the change in time lowers the impact force while decreasing the change in time increases the force.

24. E is correct.

Angular momentum is always conserved unless a system experiences a net torque greater than zero. This is the rotational equivalent of Newton's First Law of motion.

25. D is correct.

$F \Delta t = m \Delta v$

$F = (m \Delta v) / (\Delta t)$

$F = (6.8 \text{ kg}) \cdot (-3.2 \text{ m/s} - 5.4 \text{ m/s}) / (2 \text{ s})$

$F = (-58.48 \text{ kg·m/s}) / (2 \text{ s})$

$F = -29.2 \text{ N}$

$|F| = 29.2 \text{ N}$

26. A is correct.

Before collision, the total momentum of the system = 0 kg·m/s.

Momentum is conserved in the explosion.

The momentum of the moving rifle and bullet are in opposite directions:

Therefore, $p = 0$

The total momentum after the explosion = 0 kg·m/s

27. E is correct.

$$p = mv$$

Conservation of momentum:

$$p_{initial} = p_{final}$$

$$0 \text{ kg·m/s} = (0.01 \text{ kg})·(300 \text{ m/s}) + (4 \text{ kg})v_{recoil}$$

$$0 \text{ kg·m/s} = 3 \text{ kg·m/s} + (4 \text{ kg})v_{recoil}$$

$$-3 \text{ kg·m/s} = (4 \text{ kg})v_{recoil}$$

$$(-3 \text{ kg·m/s}) / (4 \text{ kg}) = v_{recoil}$$

$$v_{recoil} = -0.75 \text{ m/s}$$

Velocity is negative since the gun recoils in the opposite direction of the bullet.

28. C is correct.

Since the initial velocity only has a horizontal component, the y component of the initial velocity = 0.

Use 24 m to calculate the time the ball is in the air:

$$d_y = \tfrac{1}{2}at^2$$

$$t^2 = 2d_y / a$$

$$t^2 = 2(24 \text{ m}) / (9.8 \text{ m/s}^2)$$

$$t^2 = 4.9 \text{ s}^2$$

$$t = 2.2 \text{ s}$$

Use the time in the air and the horizontal distance to calculate the horizontal speed of the ball:

$$v_x = d_x / t$$

$$v_x = (18 \text{ m}) / (2.2 \text{ s})$$

$$v_x = 8.2 \text{ m/s}$$

29. A is correct.

An object moving in a circle at constant speed is undergoing uniform circular motion. In uniform circular motion the acceleration is due to centripetal acceleration and points inward towards the center of a circle.

30. B is correct.

Impulse:

$$J = F\Delta t$$

$$J = \Delta p$$

where p is momentum

31. C is correct.

Conservation of energy:

$$KE_i + PE_i = KE_f + PE_f$$

$$KE_i + PE_i = KE_f + 0$$

$$KE_f = \tfrac{1}{2}mv_i^2 + mgh_i$$

$$KE_f = \tfrac{1}{2}(4 \text{ kg}) \cdot (20 \text{ m/s})^2 + (4 \text{ kg}) \cdot (10 \text{ m/s}^2) \cdot (10 \text{ m})$$

$$KE_f = 800 \text{ J} + 400 \text{ J}$$

$$KE_f = 1{,}200 \text{ J}$$

32. E is correct.

The force needed to stop a car can be related to KE and work:

$$KE = W$$

$$\tfrac{1}{2}mv^2 = Fd$$

$$F = \tfrac{1}{2}mv^2 / d$$

Momentum is included in the KE term.

$$p = mv$$

$$F = \tfrac{1}{2}(mv)v / d$$

$$F = \tfrac{1}{2}(p)v / d$$

If there is less stopping distance the force increases as they are inversely proportional.

If the momentum or mass increase the force increases as they are directly proportional.

33. C is correct.

Impulse:

$$J = F\Delta t$$

Assuming no energy lost in the collision, from Newton's Third Law, the force experienced by these two objects is equal and opposite.

Therefore, the magnitudes of impulse are the same.

34. B is correct.

Balance the counterclockwise (CCW) torque with the clockwise (CW) torque. Let the axis of rotation be at the point where the rope attaches to the bar. This placement causes the torque from the rope to be zero since the lever arm is zero.

$$\Sigma \tau : \tau_1 - \tau_2 = 0$$

$$\tau_1 = \tau_2$$

The CCW torque due to the weight of the 6 kg mass:

$$\tau = r_1 F_1$$

$$r_1 F_1 = (x) \cdot (6 \text{ kg}) \cdot (9.8 \text{ m/s}^2)$$

The CW torque due to the weight of the 30 kg mass:

$$r_2 F_2 = (5 \text{ m} - x) \cdot (30 \text{ kg}) \cdot (9.8 \text{ m/s}^2)$$

Set the two expressions equal to each other

$$(9.8 \text{ m/s}^2) \cdot (x) \cdot (6 \text{ kg}) = (5 \text{ m} - x) \cdot (30 \text{ kg}) \cdot (9.8 \text{ m/s}^2)$$

Cancel g and kg from each side of the equation:

$$6x = 30(5 \text{ m} - x)$$

$$6x = 150 \text{ m} - 30x$$

$$36x = 150 \text{ m}$$

$$x = 4.2 \text{ m}$$

35. E is correct. If the block is at rest then the force of static friction is equal to the force of gravity at angle θ.

$$F_f = mg \sin \theta$$

36. C is correct. $F_{net} = 0$ is necessary to maintain constant velocity.

If 45 N must be exerted on the block to maintain constant velocity, the force due to kinetic friction against the block equals 45 N.

For a horizontal surface and no other vertical forces acting, the normal force on the block equals its weight.

$$N = mg$$

$$F_{friction} = \mu_k N$$

$$F_{friction} = \mu_k mg$$

$$\mu_k = (F_{friction}) / mg$$

$$\mu_k = (45 \text{ N}) / [(30 \text{ kg}) \cdot (10 \text{ m/s}^2)]$$

$$\mu_k = 0.15$$

37. B is correct. Newton's Second Law:

$$F = ma$$

The impulse-momentum relationship can be derived by multiplying Δt on both sides:

$$F\Delta t = ma\Delta t$$

$$F\Delta t = m\Delta v$$

$$J = m\Delta v$$

Thus the impulse is equal to the change in momentum.

38. C is correct.

Force X acts perpendicular to the short arm of the rectangle, this is the lever arm.

$$\tau = rF$$

$$\tau = (0.5 \text{ m}) \cdot (15 \text{ N})$$

$$\tau = 7.5 \text{ N·m}$$

Since the torque causes the plate to rotate clockwise its sign is negative.

$$\tau = -7.5 \text{ N·m}$$

39. E is correct.

$$\tau = rF$$

Force Z acts directly at the pivot so the lever arm equals zero.

$$\tau = (0 \text{ m}) \cdot (30 \text{ N})$$

$$\tau = 0 \text{ N·m}$$

40. A is correct.

$$\tau = rF$$

Force Y acts perpendicular to the long arm of the rectangle, this is the lever arm.

$$\tau = (0.6 \text{ m}) \cdot (25 \text{ N})$$

$$\tau = 15 \text{ N·m}$$

The torque is clockwise, so its sign is negative.

$$\tau = -15 \text{ N·m}$$

41. B is correct.

The tension in the string provides the centripetal force.

$$T = mv^2 / r$$

$$m = 50 \text{ g} = 0.05 \text{ kg}$$

$$T = [(0.05 \text{ kg}) \cdot (20 \text{ m/s})^2] / (2 \text{ m})$$

$$T = [(0.05 \text{ kg}) \cdot (400 \text{ m}^2/\text{s}^2)] / (2 \text{ m})$$

$$T = (20 \text{ kg·m}^2/\text{s}^2) / (2 \text{ m})$$

$$T = 10 \text{ N}$$

42. A is correct.

$$F = ma$$

Newton's Third Law states that each force is paired with an equal and opposite reaction force. Therefore, the small car and the truck each receive the same force.

43. C is correct.

Choose the axis of rotation at the point where the bar attaches to the wall. Since the lever arm of the force that the wall exerts is zero, the torque at that point is zero and can be ignored.

The two other torques present arise from the weight of the bar exerting force downward and the cable exerting force upward. The weight of the bar acts at the center of mass, so its lever arm is 1 m. The lever arm for the cable is 2 m, since it acts the full 2 m away from the wall at the end of the bar.

Since torque is calculated with a cross product, only the perpendicular component of force creates torque, so a sin 30° term must be used for the cable.

The sum of torques = 0, since the bar is in rotational equilibrium.

Let the torque of the cable be positive and the torque of the weight be negative.

torque upward (cable) + torque downward (weight) = 0

$(F_T \sin 30°)·(2 \text{ m}) − (10 \text{ kg})·(10 \text{ m/s}^2)·(1 \text{ m}) = 0$

$F_T = [(10 \text{ kg})·(10 \text{ m/s}^2)·(1 \text{ m})] / [(2 \text{ m})·(\sin 30°)]$

$F_T = [(10 \text{ kg})·(10 \text{ m/s}^2)·(1 \text{ m})] / [(2 \text{ m})·(0.5)]$

$F_T = 100 \text{ N}$

44. B is correct.

Momentum is defined as:

$p = mv$

$m_A = 2m_B$

$p_A = 2m_B v$

$p_B = m_B v$

$p_A = 2p_B$

If both objects reach the ground at the same time they have equal velocities.

However because B is twice the mass it has twice the momentum as object A

45. D is correct.

Use conservation of momentum to make equations for momenta along the *x*-axis and the *y*-axis. Since the mass ratio is 1 : 4, one car has a mass of *m* and the other has a mass of 4*m*. The entangled cars after the collision have a combined mass of 5*m*.

Let the car of mass *m* be traveling in the positive *x* direction and the car of mass 4*m* be traveling in the positive *y* direction. The choice of directions here is arbitrary, but the angle of impact is important.

$p_{\text{initial}} = p_{\text{final}}$ for both the *x*- and *y*-axes

$p = mv$

For the *x*-axis:

$$m_iv_i = m_fv_{fx}$$

$$m(12 \text{ m/s}) = 5mv_x, \text{ cancel } m$$

$$12 \text{ m/s} = 5v_x$$

$$v_x = 2.4 \text{ m/s}$$

For the *y*-axis:

$$m_iv_i = m_fv_{fy}$$

$$4m(12 \text{ m/s}) = 5mv_y, \text{ cancel } m$$

$$4(12 \text{ m/s}) = 5v_y$$

$$v_y = 9.6 \text{ m/s}$$

The question asks for the magnitude of the final velocity, so combine the *x* and *y* components of the final velocity using the Pythagorean Theorem.

$$v^2 = (2.4 \text{ m/s})^2 + (9.6 \text{ m/s})^2$$

$$v^2 = 5.76 \text{ m}^2/\text{s}^2 + 92.16 \text{ m}^2/\text{s}^2$$

$$v = 9.9 \text{ m/s}$$

46. C is correct.

Use conservation of momentum on the horizontal plane. The horizontal component of the anchor's momentum equals the momentum of the fisherman moving the opposite way.

Use *m* for the fisherman's mass and 2*m* for the anchor's mass.

$$p = mv$$

$$p_{boat} = p_{anchor}$$

$$m_bv_b = m_av_a$$

$$m_b(2.9 \text{ m/s}) = 2m_av \cos 5°, \text{ cancel } m$$

$$v = (2.9 \text{ m/s}) / (2 \cos 5°)$$

$$v = (2.9 \text{ m/s}) / (2)·(0.996)$$

$$v = 1.5 \text{ m/s}$$

47. B is correct.

$$\text{weight} = \text{mass} \times \text{gravity}$$

$$W = mg$$

$$m = W / g$$

$$m = (98 \text{ N}) / (9.8 \text{ m/s}^2)$$

$$m = 10 \text{ kg}$$

Newton's Second Law:

$$F = ma$$
$$F = (10 \text{ kg}) \cdot (10 \text{ m/s}^2)$$
$$F = 100 \text{ N}$$

48. A is correct. KE is constant and conserved because speed is constant.

PE increases because the cart is at a greater height at point B.

The cart as a system is not isolated since the winch does work on it and so its energy is not conserved.

Conservation of energy: PE increase of the cart = work done by the winch

49. D is correct. The vertical component of the initial velocity:

$$v_{iy} = (140 \text{ m/s}) \sin 35°$$
$$v_{iy} = (140 \text{ m/s}) \cdot (0.57)$$
$$v_{iy} = 79.8 \text{ m/s}$$

The initial velocity upward, time elapsed, and acceleration due to gravity is known.

Determine the final velocity after 4 s.

$$v_y = v_{iy} + at$$
$$v_y = 79.8 \text{ m/s} + (-9.8 \text{ m/s}^2) \cdot (4 \text{ s})$$
$$v_y = 41 \text{ m/s}$$

50. C is correct.

$$\text{impulse} = \text{force} \times \text{time}$$
$$J = F\Delta t$$

51. D is correct. Conservation of momentum: the momentum of the fired bullet is equal and opposite to that of the rifle.

$$p = mv$$
$$p_{before} = p_{after}$$
$$0 = p_{rifle} + p_{bullet}$$
$$-p_{rifle} = p_{bullet}$$
$$-(2 \text{ kg})v = (0.01 \text{ kg}) \cdot (220 \text{ m/s})$$
$$v = (0.01 \text{ kg}) \cdot (220 \text{ m/s}) / (-2 \text{ kg})$$
$$v = -1.1 \text{ m/s}$$

Thus, the velocity of the rifle is 1.1 m/s in the opposite direction as the bullet.

52. D is correct.

Airbags reduce force by increasing the time of contact between the passenger and surface.

In a collision, an impulse is experienced by a passenger:

$$J = F\Delta t$$

$$F = J / \Delta t$$

The impulse is a constant but the force experienced by the passenger is inversely related to time of contact. Airbags increase the time of impact and thus reduce the forces experienced by the person.

53. A is correct.

Since Force I is perpendicular to the beam, the entire force acts to produce torque without any horizontal force component.

$$\tau = rF$$

$$\tau = (0.5 \text{ m}) \cdot (10 \text{ N})$$

$$\tau = 5 \text{ N·m}$$

Because the force causes the beam to rotate clockwise against the positive counterclockwise direction, the torque sign should be negative:

$$\tau = -5 \text{ N·m}$$

54. E is correct.

To calculate torque, use the 35° angle.

For torque:

$$\tau = rF \sin \theta$$

$$\tau = (1 \text{ m}) \cdot (5 \text{ N}) \sin 35°$$

$$\tau = 2.9 \text{ N·m}$$

The torque is counterclockwise, so the sign is positive.

55. B is correct.

Force III acts purely in tension with the beam and has no component acting vertically against the beam. Torque can only be calculated using a force with some component perpendicular to the length vector. Because Force III has no perpendicular component to the length vector, torque is zero.

$$\tau = rF$$

$$\tau = (1 \text{ m}) \cdot (0 \text{ N})$$

$$\tau = 0 \text{ N·m}$$

56. C is correct.

Impulse can be written as:

$$J = m\Delta v$$

$$J = F\Delta t$$

Impulse is the change in momentum of an object. Because the yellow ball bounced higher, it can be concluded that its upward velocity after the collision must be higher than that of the red ball:

$$\Delta v_{yellow} > \Delta v_{red}$$

Thus, because the mass of both balls are the same, the yellow ball must have a greater impulse according to the impulse equation:

$$m\Delta v_{yellow} > m\Delta v_{red}$$

57. D is correct.

$$J = F\Delta t$$

$$J = (4.5 \text{ N}) \cdot (1.4 \text{ s})$$

$$J = (4.5 \text{ kg} \cdot \text{m/s}^2) \cdot (1.4 \text{ s})$$

$$J = 6.3 \text{ kg} \cdot \text{m/s}$$

58. A is correct.

Both trucks experience the same acceleration due to gravity so their acceleration and velocity are equal because these do not depend on mass:

$$v_f = v_0 + a\Delta t$$

However, their momentum are different and the heavier truck has a larger momentum because of its larger mass.

$$p = mv$$

$$m_H > m_L$$

$$p_H = m_H v$$

$$p_L = m_L v$$

$$p_H > p_L$$

59. E is correct.

The time elapsed from release until collision is calculated by:

time from release until collision = round trip time / 2

$t = (4 \text{ s}) / 2$

$t = 2 \text{ s}$

The time of contact is negligible to the round trip time, so this calculation ignores it. Since this collision is elastic, the time from release until the collision is the same as the time from the collision until the ball reaches the same height again.

Given this time in the air, find the velocity of the ball immediately before impact:

$v = v_i + at$

$v = 0 + (9.8 \text{ m/s}^2) \cdot (2 \text{ s})$

$v = 19.6 \text{ m/s}$

Find the KE of the ball before impact:

$\text{KE} = \frac{1}{2}mv^2$

$\text{KE} = \frac{1}{2}(0.078 \text{ kg}) \cdot (19.6 \text{ m/s})^2$

$\text{KE} = 15 \text{ J}$

The KE of the ball is stored as elastic energy during the collision and is then converted back to KE to send the ball upward in the opposite direction. This stored elastic energy is equivalent to the KE before the collision.

60. B is correct.

Consider the system to be the set containing both carts.

The force on the initial object provides and impulse to the system of:

$I = F\Delta t$

An impulse causes a change in the momentum of the system:

$I = \Delta p$

The initial momentum of the system is zero, and momentum is conserved during the collision. Since the two carts stick together after the collision, the final momentum is:

$p_f = v_f(m_A + m_A) = \Delta p = F\Delta t$

Therefore:

$v_f = F\Delta t / (m_A + m_A)$

$v_f = (3 \text{ N}) (2 \text{ s}) / (5 \text{ kg} + 10 \text{ kg})$

$v_f = 0.4 \text{ m/s}$

We want to hear from you

Your feedback is important to us because we strive to provide the highest quality prep materials. If you have any questions, comments or suggestions, email us, so we can incorporate your feedback into future editions.

Customer Satisfaction Guarantee

If you have any concerns about this book, including printing issues, contact us and we will resolve any issues to your satisfaction.

info@sterling-prep.com

Work and Energy – Explanations

1. D is correct.

The final velocity in projectile motion is related to the maximum height of the projectile through conservation of energy:

KE = PE

$\frac{1}{2}mv^2 = mgh$

When the stone thrown straight up passes its starting point on its way back down, its downward speed is equal to its initial upward velocity (2D motion). The stone thrown straight downward contains the same magnitude of initial velocity as the stone thrown upward, and thus both the stone thrown upward and the stone thrown downward have the same final speed.

A stone thrown horizontally (or for example, a stone thrown at 45º) does not achieve the same height *h* as a stone thrown straight up, so it has smaller final vertical velocity.

2. B is correct.

Work = force × displacement × cos *θ*

W = *Fd* cos *θ*, where *θ* is the angle between the vectors *F* and *d*

W = (5 N)·(10 m) cos 45º

W = (50 J)·(0.7)

W = 35 J

3. A is correct.

KE = $\frac{1}{2}mv^2$

KE is influenced by mass and velocity. However, since velocity is squared, its influence on KE is greater than the influence of mass.

4. B is correct.

Work = force × displacement × cos *θ*

W = *Fd* cos *θ*

cos 90° = 0

W = 0

Since the force of gravity acts perpendicular to the distance traveled by the ball, the force due to gravity does no work in moving the ball.

5. E is correct.

$$KE = \frac{1}{2}mv^2$$

$$KE = \frac{1}{2}(5 \text{ kg}){\cdot}(2 \text{ m/s})^2$$

$$KE = 10 \text{ J}$$

6. A is correct.

$$W = Fd \cos \theta$$

$$\cos \theta = 1$$

$$F = W / d$$

$$F = (360 \text{ J}) / (8 \text{ m})$$

$$F = 45 \text{ N}$$

$$F = ma$$

$$m = F / a$$

$$m = (45 \text{ N}) / (10 \text{ m/s}^2)$$

$$m = 4.5 \text{ kg}$$

7. D is correct.

On a displacement (x) vs. force (F) graph, the displacement is the y-axis and the force is the x-axis.

The slope is x / F, (in units of m/N) which is the reciprocal of the spring constant k, which is measured in N/m.

8. C is correct.

Work done by a spring equation:

$$W = \frac{1}{2}kx^2$$

$$W = \frac{1}{2}(22 \text{ N/m}){\cdot}(3 \text{ m})^2$$

$$W = 99 \text{ J}$$

9. A is correct.

The force due to gravity always acts downward. When the ball is traveling upward, the gravitational force applied over the traveled distance is negative, and therefore the work done by gravity is negative.

When the ball travels downward, the gravitational force is applied over the traveled distance is positive, and therefore the work done by gravity is positive.

10. B is correct. Work done by gravity is an object's change in gravitational PE.

$$W = -PE$$
$$A_1 = 400 \text{ J}$$

By the work-energy theorem,

$$W = KE$$
$$B_1 = 400 \text{ J}$$

11. D is correct. Work is calculated as the product of force and displacement parallel to the direction of the applied force:

$$W = Fd \cos \theta$$

where some component of d is in the direction of the force.

12. B is correct.

Work only depends on force and distance:

$$W = Fd \cos \theta$$

Power = W / t is the amount of work done in a unit of time.

13. A is correct.

The area under the curve on a graph is the product of the values of $y \times x$.

Here, the y value is force and the x value is distance:

$$Fd = W$$

14. C is correct.

This is the conservation of energy. The only force acting on the cat is gravity.

$$KE = PE_g$$
$$KE = mgh$$
$$KE = (3 \text{ kg}) \cdot (10 \text{ m/s}^2) \cdot (4 \text{ m})$$
$$KE = 120 \text{ J}$$

15. B is correct.

Although the book is stationary with respect to the plank, the plank is applying a force to the book causing it to accelerate in the direction of the force. Since the displacement of the point of application of the force is in the same direction as the force, the work done is positive. Choices D and E are not correct because work is a scalar and has no direction.

16. D is correct.

$$W = Fd$$
$$d = W / F$$
$$d = (350 \text{ J}) / (900 \text{ N})$$
$$d = 0.39 \text{ m}$$

17. E is correct.

Conservation of energy between kinetic energy and potential energy:

$$KE = PE$$
$$KE = \tfrac{1}{2}mv^2 \text{ and } PE = mgh$$

Set the equations equal to each other:

$$\tfrac{1}{2}mv^2 = mgh, \text{ cancel } m \text{ from both sides}$$
$$\tfrac{1}{2}v^2 = gh$$

h is only dependent on the initial v, which is equal between both objects, so the two objects rise to the same height.

18. A is correct.

$$\text{Work} = \text{Power} \times \text{time}$$
$$P_1 = W / t$$
$$P_2 = (3 \text{ W}) / (1/3 \, t)$$
$$P_2 = 3(3/1){\cdot}(W / t)$$
$$P_2 = 9(W / t)$$
$$P_2 = 9(P_1)$$

19. D is correct.

Conservation of energy:

$$KE = PE$$
$$KE = mgh$$
$$W = mg$$
$$KE = Wh$$
$$KE = (450 \text{ N}){\cdot}(9 \text{ m})$$
$$KE = 4{,}050 \text{ J}$$

20. A is correct.

$$F_1 = -kx_1$$

Solve for the spring constant k:

$$k = F / x_1$$
$$k = (160 \text{ N}) / (0.23 \text{ m})$$
$$k = 696 \text{ N/m}$$

$$F_2 = -kx_2$$
$$F_2 = (696 \text{ N/m}) \cdot (0.34 \text{ m})$$
$$F_2 = 237 \text{ N}$$

21. B is correct. There is a frictional force since the net force = 0

The mule pulls in the same direction as the direction of travel so $\cos \theta = 1$

$$W = Fd \cos \theta$$
$$d = v \Delta t$$
$$W = Fv \Delta t$$

22. D is correct.

$$W = Fd \cos \theta$$
$$F_T = W / (d \times \cos \theta)$$
$$F_T = (540 \text{ J}) / (18 \text{ m} \times \cos 32°)$$
$$F_T = (540 \text{ J}) / (18 \text{ m} \times 0.848)$$
$$F_T = 35 \text{ N}$$

23. B is correct.

$$F = -kx$$
$$ma = -kx$$

By adding an extra 120 grams, the mass is doubled:

$$2ma = -kx$$

Since acceleration and the spring constant are constant, only x changes.

Thus after the addition of 120 g, x doubles:

$$PE_1 = \tfrac{1}{2}kx^2$$
$$PE_2 = \tfrac{1}{2}k(2x)^2$$
$$PE_2 = \tfrac{1}{2}k(4x^2)$$
$$PE_2 = 4(\tfrac{1}{2}kx^2)$$

The potential energy increases by a factor of 4.

24. C is correct.

The force due to kinetic friction is related to the normal force on an object.

The normal force is equal and opposite to the object's weight:

$$F_f = \mu_k F_n$$

$$F_f = \mu_k mg$$

Therefore, the frictional force increases for larger masses.

As the force increases, so does the work done on the object, because:

$$W = F \times d$$

25. E is correct.

The hammer does work on the nail as it drives it into the wood. The amount of work done is proportional to the amount of kinetic energy lost by the hammer:

$$\Delta KE = \Delta W$$

26. A is correct.

The only force doing work is the road's friction, so the work done by the road's friction is the total work. This work equals the change in KE.

$$W = \Delta KE$$

$$W = KE_f - KE_i$$

$$W = \tfrac{1}{2}mv_2^2 - \tfrac{1}{2}mv_1^2$$

$$W = 0 - [\tfrac{1}{2}(1,500 \text{ kg}) \cdot (25 \text{ m/s})^2]$$

$$W = -4.7 \times 10^5 \text{ J}$$

27. D is correct.

$$KE = \tfrac{1}{2}mv^2$$

$$KE_{car} = \tfrac{1}{2}(1,000 \text{ kg}) \cdot (4.72 \text{ m/s})^2$$

$$KE_{car} = 11,139 \text{ J}$$

Calculate the KE of the 2,000 kg truck with 20 times the KE:

$$KE_{truck} = KE_{car} \times 20$$

$$KE_{truck} = (11,139 \text{ J}) \times 20$$

$$KE_{truck} = 222.7 \text{ kJ}$$

Calculate the speed of the 2,000 kg truck:

$$KE = \tfrac{1}{2}mv^2$$

$$v^2 = 2KE \,/\, m$$

$$v^2 = 2(222.7 \text{ kJ}) \,/\, (2,000 \text{ kg})$$

$$v_{truck} = \sqrt{[2(222.7 \text{ kJ}) / (2{,}000 \text{ kg})]}$$

$$v_{truck} = 14.9 \text{ m/s}$$

28. E is correct.

Gravity and the normal force are balanced, vertical forces.

Since the car is slowing (i.e. accelerating backwards) there is a net force backwards, due to friction (i.e. braking).

Newton's First Law of Motion states that in the absence of any forces, the car would keep moving forward.

29. B is correct.

Energy is always conserved so the work needed to lift the piano is 0.15 m is equal to the work needed to pull the rope 1 m:

$$W_1 = W_2$$

$$F_1 d_1 = F_2 d_2$$

$$F_1 d_1 / d_2 = F_2$$

$$F_2 = (6{,}000 \text{ N}){\cdot}(0.15 \text{ m}) / 1 \text{ m}$$

$$F_2 = 900 \text{ N}$$

30. C is correct. The area under the curve on a graph is the product of the values of $y \times x$.

Here, the y value is force and the x value is distance:

$$Fd = W$$

31. B is correct.

The vast majority of the Earth's energy comes from the sun, which produces radiation that penetrates the Earth's atmosphere. Likewise, radiation is emitted from the Earth's atmosphere.

32. C is correct.

$$W = Fd$$

$$W = \Delta KE$$

$$F \times d = \tfrac{1}{2}mv^2$$

If v is doubled:

$$F \times d_2 = \tfrac{1}{2}m(2v)^2$$

$$F \times d_2 = \tfrac{1}{2}m(4v^2)$$

$$F \times d_2 = 4(\tfrac{1}{2}mv^2)$$

For equations to remain equal to each other, d_2 must be 4 times d.

33. D is correct.

Work = Power × time

$P = W / t$

$W = Fd$

$P = (Fd) / t$

$P = [(2,000 \text{ N}) \cdot (320 \text{ m})] / (60 \text{ s})$

$P = 10,667 \text{ W} = 10.7 \text{ kW}$

34. E is correct.

Find acceleration:

$\Delta x = v_0 t + \frac{1}{2} a t^2$

$3 \text{ m} = 0 + (\frac{1}{2}) \cdot (a) \cdot (3 \text{ s})^2$

$a = 0.67 \text{ m/s}^2$

Find power:

Power = Work / time

$P = W / t$

Work = Force × distance

$W = Fd$

$W = (ma)d$

Therefore,

$P = (ma_{total})d / t$

$P = (25 \text{ kg}) \cdot (0.67 \text{ m/s}^2 + 9.8 \text{ m/s}^2) \cdot (3 \text{ m}) / (3 \text{ s})$

$P = 262 \text{ J}$

35. B is correct.

The bag was never lifted off the ground and moved horizontally at constant velocity.

$F = 0$

$W = Fd$

$W = 0 \text{ J}$

Because there is no acceleration, the force is zero and thus the work is zero.

36. B is correct.

$F = ma$

$a = F / m$

$a = (9{,}600 \text{ N}) / (1{,}000 \text{ kg})$

$a = 9.6 \text{ m/s}^2$

$v_f^2 = v_0^2 + 2a\Delta d$

$(v_f^2 - v_0^2) / 2a = \Delta d$

Note that acceleration is negative due to it acting opposite the velocity.

$\Delta d = [(22 \text{ m/s})^2 - (30 \text{ m/s})^2] / 2(-9.6 \text{ m/s}^2)$

$\Delta d = (484 \text{ m}^2/\text{s}^2 - 900 \text{ m}^2/\text{s}^2) / (-19.2 \text{ m/s}^2)$

$\Delta d = (-416 \text{ m}^2/\text{s}^2) / (-19.2 \text{ m/s}^2)$

$\Delta d = 21.7 \text{ m} \approx 22 \text{ m}$

Or using energy conservation to solve the problem:

$W = |\Delta KE|$

$Fd = |\tfrac{1}{2}m(v_f^2 - v_0^2)|$

$d = |m(v_f^2 - v_0^2) / 2F|$

$d = |(1{,}000 \text{ kg}) \cdot [(22 \text{ m/s})^2 - (30 \text{ m/s})^2] / (2) \cdot (9{,}600 \text{ N})|$

$d = |(1{,}000 \text{ kg}) \cdot (484 \text{ m}^2/\text{s}^2 - 900 \text{ m}^2/\text{s}^2) / 19{,}200 \text{ N}|$

$d = 22 \text{ m}$

37. C is correct.

$W = 100 \text{ J}$

Work = Power × time

$P = W / t$

$P = 100 \text{ J} / 50 \text{ s}$

$P = 2 \text{ W}$

38. D is correct.

$v_f^2 = v_0^2 + 2a\Delta x$

$v_f^2 = 0 + 2a\Delta x$

$v_f = \sqrt{2a\Delta x}$

$v_f = \sqrt{[2(10 \text{ m/s}^2) \cdot (58 \text{ m})]}$

$v_f = \sqrt{(1{,}160 \text{ m}^2/\text{s}^2)}$

$v_f = 34 \text{ m/s}$

39. E is correct.

$PE = mgh$

If height and gravity are constant then potential energy is directly proportional to mass.

As such, if the second stone has four times the mass of the first, then it must have four times the potential energy of the first stone.

$m_2 = 4m_1$

$PE_2 = 4PE_1$

Therefore, the second stone has four times the potential energy.

40. B is correct.

$W = Fd$

$W = mgh$, work done by gravity

$W = (1.3 \text{ kg}) \cdot (10 \text{ m/s}^2) \cdot (6 \text{ m})$

$W = 78 \text{ J}$

41. A is correct.

$PE = mgh$

42. A is correct.

$F_{\text{spring}} = F_{\text{centripetal}}$

$F_{\text{spring}} = kx$

$kx = 15 \text{ N}$

$x = (15 \text{ N}) / (65 \text{ N/m})$

$x = 0.23 \text{ m}$

$PE_{\text{spring}} = \frac{1}{2}kx^2$

$PE_{\text{spring}} = \frac{1}{2}(65 \text{ N/m}) \cdot (0.23 \text{ m})^2$

$PE_{\text{spring}} = 1.7 \text{ J}$

43. C is correct.

total time $= (3.5 \text{ h/day}) \cdot (7 \text{ days}) \cdot (5 \text{ weeks})$

total time $= 122.5 \text{ h}$

cost $= (8.16 \text{ cents/kW} \cdot \text{h}) \cdot (122.5 \text{ h}) \cdot (0.12 \text{ kW/1})$

cost $= 120 \text{ cents} = \$1.20$

44. E is correct.

$x = 5.1$ m × (cos 32°)

$x = 4.33$ m

$h = 5.1$ m − 4.33 m

$h = 0.775$ m

$W = Fd$

$W = mg × h$

$m = W / gh$

$m = (120$ J$) / (9.8$ m/s^2)·(0.775 m)

$m = 15.8$ kg

45. D is correct.

Potential energy of spring:

$PE = \frac{1}{2}k\Delta x^2$

111 J $= \frac{1}{2}k(2.9$ m$)^2 − (1.4$ m$)^2$

111 J $= \frac{1}{2}k(8.41$ m$^2) − (1.96$ m$^2)$

111 J $= \frac{1}{2}k(6.45$ m$^2)$

$k = 2(111$ J$) / (6.45$ m$^2)$

$k = 34$ N/m

Unit check:

J = kg·m^2/s^2

J/m^2 = (kg·m^2/s^2)·(1/m^2)

J/m^2 = (kg/s^2)

N/m = (kg·m/s^2)·(1/m)

N/m = (kg/s^2)

46. E is correct.

Potential energy, kinetic energy and work are all measured in joules:

J = kg·m^2/s^2

KE = $\frac{1}{2}mv^2$ = kg(m/s)^2 = J

PE = mgh = kg(m/s^2)·(m/1) = J

W = Fd = J

47. A is correct.

Potential energy of spring:

$$PE = \tfrac{1}{2}kx^2$$

Kinetic energy of mass:

$$KE = \tfrac{1}{2}mv^2$$

Set equal to each other and rearrange:

$\tfrac{1}{2}kx^2 = \tfrac{1}{2}mv^2$, cancel ½ from both sides of the expression

$$kx^2 = mv^2$$

$$x^2 = (mv^2) / k$$

$$x^2 = (m / k)v^2$$

Since *m* / *k* is provided:

$$x^2 = (0.038 \text{ kg·m/N})·(18 \text{ m/s})^2$$

$$x^2 = 12.3 \text{ m}^2$$

$$x = \sqrt{12.3} \text{ m}$$

$$x = 3.4 \text{ m}$$

48. A is correct.

$$m_t = 2m_c$$

$$v_t = 2v_c$$

KE of the truck:

$$KE_t = \tfrac{1}{2}m_t v_t^2$$

Replace mass and velocity of the truck with the equivalent mass and velocity of the car:

$$KE_t = \tfrac{1}{2}(2m_c)·(2v_c)^2$$

$$KE_t = \tfrac{1}{2}(2m_c)·(4v_c^2)$$

$$KE_t = \tfrac{1}{2}(8m_c v_c^2)$$

The truck has 8 times the kinetic energy of the car.

49. E is correct. When a car stops the KE is equal to the work done by the force of friction from the brakes.

Through friction the KE is transformed into heat.

50. B is correct. When the block comes to rest at the end of the spring, the upward force of the spring balances the downward force of gravity.

$$F = kx$$

$$mg = kx$$

$x = mg / k$

$x = (30 \text{ kg}){\cdot}(10 \text{ m/s}^2) / 900 \text{ N/m}$

$x = 0.33 \text{ m}$

51. D is correct.

$KE = \frac{1}{2}mv^2$

$KE = \frac{1}{2}(0.33 \text{ kg}){\cdot}(40 \text{ m/s})^2$

$KE = 264 \text{ J}$

52. C is correct. Work is the area under a force vs. position graph.

area $= Fd = W$

The area of the triangle as the object moves from 0 to 4 m:

$A = \frac{1}{2}bh$

$A = \frac{1}{2}(4 \text{ m}{\cdot})(10 \text{ N})$

$A = 20 \text{ J}$

$W = 20 \text{ J}$

53. C is correct.

$KE = PE$

$\frac{1}{2}mv^2 = mgh$

$v^2 / 2g = h$

If v is doubled:

$h_B = v_B{}^2 / 2g$

$v_J = 2v_B$

$(2v_B)^2 / 2g = h_J$

$4(v_B{}^2 / 2g) = h_J$

$4h_B = h_J$

James's ball travels 4 times higher than Bob's ball.

54. B is correct.

Hooke's Law is given as:

$F = -kx$

The negative is only by convention to demonstrate that the spring force is a restoring force. Graph B is correct because force is linearly increasing with increasing distance. All other graphs are either constant or exponential.

55. C is correct.

A decrease in the KE for the rocket causes either a gain in its gravitational PE, or the transfer of heat, or a combination.

The rocket loses some KE due to air resistance (friction).

Thus, some of the rocket's KE is converted to heat that causes the temperature of the air surrounding the rocket to increase. Therefore, the average KE of the air molecules increases.

56. D is correct.

Kinetic energy is given as:

$$KE_1 = \frac{1}{2}mv^2$$

$$KE_2 = \frac{1}{2}m(4v)^2$$

$$KE_2 = \frac{1}{2}m(16v^2)$$

Increasing the velocity by a factor of 4 increases the KE by a factor of 16.

57. C is correct.

Energy is conserved and converted from potential to kinetic.

$$PE = KE$$

$$\frac{1}{2}kx^2 = \frac{1}{2}mv^2$$

$$kx^2 = mv^2$$

$$x\sqrt{k} = v\sqrt{m}$$

The velocity and the compression distance of the spring are directly proportional. Thus if the spring is compressed by four times the original distance then the velocity is four times the original.

$$x_2 = 4x_1$$

$$v_2 = 4v_1$$

58. C is correct.

Force: $F = ma$ (N)

Work: $W = Fd$ (N·m)

Power: $P = W / t$ (N·m/s)

59. E is correct.

$$W_{net} = \Delta KE$$

$$\Delta KE = KE_f - KE_i$$

$$\Delta KE + KE_i = KE_f$$

60. D is correct.

$v = (70 \text{ km/h}) \cdot (1,000 \text{ m/km}) \cdot (1 \text{ h/60 min}) \cdot (1 \text{ min/60 s})$

$v = 19.4 \text{ m/s}$

Force acting against the car:

$F = mg \sin \theta$

$F = (1,320 \text{ kg}) \cdot (9.8 \text{ m/s}^2) \sin 5°$

$F = (1,320 \text{ kg}) \cdot (9.8 \text{ m/s}^2) \cdot (0.09)$

$F = 1,164 \text{ N}$

$N = \text{kg} \cdot \text{m/s}^2$

Rate of energy is power:

$\text{Watts} = \text{kg} \cdot \text{m}^2/\text{s}^3$

Multiply velocity by the downward force:

$P = Fv$

$P = (1,164 \text{ N}) \cdot (19.4 \text{ m/s})$

$P = 22.6 \text{ kW}$

Our guarantee – the highest quality preparation materials.

We expect our books to have the highest quality content and be error-free.

Be the first to report an error, typo or inaccuracy and receive a
$10 reward for a content error or
$5 reward for a typo or grammatical mistake.

info@sterling-prep.com

Waves and Periodic Motion – Explanations

1. B is correct.

Frequency is the measure of the amount of cycles per second a wave experiences, which is independent of the wave's amplitude.

2. D is correct.

Hooke's Law:

$F = kx$

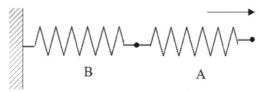

It is known that the force on each spring must be equal if they are in static equilibrium, therefore:

$F_A = F_B$

Therefore, the expression can be written as:

$k_A L_A = k_B L_B$

Solve for the spring constant of spring B:

$k_B = (k_A L_A) / L_B$

3. B is correct.

Wave motion is the result of oscillating (or vibrating) particles traveling in a perpendicular direction to their oscillations.

4. C is correct.

speed = wavelength × frequency

$v = \lambda f$

$v = (0.25 \text{ m}) \cdot (1{,}680 \text{ Hz})$

$v = 420 \text{ m/s}$

5. A is correct.

$E_{total} = PE + KE$

$E_{stored} = \frac{1}{2}kA^2$

Stored energy is potential energy. In simple harmonic motion, the equation for gravitational potential energy is similar to the equation for the potential energy of a spring.

$PE = \frac{1}{2}kx^2$ or $\frac{1}{2}kA^2$,

where k is a constant and A (or x) is the distance from equilibrium

A is the amplitude of a wave in simple harmonic motion (SHM).

---

6. E is correct. The period of the spring's oscillation is:

$$T = 2\pi\sqrt{(L / g)}$$
$$T = 2\pi\sqrt{(0.03 \text{ m} / 9.8 \text{ m/s}^2)}$$
$$T = 2\pi(0.055 \text{ s})$$
$$T = 0.35 \text{ s}$$

The frequency is the reciprocal of the period.

$$f = 1 / T$$
$$f = 1 / (0.35 \text{ s})$$
$$f = 2.9 \text{ Hz}$$

7. C is correct. $T = 1 / f$

8. D is correct. The period of a pendulum:

$$T = 2\pi\sqrt{(L / g)}$$

The period only depends on the pendulum's length and gravity.

In an elevator, gravity only changes if the elevator is accelerating in either direction.

9. A is correct.

The period is the reciprocal of the frequency:

$$T = 1 / f$$
$$T = 1 / 100 \text{ Hz}$$
$$T = 0.01 \text{ s}$$

10. E is correct.

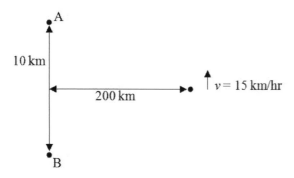

Convert v to m/s:

$$v = (15 \text{ km/1 h}) \cdot (1 \text{ h/60 min}) \cdot (1 \text{ min/60 s}) \cdot (10^3 \text{ m/1 km})$$
$$v = 4.2 \text{ m/s}$$

Convert frequency to λ:

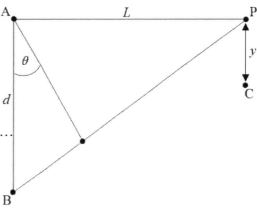

$$\lambda = c / f$$

$$\lambda = (3 \times 10^8 \text{ m/s}) / (4.7 \times 10^6 \text{ Hz})$$

$$\lambda = 63.8 \text{ m}$$

According to Young's Equation:

$$\lambda = yd / mL, \text{ where } m = 0, 1, 2, 3, 4...$$

Solve for y by rearranging to isolate y:

$$y = \lambda L m / d$$

y = distance travelled by the ship:

$$y = vt$$

Since the first signal came at the point of maximum intensity, m = 0 at that time, at the next maximum m = 1.

Therefore:

$$t = mL\lambda / vd$$

$$t = (1) \cdot (200{,}000 \text{ m}) \cdot (63.8 \text{ m}) / (4.2 \text{ m/s}) \cdot (10{,}000 \text{ m})$$

$$t = 304 \text{ s}$$

Convert time from seconds to minutes:

$$t = (304 \text{ s}) \cdot (1 \text{ min}/60 \text{ s})$$

$$t = 5.06 \text{ min} \approx 5.1 \text{ min}$$

For all m values greater than 1, the calculated times are beyond the answer choices so 5.1 min is the correct answer.

11. D is correct.

The tension in the rope is given by the equation:

$$T = (mv^2) / L$$

where v is the velocity of the wave and L is the length of the rope.

Substituting:

$$v = L / t$$

$$T = [m(L / t)^2] / L$$

$$T = mL / t^2$$

$$t^2 = mL / T$$

$$t = \sqrt{(mL / T)}$$

$$t = \sqrt{[(2.31 \text{ kg}) \cdot (10.4 \text{ m}) / 74.4 \text{ N}]}$$

$$t = \sqrt{(0.323 \text{ s}^2)} = 0.57 \text{ s}$$

12. A is correct.

$$f_A = 2 f_B$$

frequency = 1 / period

$$f = 1 / T$$

The period is the reciprocal of the frequency:

$$T = 1 / f$$

$$f_A = 2 f_B$$

$$T_A = \tfrac{1}{2} f_B$$

$$T_A = \tfrac{1}{2} T_B$$

$$T = 2\pi \sqrt{(L / g)}$$

$$L_B = g(T_B / 2\pi)^2$$

$$L_A = g(\tfrac{1}{2} T_B / 2\pi)^2$$

$$L_A = \tfrac{1}{4} g(T_B / 2\pi)^2$$

$$L_A = \tfrac{1}{4} L_B$$

13. B is correct. $F = -kx$

Since the motion is simple harmonic, the restoring force is proportional to displacement.

Therefore, if the displacement is 5 times greater, then so is the restoring force.

14. C is correct.

$$\text{Period} = (60\ \text{s}) / (10\ \text{oscillations})$$

$$T = 6\ \text{s}$$

The period is the time for one oscillation.

If 10 oscillations take 60 s, then one oscillation takes 6 s.

15. E is correct. Conservation of Energy:

$$\text{total ME} = \Delta KE + \Delta PE = \text{constant}$$

$$\tfrac{1}{2} m v^2 + \tfrac{1}{2} k x^2 = \text{constant}$$

16. B is correct. A displacement from the position of maximum elongation to the position of maximum compression represents *half* a cycle. If it takes 1 s, then the time required for a complete cycle is 2 s.

$$f = 1 / T$$

$$f = 1 / 2\ \text{s}$$

$$f = 0.5\ \text{Hz}$$

17. C is correct.

Sound waves are longitudinal waves.

18. E is correct.

speed = wavelength × frequency

speed = wavelength / period

$v = \lambda / T$

$\lambda = vT$

$\lambda = (362 \text{ m/s}) \cdot (0.004 \text{ s})$

$\lambda = 1.5 \text{ m}$

19. A is correct.

$a = -A\omega^2 \cos (\omega t)$

where A is the amplitude, or displacement from resting position.

20. D is correct.

The acceleration of a simple harmonic oscillation is:

$a = -A\omega^2 \cos (\omega t)$

Its maximum occurs when cos (ωt) is equal to 1

$a_{max} = -\omega^2 x$

If ω is doubled:

$a = -(2\omega)^2 x$

$a = -4\omega^2 x$

The maximum value of acceleration changes by a factor of 4.

21. B is correct.

Resonant frequency of a spring and mass system in any orientation:

$\omega = \sqrt{(k / m)}$

$f = \omega / 2\pi$

$T = 1 / f$

$T = 2\pi\sqrt{(m / k)}$

Period of a spring does not depend on gravity.

The period remains constant because only mass and the spring constant affect the period.

22. E is correct.

$$v = \lambda f$$

$$\lambda = v / f$$

An increase in v and a decrease in f must increase λ.

23. B is correct.

Frequency is the measure of oscillations or vibrations per second.

> frequency = 60 vibrations in 1 s
>
> frequency = 60 Hz
>
> speed = 30 m / 1 s
>
> speed = 30 m/s

24. A is correct.

$$T = (mv^2) / L$$

$$m = TL / v^2$$

$$m = (60 \text{ N}) \cdot (16 \text{ m}) / (40 \text{ m/s})^2$$

$$m = (960 \text{ N} \cdot \text{m}) / (1{,}600 \text{ m}^2/\text{s}^2)$$

$$m = 0.6 \text{ kg}$$

25. E is correct.

Amplitude is independent of frequency.

26. C is correct.

$$f = \text{\# cycles} / \text{time}$$

$$f = 60 \text{ drips} / 40 \text{ s}$$

$$f = 1.5 \text{ Hz}$$

27. D is correct. Transverse waves are characterized by their crests and valleys, which are caused by the particles of the wave traveling "up and down" with respect to the lateral movement of the wave.

The particles in longitudinal waves travel parallel to the direction of the wave.

28. B is correct. For a particle in simple harmonic motion, at each end of its oscillation when the amplitude is maximum, the particle's velocity is zero since it is stopped and about to "turn around" in its motion. At this point, the particle's acceleration is at a maximum and directed toward the equilibrium position since the particle is at the farthest distance from equilibrium and requires the largest acceleration to get there.

Once the particle reaches the equilibrium position, it stops moving; since the acceleration is always directed toward equilibrium, the acceleration is zero at the equilibrium position. But due to the previous acceleration the particle just experienced, its velocity reaches a maximum as it passes through the equilibrium position, then decreases.

29. E is correct.

The speed of a wave is determined by the characteristics of the medium (and the type of wave). Speed is independent of amplitude.

30. A is correct.

$f = 1$ / period

$f = $ # cycles / second

$f = 1$ cycle / 2 s

$f = $ ½ Hz

31. B is correct.

$f = v / \lambda$

$\lambda = v / f$

$\lambda = (340$ m/s$) / (2,100$ Hz$)$

$\lambda = 0.16$ m

32. D is correct.

Period $(T) = 2\pi\sqrt{(L / g)}$

The period is independent of the mass.

33. E is correct.

$v = \omega x$

$\omega = v / x$

$\omega = (15$ m/s$) / (2.5$ m$)$

$\omega = 6.0$ rad/s

34. D is correct.

Unpolarized light on a polarizer reduces the intensity by ½.

$I = (½)I_0$

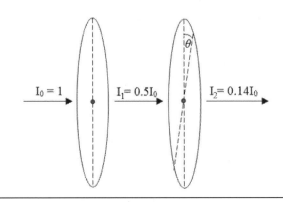

After that, the light is further reduced in intensity by the second filter.

Law of Malus:

$I = I_0 \cos^2 \theta$

$(0.14\ I_0) = (0.5\ I_0) \cos^2 \theta$

$0.28 = \cos^2 \theta$

$\cos^{-1} \sqrt{(0.28)} = \theta$

$\theta = 58°$

35. C is correct.

At a maximum distance from equilibrium, the energy in the system is potential energy and the speed is zero, therefore kinetic energy is also zero. Since there is no kinetic energy, the mass has no velocity.

36. D is correct.

$v = \lambda f$

$f = v\ /\ \lambda$

$f = (240\ \text{m/s})\ /\ (0.1\ \text{m})$

$f = 2{,}400\ \text{Hz}$

37. B is correct.

In a transverse wave the vibrations of particles are perpendicular to the direction of travel of the wave. Transverse waves have crests and troughs that move along the wave.

In a longitudinal wave the vibrations of particles are parallel to the direction of travel of the wave. Longitudinal waves have compressions and rarefactions that move along the wave.

38. C is correct.

$v = \sqrt{(T\ /\ \mu)},$

where μ is the linear density of the wire.

$T = v^2 \mu$

$\mu = \rho A$

where A is the cross-sectional area of the wire.

$\mu = (2{,}700\ \text{kg/m}^3)\pi(4.6 \times 10^{-3}\ \text{m})^2$

$\mu = 0.045\ \text{kg/m}$

$T = (36\ \text{m/s})^2 \cdot (0.045\ \text{kg/m})$

$T = 58\ \text{N}$

39. D is correct.

Refraction is the change in direction of a wave, caused by the change in the wave's speed. Examples of waves include sound waves and light waves. Refraction is seen most often when a wave passes from one medium to a different medium (e.g. from air to water and vice versa).

40. C is correct.

f = # cycles / second

f = 2 cycles / 1 s

f = 2 Hz

41. A is correct.

pitch = frequency

A higher pitch means a greater f.

42. C is correct.

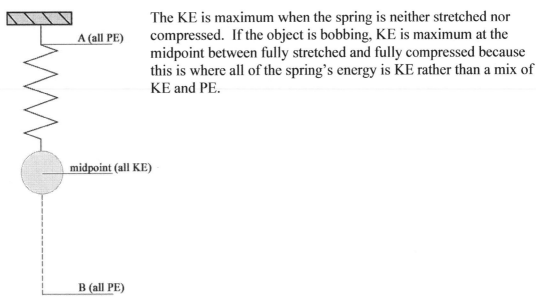

The KE is maximum when the spring is neither stretched nor compressed. If the object is bobbing, KE is maximum at the midpoint between fully stretched and fully compressed because this is where all of the spring's energy is KE rather than a mix of KE and PE.

43. B is correct.

Torque = $rF \sin \theta$

$F = ma$, substitute mg for F

$\tau = rmg \sin \theta$

$\tau = (1 \text{ m}) \cdot (0.5 \text{ kg}) \cdot (10 \text{ m/s}^2) \sin 60°$

$\tau = (5 \text{ kg·m}^2/\text{s}^2) \times 0.87$

$\tau = 4.4 \text{ N·m}$

44. E is correct. The Doppler effect can be observed to occur in all types of waves.

45. A is correct.

$v = \sqrt{(T / \mu)}$ where μ is the linear density of the wire.

$F_T = ma$

$F_T = (2{,}500 \text{ kg}){\cdot}(10 \text{ m/s}^2)$

$F_T = 25{,}000 \text{ N}$

$v = \sqrt{(25{,}000 \text{ N} / 0.65 \text{ kg/m})}$

$v = 196 \text{ m/s}$

The weight of the wire can be assumed to be negligible compared to the cement block.

46. B is correct. $f = \frac{1}{2}\pi[\sqrt{(g / L)}]$, frequency is independent of mass

47. A is correct.

$T = 2\pi\sqrt{(L / g)}]$

$T = 2\pi\sqrt{(3.3 \text{ m} / 10 \text{ m/s}^2)}$

$T = 3.6 \text{ s}$

48. C is correct. $f = (1/2\pi)\sqrt{(k / m)}$

If k increases by a factor of 2, then f increases by a factor of $\sqrt{2}$ (or 1.41).

Increasing by a factor of 1.41 or 41%

49. D is correct. In simple harmonic motion, the acceleration is greatest at the ends of motions (points A and D) where velocity is zero.

Velocity is greatest at the nadir where acceleration is equal to zero (point C).

50. A is correct.

At the lowest point, the KE is at a maximum and the PE is at a minimum.

The loss of gravitational PE equals the gain in KE:

$mgh = \frac{1}{2}mv^2$, cancel m from both sides of the expression

$gh = \frac{1}{2}v^2$

$(10 \text{ m/s}^2){\cdot}(10 \text{ m}) = \frac{1}{2}v^2$

$(100 \text{ m}^2/\text{s}^2) = \frac{1}{2}v^2$

$200 \text{ m}^2/\text{s}^2 = v^2$

$v = 14 \text{ m/s}$

51. A is correct.

Pitch is equivalent to frequency and amplitude. It is a measurement of wave energy but does not relate to speed which is constant.

52. C is correct.

Because wind is blowing in the reference frame of both the train and the observer, it does not need to be taken into account.

$$f_{observed} = [v_{sound} / (v_{sound} - v_{source})]f_{source}$$

$$f_{observed} = [340 \text{ m/s} / (340 \text{ m/s} - 50 \text{ m/s})] \cdot 500 \text{ Hz}$$

$$f_{observed} = 586 \text{ Hz}$$

$$\lambda = v / f$$

$$\lambda = 340 \text{ m/s} / 586 \text{ Hz}$$

$$\lambda = 0.58 \text{ m}$$

53. B is correct.

$$PE = \frac{1}{2}kx^2$$

Doubling the amplitude x increases PE by a factor of 4.

54. E is correct.

The elastic modulus is given by:

$$E = \text{tensional strength} / \text{extensional strain}$$

$$E = \sigma / \varepsilon$$

55. D is correct.

Resonance is the phenomenon where one system transfers its energy to another at that system's resonant frequency (natural frequency). It is forced vibration with the least energy input.

56. A is correct.

Period of a pendulum:

$$T_P = 2\pi\sqrt{(L / g)}$$

Period of a spring:

$$T_S = 2\pi\sqrt{(m / k)}$$

The period of a spring does not depend on gravity and is unaffected.

57. E is correct.

At the top of its arc, the pendulum comes to rest momentarily; the KE and the velocity equal zero.

Since its height above the bottom of its arc is at a maximum at this point, its (angular) displacement from the vertical equilibrium position is at a maximum also.

The pendulum constantly experiences the forces of gravity and tension, and is therefore continuously accelerating.

58. D is correct.

The Doppler effect is the observed change in frequency when a sound source is in motion relative to an observer (away or towards). If the sound source moves with the observer then there is no relative motion between the two and the Doppler effect does not occur.

59. C is correct.

The amplitude of a wave is the magnitude of its oscillation from its equilibrium point.

60. A is correct.

$$f = (1/2\pi)\sqrt{(k/m)}$$

An increase in m causes a decrease in f.

We want to hear from you

Your feedback is important to us because we strive to provide the highest quality prep materials. If you have any questions, comments or suggestions, email us, so we can incorporate your feedback into future editions.

Customer Satisfaction Guarantee

If you have any concerns about this book, including printing issues, contact us and we will
resolve any issues to your satisfaction.

info@sterling-prep.com

Sound – Explanations

1. B is correct.

Intensity is inversely proportional to distance (in W/m², not dB).

$$I_2 / I_1 = (d_1 / d_2)^2$$

$$I_2 / I_1 = (3 \text{ m} / 30 \text{ m})^2$$

$$100 \, I_2 = I_1$$

The intensity is 100 times greater at 3 m away than 30 m away.

Intensity to decibel relationship:

$$I \, (dB) = 10 \log_{10} (I / I_0)$$

The intensity to dB relationship is logarithmic. Thus if I_1 is 100 times the original intensity then it is two times the dB intensity because:

$$\log_{10} (100) = 2$$

Thus the decibel level at 3 m away is:

$$I \, (dB) = (2) \cdot (20 \text{ dB})$$

$$I = 40 \text{ dB}$$

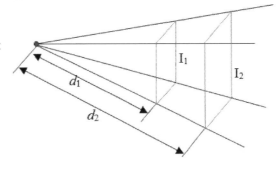

2. A is correct.

$$\text{distance} = \text{velocity} \times \text{time}$$

$$d = vt$$

$$t = d / v$$

$$t = (6{,}000 \text{ m}) / (340 \text{ m/s})$$

$$t = 18 \text{ s}$$

3. B is correct.

Resonance occurs when a wave oscillates at a relative maximum amplitude, which translates into greater energy of the system. When this energy exceeds the stability of the glass, the glass shatters.

4. C is correct.

The third harmonic is shown in the figure below:

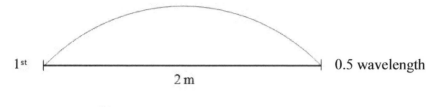

1st 2 m   0.5 wavelength

2nd 1 wavelength

3rd 1.5 wavelength

There are $(3/2)\lambda$ in the 2 m wave in the third harmonic

$$L = (n / 2)\lambda \text{ (for n harmonic)}$$
$$L = (3 / 2)\lambda \text{ (for 3}^{rd}\text{ harmonic)}$$
$$L(2 / 3) = \lambda$$
$$\lambda = (2 \text{ m}) \cdot (2 / 3)$$
$$\lambda = 4/3 \text{ m}$$

5. B is correct.

6. E is correct.

Snell's law:

$$n_1 \sin \theta_1 = n_2 \sin \theta_2$$

Solve for θ_2:

$$(n_1 / n_2) \sin \theta_1 = \sin \theta_2$$
$$\sin \theta_1 = (n_1 / n_2) \sin \theta_2$$
$$\theta_2 = \sin^{-1}[(n_1 / n_2) \sin \theta_1]$$

Substituting the given values:

$$\theta_2 = \sin^{-1}[(1 / 1.5) \sin 60°]$$
$$\theta_2 = \sin^{-1}(0.67 \sin 60°)$$

7. D is correct.

For a standing wave, the length and wavelength are related:

$L = (n / 2)\lambda$ (for n harmonic)

From the diagram, the wave is the 6th harmonic:

$L = (6 / 2)\lambda$

$\lambda = (2 \text{ m}) \cdot (2 / 6)$

$\lambda = 0.667 \text{ m}$

$f = v / \lambda$

$f = (92 \text{ m/s}) / (0.667 \text{ m})$

$f = 138 \text{ Hz}$

8. A is correct.

$v = d / t$

$v = (0.6 \text{ m}) / (0.00014 \text{ s})$

$v = 4{,}286 \text{ m/s}$

$\lambda = v / f$

$\lambda = (4{,}286 \text{ m/s}) / (1.5 \times 10^{6} \text{ Hz})$

$\lambda = 0.0029 \text{ m} = 2.9 \text{ mm}$

9. C is correct.

The wave velocity is increased by a factor of 1.3.

$v^2 = T / \rho_L$

$T = v^2 \times \rho_L$

Increasing v by a factor of 1.3:

$T = (1.3v)^2 \rho_L$

$T = 1.69v^2 \rho_L$

T increases by 69%

10. D is correct.

$\rho_L = \rho A$

$\rho_L = \rho(\pi r^2)$

Thus if the diameter decreases by a factor of 2, then the radius decreases by a factor of 2, and the area decreases by a factor of 4. The linear mass density decreases by a factor of 4.

11. B is correct.

The v and period (T) of wire C are equal to wire A so the ρ_L must be equal as well.

$\rho_{LA} = \rho_{LC}$

$\rho_A A_A = \rho_C A_C$

$A_C = (\rho_A A_A) / \rho_C$

$(\pi / 4)\cdot(d_C)^2 = (7 \text{ g/cm}^3)(\pi / 4)\cdot(0.6 \text{ mm})^2 / (3 \text{ g/cm}^3)$

$(d_C)^2 = (7 \text{ g/cm}^3)\cdot(0.6 \text{ mm})^2 / (3 \text{ g/cm}^3)$

$d_C^2 = 0.84 \text{ mm}^2$

$d_C = \sqrt{(0.84 \text{ mm}^2)} = 0.92 \text{ mm}$

12. A is correct.

$A = \pi r^2$

If d increases by a factor of 4, r increases by a factor of 4.

A increases by a factor of 16.

13. E is correct. Since the bird is moving toward the observer, the $f_{observed}$ must be higher than f_{source}.

Doppler shift for an approaching sound source:

$f_{observed} = (v_{sound} / v_{sound} - v_{source})f_{source}$

$f_{observed} = [340 \text{ m/s} / (340 \text{ m/s} - 10 \text{ m/s})]f_{source}$

$f_{observed} = (340 \text{ m/s} / 330 \text{ m/s})\cdot(60 \text{ kHz})$

$f_{observed} = (1.03)\cdot(60 \text{ kHz})$

$f_{observed} = 62 \text{ kHz}$

14. C is correct. When an approaching sound source is heard, the observed frequency is higher than the frequency from the source due to the Doppler effect.

15. D is correct. Sound requires a medium of solid, liquid or gas substances to be propagated through. A vacuum is none of these.

16. E is correct.   πιτχη = φρεθυενχψ

According to the Doppler effect pitch increases as the sound source moves towards the observer because consecutive waves which are closer together have a higher frequency and therefore a higher pitch.

Conversely, as the sound source moves away from the observer, its pitch decreases.

17. C is correct.

If waves are out of phase, the combination has its minimum amplitude of (0.6 – 0.4) Pa = 0.2 Pa.

If waves are in phase, the combination has its maximum amplitude of (0.6 + 0.4) Pa = 1.0 Pa.

When the phase difference has a value between in phase and out of phase, the amplitude will be between 0.2 Pa and 0.4 Pa.

18. B is correct.

$$I = P / A$$
$$I = P / \pi d^2$$

Intensity at 2*d*:

$$I_2 = P / \pi(2d)^2$$
$$I_2 = P / 4\pi d^2$$
$$I_2 = \frac{1}{4}P / \pi d^2$$

The new intensity is ¼ the original.

19. A is correct.

speed of sound = √[resistance to compression / density]

$$v_{sound} = \sqrt{(E / \rho)}$$

Low resistance to compression and high density result in low velocity because this minimizes the term under the radical and thus minimizes velocity.

20. B is correct.

Pipes resonate at harmonic frequencies, which are integer multiples of the pipe's fundamental frequency.

At these frequencies, there are antinodes on the wave at each end of the open pipe.

21. E is correct.

For a pipe open at both ends, the resonance frequency:

$$f_n = nf_1$$

where n = 1, 2, 3, 4…

Therefore only a multiple of 200 Hz can be a resonant frequency.

22. D is correct.

Unlike light, sound waves require a medium to travel through and its speed is dependent upon the medium.

Sound is fastest in solids, then liquids and slowest in air: $v_{solid} > v_{liquid} > v_{air}$

---

23. B is correct.

Magnetic fields are induced by currents or moving charges.

24. C is correct.

$$\lambda = v / f$$

$$\lambda = (5{,}000 \text{ m/s}) / (620 \text{ Hz})$$

$$\lambda = 8.1 \text{ m}$$

25. E is correct.

Sound intensity radiating spherically:

$$I = P / 4\pi r^2$$

If r is doubled:

$$I = P / 4\pi(2r)^2$$

$$I = \tfrac{1}{4}P / 4\pi r^2$$

The intensity is reduced by a factor of ¼.

26. D is correct.

As the sound propagates through a medium it spreads out in an approximately spherical pattern. Thus the power is radiated along the surface of the sphere and the intensity can be given by:

$$I = P / (4\pi r^2) \leftarrow \text{for surface area of a sphere}$$

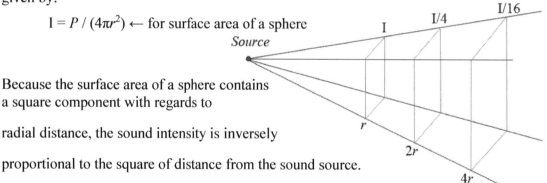

Because the surface area of a sphere contains a square component with regards to

radial distance, the sound intensity is inversely

proportional to the square of distance from the sound source.

27. B is correct.

The closed end is a node and the open end is an antinode.

$$\lambda = (4 / n)L$$

where n = 1, 3, 5 …

For the fundamental n = 1:

$$\lambda = (4 / 1) \cdot (1.5 \text{ m})$$

$$\lambda = 6 \text{ m}$$

The 1.5 m tube (open at one end) is a quarter of a full wave, so the wavelength is 6 m.

---

28. A is correct. The 1.5 m is ¼ a full wave, so the wavelength is 6 m, for the fundamental.

$f = v / \lambda$

$f = (960 \text{ m/s}) / 6 \text{ m}$

$f = 160 \text{ Hz}$

29. E is correct.

For a closed-ended pipe the wavelength to the harmonic relationship is:

$\lambda = (4 / n)L$

where n = 1, 3, 5…

For the 5th harmonic n = 5

$\lambda = (4 / 5) \cdot (1.5 \text{ m})$

$\lambda_n = 1.2 \text{ m}$

Closed end tube				
Harmonic # (n)	# of waves in tube	# of nodes	# of antinodes	Wavelength to length
1	1/4	1	1	$\lambda = 4 L$
3	3/4	2	2	$\lambda = 4/3\, L$
5	5/4	3	3	$\lambda = 4/5\, L$
7	7/4	4	4	$\lambda = 4/7\, L$

30. A is correct.

$f = v / \lambda$

$f = (340 \text{ m/s}) / (6 \text{ m})$

$f = 57 \text{ Hz}$

31. C is correct. Wavelength to harmonic number relationship in a standing wave on a string:

$\lambda = (2L / n)$

where n = 1, 2, 3, 4, 5 …

For the 3rd harmonic:

$\lambda = (2) \cdot (0.34 \text{ m}) / 3$

$\lambda = 0.23 \text{ m}$

32. D is correct. Beat frequency equation:

$f_{beat} = | f_2 - f_1 |$

If one of the tones increases in frequency, then the beat frequency increases or decreases, but this cannot be determined unless the two tones are known.

33. A is correct. For a closed-ended pipe, the wavelength to harmonic relationship is:

$\lambda = (4 / n)L$

where n = 1, 3, 5, 7…

The lowest three tones are n = 1, 3, 5

$\lambda = (4 / 1)L; \lambda = (4 / 3)L; \lambda = (4 / 5)L$

34. E is correct.

The sound was barely perceptible, the intensity at Mary's ear is $I_0 = 9.8 \times 10^{-12}$ W/m^2.

Since the mosquito is 1 m away, imagine a sphere 1 m in radius around the mosquito.

If 9.8×10^{-12} W emanates from each area 1 m^2, then the surface area is $4\pi(1 \text{ m})^2$.

This is the power produced by one mosquito:

$P = 4\pi r^2 I_0$

$P = 4\pi(1 \text{ m})^2 \times (9.8 \times 10^{-12} \text{ W/m}^2)$

$P = 1.2 \times 10^{-10}$ W

energy = power × time

$E = Pt$

Energy produced in 200 s:

$Pt = (1.2 \times 10^{-10} \text{ W}) \cdot (200 \text{ s})$

$E = 2.5 \times 10^{-8}$ J

35. A is correct.

$v = c / \text{n}$

where c is the speed of light in a vacuum

$v = \Delta x / \Delta t$

$\Delta x / \Delta t = c / \text{n}$

$\Delta t = \text{n} \Delta x / c$

$\Delta t = (1.33) \cdot (10^3 \text{ m}) / (3 \times 10^8 \text{ m/s})$

$\Delta t = 4.4 \times 10^{-6}$ s

36. E is correct.

When waves interfere constructively (i.e. in phase), the sound level is amplified. When they interfere destructively (i.e. out of phase), they cancel and no sound is heard. Acoustic engineers work to ensure that there are no "dead spots" and the sound waves add.

An engineer should minimize destructive interference which can distort sound.

37. B is correct.

Velocity of a wave on a string in tension can be calculated by:

$v = \sqrt{(TL / m)}$

Graph B gives a curve of a square root relationship which is how velocity and tension are related.

$y = x^{\frac{1}{2}}$

38. D is correct. From the diagram, the wave is a 6th harmonic standing wave.

Find wavelength:

$\lambda = (2L / n)$

$\lambda = (2) \cdot (4 \text{ m}) / (6)$

$\lambda = 1.3 \text{ m}$

Find frequency:

$f = v / \lambda$

$f = (20 \text{ m/s}) / (1.3 \text{ m})$

$f = 15.4 \text{ Hz}$

1st

2nd

3rd

39. E is correct. Sound wave velocity is independent of frequency and does not change.

40. C is correct.

First, find the frequency of the string, then the length of the pipe excited to the second overtone using that frequency.

The speed of sound in the string is:

$v_{string} = \sqrt{T/\mu}$

where T is the tension in the string, and μ is linear mass density.

$v_{string} = \sqrt{[(75 \text{ N}) / (0.00040 \text{ kg})]}$

$v_{string} = 433.01 \text{ m/s}$

The wavelength of a string of length L_{string} vibrating in harmonic n_{string} is:

$\lambda_{string} = 2L_{string} / n_{string}$

Therefore, the vibration frequency of the string is:

$f = v_{string} / \lambda_{string}$

$f = [(n_{string})(v_{string})] / 2L_{string}$

$f = [(6)(433.01 \text{ m/s})] / (2 \times 0.50 \text{ m})$

$f = (2,598.06 \text{ m/s}) / 1 \text{ m}$

$f = 2,598.1 \text{ Hz}$

Now, consider the open pipe. The relationship between length, wavelength and harmonic number for an open pipe is the same as that for a string.

Therefore:

$L_{pipe} = n_{pipe} (\lambda_{pipe} / 2)$

However, since $\lambda_{pipe} = v_{air} / f$:

$L_{pipe} = n_{pipe} (v_{air} / 2f)$

Noting that the second overtone is the third harmonic ($n_{pipe} = 3$):

$L_{pipe} = (3 \times 345 \text{ m/s}) / (2 \times 2{,}598.1 \text{ Hz})$

$L_{pipe} = 0.20 \text{ m}$

Note that it is not necessary to calculate the frequency; its value cancels out.

There is less chance for error if the two steps that use frequency are skipped.

In $L_{pipe} = n_{pipe} (v_{air} / 2f)$ substitute $f = [(n_{string})(v_{string})] / 2L_{string}$

which gives:

$L_{pipe} = L_{string} (v_{air} / v_{string}) \cdot (n_{pipe} / n_{string})$

It yields the same answer but with fewer calculations.

41. A is correct.

$v = \sqrt{(T / \mu)}$

$\mu = m / L$

$v = \sqrt{(TL / m)}$

$v_2 = \sqrt{(T(2L) / m)}$

$v_2 = \sqrt{2} \sqrt{(TL / m)}$

$v_2 = v\sqrt{2}$

42. C is correct.

For a standing wave, the resonance frequency:

$f_n = nf_1$

where n is the harmonic number, n = 1, 2, 3, 4 …

Therefore, only a multiple of 500 Hz can be a resonant frequency.

43. D is correct.

The angle of incidence always equals the angle of reflection.

A light beam entering a medium with a greater refractive index than the incident medium refracts *toward* the normal. Thus, the angle of refraction is less than the angles of incidence and reflection.

Snell's law:

$n_1 \sin \theta_1 = n_2 \sin \theta_2$

where $n_1 < n_2$

For Snell's law to be true, then:

$\theta_1 > \theta_2$

44. A is correct. Speed of sound in gas:

$$v_{sound} = \sqrt{(yRT / M)}$$

where y = adiabatic constant, R = gas constant, T = temperature and M = molecular mass

The speed of sound in a gas is only dependent upon temperature and not frequency or wavelength.

45. B is correct. Waves only transport energy and not matter.

46. E is correct.

$$v = \lambda f$$

$$\lambda = v / f$$

$$\lambda = (344 \text{ m/s}) / (700 \text{ s}^{-1})$$

$$\lambda = 0.5 \text{ m}$$

The information about the string is unnecessary, as the only contributor to the wavelength of the sound in air is the frequency and the speed.

47. C is correct.

$$v = \lambda f$$

$$f = v / \lambda$$

Distance from sound source is not part of the equation for frequency.

48. A is correct. Velocity of a wave in a rope:

$$v = \sqrt{[T / (m / L)]}$$

$$t = d / v$$

$$d = L$$

$$t = d / \sqrt{[T / (m / L)]}$$

$$t = (8 \text{ m}) / [40 \text{ N} / (2.5 \text{ kg} / 8 \text{ m})]^{\frac{1}{2}}$$

$$t = 0.71 \text{ s}$$

49. C is correct.

Intensity to decibel relationship:

$$I \text{ (dB)} = 10 \log_{10} (I_1 / I_0)$$

where I_0 = threshold of hearing

$$dB = 10\log_{10}[(10^{-5} \text{ W/m}^2) / (10^{-12} \text{ W/m}^2)]$$

$$I = 70 \text{ decibels}$$

50. E is correct.

The diagram represents the described scenario.

The wave is in the second harmonic with a wavelength of:

$$\lambda = (2 / n)L$$

$$\lambda = (2 / 2){\cdot}(1 \text{ m})$$

$$\lambda = 1 \text{ m}$$

$$f = v / \lambda$$

$$f = (3.8 \times 10^4 \text{ m/s}) / (1 \text{ m})$$

$$f = 3.8 \times 10^4 \text{ Hz}$$

The lowest frequency corresponds to the lowest possible harmonic number.

For this problem, n = 2.

51. D is correct. The speed of light travelling in a vacuum is *c*.

$$c = \lambda v$$

$$c = \lambda f$$

$$f = c / \lambda$$

Frequency and wavelength are inversely proportional so an increase in frequency results in a decreased wavelength.

52. B is correct.

Radio waves are electromagnetic waves while all other choices are mechanical waves.

53. D is correct.

Find the extreme path difference (EPD) which is the path length from speaker 1 to the microphone minus the path length from speaker 2.

$$EPD = | L_1 - L_2 |$$

$$L = \text{path} / \lambda$$

$$EPD = | (1 \text{ m} / 0.8 \text{ m}) - (1 \text{ m} / 0.8 \text{ m}) |$$

$$EPD = 0$$

For constructive interference:

$$EPD = m\lambda$$

where m = 0, 1, 2, 3 …

For destructive interference:

$$EPD = \tfrac{1}{2}(2m - 1)\lambda$$

where m = 1, 2, 3 …

The wave is constructively interfering because EPD = 0 which can only be produced when m = 0.

Thus point m must be an antinode.

54. C is correct. Doppler equation for receding source of sound:

$f_{observed} = [v_{sound} / (v_{sound} + v_{source})] f_{source}$

$f_{observed} = [(342 \text{ m/s}) / (342 \text{ m/s} + 30 \text{ m/s})] \cdot (1,200 \text{ Hz})$

$f_{observed} = 1,103 \text{ Hz}$

The observed frequency is always lower when the source is receding.

55. E is correct.

$f_1 = 600 \text{ Hz}$

$f_2 = 300 \text{ Hz}$

$f_2 = \frac{1}{2} f_1$

$\lambda_1 = v / f_1$

$\lambda_2 = v / (\frac{1}{2} f_1)$

$\lambda_2 = 2 (v / f_1)$

The wavelength of the 300 Hz frequency is twice as long as the wavelength of the 600 Hz frequency.

56. C is correct.

$f_2 = 2f_1$

$f = v / \lambda$

$v / \lambda_2 = (2)v / \lambda_1$, cancel v from both sides of the expression

$1 / \lambda_2 = 2 / \lambda_1$

$\lambda = (2 / n)L$, for open-ended pipes

$1 / (2 / n)L_2 = 2 / (2 / n)L_1$

$L_1 = 2L_2$

$L_1 / L_2 = 2$

57. A is correct.

Resonance occurs when energy gets transferred from one oscillator to another of similar f by a weak coupling. Dispersion is the spreading of waves due to the dependence of wave speed on frequency.

Interference is the addition of two waves in the same medium, which is what happens when waves from both strings combine, but that is not the excitation of the C_4 string.

58. C is correct.

> frequency = 1 / period
>
> $f = 1 / T$
>
> $f = 1 / 10$ s
>
> $f = 0.1$ Hz

Find wavelength:

> $\lambda = v / f$
>
> $\lambda = (4.5 \text{ m/s}) / (0.1 \text{ Hz})$
>
> $\lambda = 45$ m

59. D is correct.

> $v = \sqrt{K / \rho}$
>
> where K = bulk modulus (i.e. resistance to compression) and ρ = density.

Since ρ for water is greater than for air, the greater v for water implies that water's bulk modulus (K) must be much greater than for air.

60. C is correct.

When visible light strikes glass, it causes the electrons of the atoms in the glass to vibrate at their non-resonant frequency. The vibration is passed from one atom to the next transferring the energy of the light. Finally, the energy is passed to the last atom before the light is re-mitted out of the glass at its original frequency.

If the light energy were converted into internal energy the glass would heat up and not transfer the light.

Electrostatics and Electromagnetism – Explanations

1. C is correct. Since charge is quantized, the charge Q must be a whole number (n) times the charge on a single electron:

Charge = # electrons × electron charge

$Q = n(e^-)$

$n = Q / e^-$

$n = (-1 \text{ C}) / (-1.6 \times 10^{-19} \text{ C})$

$n = 6.25 \times 10^{18} \approx 6.3 \times 10^{18}$ electrons

2. D is correct. In Gaus's Law, the area is a vector perpendicular to the plane. Only the component of the electric field strength parallel is used.

Gaus's Law:

$\Phi = EA \cos \theta$

where Φ is electric flux (scalar), E is electric field strength and A is area vector.

Solve:

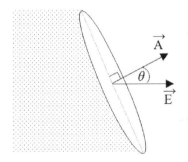

$\Phi = EA \cos (\pi / 6)$

$A = \pi r^2 = \pi / 4 \, D^2$

$\Phi = (740 \text{ N/C}) \cdot (\pi / 4) \cdot (1 \text{ m})^2 \cos (\pi / 6)$

$\Phi = 160\pi \text{ N·m}^2/\text{C}$

For calculation, use radians mode, not degree mode.

3. A is correct. The vector E_1 is due to charge Q at $x = -10^{-3}$ m.

The magnitude of the negative charge's electric field:

$| E_2 | = kQ_2 / d_2^2$

$| E_2 | = (9 \times 10^9 \text{ N·m}^2/\text{C}^2) \cdot [(-1.3 \times 10^{-9} \text{ C}) / (+10^{-3} \text{ m})^2]$

$| E_2 | = 1.17 \times 10^7$ N/C to the left

The magnitude of the positive charge's electric field:

$| E_1 | = kQ_1 / d_1^2$

$| E_1 | = (9 \times 10^9 \text{ N·m}^2/\text{C}^2) \cdot [(1.3 \times 10^{-9} \text{ C}) / (2 \times 10^{-3} \text{ m})^2]$

$| E_1 | = 2.9 \times 10^6$ N/C to the right

$\Delta E = E_2 - E_1$

$\Delta E = (1.17 \times 10^7 \text{ N/C}) - (2.9 \times 10^6 \text{ N/C})$

$\Delta E = 8.8 \times 10^6$ N/C, to the left

The point of observation is closer to the negative charge, thus vector to the left is longer.

4. C is correct. Coulomb's law:

$$F_1 = kQ_1Q_2 / r^2$$

If r is increased by a factor of 4:

$$F_e = kQ_1Q_2 / (4r)^2$$
$$F_e = kQ_1Q_2 / (16r^2)$$
$$F_e = (1/16)kQ_1Q_2 / r^2$$
$$F_e = (1/16)F_1$$

As the distance increases by a factor of 4, the force decreases by a factor of $4^2 = 16$.

5. E is correct. Calculate the distance between the two charges using the Pythagorean Theorem:

$$r^2 = (1 \text{ nm})^2 + (4 \text{ nm})^2$$
$$r^2 = 17 \text{ nm}^2$$
$$r = 4.1 \text{ nm}$$
$$F = kQ_1Q_2 / r^2$$
$$F = [(9 \times 10^9 \text{ N·m}^2/\text{C}^2)·(1.6 \times 10^{-19} \text{ C})·(1.6 \times 10^{-19} \text{ C})] / (4.1 \times 10^{-9} \text{ m})^2$$
$$F = 1.4 \times 10^{-11} \text{ N}$$

6. A is correct.

7. D is correct. Gravitational Force: F_g

$$F_g = Gm_1m_2 / r^2$$
$$F_g = [(6.673 \times 10^{-11} \text{ N·m}^2/\text{kg}^2)·(54,000 \text{ kg})·(51,000 \text{ kg})] / (180 \text{ m})^2$$
$$F_g = 0.18 \text{ N·m}^2 / (32,400 \text{ m}^2)$$
$$F_g = 5.7 \times 10^{-6} \text{ N}$$

Electrostatic Force: F_e

$$F_e = kQ_1Q_2 / r^2$$
$$F_e = [(9 \times 10^9 \text{ N·m}^2/\text{C}^2)·(15 \times 10^{-6} \text{ C})·(11 \times 10^{-6} \text{ C})] / (180 \text{ m})^2$$
$$F_e = (1.49 \text{ N·m}^2) / (32,400 \text{ m}^2)$$
$$F_e = 4.6 \times 10^{-5} \text{ N}$$

Net Force:

$$F_{net} = F_g - F_e$$
$$F_{net} = (5.7 \times 10^{-6} \text{ N}) - (4.6 \times 10^{-5} \text{ N})$$
$$F_{net} = -4 \times 10^{-5} \text{ N}$$

Because the charges are opposite, subtract F_e from F_g.

Force is expected to be negative since asteroid's charges have the same sign and will repel each other.

8. B is correct. Newton's Third Law also applies to electrostatic forces.

Newton's Third Law states for every force there is an equal and opposite reaction force:

Electrostatic Force:

$$F_1 = kQ_1Q_2 / r^2$$
$$F_2 = kQ_1Q_2 / r^2$$
$$F_1 = F_2$$

9. D is correct.

Forces balance to yield:

$$F_{electric} = F_{gravitation}$$
$$F_{electric} = mg$$

The values for an electric field are provided.

Electrostatic Force:

$$F_e = kQ_1Q_2 / r^2$$

Electric Field:

$$E = kQ_{source} / r^2$$
$$F_e = QE$$

$QE - mg = 0$, where Q is the charge on the ball

$$QE = mg$$
$$Q = mg / E$$
$$Q = (0.008 \text{ kg}) \cdot (9.8 \text{ m/s}^2) / (3.5 \times 10^4 \text{ N/C})$$
$$Q = -2.2 \times 10^{-6} \text{ C}$$

If the electric field points down, then a positive charge experiences a downward force.

The charge must be negative, so the electric force balances gravity.

10. A is correct.

$$a = qE / m$$

The electron moves against the electric field, in the upward direction, so its acceleration:

$$a_e = qE / m_e$$

The proton moves with the electric field, which is down, so:

$$a_p = qE / m_p$$

However, the masses considered are small to where the gravity component is negligible.

$$m_p / m_e = (1.67 \times 10^{-27} \text{ kg}) / (9.11 \times 10^{-31} \text{ kg})$$
$$m_p / m_e = 1,830$$

The mass of an electron is about 1,830 times smaller than the mass of a proton.

$$(1,830)m_e = m_p$$

$$a_p = qE / (1,830)m_e$$

$$a_p = a_e / (1,830)$$

$$a_e = 1,830a_p$$

11. D is correct.

Calculate the strength of the field at point P due to only one charge:

$$E = kQ / r^2$$

$$E_1 = (9 \times 10^9 \text{ N·m}^2/\text{C}^2)·[(2.3 \times 10^{-11} \text{ C}) / (5 \times 10^{-3} \text{ m})^2]$$

$$E_1 = 8.3 \times 10^3 \text{ N/C}$$

Both electric field vectors point toward the negative charge, so the magnitude of each field at point P is doubled:

$$E_T = 2E_1$$

$$E_T = 2(8.3 \times 10^3 \text{ N/C})$$

$$E_T = 1.7 \times 10^4 \text{ N/C}$$

12. E is correct.

$$\text{charge} = \text{\# electrons} \times \text{electron charge}$$

$$Q = ne^-$$

$$n = Q / e^-$$

$$n = (-10 \times 10^{-6} \text{ C}) / (-1.6 \times 10^{-19} \text{ C})$$

$$n = 6.3 \times 10^{13} \text{ electrons}$$

13. C is correct.

Coulomb's law:

$$F_e = kQ_1Q_2 / r^2$$

If the separation is halved then r decreases by ½:

$$F_2 = kq_1q_2 / (½r)^2$$

$$F_2 = 4(kq_1q_2 / r^2)$$

$$F_2 = 4F_e$$

14. E is correct.

Coulomb's law:

$$F = kQ_1Q_2 / r^2$$

Doubling both the charges and distance:

$$F = [k(2Q_1) \cdot (2Q_2)] / (2r)^2$$

$$F = [4k(Q_1) \cdot (Q_2)] / (4r^2)$$

$$F = (4/4)[kQ_1Q_2 / (r^2)]$$

$$F = kQ_1Q_2 / r^2, \text{ remains the same}$$

15. D is correct.

Like charges repel each other.

From Newton's Third Law, the magnitude of the force experienced by each charge is equal.

16. A is correct.

Coulomb's law:

$$F = kQ_1Q_2 / r^2$$

The Coulomb force between opposite charges is attractive.

Since the strength of force is inversely proportional to the square of the separation distance (r^2), the force decreases as the charges are pulled apart.

17. B is correct.

Electric fields exists when a voltage is present between two conductors.

When there is a voltage difference between the conductors, electrons move through the electric field from one conductor to the other.

18. D is correct.

Voltage is related to the number of coils in a wire. More coils yields a higher voltage.

Turns ratio:

$$V_s / V_p = n_s / n_p$$

In this case:

$$n_s < n_p$$

Therefore,

$$V_s < V_p$$

Because the secondary voltage (V_s) is lower than the primary voltage (V_p) the transformer is a step-down transformer.

19. B is correct.

Coulomb's Law:

$$F_1 = kQ_1Q_2 / r^2$$
$$F_2 = kQ_1Q_2 / r^2$$
$$F_1 = F_2$$

Newton's Third Law: the force exerted by one charge on the other has the same magnitude as the force the other exerts on the first.

20. E is correct.

$$F_e = kQ_1Q_2 / r^2$$
$$F_e = (9 \times 10^9 \text{ N·m}^2/\text{C}^2) \cdot (-1.6 \times 10^{-19} \text{ C}) \cdot (-1.6 \times 10^{-19} \text{ C}) / (0.03 \text{ m})^2$$
$$F_e = 2.56 \times 10^{-25} \text{ N}$$

21. A is correct.

According to Lenz's Law, inserting a magnet into the coil causes the magnetic flux through the coil to change. This produces an emf in the coil which drives a current through the coil:

Lenz's Law:

$$\text{emf} = -N\Delta BA / \Delta t$$

The brightness of the bulb changes with a change in the current but it cannot be known if the bulb gets brighter or dimmer without knowing the orientation of the coil with respect to the incoming magnetic pole of the magnet.

22. C is correct.

Charge = # electrons × electron charge

$$Q = ne^-$$
$$n = Q / e^-$$
$$n = (8 \times 10^{-6} \text{ C}) / (1.6 \times 10^{-19} \text{ C})$$
$$n = 5 \times 10^{13} \text{ electrons}$$

23. A is correct.

An object with a charge can attract another object of opposite charge or a neutral charge.

Like charges cannot attract, but the type of charge does not matter otherwise.

24. B is correct.

$$1 \text{ amp} = 1 \text{ C} / \text{s}$$

The ampere is the unit to express flow rate of electric charge known as current.

25. A is correct.

Initially, the current will flow clockwise but after 180° of rotation the current will reverse itself. After 360° of rotation the current will reverse itself again. Thus there are 2 current reverses in 1 revolution.

26. D is correct.

$$W = Q\Delta V$$

$$V = kQ / r$$

Consider the charge Q_1 to be fixed and move charge Q_2 from initial distance r_i to final distance r_f.

$$W = Q_2(V_f - V_i)$$

$$W = Q_2[(kQ_1 / r_f) - (kQ_1 / r_i)]$$

$$W = kQ_1Q_2(1 / r_f - 1 / r_i)$$

$$W = (9 \times 10^9 \text{ N·m}^2/\text{C}) \cdot (2.3 \times 10^{-8} \text{ C}) \cdot (2.5 \times 10^{-9} \text{ C}) \cdot [(1 / 0.01 \text{ m}) - (1 / 0.1 \text{ m})]$$

$$W = 4.7 \times 10^{-5} \text{ J}$$

27. E is correct.

The electric field is oriented in a way that a positively-charged particle would be forced to move to the top because negatively-charged particles move to the bottom of the cube to be closer to the source of the electric field.

Therefore, all the positively charged particles are forced upward and the negatively-charged ones downward, leaving the top surface positively charged.

28. C is correct.

The magnitude of the force between the center charge and each charge at a vertex is 5 N. The net force of these two forces is directed toward the third vertex.

To determine the magnitude of the net force, calculate the magnitude of the component of each force acting in that direction:

$$F_{net} = F_1 \sin (½ \, \theta) + F_2 \sin (½ \, \theta) \qquad \text{(see diagram)}$$

Since it is an equilateral triangle $\theta = 60°$,

$$F_{net} = (5 \text{ N} \sin 30°) + (5 \text{ N} \sin 30°)$$

$$F_{net} = (5 \text{ N}) \cdot (½) + (5 \text{ N}) \cdot (½)$$

$$F_{net} = 5 \text{ N}$$

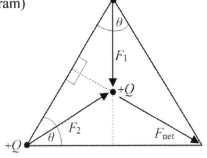

29. D is correct. Equilibrium:

$$F = kq_1q_2 / r_1^2$$

$$F_{\text{attractive on } q2} = F_{\text{repulsive on } q2}$$

$$kq_1q_2 / r_1^2 = kq_2Q / r_2^2$$

$$q_1 = Qr_1^2 / r_2^2$$

$$q_1 = (7.5 \times 10^{-9}\ \text{C}) \cdot (0.2\ \text{m})^2 / (0.1\ \text{m})^2$$

$$q_1 = 30 \times 10^{-9}\ \text{C}$$

30. A is correct. Gamma rays have the highest frequency on the electromagnetic spectrum, with frequencies greater than 3×10^{19} Hz.

31. A is correct.

The strength of the electrostatic field due to a single point charge is given by:

$$E = kQ / r^2,\ \text{assumes that the source charge is in vacuum}$$

E depends on both the magnitude of the source charge Q and the distance r from Q.

The sign of the source charge affects only the direction of the electrostatic field vectors.

The sign of the source charge does not affect the strength of the field.

32. B is correct.

$$F = qvB$$

$$F = mv^2 / r$$

$$mv^2 / r = qvB,\ \text{cancel } v \text{ from both sides of the expression}$$

$$mv / r = qB$$

$$r = (mv) / (qB)$$

If the velocity doubles, the radius also doubles.

33. C is correct.

Coulomb's law:

$$F_e = kQ_1Q_2 / r^2$$

$$1\ \text{N} = kQ_1Q_2 / r^2$$

Doubling charges and keeping distance constant:

$$k(2Q_1) \cdot (2Q_2) / r^2 = 4kQ_1Q_2 / r^2$$

$$4kQ_1Q_2 / r^2 = 4F_e$$

$$4F_e = 4(1\ \text{N}) = 4\ \text{N}$$

34. D is correct.

The Na^+ ion is positively charged and attracts the oxygen atom. Oxygen is slightly negative because it is more electronegative than the hydrogen atoms to which it is bonded.

35. C is correct.

Charge = # of electrons × electron charge

$$Q = ne^-$$
$$Q = (30) \cdot (-1.6 \times 10^{-19} \text{ C})$$
$$Q = -4.8 \times 10^{-18} \text{ C}$$

36. E is correct.

Cyclotron frequency is given as:

$$f = qB \, / \, 2\pi m$$

This expression does not take speed into consideration.

37. B is correct.

The repulsive force between two particles is:

$$F = kQ_1Q_2 \, / \, r^2$$

As r increases, F decreases

Using $F = ma$, a also decreases

38. A is correct.

Electric potential difference = Volts

$$1 \text{ V} = (\text{kg} \cdot \text{m}^2) \, / \, (\text{A} \cdot \text{s}^3)$$
$$1 \text{ A} = 1 \text{ C} \, / \, \text{s}$$
$$\text{V} = [(\text{kg} \cdot \text{m}^2) \, / \, \text{s}^3] \cdot (\text{s} \, / \, \text{C})$$
$$\text{V} = (\text{kg} \cdot \text{m}^2) \, / \, (\text{s}^2 \cdot \text{C})$$

39. C is correct.

The Coulomb is the basic unit of electrical charge in the SI unit system and is equal to one ampere per second.

$$1 \text{ C} = 1 \text{ A/s}$$

40. A is correct.

By the Law of Conservation of Charge, charge cannot be created nor destroyed.

41. B is correct. Coulomb's Law:

$$F = kQ_1Q_2 / r^2$$

If both charges are doubled,

$$F = k(2Q_1)\cdot(2Q_2) / r^2$$
$$F = 4kQ_1Q_2 / r^2$$

F increases by a factor of 4.

42. C is correct. Coulomb's law:

$$F = kQ_1Q_2 / r^2$$
$$Q_1 = Q_2$$

Therefore:

$$Q_1Q_2 = Q^2$$
$$F = kQ^2 / r^2$$

Rearranging:

$$Q^2 = Fr^2 / k$$
$$Q = \sqrt{(Fr^2 / k)}$$
$$Q = \sqrt{[(4 \text{ N})\cdot(0.01 \text{ m})^2 / (9 \times 10^9 \text{ N·m}^2/\text{C}^2)]}$$
$$Q = 2 \times 10^{-7} \text{ C}$$

43. A is correct. Magnetic flux:

$$\Phi = BA$$

where *B* is magnetic field and A is area perpendicular to *B*.

If the coil is vertical and *B* is downward, there is no area for Φ to occur.

$$\Phi = 0$$

44. C is correct.

Coulomb's law:

$$F = kQ_1Q_2 / r^2$$

When each particle has lost ½ its charge:

$$F_2 = k(\tfrac{1}{2}Q_1)\cdot(\tfrac{1}{2}Q_2) / r^2$$
$$F_2 = (\tfrac{1}{4})kQ_1Q_2 / r^2$$
$$F_2 = (\tfrac{1}{4})F$$

F decreases by a factor of ¼

45. B is correct.

T = period

T = time to complete 1 cycle

If velocity is tripled:

$v = d / t$

$t = d / v$

$(1/3)t = d / 3v$

So, T must be divided by 3:

New period = T / 3

46. C is correct. An electrostatic field shows the path that would be taken by a positively-charged particle.

As this positive particle moves closer to the negatively-charged one, the force between them increases.

Coulomb's law:

$F = kQ_1Q_2 / r^2$

By convention, electric field vectors always point towards negative source charges.

Since electrical field strength is inversely proportional to the square of the distance from the source charge, the magnitude of the electric field progressively increases as an object moves towards the source charge.

47. E is correct. Protons are charges so they have an electric field.

Protons have mass so they have a gravitational field.

Protons spin on their axes so they have a magnetic field (moving electric charge).

48. A is correct.

$W = Q\Delta V$

$V = kq / r$

$W = (kQq) \cdot (1 / r_2 - 1 / r_1)$

$W = (kQq) \cdot (1 / 2 \text{ m} - 1 / 6 \text{ m})$

$W = (kQq) \cdot (1 / 3 \text{ m})$

$W = (9 \times 10^9 \text{ N·m}^2/\text{C}^2) \cdot (3.1 \times 10^{-5} \text{ C}) \cdot (-10^{-6} \text{ C}) / (1 / 3 \text{ m})$

$W = -0.093 \text{ J} \approx -0.09 \text{ J}$

The negative sign indicates that the electric field does the work on charge q.

49. D is correct.

charge = # electrons × electron charge

$Q = ne^-$

$n = Q / e^-$

$n = (-600 \times 10^{-9}\, C) / (-1.6 \times 10^{-19}\, C)$

$n = 3.8 \times 10^{12}$ electrons

50. C is correct.

$E\ (N/C) = F\ (N) / q\ (C)$

Coulombs (C) are the equivalent of mass in electricity.

51. E is correct.

All the electromagnetic waves travel through space (vacuum) at the same speed:

$c = 3 \times 10^8$ m/s

52. A is correct.

As the proton of charge q moves in the direction of the electric field lines it moves away from a positive charge (because field lines emanate from positive charge).

Electric Potential Energy:

$U = kQq / r$

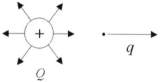

As distance increases, the potential energy decreases because they are inversely proportional.

Electrical potential:

$V = kQ / r$

Electrical potential is inversely proportional to distance and decreases as distance increases.

53. B is correct.

1 watt = 1 J/s

54. D is correct.

An object that is electrically polarized has had its charge separated into opposites and thus rearrange themselves within distinct regions.

55. A is correct.

Because point P is symmetric about Q_1 and Q_2 and both charges have the same positive magnitude, the electric field cancels midway between the charges.

$$E = kQ / r^2$$
$$E_1 = -E_2$$
$$E_{tot} = E_1 + E_2$$
$$E_{tot} = (-E_2 + E_2)$$
$$E_{tot} = 0 \text{ N/C}$$

56. E is correct.

Force due to motion:

$$F = ma$$
$$F = (0.001 \text{ kg}) \cdot (440 \text{ m/s}^2)$$
$$F = 0.44 \text{ N}$$

Force due to charge:

$$F = kQ_1Q_2 / r^2$$
$$Q_1 = Q_2$$
$$Q_1Q_2 = Q^2$$
$$F = kQ^2 / r^2$$

Rearranging:

$$Q^2 = Fr^2 / k$$
$$Q = \sqrt{(Fr^2 / k)}$$
$$Q = \sqrt{[(0.44 \text{ N}) \cdot (0.02 \text{ m})^2 / (9 \times 10^9 \text{ N} \cdot \text{m}^2/\text{C}^2)]}$$
$$Q = 1.4 \times 10^{-7} \text{ C} = 140 \text{ nC}$$

57. D is correct. A sphere or any conduction object that acquires a net charge has the charge collect on the surface. This is due to excess charge repelling itself and moving to the surface to increase distance between themselves.

58. B is correct.

$$F = kQ_1Q_2 / r^2$$

	Force from +	Force from −
x direction	→	→
y direction	↑	↓

Net force = →

---

59. A is correct.

A charged particle only experiences a magnetic force if it moves with a perpendicular velocity component to the field. Thus, there must not be a magnetic field or the particle moves parallel to the field.

60. B is correct.

Coulomb's law: the strength of the electrostatic force between two point charges.

$F = kQ_1Q_2 / r^2$

$F = [(9 \times 10^9 \text{ N·m}^2/\text{C}^2)·(+3 \text{ C})·(-6 \text{ C})] / (0.5 \text{ m})^2$

$F = 1.3 \times 10^{12} \text{ N}$

F is positive to indicate an attractive force.

We want to hear from you

Your feedback is important to us because we strive to provide the highest quality prep materials. If you have any questions, comments or suggestions, email us, so we can incorporate your feedback into future editions.

Customer Satisfaction Guarantee

If you have any concerns about this book, including printing issues, contact us and we will
resolve any issues to your satisfaction.

info@sterling-prep.com

Circuit Elements and DC Circuits – Explanations

1. B is correct.

$R = \rho L / A$, where ρ is the resistivity of the wire material.

If the length L is doubled, the resistance R is doubled.

If the radius r is doubled, the area $A = \pi r^2$ is quadrupled and the resistance R is decreased by ¼.

If these two changes are combined:

$R_{new} = \rho(2L) / \pi(2r)^2$

$R_{new} = (2/4) \cdot (\rho L / \pi r^2)$

$R_{new} = (2/4)R = ½R$

2. D is correct. Internal resistance of battery is in series with resistors in circuit:

$R_{eq} = R_1 + R_{battery}$

where R_{eq} is equivalent resistance and R_1 is resistor connected to battery

$V = IR_{eq}$

$V = I(R_1 + R_{battery})$

$R_{battery} = V / I - R_1$

$R_{battery} = (12 \text{ V} / 0.6 \text{ A}) - 6 \text{ }\Omega$

$R_{battery} = 14 \text{ }\Omega$

3. C is correct. An ohm Ω is defined as the resistance between two points of a conductor when a constant potential difference of 1 V, applied to these points, produces in the conductor a current of 1 A.

A series circuit experiences the same current through all resistors regardless of their resistance.

However, the voltage across each resistor can be different.

Since the light bulbs are in series, the current through them is the same.

4. D is correct.

$V = kQ / r$

$V_B = kQ / r_B$

$V_B = (9 \times 10^9 \text{ N·m}^2/\text{C}^2) \cdot (1 \times 10^{-6} \text{ C}) / 3.5 \text{ m}$

$V_B = 2,571 \text{ V}$

$V_A = kQ / r_A$

$V_A = (9 \times 10^9 \text{ N·m}^2/\text{C}^2) \cdot (1 \times 10^{-6} \text{ C}) / 8 \text{ m}$

$V_A = 1,125$ V

Potential difference:

$$\Delta V = V_B - V_A$$

$$\Delta V = 2,571 \text{ V} - 1,125 \text{ V}$$

$$\Delta V = 1,446 \text{ V}$$

5. E is correct.

The capacitance of a parallel place capacitor demonstrates the influence of material, separation distance and geometry in determining the overall capacitance.

$$C = k\mathcal{E}_0 A / d$$

where k = dielectric constant or permittivity of material between the plates, A = surface area of the conductor and d = distance of plate separation

6. A is correct.

$$E = qV$$

$$E = \frac{1}{2}m(\Delta v)^2$$

$$qV = \frac{1}{2}m(v_f^2 - v_i^2)$$

$$v_f^2 = (2qV / m) + v_i^2$$

$$v_f^2 = [2(1.6 \times 10^{-19} \text{ C}) \cdot (100 \text{ V}) / (1.67 \times 10^{-27} \text{ kg})] + (1.5 \times 10^5 \text{ m/s})^2$$

$$v_f^2 = (1.9 \times 10^{10} \text{ m}^2/\text{s}^2) + (2.3 \times 10^{10} \text{ m}^2/\text{s}^2)$$

$$v_f^2 = 4.2 \times 10^{10} \text{ m}^2/\text{s}^2$$

$$v_f = 2.04 \times 10^5 \text{ m/s} \approx 2 \times 10^5 \text{ m/s}$$

7. C is correct.

Power = current^2 × resistance

$$P = I^2 R$$

Double current:

$$P_2 = (2I)^2 R$$

$$P_2 = 4(I^2 R)$$

$$P_2 = 4P$$

Power is quadrupled

8. D is correct.

A magnetic field is created only by electric charges in motion.

A stationary charged particle does not generate a magnetic field.

9. B is correct.

Combining the power equation with Ohm's law:

$P = (\Delta V)^2 / R$, where $\Delta V = 120$ V is a constant

To increase power, decrease the resistance.

A longer wire increases resistance, while a thicker wire decreases it:

$A = \pi r^2$

$R = \rho L / A$

Larger radius of the cross-sectional area means A is larger (denominator) which lowers *R*.

10. E is correct.

$W = k q_1 q_2 / r$

$r = \Delta x$

$r = 2$ mm $- (- 2$ mm$)$

$r = 4$ mm

$W = [(9 \times 10^9 \text{ N·m}^2/\text{C}^2) \cdot (4 \times 10^{-6} \text{ C}) \cdot (8 \times 10^{-6} \text{ C})] / (4 \times 10^{-3} \text{ m})$

$W = (0.288 \text{ N·m}^2) / (4 \times 10^{-3} \text{ m})$

$W = 72$ J

11. A is correct.

$V = IR$

$I = V / R$

$I = (220 \text{ V}) / (400 \text{ }\Omega)$

$I = 0.55$ A

12. E is correct.

A parallel circuit experiences the same potential difference across each resistor.

However, the current through each resistor can be different.

13. D is correct.

$E = q\text{V}$

$E = \frac{1}{2} m v^2$

$q\text{V} = \frac{1}{2} m v^2$

$v^2 = 2q\text{V} / m$

$v^2 = [2(1.6 \times 10^{-19} \text{ C}) \cdot (990 \text{ V})] / (9.11 \times 10^{-31} \text{ kg})$

$v^2 = 3.5 \times 10^{14} \text{ m}^2/\text{s}^2$

$v = 1.9 \times 10^7$ m/s

14. B is correct. Calculate magnetic field perpendicular to loop:

$B_{Perp2} = (12\ T) \cos 30°$

$B_{Perp2} = 10.4\ T$

$B_{Perp1} = (1\ T) \cos 30°$

$B_{Perp1} = 0.87\ T$

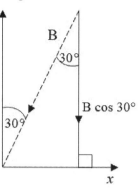

Use Faraday's Law to calculate generated voltage:

$V = N\Delta BA\ /\ \Delta t$

$V = N\Delta B(\pi r^2)\ /\ \Delta t$

$V = [(1)\cdot(10.4\ T - 0.87\ T)\cdot(\pi(0.5\ m)^2)]\ /\ (5\ s - 0\ s)$

$V = [(1)\cdot(10.4\ T - 0.87\ T)\cdot(0.785\ m^2)]\ /\ (5\ s)$

$V = 1.5\ V$

Use Ohm's Law to calculate current:

$V = IR$

$I = V\ /\ R$

$I = (1.5\ V)\ /\ (12\ Ω)$

$I = 0.13\ A$

15. C is correct. Ohm's Law:

$V = IR$

$V = (10\ A)\cdot(35\ Ω)$

$V = 350\ V$

16. A is correct. The magnitude of the acceleration is given by:

$F = ma$

$a = F\ /\ m$

$F = qE_0$

$a = qE_0\ /\ m$

Bare nuclei = no electrons

^1H has 1 proton and ^4He has 2 protons and 2 neutrons

Thus ^1H has ½ the charge ad ¼ the mass of ^4He.

$a_H = q_H E_0\ /\ m_H$

$a_{He} = q_{He} E_0\ /\ m_{He}$

$a_H = (½q_{He})E_0\ /\ (¼m_{He})$

$a_H = 2(q_{He}E_0\ /\ m_{He})$

$a_H = 2a_{He}$

17. B is correct.

The current will change as the choice of lamp arrangement changes.

Since $P = V^2/R$, power increases as resistance decreases.

To rank the power in increasing order, the equivalent resistance must be ranked in decreasing order.

For arrangement B, the resistors are in series, so:

$R_{eq} = R + R = 2R$

For arrangement C, the resistors are in parallel, so:

$1/R_{eq} = 1/R + 1/R$

$R_{eq} = R/2$

The ranking of resistance in decreasing order is B to A to C, which is therefore the ranking of power in increasing order.

18. D is correct.

$C = k\varepsilon_0 A / d$

where k = dielectric constant or permittivity of material between the plates, A = area and d = distance of plate separation

$C = (2.1)\cdot(8.854 \times 10^{-12} \text{ F/m})\cdot(0.01 \text{ m} \times 0.01 \text{ m}) / (0.001 \text{ m})$

$C = (1.9 \times 10^{-15} \text{ F/m}) / (0.001 \text{ m})$

$C = 1.9 \times 10^{-12} \text{ F} = 1.9 \text{ pF}$

19. A is correct.

Current remains constant across resistors in series and voltage remains constant across resistors in parallel.

Equivalent resistors of R_2 and R:

$R_{eq} = R_2 + R$

$V = IR_{eq}$

$I_2 = V / R_{eq}$

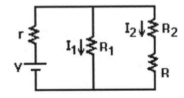

If R decreases, then R_{eq} decreases.

If R_{eq} decreases, then I_2 increases.

Assume a node where I_1 and I_2 start with current I_0

By Kirchhoff's Current Law:

$I_0 = I_1 + I_2$

Thus if I_2 increases I_1 decreases to keep I_0 constant.

---

20. C is correct.

$$V = IR$$

$$I = V / R$$

Ohm's law states that the current between two points is directly proportional to the potential difference between the points.

21. E is correct. Root mean square voltage equation:

$$V_{rms} = V_{max} / \sqrt{2}$$

$$V_{rms} = 12 / \sqrt{2}$$

$$V_{rms} = (12 / \sqrt{2}) \cdot (\sqrt{2} / \sqrt{2})$$

$$V_{rms} = (12\sqrt{2}) / 2$$

$$V_{rms} = 6\sqrt{2} \text{ V}$$

22. C is correct. By definition:

$$V_{rms} = V_{max} / \sqrt{2}$$

Therefore:

$$V_{max} = V_{rms}\sqrt{2}$$

$$V_{max} = (150 \text{ V})\sqrt{2}$$

$$V_{max} = 212 \text{ V}$$

23. D is correct.

Kirchhoff's junction rule states that the sum of all currents coming into a junction is the sum of all currents leaving a junction. This is a statement of conservation of charge because it defines that no charge is created nor destroyed in the circuit.

24. A is correct.

Voltage remains constant across parallel capacitors.

$$V = Q / C$$

Capacitors are added in parallel to produce the equivalent capacitance (Q_{eq}) of the circuit.

$$Q_1 + Q_2 + Q_3 + Q_4 = Q_{eq}$$

$$4Q = Q_{eq}$$

$$Q = Q_{eq} / 4$$

25. B is correct.

If two conductors are connected by copper wire, each conductor will be at the same potential because current can flow through the wire and equalize the difference in potential.

26. C is correct.

Electromagnetic induction is the production of an electromotive force across a conductor.

When a changing magnetic field is brought near a coil, a voltage is generated in the coil thus inducing a current.

The voltage generated can be calculated by Faraday's Law:

$$\text{emf} = -N\Delta\phi \,/\, \Delta t$$

where N = number of turns and $\Delta\phi$ = change in magnetic flux

27. A is correct.

Current is constant across resistors connected in series.

28. D is correct.

By convention, the direction of electric current is the direction that a positive charge migrates.

Therefore, current flows from a point of high potential to a point of lower potential.

29. E is correct.

$$PE_e = PE_1 + PE_2 + PE_3$$

$$PE_e = (kQ_1Q_2) \,/\, r_1 + (kQ_2Q_3) \,/\, r_2 + (kQ_1Q_3) \,/\, r_3$$

$$PE_e = kQ^2 \,[(1 \,/\, r_1) + (1 \,/\, r_2) + (1 \,/\, r_3)]$$

$r_1 = 4$ cm and $r_2 = 3$ cm are known, use Pythagorean Theorem to find r_3:

$$r_3{}^2 = r_1{}^2 + r_2{}^2$$

$$r_3{}^2 = (4 \text{ cm})^2 + (3 \text{ cm})^2$$

$$r_3{}^2 = 16 \text{ cm}^2 + 9 \text{ cm}^2$$

$$r_3{}^2 = 25 \text{ cm}^2$$

$$r_3 = 5 \text{ cm}$$

$$PE_e = (9 \times 10^9 \text{ N·m}^2/\text{C}^2){\cdot}(3.8 \times 10^{-9} \text{ C})^2 \times [(1 \,/\, 0.04 \text{ m}) + (1 \,/\, 0.03 \text{ m}) + (1 \,/\, 0.05 \text{ m})]$$

$$PE_e = (1.2 \times 10^{-7} \text{ N·m}^2){\cdot}(25 \text{ m}^{-1} + 33 \text{ m}^{-1} + 20 \text{ m}^{-1})$$

$$PE_e = (1.2 \times 10^{-7} \text{ N·m}^2){\cdot}(78 \text{ m}^{-1})$$

$$PE_e = 1 \times 10^{-5} \text{ J}$$

30. A is correct.

The magnetic force acting on a charge q moving at velocity v in a magnetic field B is given by:

$$F = qv \times B$$

If q, v, and the angle between v and B are the same for both charges, then the magnitude of the force F is the same on both charges.

However, if the charges carry opposite signs, each experiences oppositely-directed forces.

31. C is correct. By convention, the direction of electric current is the direction that a positive charge migrates.

Electrons flow from regions of low potential to regions of high potential.

Electric Potential Energy:

$$U = (kQq) / r$$

Electric Potential:

$$V = (kQ) / r$$

Because the charge of an electron (q) is negative, as the electron moves opposite to the electric field, it must be getting closer to the positive charge Q. As this occurs, an increasingly negative potential energy U is produced; thus, potential energy is decreasing.

Conversely, as the electron approaches Q, the electric potential V increases with less distance. This is because the product is positive and reducing r increases V.

32. E is correct. Magnets provide magnetic forces.

Generators convert mechanical energy into electrical energy, turbines extract energy from fluids (e.g. air and water), and transformers transfer energy between circuits.

33. B is correct.

$$PE = -k q_1 q_2 / r$$

If radius increases, PE decreases.

34. C is correct.

$$R = (\rho L) / (\pi r^2)$$

$$R_A = (\rho L) / (\pi r^2)$$

$$R_B = [\rho(2L)] / [\pi(2r)^2]$$

$$R_B = (2/4) \cdot [(\rho L) / (\pi r^2)]$$

$$R_B = \tfrac{1}{2}[(\rho L) / (\pi r^2)]$$

$$R_B = \tfrac{1}{2} R_A$$

35. D is correct.

By convention, current flows from high to low potential, but it represents the flow of positive charges.

Electron flow is in the opposite direction, from low potential to high potential.

36. C is correct.

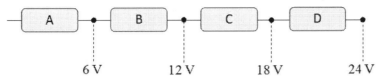

6 V   12 V   18 V   24 V

Batteries in series add voltage like resistors in series add resistance.

The resistances of the lights they power are not needed to solve the problem.

37. B is correct.

$$C = (k\mathcal{E}_0 A) / d$$

$$k = (Cd) / A\mathcal{E}_0$$

If capacitance increases by a factor of 4:

$$k_2 = (4C)d / A\mathcal{E}_0$$

$$k_2 = 4(Cd / A\mathcal{E}_0)$$

$$k_2 = 4k$$

38. E is correct.

$$C = (k\mathcal{E}_0 A) / d$$

$$C = [(1)\cdot(8.854 \times 10^{-12}\text{ F/m})\cdot(0.4\text{ m}^2)] / (0.04\text{ m})$$

$$C = 8.854 \times 10^{-11}\text{ F}$$

$$V = Q / C$$

$$V = (6.8 \times 10^{-10}\text{ C}) / (8.854 \times 10^{-11}\text{ F})$$

$$V = 7.7\text{ V}$$

39. A is correct.

Since force is the cross-product of velocity and magnetic field strength:

$$F = qv \times B$$

The force is at a maximum when v and B are perpendicular:

$$F = qvB \sin 90°$$

$$\sin 90° = 1$$

$$F = qvB$$

40. E is correct.

Current is defined as the flow of charge per unit of time:

$$A = C / s$$

$$C = A{\cdot}s$$

41. C is correct.

$$\Delta V = \Delta E \, / \, q$$

$$\Delta V = (1 \, / \, q) \cdot (\tfrac{1}{2} m v_f{}^2 - \tfrac{1}{2} m v_i{}^2)$$

$$\Delta V = (m \, / \, 2q) \cdot (v_f{}^2 - v_i{}^2)$$

$$\Delta V = [(1.67 \times 10^{-27} \text{ kg}) \, / \, (2) \cdot (1.6 \times 10^{-19} \text{ C})] \times [(3.2 \times 10^5 \text{ m/s})^2 - (1.7 \times 10^5 \text{ m/s})^2]$$

$$\Delta V = 384 \text{ V}$$

42. E is correct.

$$Q = VC$$

Even though the capacitors have different capacitances, the voltage across each capacitor is inversely proportional to the capacitance of that capacitor.

Like current, charge is conserved across capacitors in series.

43. A is correct.

Calculate capacitance:

$$C = k \mathcal{E}_o A \, / \, d$$

$$C = [(1) \cdot (8.854 \times 10^{-12} \text{ F/m}) \cdot (0.6 \text{ m}^2)] \, / \, (0.06 \text{ m})$$

$$C = 8.854 \times 10^{-11} \text{ F}$$

Find potential difference:

$$C = Q \, / \, V$$

$$V = Q \, / \, C$$

$$V = (7.08 \times 10^{-10} \text{ C}) \, / \, (8.854 \times 10^{-11} \text{ F})$$

$$V = 8 \text{ V}$$

44. B is correct.

"In a perfect conductor" and "in the absence of resistance" have the same meanings, and current can flow in conductors of varying resistances.

A semi-perfect conductor has resistance.

45. C is correct.

Faraday's Law: a changing magnetic environment causes a voltage to be induced in a conductor. Metal detectors send quick magnetic pulses that cause a voltage (by Faraday's Law) and subsequent current to be induced in the conductor.

By Lenz's Law, an opposing magnetic field will then arise to counter the changing magnetic field. The detector picks up the magnetic field and notifies the operator.

Thus, metal detectors use Faraday's Law and Lenz's Law to detect metal objects.

46. E is correct.

$E = q\text{V}$

$E = (7 \times 10^{-6} \text{ C}){\cdot}(3.5 \times 10^{-3} \text{ V})$

$E = 24.5 \times 10^{-9} \text{ J}$

$E = 24.5 \text{ nJ}$

47. B is correct.

$R_1 = \rho L_1 / A_1$

$R_2 = \rho(4L_1) / A_2$

$R_1 = R_2$

$\rho L_1 / A_1 = \rho(4L_1) / A_2$

$A_2 = 4A_1$

$(\pi / 4)d_2{}^2 = (\pi / 4){\cdot}(4)d_1{}^2$

$d_2{}^2 = 4d_1{}^2$

$d_2 = 2d_1$

48. D is correct. The total resistance of a network of series resistors increases as more resistors are added.

$\text{V} = IR$

An increase in the total resistance results in a decrease in the total current through the network.

49. A is correct. This is a circuit with two resistors in series.

Combine the two resistors into one resistor:

$R_T = R + R_{int}$

$R_T = 0.5 \; \Omega + 0.1 \; \Omega$

$R_T = 0.6 \; \Omega$

Ohm's law:

$\text{V} = IR$

$I = \text{V} / R$

$I = 9 \text{ V} / 0.6 \; \Omega$

$I = 15 \text{ A}$

50. C is correct.

Energy stored in capacitor:

$U = \frac{1}{2}(Q^2 / \text{C})$

Capacitance:

$$C = k\mathcal{E}_0 A \,/\, d$$

$$U = \tfrac{1}{2}(Q^2 d) \,/\, (k\mathcal{E}_0 A)$$

$$Q = \sqrt{[(2U \times k\mathcal{E}_0 A) \,/\, d]}$$

$$Q = \sqrt{\{[(2)\cdot(10 \times 10^3 \text{ J})\cdot(1)\cdot(8.854 \times 10^{-12} \text{ F/m})\cdot(2.4 \times 10^{-5} \text{ m}^2)] \,/\, 0.0016 \text{ m}\}}$$

$$Q = 52 \text{ μC}$$

51. B is correct.

Potential energy:

$$U = (kQq) \,/\, r$$

Electric Potential:

$$V = (kQ) \,/\, r$$

As r increases, the potential energy U decreases as does the electric potential V.

Movement in the direction of the electric field is movement away from a positive charge.

52. D is correct.

Electric field energy density:

$$\eta_E = \tfrac{1}{2}E^2 \times \mathcal{E}_0$$

$$\eta_E = \tfrac{1}{2}(8.6 \times 10^6 \text{ V/m})^2\cdot(8.854 \times 10^{-12} \text{ F/m})$$

$$\eta_E = 330 \text{ J/m}^3$$

53. A is correct.

$$\text{Resistance} = \text{Ohms}$$

$$\Omega = V \,/\, A$$

$$\Omega = [(\text{kg}\cdot\text{m}^2) \,/\, (A\cdot s^3)] \,/\, A$$

$$\Omega = (\text{kg}\cdot\text{m}^2) \,/\, (A^2\cdot s^3)$$

$$\Omega = (\text{kg}\cdot\text{m}^2\cdot s^2) \,/\, (C^2\cdot s^3)$$

$$\Omega = (\text{kg}\cdot\text{m}^2) \,/\, (C^2\cdot s) = \text{kg}\cdot\text{m}^2 \,/\, s\cdot C^2$$

54. E is correct. Ohm's Law:

$$V = IR$$

If V is constant, then I and R are inversely proportional.

An increase in R results in a decrease in I.

55. D is correct.

Electric Potential:

$$V = kQ / r$$

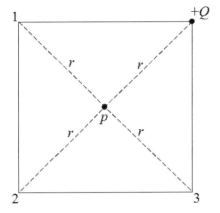

All other positions on the square (1, 2 or 3) are equidistant from point *p*, as is charge +*Q*.

Thus, a negative charge placed at any of these locations would have equal magnitude potential but an opposite sign because the new charge is negative.

Thus: $| V | = | -V |$

$$V + (-V) = 0$$

56. B is correct.

Electric field energy density:

$$\eta_E = \tfrac{1}{2}E^2 \times \mathcal{E}_0$$

$$\eta_E = \tfrac{1}{2}(6 \text{ N/C})^2 \cdot (8.854 \times 10^{-12} \text{ F/m})$$

$$\eta_E = 1.6 \times 10^{-10} \text{ J/m}^3$$

57. A is correct.

Ohm's law:

$$V = IR$$

Increasing V and decreasing *R* increases *I*.

58. D is correct.

$$C_{Eq1} = C_2 + C_3$$

$$C_{Eq1} = 18 \text{ pF} + 24 \text{ pF}$$

$$C_{Eq1} = 42 \text{ pF}$$

Voltage drops is equal in capacitors in parallel, so:

$$C_{Eq1} = Q_1 / V_1$$

$$Q_1 = C_{Eq1} \times V_1$$

$$Q_1 = (42 \times 10^{-12} \text{ F}) \cdot (240 \text{ V})$$

$$Q_1 = 1 \times 10^{-8} \text{ C}$$

Charge is equal in capacitors in series, so:

$$1 / C_{Eq2} = 1 / C_{Eq1} + 1 / C_1$$

$$1 / C_{Eq2} = 1 / 42 \text{ pF} + 1 / 9 \text{ pF}$$

$$1 / C_{Eq2} = 7.4 \text{ pF}$$

$$1 / C_{Eq2} = V_{system} / Q_1$$

$$V_{system} = Q_1 / C_{Eq2}$$

$$V_{system} = (1 \times 10^{-8}\,\text{C}) / (7.4 \times 10^{-12}\,\text{F})$$

$$V_{system} = 1{,}350\,\text{V}$$

59. A is correct.

Energy stored in a capacitor:

$$U = \tfrac{1}{2}Q^2 / C$$

$$U_2 = Q^2 / 2(2C)$$

$$U_2 = \tfrac{1}{2}Q^2 / 2C$$

$$U_2 = \tfrac{1}{2}U$$

Decreases by half.

60. C is correct.

The total resistance of a network of series resistors increases as more resistors are added to the network.

An increase in the total resistance results in a decrease in the total current through the network.

A decrease in current results in a decrease in the voltage across the original resistor:

$$V = IR$$

Our guarantee – the highest quality preparation materials.

We expect our books to have the highest quality content and be error-free.

Be the first to report an error, typo or inaccuracy and receive a
$10 reward for a content error or
$5 reward for a typo or grammatical mistake.

info@sterling-prep.com

Light and Optics – Explanations

1. A is correct.

Soap film that reflects a given wavelength of light exhibits constructive interference.

The expression for constructive interference of a thin film:

$2t = (m + \frac{1}{2})\lambda$

where t = thickness, m = 0, 1, 2, 3… and λ = wavelength

To find the minimum thickness set m = 0:

$2t = (0 + \frac{1}{2})\lambda = \frac{1}{2}\lambda$

$t = \frac{1}{4}\lambda$

2. A is correct. By the law of reflection, the angle of incidence is equal to the angle of reflection.

Thus, as the angle of incidence increases, the angle of reflection increases as well to be equal to the angle of incidence.

3. B is correct.

If image is twice her height and upright, then:

$2h_o = h_i$

$m = h_i / h_o$

$m = -d_i / d_o$

$m = 2h_o / h_o$

$m = 2$

$2 = -d_i / d_o$

$-2d_o = d_i$

Use lens equation to solve:

$1 / f = 1 / d_o + 1 / d_i$

$1 / 100 \text{ cm} = 1 / d_o + (-1 / 2 d_o)$

$1 / 100 \text{ cm} = 1 / 2 d_o$

$2d_o = 100 \text{ cm}$

$d_o = 50 \text{ cm}$

4. D is correct. If a person's eye is too long, the light entering the eye is focused in front of the retina causing myopia. This condition is also referred to as nearsightedness.

Hyperopia is also referred to as farsightedness.

5. E is correct.

Visible light:

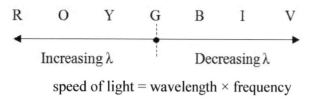

speed of light = wavelength × frequency

$c = \lambda f$

Wavelength to frequency:

$f = c / \lambda$

Frequency and wavelength are inversely proportional:

As λ increases, f decreases.

As λ decreases, f increases.

Thus, because $E = hf$:

6. B is correct.

The lens equation:

$1 / f = 1 / d_o + 1 / d_i$

$1 / d_i = 1 / f - 1 / d_o$

$1 / d_i = -1 / 3 \, m - 1 / 4 \, m$

$1 / d_i = (-3 \, m - 4 \, m) / 12 \, m$

$1 / d_i = -7 \, m / 12 \, m$

$d_i = -12 / 7 \, m$

Magnification:

$m = -d_i / d_o$

$m = -(-12 / 7 \, m) / 4 \, m$

$m = 3 / 7$

Height of the candle image:

$h_i = m h_o$

$h_i = (3/7) \cdot (18 \, cm)$

$h_i = 54 / 7 \, cm$

$h_i = 7.7 \, cm$

7. C is correct.

$\theta_{\text{syrup}} = \tan^{-1} (0.9 \text{ m} / 0.66 \text{ m})$

$\theta_s = \tan^{-1} (1.36)$

$\theta_s = 53.7°$

$\theta_{\text{oil}} = \tan^{-1} [(2 \text{ m} - 0.9 \text{ m}) / 1.58 \text{ m}]$

$\theta_o = \tan^{-1} (0.7)$

$\theta_o = 34.8°$

$n_o \sin \theta_o = n_{\text{air}} \sin \theta_{\text{air}}$

$n_o \sin 34.8° = (1) \sin 90°$

$n_o = 1 / (\sin 34.8°)$

$n_o = 1.75$

8. D is correct.

$\theta_{\text{syrup}} = \tan^{-1} (0.9 \text{ m} / 0.66 \text{ m})$

$\theta_s = \tan^{-1} (1.36)$

$\theta_s = 53.7°$

$\theta_{\text{oil}} = \tan^{-1} [(2 \text{ m} - 0.9 \text{ m}) / 1.58 \text{ m}]$

$\theta_o = \tan^{-1} (0.7)$

$\theta_o = 34.8°$

$n_o \sin \theta_o = n_{\text{air}} \sin \theta_{\text{air}}$

$n_o \sin 34.8° = (1) \sin 90°$

$n_o = 1 / (\sin 34.8°)$

$n_o = 1.75$

$n_s \sin \theta_s = n_o \sin \theta_o$

$n_s = n_o \sin \theta_o / \sin \theta_s$

$n_s = (1.75)·(\sin 34.8°) / (\sin 53.7°)$

$n_s = 1.24$

9. A is correct.

10. D is correct.

Geometrical optics, or ray optics, describes light propagation in terms of rays and fronts to approximate the path along which light propagates in certain circumstances.

11. D is correct.

First find the critical angle:

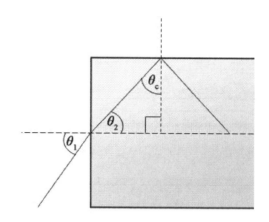

$$n_{fiber} \sin \theta_c = n_{air} \sin \theta_{air}$$

$$(1.26) \sin \theta_c = (1) \sin 90°$$

$$\sin \theta_c = 1 / 1.26$$

$$\theta_c = \sin^{-1} (1 / 1.26)$$

$$\theta_c = 52.5°$$

Find θ_2:

$$\theta_2 + \theta_c + 90° = 180°$$

$$(\theta_2 + 52.5° + 90°) = 180°$$

$$\theta_2 = 37.5°$$

Find θ_1:

$$n_{air} \sin \theta_1 = n_{fiber} \sin \theta_2$$

$$(1) \sin \theta_1 = (1.26) \sin 37.5°$$

$$\sin \theta_1 = 0.77$$

$$\theta_1 = \sin^{-1} (0.77)$$

$$\theta_1 = 50°$$

12. A is correct.

If the power of the lens is 10 diopters,

$$1 / f = 10 \text{ D}$$

where f is the focal length in m

Lens equation:

$$1 / f = 1 / d_o + 1 / d_i$$

$$10 \text{ m}^{-1} = 1 / 0.5 \text{ m} + 1 / d_i$$

$$1 / d_i = 10 \text{ m}^{-1} - 1 / 0.5 \text{ m}$$

$$1 / d_i = 8 \text{ m}^{-1}$$

$$d_i = 1 / 8 \text{ m}$$

$$d_i = 0.13 \text{ m}$$

13. D is correct. Most objects observed by humans are virtual images, or objects which reflect incoming light to project an image.

14. E is correct.

An image from a convex mirror will always have the following characteristics, regardless of object distance:

- located behind convex mirror
- virtual
- upright
- reduced in size from object (image < object)

15. A is correct.

The mirror has a positive focal length which indicates that the mirror is concave.

The object is at a distance greater than the focal length, therefore it is inverted.

Use lens equation to solve image distance:

$$1/f = 1/d_o + 1/d_i$$

$$1/10 \text{ m} = 1/20 \text{ m} + 1/d_i$$

$$d_i = 20 \text{ cm}$$

The image distance is positive so the image is real.

Use the magnification equation to determine if it is upright or inverted.

$$m = -d_i/d_o$$

$$m = h_i/h_o$$

$$-(20 \text{ m}/20 \text{ m}) = h_i/h_o$$

$$-1 = h_i/h_o$$

The object height h_o is always positive so the image height h_i must be negative to satisfy the equation.

A negative image height indicates an inverted image.

16. E is correct.

For a converging lens, if an object is placed beyond $2f$ from the lens, the image is real, inverted and reduced.

Use the lens equation to determine if the image is real (or vitual):

Assume $f = 1$ m and $d_o = 3f$ (because $d_o > 2f$)

$$1/f = 1/d_o + 1/d_i$$

$$1/f = 1/3f + 1/d_i$$

$$d_i = 1.5$$

A positive d_i indicates a real image.

Use the magnification equation to determine if the image is inverted and reduced.

$$m = -d_i / d_o$$

$$m = -(1.5 \text{ m} / 3 \text{ m})$$

$$m = -\tfrac{1}{2}$$

$$|m| = \tfrac{1}{2}$$

$$|m| < 1$$

A negative magnification factor with an absolute value less than 1 a reduced and inverted image.

17. C is correct.

Radio waves range from 3 kHz to 300 GHz, which is lower than all forms of radiation listed.

Since the energy of radiation is proportional to frequency ($E = hf$), radio waves have the lowest energy.

18. B is correct.

A medium's index of refraction is the ratio of the speed of refracted light in a vacuum to its speed in the reference medium.

$$n = c / v$$

$$n = 2.43$$

$$2.43 = c / v_{\text{diamond}}$$

$$c = 2.43(v_{\text{diamond}})$$

19. D is correct.

$$1 / f = 1 / d_o + 1 / d_i$$

$$1 / 20 \text{ cm} = 1 / 15 \text{ cm} + 1 / d_i$$

$$3 / 60 \text{ cm} - 4 / 60 \text{ cm} = 1 / d_i$$

$$-1 / 60 \text{ cm} = 1 / d_i$$

$$d_i = -60 \text{ cm}$$

The negative sign indicates that the image is projected back the way it came.

20. B is correct.

Red paper absorbs all colors but reflects only red light giving it the appearance of being red. Cyan is the complementary color to red, so when the cyan light shines upon the red paper, no light is reflected and the paper appears black.

21. B is correct.

$$1/f = 1/d_o + 1/d_i$$

If $d_i = f$,

$$1/d_o = 0$$

Thus, d_o must be large.

22. E is correct. Since the index of refraction depends on the frequency, and the focal length depends on the refraction of the beam in the lens, dispersion causes the focal length to depend on frequency.

23. C is correct. Use the equation for magnification:

$$m = -d_i / d_o$$

$$d_i = d_o$$

$$m = 1$$

Thus, there is no magnification, so the image is the same size as the object.

24. E is correct.

25. C is correct.

26. C is correct. First, find the angle that the ray makes with the normal of the glass:

$$180° = x + 90° + 54°$$

$$x = 36°$$

Find θ_1:

$$\theta_1 = 90° - 36°$$

$$\theta_1 = 54°$$

Referring to the diagram, $\theta_1 = 54°$

Snell's Law:

$$n_1 \sin \theta_1 = n_2 \sin \theta_2$$

$$\sin^{-1} [(n_1 / n_2) \sin \theta_1] = \theta_2$$

$$\theta_2 = \sin^{-1}[(1.45 / 1.35) \sin 54°]$$

$$\theta_2 = 60°$$

Solve for the angle with the horizontal:

$$\theta_H = 60° - 54°$$

$$\theta_H = 6°$$

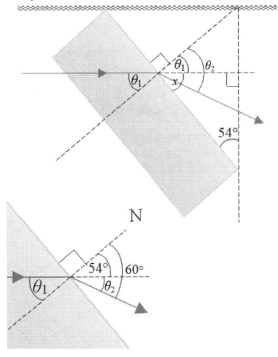

27. A is correct. The angle at which the ray is turned is the sum of the angles if reflected off each mirror once:

$$\theta_{turned} = \theta_1 + \theta_2 + \theta_3 + \theta_4$$

By law of reflection:

$$\theta_1 = \theta_2$$

$$\theta_3 = \theta_4$$

Note the triangle formed (sum of interior angles is 180°):

$$30° + (90° - \theta_2) + (90° - \theta_3) = 180°$$

$$\theta_2 + \theta_3 = 30°$$

Given:

$$\theta_2 + \theta_3 = \theta_1 + \theta_4$$

Thus:

$$\theta_{turned} = 30° + 30°$$

$$\theta_{turned} = 60°$$

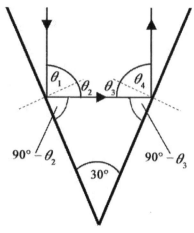

Note: figure is not to scale

In general: for two plane mirrors that meet at an angle of $\theta \leq 90°$ the ray that is deflected off both mirrors is deflected through an angle of 2θ.

28. E is correct.

29. A is correct.

The angle of incidence is < the angle of refraction if the light travels into a less dense medium.

The angle of incidence is > the angle of refraction if the light travels into a denser medium.

The angle of incidence is = the angle of refraction if the densities of the mediums are equal.

30. E is correct. Plane mirrors do not distort the size or the shape of an object since light is reflected at the same angle it was received by the mirror.

Magnification equation:

$$m = -d_i / d_o$$

$$m = h_i / h_o$$

For a plane mirror m = 1:

$$1 = -d_i / d_o$$

$$-d_i = d_o$$

$$1 = h_i / h_o$$

$$h_i = h_o$$

So image size is the same as object size and located behind the mirror because d_i is negative.

31. C is correct.

A spherical concave mirror has a focal length of:

$$f = R / 2$$

32. B is correct.

Refracted rays bend further from the normal than the original incident angle when the refracting medium is optically less dense than the incident medium. Therefore, $n_1 > n_2$.

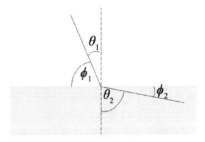

The index of refraction for a medium can never be less than 1.

33. B is correct.

If a person's eye is too short, then the light entering the eye is focused behind the retina causing farsightedness (hyperopia).

34. A is correct.

Hot air is less dense than cold air. Light traveling through both types of air experiences refractions, which appear as shimmering or "wavy" air.

35. E is correct.

Chromatic aberration occurs when a lens focuses different wavelengths of color at different positions in the focal plane.

It always occurs in the following pattern for converging lens:

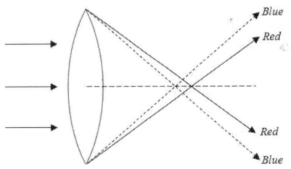

36. B is correct.

$$1 / f_{\text{total}} = 1 / f_1 + 1 / f_2$$
$$1 / f_{\text{total}} = 1 / 2\ \text{m} + 1 / 4\ \text{m}$$
$$1 / f_{\text{total}} = 3 / 4\ \text{m}$$
$$f_{\text{total}} = 4 / 3\ \text{m}$$

37. C is correct.

The angle in the water respective to the normal:

$\theta = \tan^{-1}(37.5 \text{ ft} / 50 \text{ ft})$

$\theta = \tan^{-1}(0.75)$

$\theta = 36.9°$

$n_{air} \sin(90 - \theta) = n_{water} \sin\theta$

$(1) \sin(90 - \theta) = (1.33) \sin 36.9°$

$\sin(90 - \theta) = 0.8$

$(90 - \theta) = \sin^{-1}(0.8)$

$(90 - \theta) = 52.9$

$\theta = 37.1° \approx 37°$

38. A is correct.

Violet light has the highest energy and frequency, and therefore has the shortest wavelength.

39. E is correct.

Objects directly in front of plane mirrors are reflected in their likeness, since plane mirrors are not curved and therefore reflect light perpendicularly to their surface.

40. B is correct.

A virtual image can be formed by both a diverging lens and converging lens.

Diverging lens → reduced and virtual image

Converging lens → enlarged and virtual image

41. B is correct.

Neon light is the light emitted from neon atoms as their energized electrons cascade back down to ground level. When this occurs, energy is released in the form of light at very specific wavelengths known as the emission spectrum.

When this light is passed through a prism, a series of bright discontinuous spots or lines will be seen due to the specific wavelengths of emission spectrum of neon.

42. E is correct.

The law of reflection states that the angle of incidence is equal to the angle of reflection (with respect to the normal) and is true for all mirrors.

$\theta_i = \theta_r$

43. C is correct.

A concave lens always forms an image that is virtual, upright and reduced in size.

44. B is correct.

Virtual images are always upright.

There is no correlation between the size and nature – virtual or real – of an image.

Images may be larger, smaller, or the same size as the object.

45. E is correct.

46. D is correct.

$$1 / f = 1 / d_o + 1 / d_i$$

$$1 / 6 \text{ m} = 1 / 3 \text{ m} + 1 / d_i$$

$$1 / d_i = 1 / 6 \text{ m} - 1 / 3 \text{ m}$$

$$1 / d_i = -1 / 6 \text{ m}$$

$$d_i = -6 \text{ m}$$

where the negative sign indicates the image is on the same side as the object.

The image is upright and virtual, since the rays must be extended to intersect.

47. A is correct.

A diverging lens (concave) always produces an image that is virtual, upright and reduced in size.

48. C is correct.

Thin lens formula:

$$1 / f = 1 / d_o + 1 / d_i$$

d_i is negative because the image is virtual

$$1 / f = 1 / 14 \text{ cm} + 1 / -5 \text{ cm}$$

$$f = -7.8 \text{ cm}$$

The focus is negative because the lens is diverging.

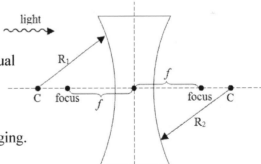

Lens maker formula:

$$1 / f = (n - 1) \cdot (1 / R_1 - 1 / R_2)$$

R_1 is negative by convention because the light ray passes its center of curvature before the curved surface.

$$1 / (-7.8 \text{ cm}) = (n - 1) \cdot (1 / -15 \text{ cm} - 1 / 15 \text{ cm})$$

$$(1 / -7.8 \text{ cm}) \cdot (15 \text{ cm} / -2) + 1 = n$$

$$n = 2$$

49. E is correct.

The magnification equation relates the image and object distance:

$m = -d_i / d_o$

or

The magnification equation relates the image and object height:

$m = h_i / h_o$

50. D is correct.

For a concave mirror, if an object is located between the focal point and center of curvature the image is formed beyond the center of curvature.

In this problem, Mike does not see his image because he is in front of where it forms.

51. D is correct. For a concave spherical mirror the produced image characteristics depend upon the placement of the object in relation to the focal point and center of curvature. The image can be smaller, larger or the same size as the object.

52. A is correct. Lens power is the reciprocal of the focal length in meters:

$P = 1 / f$

If the effective focal length of the lens combination is less than the focal length of either individual lens, then the power of the combination must be greater than the power of either individual lens.

53. B is correct. A medium's index of refraction is the ratio of the speed of refracted light in a vacuum to its speed in the reference medium.

$n = c / v$

54. E is correct.

As it is a plane mirror, the image is not distorted.

Only some of the light rays are reflected, the others create an image behind the mirror's surface.

For a plane mirror:

$m = 1$

$m = -d_i / d_o$

$1 = -d_i / d_o$

$d_o = -d_i$

The negative indicates the image is virtual and behind the mirror.

55. C is correct.

The radius length is the center of curvature, $r = 50$ cm

Find the focal length:

$f = r / 2$

$f = 50$ cm $/ 2$

$f = 25$ cm

For a concave mirror with an object between the center of curvature and the focal length, the resulting image is real and inverted.

56. B is correct.

Find index of refraction of glass:

Snell's Law:

$n_1 \sin \theta_1 = n_2 \sin \theta_2$

$n_g \sin 48° = (1.33) \sin 68°$

$n_g = (1.33) \sin 68° / \sin 48°$

$n_g = 1.66$

Find refracted angle of ray:

$(1.66) \sin 29° = (1.33) \sin \theta$

$\sin \theta = (1.66) \sin 29° / (1.33)$

$\sin \theta = 0.605$

$\theta = \sin^{-1} (0.605)$

$\theta = 37°$

57. E is correct.

58. D is correct. The refractive index is given by:

$n = c / v$

Because $v \approx c$ in air,

$n_{air} \approx n_{vacuum}$

$n_{air} = 1$

$n_{vacuum} = 1$

All other transparent materials slow the speed of light.

Thus, n is greater than 1 because $v_{other\ materials} < c$.

59. D is correct. Lens maker formula:

$$1 / f = (n - 1) \cdot (1 / R_1 - 1 / R_2)$$

For a flat surface:

$$R_2 = \infty$$

$$1 / f = (1.64 - 1) \cdot [(1 / 33 \text{ cm}) - (1 / \infty)]$$

$$1 / f = (0.64) \cdot (1 / 33 \text{ cm})$$

$$f = 51.6 \text{ cm} \approx 52 \text{ cm}$$

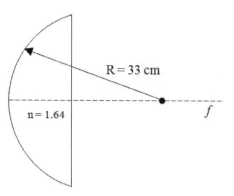

60. C is correct. Water doesn't absorb visible light very easily ($\lambda = 400$ to 700 nm) but absorbs infrared light ($\lambda = 700$ nm to 1 mm) from vibrational motion of the molecule. It also absorbs microwaves through rotational motion.

We want to hear from you

Your feedback is important to us because we strive to provide the highest quality prep materials. If you have any questions, comments or suggestions, email us, so we can incorporate your feedback into future editions.

Customer Satisfaction Guarantee

If you have any concerns about this book, including printing issues, contact us and we will
resolve any issues to your satisfaction.

info@sterling-prep.com

Heat and Thermodynamics – Explanations

1. B is correct.

Ideal gas law:

$$PV = nRT$$

$$P_0 = nRT / V_0$$

If isothermal expansion, then n, R and T are constant

$$P = nRT / (1/3\ V_0)$$

$$P = 3(nRT / V_0)$$

$$P = 3P_0$$

2. C is correct.

Area expansion equation:

$$\Delta A = A_0(2\alpha\Delta T)$$

$$\Delta A = (\pi / 4)\cdot(1.2\ \text{cm})^2\cdot(2)\cdot(19 \times 10^{-6}\ \text{K}^{-1})\cdot(200\ °\text{C})$$

$$\Delta A = 8.6 \times 10^{-3}\ \text{cm}^2$$

$$\Delta A = A_f - A_0$$

$$8.6 \times 10^{-3}\ \text{cm}^2 = (\pi / 4)\cdot[d_f^2 - (1.2\ \text{cm})^2]$$

$$d_f = 1.2\ \text{cm}$$

3. D is correct.

$$1\ \text{Watt} = 1\ \text{J/s}$$

$$\text{Power} \times \text{Time} = Q$$

$$Q = mc\Delta T$$

$$P \times t = mc\Delta T$$

$$t = (mc\Delta T) / P$$

$$t = (90\ \text{g})\cdot(4.186\ \text{J/g·°C})\cdot(30\ °\text{C} - 10\ °\text{C}) / (50\ \text{W})$$

$$t = 151\ \text{s}$$

4. A is correct.

Convert 15 minutes to seconds:

$$t = (15\ \text{min/1})\cdot(60\ \text{s/1 min})$$

$$t = 900\ \text{s}$$

Find total energy generated:

$$Q = P \times t$$

$$Q = (1{,}260 \text{ J/s}){\cdot}(900 \text{ s})$$

$$Q = 1{,}134 \text{ kJ}$$

Find mass of water needed to carry away energy:

$$Q = mL_v$$

$$m = Q / L_v$$

$$m = (1{,}134 \text{ kJ}) / (22.6 \times 10^2 \text{ kJ/kg})$$

$$m = 0.5 \text{ kg}$$

$$m = 500 \text{ g}$$

5. C is correct.

Phase changes occur at constant temperature. Once the phase change is complete the temperature of the substance then either increases or decreases.

For example, water remains at 0 °C until it has completely changed phase to ice before the temperature decreases further.

6. E is correct.

L_f stands for the latent heat of fusion, which is the energy needed to melt a substance.

$$L_f = (334 \text{ kJ/kg}){\cdot}(55 \text{ kg})$$

$$L_f = 1.8 \times 10^4 \text{ kJ}$$

7. D is correct.

Metals are good heat and electrical conductors because of their bonding structure. In metallic bonding, the outer electrons are held loosely and can travel freely. Electricity and heat require high electron mobility. Thus, the looseness of the outer electrons in the materials allows them to be excellent conductors.

8. A is correct.

Find heat of phase change from steam to liquid:

$$Q_1 = mL_v$$

Find heat of phase change from liquid to solid:

$$Q_2 = mL_f$$

Find heat of temperature from 100 °C to 0 °C:

$$Q_3 = mc\Delta T$$

Total heat:

$$Q_{net} = Q_1 + Q_2 + Q_3$$
$$Q_{net} = mL_v + mL_f + mc\Delta T$$

To find mass:

$$Q_{net} = m(L_v + c\Delta T + L_f)$$
$$m = Q_{net} / (L_v + c\Delta T + L_f)$$

Solve:

$$Q_{net} = 200 \text{ kJ}$$
$$Q_{net} = 2 \times 10^5 \text{ J}$$
$$m = (2 \times 10^5 \text{ J}) / [(22.6 \times 10^5 \text{ J/kg}) + (4,186 \text{ J/kg·K})\cdot(100 \text{ °C} - 0 \text{ °C}) + (33.5 \times 10^4 \text{ J/kg})]$$
$$m = 0.066 \text{ kg}$$

9. C is correct. Fusion is the process whereby a substance changes from a solid to liquid (i.e. melting).

Condensation is the process whereby a substance changes from a vapor to liquid.

Sublimation is the process whereby a substance changes directly from a solid to the gas phase without passing through the liquid phase.

10. E is correct.

$$Q = mc\Delta T$$
$$Q = (0.2 \text{ g})\cdot(14.3 \text{ J/g·K})\cdot(280 \text{ K} - 250 \text{ K})$$
$$Q = 86 \text{ J}$$

11. B is correct.

Heat needed to raise temperature of aluminum:

$$Q_A = m_A c_A \Delta T$$

Heat needed to raise temperature of water:

$$Q_W = m_W c_W \Delta T$$

Total heat to raise temperature of system:

$$Q_{net} = Q_A + Q_W$$
$$Q_{net} = m_A c_A \Delta T + m_W c_W \Delta T$$
$$Q_{net} = \Delta T(m_A c_A + m_W c_W)$$
$$Q_{net} = (98 \text{ °C} - 18 \text{ °C})\cdot[(0.5 \text{ kg})\cdot(900 \text{ J/kg·K}) + (1 \text{ kg})\cdot(4,186 \text{ J/kg·K})]$$
$$Q_{net} = 370,880 \text{ J}$$

Time to produce Q_{net} with 500 W:

$$Q_{net} = (500 \text{ W})t$$

$$t = Q_{net} / (500 \text{ W})$$

$$t = (370{,}880 \text{ J}) / 500 \text{ W}$$

$$t = 741.8 \text{ s}$$

Convert to minutes:

$$t = (741.8 \text{ s}/1) \cdot (1 \text{ min}/60 \text{ s})$$

$$t = 12.4 \text{ min} \approx 12 \text{ min}$$

12. A is correct.

When a substance goes through a phase change, the temperature doesn't change.

It can be assumed that the lower plateau is L_f and the upper plateau is L_v.

Count the columns: $L_f = 2$, $L_v = 7$

$$L_v / L_f = 7 / 2$$

$$L_v / L_f = 3.5$$

13. B is correct. Specific heat is the amount of heat (i.e. energy) needed to raise the temperature of the unit mass of a substance by a given amount (usually one degree).

14. E is correct.

Find ½ of KE of the BB:

$$KE = \tfrac{1}{2}mv^2$$

$$\tfrac{1}{2}KE = \tfrac{1}{2}(\tfrac{1}{2}mv^2)$$

$$\tfrac{1}{2}KE_{BB} = \tfrac{1}{2}(\tfrac{1}{2}) \cdot (0.0045 \text{ kg}) \cdot (46 \text{ m/s})^2$$

$$\tfrac{1}{2}KE_{BB} = 2.38 \text{ J}$$

The $\tfrac{1}{2}KE_{BB}$ is equal to energy taken to change temperature:

$$Q = \tfrac{1}{2}KE_{BB}$$
$$Q = mc\Delta T$$

$$mc\Delta T = \tfrac{1}{2}KE_{BB}$$

$$\Delta T = \tfrac{1}{2}KE_{BB} / mc$$

Calculate to find ΔT:

$$\Delta T = (2.38 \text{ J}) / (0.0045 \text{ kg}) \cdot (128 \text{ J/kg·K})$$

$$\Delta T = 4.1 \text{ K}$$

15. C is correct.

Vaporization is the process whereby a substance changes from a liquid to a gas. The process can be either boiling or evaporation.

Sublimation is the process whereby a substance changes from a solid to a gas.

16. A is correct.

Carnot efficiency:

η = work done / total energy

$\eta = W / Q_H$

$\eta = 5 \text{ J} / 18 \text{ J}$

$\eta = 0.28$

The engine's efficiency:

$\eta = (T_H - T_C) / T_H$

$0.28 = (233 \text{ K} - T_C) / 233 \text{ K}$

$(0.28) \cdot (233 \text{ K}) = (233 \text{ K} - T_C)$

$65.2 \text{ K} = 233 \text{ K} - T_C$

$T_C = 168 \text{ K}$

17. D is correct.

Heat needed to change temperature of a mass:

$Q = mc\Delta T$

Calculate to find Q:

$Q = (0.92 \text{ kg}) \cdot (113 \text{ cal/kg} \cdot {}^\circ\text{C}) \cdot (96 \,{}^\circ\text{C} - 18 \,{}^\circ\text{C})$

$Q = 8,108.9 \text{ cal}$

Convert to joules:

$Q = (8,108.9 \text{ cal}) \cdot (4.186 \text{ J/cal})$

$Q = 33,940 \text{ J}$

18. B is correct.

During a change of state the addition of heat does not change the temperature (i.e. a measure of the kinetic energy). The heat energy added only adds to the potential energy of the substance until the substance completely changes state.

19. E is correct.

20. A is correct.

Specific heat of A is larger than B:

$$c_A > c_B$$

Energy to raise the temperature:

$$Q = mc\Delta T$$

If m and ΔT are equal for A and B:

$$Q_A = m_A c_A \Delta T_A$$

$$Q_B = m_B c_B \Delta T_B$$

$$Q_A > Q_B$$

This is valid because all other factors are equal and the magnitude of Q only depends on c.

21. D is correct.

Find kinetic energy of meteor:

$$KE = \tfrac{1}{2}mv^2$$

$$KE = \tfrac{1}{2}(0.0065 \text{ kg}) \cdot (300 \text{ m/s})^2$$

$$KE = 292.5 \text{ J}$$

Find temperature rise:

$$Q = KE$$

$$Q = mc\Delta T$$

$$mc\Delta T = KE$$

$$\Delta T = KE / mc$$

Convert KE to calories:

$$KE = (292.5 \text{ J/1}) \cdot (1 \text{ cal/4.186 J})$$

$$KE = 69.9 \text{ cal}$$

Calculate ΔT:

$$\Delta T = (69.9 \text{ cal}) / [(0.0065 \text{ kg}) \cdot (120 \text{ cal/kg} \cdot °C)]$$

$$\Delta T = 89.6 \text{ }°C \approx 90 \text{ }°C$$

22. A is correct.

When a liquid freezes it undergoes a phase change from liquid to solid. In order for this to occur heat energy must be dissipated (removed). During any phase change the temperature remains constant.

23. B is correct.

For an isothermal process:

$$\Delta U = 0$$

$$\Delta U = Q - W$$

$$Q = W$$

Work to expand gas in isothermal process:

$$W = nRT \ln(V_f / V_i)$$

Calculate moles using ideal gas law:

$$PV = nRT$$

$$n = (PV) / (RT)$$

$$n = [(130 \times 10^3 \text{ Pa}) \cdot (0.2 \text{ m}^3)] / [(8.314 \text{ J/mol·K}) \cdot (300 \text{ K})]$$

$$n = 10.4 \text{ mol}$$

Use moles in work calculation:

$$W = (10.4 \text{ mol}) \cdot (8.314 \text{ J/mol·K}) \cdot (300 \text{ K}) \cdot [\ln (0.2 \text{ m}^3 / 0.05 \text{ m}^3)]$$

$$W = 36 \text{ kJ}$$

$$W = Q$$

$$Q = 36 \text{ kJ}$$

The heat value is positive because heat is added to the system to do work.

24. D is correct.

Find the potential energy of 1 kg of water:

$$PE = mgh$$

$$PE = (1 \text{ kg}) \cdot (9.8 \text{ m/s}^2) \cdot (30 \text{ m})$$

$$PE = 294 \text{ J}$$

Assume all potential energy is converted to heat for maximum temperature increase:

$$PE = Q$$

$$Q = mc\Delta T$$

$$mc\Delta T = PE$$

$$\Delta T = PE / mc$$

$$\Delta T = (294 \text{ J}) / (1 \text{ kg}) \cdot (4{,}186 \text{ J/kg·K})$$

$$\Delta T = 0.07 \text{ °C}$$

For temperature differences it is not necessary to convert to Kelvin because a temperature change in Kelvin is equal to a temperature change in Celsius.

25. A is correct.

Find heat from phase change:

$$Q = mL_f$$

$$Q = (0.75 \text{ kg}) \cdot (33{,}400 \text{ J/kg})$$

$$Q = 25{,}050 \text{ J}$$

Because the water is freezing, Q should be negative due to heat being released.

$$Q = -25{,}050 \text{ J}$$

Find change in entropy:

$$\Delta S = Q / \text{T}$$

$$\Delta S = -25{,}050 \text{ J} / (0 \text{ °C} + 273 \text{ K})$$

$$\Delta S = -92 \text{ J} / \text{K}$$

A negative change in entropy indicates that the disorder of the isolated system has decreased. When water freezes the entropy is negative because water is more disordered than ice. Thus, disorder has decreased.

26. A is correct.

Copper has a larger coefficient of linear expansion that iron so it expands more than iron during a given temperature change. The bimetallic bar bends due to the difference in expansion between the copper and iron.

27. D is correct.

Calculate heat needed to raise temperature:

$$Q = mc\Delta \text{T}$$

$$Q = (0.110 \text{ kg}) \cdot (4{,}186 \text{ J/kg·K}) \cdot (30 \text{ °C} - 20 \text{ °C})$$

$$Q = 4{,}605 \text{ J}$$

Calculate time needed to raise temperature with 60 W power source:

$$Q = P \times t$$

$$Q = (60 \text{ W})t$$

$$t = Q / (60 \text{ W})$$

$$t = (4{,}605 \text{ J}) / (60 \text{ W})$$

$$t = 77 \text{ s}$$

28. B is correct.

During a change of state the addition of heat does not change the temperature (i.e. a measure of the kinetic energy). The heat energy added only adds to the potential energy of the substance until the substance completely changes state.

29. E is correct. Convert to Kelvin:

$$T = -243 \ °C + 273$$

$$T = 30 \ K$$

Double temperature:

$$T_2 = (30 \ K) \cdot (2)$$

$$T_2 = 60 \ K$$

Convert back to Celsius:

$$T_2 = 60 \ K - 273$$

$$T_2 = -213 \ °C$$

30. D is correct.

31. B is correct.

Convert units:

$$1.7 \times 10^5 \ J/kg = 170 \ kJ/kg$$

Change in internal energy = heat added (Q)

$$Q = mL_v$$

$$Q = (1 \ kg) \cdot (170 \ kJ/kg)$$

$$Q = 170 \ kJ$$

32. D is correct.

$$Q = mc\Delta T$$

If m and c are constant, the relationship is directly proportional.

To double Q, T must be doubled:

$$5 \ C + 273 = 278 \ K$$

$$278 \ K \times 2 = 556 \ K$$

$$556 \ K - 273 = 283 \ C$$

33. E is correct.

34. B is correct.

When Kevin steps out of the water his body heat gives energy to the water molecules. This energy is transferred via collisions until some molecules have enough energy to break the hydrogen bonds and escape the liquid (evaporation). However, if Kevin is dry his heat is not given to the water and he feels warmer because his heat is not lost due to the evaporation of the water.

35. D is correct. Calculate heat released when 0 °C water converts to 0 °C ice:

$$Q_1 = mL_f$$

$$Q_1 = (2{,}200 \text{ kg}) \cdot (334 \times 10^3 \text{ J/kg})$$

$$Q_1 = 734{,}800 \text{ kJ}$$

Calculate heat released for temperature drop ΔT

$$Q_2 = mc\Delta T$$

$$Q_2 = (2{,}200 \text{ kg}) \cdot (2{,}050 \text{ J/kg K}) \cdot [(0 \text{ °C} - (-30 \text{ °C})]$$

$\Delta K = \Delta °C$, so units cancel:

$$Q_2 = 135{,}300 \text{ kJ}$$

Add heat released to get Q_{net}:

$$Q_{net} = Q_1 + Q_2$$

$$Q_{net} = (734{,}800 \text{ kJ}) + (135{,}300 \text{ kJ})$$

$$Q_{net} = 870{,}100 \text{ kJ}$$

36. E is correct.

Object 1 has three times the specific heat capacity and four times the mass of Object 2:

$$c_1 = 3c_2; \ m_1 = 4m_2$$

A single-phase substance obeys the specific heat equation:

$$Q = mc\Delta T$$

In this case, the same amount of heat is added to each substance, therefore:

$$Q_1 = Q_2$$

$$m_1 c_1 \Delta T_1 = m_2 c_2 \Delta T_2$$

$$m_1 c_1 \Delta T_1 = (4m_1)(3c_1)\Delta T_2$$

$$m_1 c_1 \Delta T_1 = 12 \ m_1 c_1 \Delta T_2$$

$$\Delta T_1 = 12 \ \Delta T_2$$

$$\Delta T_2 = \Delta T_1 / 12$$

37. C is correct. Conduction is a form of heat transfer in which the collisions of the molecules of the material transfer energy through the material. Higher temperature of the material causes the molecules to collide with more energy which eventually is transferred throughout the material through subsequent collisions.

Radiation is a form of heat transfer in which electromagnetic waves carry energy from the emitting object and deposit the energy to the object that absorbs the radiation.

Convection is a form of heat transfer in which mass motion of a fluid (i.e. liquids and gases) transfers energy from the source of heat.

38. A is correct. Calculate moles of oxygen, O_2, as two oxygen atoms:

$n = (5.1 \text{ g } O_2 \, / \, 1) \cdot (1 \text{ mol } O_2 \, / \, 32 \text{ g } O_2)$

$n = 0.16 \text{ mol } O_2$

Calculate P_1, using the ideal gas law:

$PV = nRT$

$P = nRT \, / \, V$

$V_1 = (100 \text{ cm}^3 \, / \, 1) \cdot (1 \text{m} \, / \, 100 \text{ cm})^3 = 1 \times 10^{-4} \text{ m}^3$

$P_1 = [(0.16 \text{ mol}) \cdot (8.314 \text{ J/mol·K}) \cdot (20 \text{ °C} + 273 \text{ K})] \, / \, (1 \times 10^{-4} \text{ m}^3)$

$P_1 = 3.9 \times 10^6 \text{ Pa}$

Calculate T_3 using the ideal gas law:

$PV = nRT$

$T = (PV) \, / \, (nR)$

$V_3 = (50 \text{ cm}^3 \, / \, 1) \cdot (1 \text{m} \, / \, 100 \text{ cm})^3 = 5 \times 10^{-5} \text{ m}^3$

$T_3 = [(1.5 \times 3.9 \times 10^6 \text{ Pa}) \cdot (5 \times 10^{-5} \text{ m}^3)] \, / \, [(0.16 \text{ mol}) \cdot (8.314 \text{ J/mol·K})]$

$T_3 = 220 \text{ K}$

$T_3 = (220 \text{ K} - 273 \text{ K})$

$T_3 = -53 \text{ °C}$

Calculate T_4 using the ideal gas law:

$V_4 = (150 \text{ cm}^3 \, / \, 1) \cdot (1 \text{m} \, / \, 100 \text{ cm})^3 = 1.5 \times 10^{-4} \text{ m}^3$

$T_4 = [(1.5 \times 3.9 \times 10^6 \text{ Pa}) \cdot (1.5 \times 10^{-4} \text{ m}^3)] \, / \, [(0.16 \text{ mol}) \cdot (8.314 \text{ J/mol·K})]$

$T_4 = 660 \text{ K}$

$T_4 = (660 \text{ K} - 273 \text{ K})$

$T_4 = 387 \text{ °C}$

39. B is correct. Steel is a very conductive material that is able to transfer thermal energy very well. The steel feels colder than the plastic because its higher thermal conductivity allows it to remove more heat and thus makes touching it feel colder.

40. B is correct. An isobaric process involves constant pressure.

An isochoric (also isometric) process involves a closed system at constant volume.

An adiabatic process occurs without transfer of heat or matter between a system and its surroundings.

An isothermal process involves the change of a system in which the temperature remains constant.

An isentropic process is an idealized thermodynamic process that is adiabatic of a frictionless system where work is transferred such that there is no transfer of heat or matter.

41. E is correct.

Carnot coefficient of performance of a refrigeration cycle:

$$C_P = T_C / (T_H - T_C)$$

$$C_P = Q_C / W$$

$$Q_C / W = T_C / (T_H - T_C)$$

$$W = (Q_C / T_C) \cdot (T_H - T_C)$$

$$W = (20 \times 10^3 \text{ J} / 293 \text{ K}) \cdot (307 \text{ K} - 293 \text{ K})$$

$$W = 955.6 \text{ J} = 0.956 \text{ kJ}$$

Power = Work / time

$$P = W / t$$

$$P = 0.956 \text{ kJ} / 1 \text{ s}$$

$$P = 0.956 \text{ kW} \approx 0.96 \text{ kW}$$

42. C is correct.

43. B is correct.

Convection is a form of heat transfer in which mass motion of a fluid (i.e. liquids and gases) transfers energy from the source of heat.

44. A is correct.

Radiation is the transmission of energy in the form of particles or waves through space or a material medium. Examples include electromagnetic radiations such as X-rays, alpha particles, beta particles, radio waves and visible light.

45. D is correct.

Convert P_3 to Pascals:

$$P_3 = (2 \text{ atm} / 1) \cdot (101,325 \text{ Pa} / 1 \text{ atm})$$

$$P_3 = 202,650 \text{ Pa}$$

Use the ideal gas law to find V_3:

$$PV = nRT$$

$$V = (nRT) / P$$

$$V_3 = [(0.008 \text{ mol}) \cdot (8.314 \text{ J/mol·K}) \cdot (2,438 \text{ K})] / (202,650 \text{ Pa})$$

$$V_3 = 8 \times 10^{-4} \text{ m}^3$$

Convert to cm^3:

$$V_3 = (8 \times 10^{-4} \text{ m}^3/1) \cdot (100^3 \text{ cm}^3/1 \text{ m}^3)$$

$$V_3 = 800 \text{ cm}^3$$

46. C is correct.

An adiabatic process involves no heat added or removed from the system.

From the First law of Thermodynamics:

$\Delta U = Q + W$

If $Q = 0$, then:

$\Delta U = W$

Because work is being done to expand the gas it is considered negative and then the change in internal energy is negative (decreases).

$-\Delta U = -W$

47. E is correct.

Standing in a breeze while wet feels colder than when dry because of the evaporation of water off the skin. Water requires heat to evaporate so this is taken from the body making a person feel colder than if they were dry and the evaporation did not occur.

48. A is correct.

Conduction is a form of heat transfer in which the collisions of the molecules of the material transfer energy through the material. Higher temperature of the material causes the molecules to collide with more energy which eventually is transferred throughout the material through subsequent collisions.

49. D is correct.

An isobaric process is a constant pressure process, so the resulting pressure is always the same.

50. B is correct.

This question is asking which type of surface has higher emissivity than others and therefore can radiate more energy over a set time period. Blackbody is an idealized radiator and has the highest emissivity. As such, a surface most similar to a blackbody (the black surface) is the best radiator of thermal energy.

A black surface is considered to be an ideal blackbody and therefore has an emissivity of 1 (perfect emissivity). The black surface will be the best radiator as compared to other surface which cannot be considered as blackbodies and have emissivity of <1.

51. E is correct. Calculate gap between the rods.

The gap in between the rods will be filled by both expanding, so total thermal expansion length is equal to 1.1 cm.

$\Delta L = L_0 \alpha \Delta T$

$\Delta L_{tot} = \Delta L_B + \Delta L_A$

$\Delta L_{tot} = (\alpha_B L_B + \alpha_A L_A) \Delta T$

Rearrange the equation for ΔT:

$$\Delta T = \Delta L_{tot} / (\alpha_B L_B + \alpha_A L_A)$$

$$\Delta T = 1.1 \text{ cm} / [(2 \times 10^{-5} \text{ K}^{-1}) \cdot (59.1 \text{ cm}) + (2.4 \times 10^{-5} \text{ K}^{-1}) \cdot (39.3 \text{ cm})]$$

$$\Delta T = 517 \text{ K} = 517 \text{ °C}$$

Measuring difference in temperature in K is the same as in °C, so it is not required to convert.

52. A is correct.

Find seconds in a day:

$$t = (24 \text{ h} / 1 \text{ day}) \cdot (60 \text{ min} / 1 \text{ h}) \cdot (60 \text{ s} / 1 \text{ min})]$$

$$t = 86,400 \text{ s}$$

Find energy lost in a day:

$$E = \text{Power} \times \text{time}$$

$$E = (60 \text{ W})t$$

$$E = (60 \text{ W}) \cdot (86,400 \text{ s})$$

$$E = 5,184,000 \text{ J}$$

Convert to kcal:

$$E = (5,184,000 \text{ J}/1) \cdot (1 \text{ cal}/4.186 \text{ J}) \cdot (1 \text{ kcal}/10^3 \text{ cal})$$

$$E = 1,240 \text{ kcal}$$

53. D is correct.
Conduction is a form of heat transfer in which the collisions of the molecules of the material transfer energy through the material. Higher temperature of the material causes the molecules to collide with more energy which eventually is transferred throughout the material through subsequent collisions.

54. B is correct.

Heat given off by warmer water is equal to that absorbed by the frozen cube. This heat is split into heat needed to melt the cube and bring temperature to equilibrium.

$$Q_{H2O,1} + Q_{alcohol,Temp1} + Q_{alcohol,Phase1} = 0$$

$$(mc\Delta T)_{H2O,1} + (mc\Delta T)_{alcohol,Temp1} + (mL_f)_{alcohol} = 0$$

$$Q_{H2O,2} + Q_{alcohol,Temp2} + Q_{alcohol,Phase2} = 0$$

$$(mc\Delta T)_{H2O,2} + (mc\Delta T)_{alcohol,Temp2} + (mL_f)_{alcohol} = 0$$

Set equal to each other to cancel heat from phase change (since they are equal):

$$(mc\Delta T)_{H2O,1} + (mc\Delta T)_{alcohol,Temp1} = (mc\Delta T)_{H2O,2} + (mc\Delta T)_{alcohol,Temp2}$$

$$(m_{alcohol})(c_{alcohol}) \cdot (\Delta T_{alcohol1} - \Delta T_{alcohol2}) = c_{H2O}(m\Delta T_{H2O,2} - m\Delta T_{H2O,1})$$

$$c_{alcohol} = (c_{H2O} / m_{alcohol}) \cdot [(m\Delta T_{H2O,2} - m\Delta T_{H2O,1}) / (\Delta T_{alcohol1} - \Delta T_{alcohol2})]$$

Solving for $c_{alcohol}$:

$$c_{alc} = [(4{,}190 \text{ J/kg·K}) / (0.22 \text{ kg})]·[(0.4 \text{ kg})·(10 - 30 \text{ °C}) - (0.35 \text{ kg})·(5 - 26 \text{ °C})]$$

$$/ [(5 \text{ °C} - (-10 \text{ °C}) - (10 \text{ °C} - (-10 \text{ °C})]$$

$$c_{alc} = (19{,}045 \text{ J/kg·K})·[(-0.65 \text{ °C}) / (-5 \text{ °C})]$$

$$c_{alc} = 2{,}475 \text{ J/kg·K}$$

55. D is correct.

Using the calculated value for c_{alc} in the problem above:

$$Q_{H2O,1} + Q_{alcohol,Temp1} + Q_{alcohol,Phase1} = 0$$

$$(mc\Delta T)_{H2O,1} + (mc\Delta T)_{alcohol} + (mL_f)_{alcohol} = 0$$

$$L_{f\,alcohol} = [-(mc\Delta T)_{H2O,1} - (mc\Delta T)_{alcohol}] / m_{alcohol}$$

Solve:

$$L_{f\,alcohol} = -[(0.35 \text{ kg})·(4{,}190 \text{ J/kg·K})·(5 \text{ °C} - 26 \text{ °C})$$

$$- (0.22 \text{ kg})·(2{,}475 \text{ J/kg·K})·(5 \text{ °C} - (-10 \text{ °C})] / (0.22 \text{ kg})$$

$$L_{f\,alcohol} = (30{,}796.5 \text{ J} - 8{,}167.5 \text{ J}) / (0.22 \text{ kg})$$

$$L_{f\,alcohol} = 103 \times 10^3 \text{ J/kg} = 10.3 \times 10^4 \text{ J/kg}$$

56. C is correct.

The silver coating reflects thermal radiation back into the bottle to reduce heat loss by radiation. Radiation is a form of heat transfer in which electromagnetic waves carry energy from an emitting object and deposit the energy in an object absorbing the radiation.

57. E is correct.

Convert calories to Joules:

$$E = (16 \text{ kcal/1})·(10^3 \text{ cal/1 kcal})·(4.186 \text{ J/1 cal})$$

$$E = 66{,}976 \text{ J}$$

Convert hours to seconds:

$$t = (5 \text{ h})·(60 \text{ min/h})·(60 \text{ s/min})$$

$$t = 18{,}000 \text{ s}$$

Find power of food:

$$P = E / t$$

$$P = (66{,}976 \text{ J}) / (18{,}000 \text{ s})$$

$$P = 3.7 \text{ W}$$

58. A is correct.

$\Delta Q = cm\Delta T$

$\Delta T = \Delta Q \,/\, cm$

$\Delta T = (50 \text{ kcal}) \,/\, [(1 \text{ kcal/kg·°C})·(5 \text{ kg})]$

$\Delta T = 10 \text{ °C}$

59. C is correct.

For melting, use L_f:

$Q = mL_f$

$Q = (30 \text{ kg})·(334 \text{ kJ/kg})$

$Q = 1 \times 10^4 \text{ kJ}$

60. B is correct.

Find temperature change:

$Q = mc\Delta T$

$\Delta T = Q \,/\, mc$

$\Delta T = (160 \times 10^3 \text{ J}) \,/\, [(6 \text{ kg})·(910 \text{ J/kg·K})]$

$\Delta T = 29 \text{ °C}$

Find final temperature:

$\Delta T = T_f - T_i$

$T_f = T_i + \Delta T$

$T_f = 12 \text{ °C} + 29 \text{ °C}$

$T_f = 41 \text{ °C}$

Atomic and Nuclear Structure – Explanations

1. A is correct. Though alpha particles have low penetrating power and high ionizing power, they are not harmless. All forms of radiation present risks and cannot be thought of as completely harmless.

2. C is correct. A beta particle (β) is a high-energy, high-speed electron (β⁻) or positron (β⁺) emitted in the radioactive decay of an atomic nucleus.

Electron emission (β⁻ decay) occurs in an unstable atomic nucleus with an excess of neutrons, whereby a neutron is converted into a proton, an electron and an electron antineutrino.

Positron emission (β⁺ decay) occurs in an unstable atomic nucleus with an excess of protons, whereby a proton is converted into a neutron, a positron and an electron neutrino.

3. E is correct. The de Broglie wavelength is given as:

$\lambda = h \,/\, p$

where h is Planck's constant and p is momentum

$p = mv$

$\lambda_1 = h \,/\, mv$

$\lambda_2 = h \,/\, m(2v)$

$\lambda_2 = \tfrac{1}{2} h \,/\, mv$

$\lambda_2 = \tfrac{1}{2}\,\lambda_1$

λ decreases by factor of 2

4. B is correct. The Bohr model places electrons around the nucleus of the atom at discrete energy levels. The Balmer series line spectra agreed with the Bohr model because the energy of the observed photons in each spectra matched the transition energy of electrons within these discrete predicted states.

5. C is correct. A radioactive element is an element that spontaneously emits radiation in the form of one or a combination of the following: alpha radiation, beta radiation, gamma radiation.

6. D is correct. This is an example of an electron capture nuclear reaction.

When this happens, the atomic number decreases by one, but the mass number stays the same.

$$^{100}_{44}\text{Ru} + \,^{0}_{-1}\text{e}^{-} \rightarrow \,^{100}_{43}\text{Tc}$$

Ru: 100 = mass number (# protons + # neutrons)

Ru: 44 = atomic number (# protons)

From the periodic table, Tc is the element with 1 less proton than Ru.

7. B is correct.

A nucleon is a particle that makes up the nucleus of an atom. The two known nucleons are protons and neutrons.

8. E is correct.

An alpha particle is composed of two neutrons and two protons, and is identical to the nucleus of a ^{4}He atom.

Total mass of two alpha particles:

$$2 \times (2 \text{ neutrons} + 2 \text{ protons}) = 8$$

Mass of a ^{9}Be atom:

$$5 \text{ neutrons} + 4 \text{ protons} = 9$$

$$\text{Mass of a } ^9\text{Be atom} > \text{total mass of two alpha particles}$$

The mass of a ^{9}Be atom is greater than the mass of two alpha particles, so its mass is also greater than twice the mass of a ^{4}He atom.

9. C is correct.

The superscript is the mass number (atomic weight), which is both neutrons and protons.

The subscript is the atomic number, which is the number of protons.

Therefore, the number of neutrons is equal to the superscript minus the subscript.

$181 – 86 = 95$, which is the greatest number of neutrons among the choices.

10. C is correct.

A nucleon inside the nucleus has a lower mass than a nucleon outside the nucleus due to mass defect. The mass defect is the mass of the nucleus minus the sum of the mass of the individual nucleons comprising the nucleus. This difference in mass is accounted for in the energy needed to bind the nucleons together to form the nucleus and can be found via:

$$E = \Delta mc^2$$

Some of the mass of a nucleon is transformed into energy needed to bind the nucleus together, and its mass inside the nucleus is therefore slightly less than if it were outside the nucleus.

11. E is correct. Balmer's equation is given by:

$$\lambda = B[(n^2) / (n^2 – 2^2)]$$

$$\lambda = (3.6 \times 10^{-7})\cdot[(12^2) / (12^2 – 2^2)]$$

$$\lambda = 3.7 \times 10^{-7} \text{ m}$$

Where c is the speed of light:

$$c = \lambda f$$

Convert wavelength to frequency:

$$f = c / \lambda$$

$$f = (3 \times 10^8 \, \text{m/s}) / (3.7 \times 10^{-7} \, \text{m})$$

$$f = 8.1 \times 10^{14} \, \text{s}^{-1} = 8.1 \times 10^{14} \, \text{Hz}$$

12. D is correct. Gamma rays are the most penetrating form of radiation because they are the highest energy and least ionizing. A gamma ray passes through a given amount of material without imparting as much of its energy into removing electrons from atoms and ionizing them as other forms of radiation do. Gamma rays retain more of their energy passing through matter and are able to penetrate further.

13. A is correct. Use the Rydberg Formula:

$$E = hf$$

$$f = c / \lambda$$

$$E = (hc) \cdot (1 / \lambda)$$

$$1 / \lambda = R(1 / n_1^2 - 1 / n_2^2), \text{ where } n_1 = 1 \text{ and } n_2 = 2$$

$$E = hcR[(1 / n_1^2) - (1 / n_2^2)]$$

$$E = (4.14 \times 10^{-15} \, \text{eV·s}) \cdot (3 \times 10^8 \, \text{m/s}) \cdot (1.097 \times 10^7 \, \text{m}^{-1}) \cdot [(1 / 1^2) - (1 / 2^2)]$$

$$E = 13.6[1 - (1 / 4)]$$

$$E = 10.2 \, \text{eV}$$

The positive energy indicates that a photon was absorbed and not emitted.

14. C is correct. In β^- (beta minus) decay, the atomic number (subscript) increases by 1 but the atomic mass stays constant.

$$^{87}_{37}\text{Rb} \rightarrow \, ^{87}_{38}\text{Sr} + \, ^{0}_{-1}\text{e} + \, ^{0}_{0}\nu$$

Sr is the element with 1 more proton (subscript) than Rb.

$^{0}_{0}\nu$ represents an electron antineutrino.

15. C is correct.

The nucleus of an atom is bound together by the strong nuclear force from the nucleons within it. The strong nuclear force must overcome the Coulomb repulsion of the protons (due to their like charges).

Neutrons help stabilize and bind the nucleus together by contributing to the strong nuclear force, so that it is greater than the Coulomb repulsion experienced by the protons.

16. A is correct.

Geiger-Muller counters operate using a Geiger-Muller tube, which consists of a high voltage shell and small rod in the center, filled with low pressure inert gas (e.g. argon). When exposed to radiation (specifically particle radiation), the radiation particles ionize atoms of the argon allowing for a brief charge to be conducted between the high voltage rod and outer shell. The electric pulse is then displayed visually or via audio to indicate radioactivity.

17. B is correct.

The half-life calculation:

$$A = A_0(\tfrac{1}{2})^{t/h}$$

where A_0 = original amount, t = time elapse and h = half-life

If three half=life pass, $t = 3h$

$$A = (1)\cdot(\tfrac{1}{2})^{3h/h}$$
$$A = (1)\cdot(\tfrac{1}{2})^{3}$$
$$A = 0.125 = 12.5\%$$

18. D is correct.

In the Lyman series, electron transitions always go from $n \geq 2$ to $n = 1$.

19. B is correct.

20. A is correct.

Alpha particles are positively charged due to their protons, while beta minus particles are negatively charged (i.e., electrons). When exposed to a magnetic field, alpha particles and electrons deflect in opposite directions due to their opposite charges and thus experience opposite forces due to the magnetic field.

21. E is correct.

Chemical reactions store and release energy in their chemical bonds, but do not convert mass into energy. However, nuclear reactions convert a small amount of mass into energy, which can be measured and calculated via the equation:

$$E = \Delta mc^2$$

22. C is correct.

The Curie is a non-SI unit of radioactivity equivalent to 3.7×10^{10} decays (disintegrations) per second. It is named after the early radioactivity researchers Marie and Pierre Curie.

23. B is correct.

The atomic numbers: $^{235}_{92}U \rightarrow {}^{141}_{56}Ba + {}^{92}_{36}Kr$

The subscripts on each side of the expression sum to 92, so adding a proton ($^{1}_{1}H$) to the right side would not balance.

The superscripts sum to 235 on the left and sum to 233 on the right.

Add two neutrons ($^{1}_{0}n + {}^{1}_{0}n$) to the right side to balance both sides of the equation.

24. D is correct.

The atomic number is the subscript and represents the number of protons. The superscript is the mass number and is the sum of protons and neutrons. The number of neutrons can be found by taking the difference between the mass number and atomic number. In this example, there are 16 protons and 18 neutrons.

25. A is correct.

$A = A_0(\frac{1}{2})^{t/h}$

where A_0 = original amount, t = time elapse and h = half-life

Consider: (2 days)·(24 hours / 1 day) = 48 hours

$A = (1)·(\frac{1}{2})^{(48/12)}$

$A = 0.5^4$

$A = 0.0625 = 1/16$

26. C is correct.

An alpha particle consists of two protons and two neutrons, and is identical to a helium nucleus, so it can be written as $^{4}_{2}He$

For a nuclear reaction to be written correctly it must be balanced, and the sum of superscripts and subscripts must be equal on both sides of the reaction. The superscripts add to 238, and the subscripts add to 92 on both sides, therefore it is the only balanced answer.

27. E is correct.

The question is asking for the λ of the emitted photon so use the Rydberg Formula:

$1/\lambda = R(1/n_1^2 - 1/n_2^2)$

$\lambda = 1/[R(1/n_1^2 - 1/n_2^2)]$

Use $n_1 = 5$ and $n_2 = 20$ because we are solving for λ of an emitted (not absorbed) photon.

$\lambda = 1/[(1.097 \times 10^7\,m^-1)·(1/5^2 - 1/20^2)]$

$\lambda = 2.43\ \mu m$

28. D is correct.

When writing a nuclear reaction, the superscript represents the mass number, while the subscript represents the atomic number. A correct nuclear reaction is balanced when the sum of superscripts (mass number) and subscripts (atomic number) is equal on both sides of the reaction.

29. C is correct.

A blackbody is an ideal system that absorbs 100% of all light incident upon it and reflects none. It also emits 100% of the radiation it generates, therefore it has perfect absorption and emissivity.

30. D is correct.

Carbon dating relies upon a steady creation of ^{14}C and knowledge of the rate of creation at various points in time to determine the approximate age of objects.

If a future archeologist is unaware of nuclear bomb testing and the higher levels of ^{14}C created, then the dates they calculate for an object would be too young. This is because a higher amount of ^{14}C would be present in samples and make them seem as if they had not had time to decay and thus appear to be younger.

31. A is correct.

Gamma radiation is an electromagnetic wave and is not a particle. Thus, when gamma radiation is emitted, the atomic number and mass number remain the same.

32. C is correct.

In β^- decay a neutron is converted to a proton and an electron and electron antineutrino are emitted. In β^+ decay a proton is converted to a neutron and a positron and an electron neutrino are emitted.

$$^{14}_{6}\text{C} \rightarrow \, ^{14}_{7}\text{N} + e^- + v_e$$

33. E is correct.

In a nuclear equation the number of nucleons must be conserved.

The sum of mass numbers and atomic numbers must be equal on both sides of the equation.

The product (i.e. daughter nuclei) should be on the right side of the equation.

34. B is correct.

The atomic number is the number of protons within the nucleus which characterizes the element's nuclear and chemical properties.

35. C is correct.

The Balmer series is the name of the emission spectrum of hydrogen when electrons transition from a higher state to the n = 2 state.

Within the Balmer series, there are four visible spectral lines with colors ranging from red to violet (i.e. ROY G BIV)

36. D is correct.

Electrons were discovered through early experiments with electricity, specifically in high voltage vacuum tubes (cathode ray tubes). Beams of electrons were observed traveling through these tubes when high voltage was applied between the anode and cathode, and the electrons struck fluorescent material at the back of the tube.

37. B is correct.

Beams a and c both deflect when an electric field is applied, indicating they have a net charge and therefore must be particles.

Beam b is undisturbed by the applied electric field, indicating it has no net charge and must be a high energy electromagnetic wave, since all other forms of radioactivity (alpha and beta radiation) are charged particles.

38. E is correct. Beam a is composed of negatively charged particles, while beam c is composed of positively charged particles; therefore both beams are deflected by the electric field.

Beam b is also composed of particles; however, these particles are neutral because they are not deflected by the electric field. An example of this kind of radiation would be a gamma ray, which consists of neutral photons.

39. C is correct. A helium nucleus is positively charged, so it is deflected away from the top plate and attracted toward the negative plate.

40. B is correct.

5.37 eV is the amount of energy required to excite the electron from the ground state to the zero energy state.

Calculate the wavelength of a photon with this energy:

$E = hf$

$f = c / \lambda$

$E = hc / \lambda$

$\lambda = hc / E$

$\lambda = (4.14 \times 10^{-15} \text{ eV·s})·(3 \times 10^8 \text{ m/s}) / (5.37 \text{ eV})$

$\lambda = 2.3 \times 10^{-7} \text{ m}$

41. D is correct.

Elements with atomic numbers of 84 and higher are radioactive because the strong nuclear force binding the nucleus together cannot overcome the Coulomb repulsion from the high number of protons within the atom. Thus, these nuclei are unstable and emit alpha radiation to decrease the number of protons within the nucleus.

42. E is correct.

Beta particles, like all forms of ionizing radiation, cannot be considered harmless.

43. A is correct.

The nuclear force is stronger than the electromagnetic force at close proximities. Thus, when two protons are close to each other, the nuclear force is in fact stronger than electromagnetic repulsion between the two.

44. B is correct.

Planck's constant quantizes the amount of energy that can be absorbed or emitted. Therefore, it sets a discrete lowest amount of energy for energy transfer.

45. E is correct.

The decay rate of any radioactive isotope or element is constant and independent of temperature, pressure, or surface area.

46. B is correct.

Larger nuclei (atomic number above 83) tend to decay because the attractive force of the nucleons (strong nuclear force) has a limited range and the nucleus is larger than this range. Therefore, these nuclei tend to emit alpha particles to decrease the size of the nucleus.

Smaller nuclei are not large enough to encounter this problem, but some isotopes have an irregular ratio of neutrons to protons and become unstable. ^{14}Carbon has 8 neutrons and 6 protons, and its neutron to proton ratio is too large, therefore it is unstable and radioactive.

47. C is correct.

Positron emission occurs during β^+ decay. In β^+ decay a proton converts to a neutron and emits a positron and electron neutrino.

The decay can be expressed as: $^{44}_{21}\text{Sc} \rightarrow\ ^{44}_{20}\text{Ca} + \text{e}^+ + \nu_\text{e}$

48. C is correct.

A scintillation counter operates by detecting light flashes from the scintillator material. When radiation strikes the scintillator crystal (often NaI), a light flash is emitted and detected by a photomultiplier tube, which then passes an electronic signal to audio or visual identification equipment.

49. B is correct.

When a Geiger counter clicks, it indicates that it has detected the radiation from one nucleus decaying. The click could be from an alpha, beta, or even gamma ray source, but cannot be determined without other information.

50. A is correct.

The Pauli Exclusion Principle states that in an atom no two electrons can have the same set of quantum numbers. Thus, every electron in an atom has a unique set of quantum numbers and a particular set belongs to only one electron.

51. D is correct.

The atomic number indicates the number of protons within the nucleus of an atom.

52. E is correct.

Gamma rays are high-energy electromagnetic radiation rays and have no charge or mass.

Due to their high energy and speed, they have high penetrating power.

53. B is correct.

Calculate mass defect:

$$m_1 = (2 \text{ protons}) \cdot (1.0072764669 \text{ amu}) + (2 \text{ neutrons}) \cdot (1.0086649156 \text{ amu})$$

$$m_1 = 4.031882765 \text{ amu}$$

$$\Delta m = 4.031882765 \text{ amu} - 4.002602 \text{ amu}$$

$$\Delta m = 0.029280765 \text{ amu}$$

Convert to kg:

$$\Delta m = (0.029280765 \text{ amu} / 1) \cdot (1.6606 \times 10^{-27} \text{ kg} / 1 \text{ amu})$$

$$\Delta m = 4.86236 \times 10^{-29} \text{ kg}$$

Find binding energy:

$$E = \Delta m c^2$$

$$E = (4.86236 \times 10^{-29} \text{ kg}) \cdot (3 \times 10^8 \text{ m/s})^2$$

$$E = 4.38 \times 10^{-12} \text{ J} \approx 4.4 \times 10^{-12} \text{ J}$$

54. E is correct.

Boron has an atomic number of five, and thus has five protons and five electrons. The $1s$ orbital is completely filled by two electrons, then the $2s$ orbital is completely filled with two electrons. Only one electron remains and it is in the $2p$ orbital, leaving it partially filled.

The electron configuration of boron: $1s^2 2s^2 2p$

55. C is correct.

$$E = mc^2$$

$$m = E / c^2$$

$$m = (3.85 \times 10^{26} \text{ J}) / (3 \times 10^8 \text{ m/s})^2$$

$$m = 4.3 \times 10^9 \text{ kg}$$

56. D is correct.

When any form of ionizing radiation interacts with the body, the high energy particles or electromagnetic waves cause atoms within the tissue to ionize. This process creates unstable ions and free radicals that are damaging and pose serious health risks.

57. B is correct.

When a gamma ray is emitted the atom must lose energy due to conservation of energy. Thus the atom will have less energy than before.

58. A is correct. The lower case symbol "n" signifies a neutron. An atomic number of zero indicates that there are no protons. A mass number of one indicates that it contains a neutron.

59. C is correct.

The uncertainty principle states that the position and momentum of a particle cannot be simultaneously measured over a set precision.

Additionally, the energy and time cannot be simultaneously known over a set precision.

Mathematically this is stated as:

$$\Delta x \Delta p > \hbar / 2$$

$$\Delta E \Delta t > \hbar / 2$$

where x = position, p = momentum, $\hbar$ = reduced Planck's constant, E = energy, t = time

60. D is correct.

$$A = A_0 (\tfrac{1}{2})^{t/h}$$

where A_o = original amount, t = time elapse and h = half-life

$$0.03 = (1) \cdot (\tfrac{1}{2})^{(t/20,000 \text{ years})}$$

$$\ln (0.03) = (t / 20,000 \text{ years}) \cdot \ln (\tfrac{1}{2})$$

$$t = 101,179 \text{ years}$$

To access these and other SAT questions at a special pricing visit:
http://SAT.Sterling-Prep.com/bookowner.htm